# Resistant Islands

To Ota Masahide (1925-2017)

Friend, mentor, inspiration
In gratitude and in the hope that our book will help
advance the causes to which you devoted your life

# Resistant Islands

## Okinawa Confronts Japan and the United States

*Second Edition*

Gavan McCormack
and
Satoko Oka Norimatsu

ROWMAN & LITTLEFIELD PUBLISHERS, INC.
*Lanham • Boulder • New York • Toronto • Plymouth, UK*

Published by Rowman & Littlefield Publishers, Inc.
A wholly owned subsidiary of The Rowman & Littlefield Publishing Group, Inc.
4501 Forbes Boulevard, Suite 200, Lanham, Maryland 20706
www.rowman.com

10 Thornbury Road, Plymouth PL6 7PP, United Kingdom

British Library Cataloguing in Publication Information Available

The previous edition of this book was cataloged by the Library of Congress
as follows:
McCormack, Gavan.
   Resistant islands : Okinawa confronts Japan and the United States / Gavan
McCormack and Satoko Oka Norimatsu.
      p.   cm. — (Asia Pacific perspectives)
   Includes bibliographical references and index.
   1. Okinawa-ken (Japan)—History. 2. Okinawa-ken (Japan)—Colonization.
3. United States—Armed Forces—Japan—Okinawa-ken—History. 4. Military
bases, American—Japan—Okinawa-ken—History. 5. Okinawa-ken (Japan)—
Relations—United States. 6. Untied States—Relations—Okinawa-ken (Japan)
7. Japan—Foreign relations—United States. 8. United States—Foreign
relations—Japan. I. Norimatsu, Satoko Oka, 1965– II. Title.
   DS894.99.O375M44 2012
   952'.29404—dc23
                                                                    2012008989
ISBN 978-1-5381-1557-2 (cloth : alk. paper)
ISBN 978-1-4422-1563-4 (pbk. : alk. paper)
ISBN 978-1-5381-1556-5 (electronic)

∞™ The paper used in this publication meets the minimum requirements of
American National Standard for Information Sciences—Permanence of Paper
for Printed Library Materials, ANSI/NISO Z39.48-1992.

Printed in the United States of America

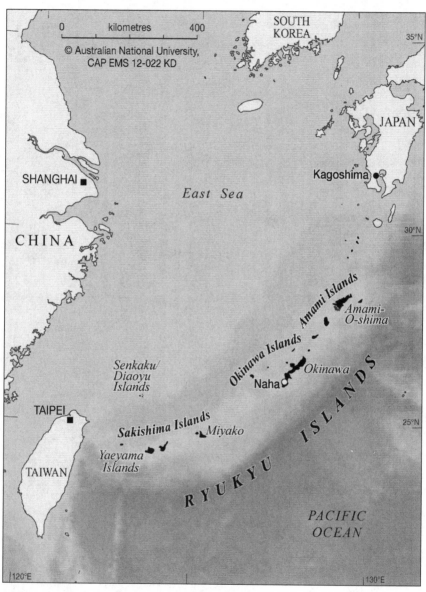

Okinawa and its surrounds.

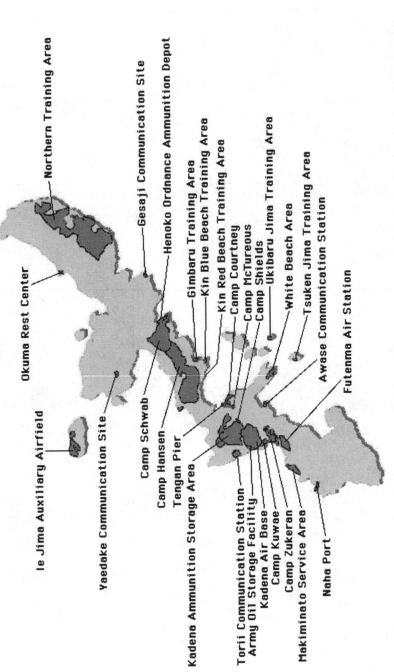

US military bases in Okinawa. *Source:* Adapted with permission from Executive Office of the Governor, Okinawa Prefecture.

Futenma Air Station. *Source: Ryukyu Shimpo.*

# Contents

# Preface to the Second Edition: Six Years On

It is a pleasure for us as authors that this updated edition is to be published, six years after publication of the English original in 2012 (four or five since publication in Japanese, Korean, and Chinese). But it is also sobering for us that although those years have seen many significant developments (which we outline in the last chapter), the key issues we wrote about have not changed: the vast majority of the people of the "Resistant Islands" continue to resist; the Japanese state continues to oppress; and the United States military presence continues to weigh heavily on Okinawa's core lands, its economy, and its society. Day after day citizens gather at the Camp Schwab gate to the reclamation and construction site for a new US base at Henoko to try to oppose or delay the delivery of reclamation/construction materials, and day after day they are roughly dragged aside to clear a way for trucks (sometimes thirty to fifty, sometimes well over a hundred) delivering those materials. Military helicopters continue to intimidate and on occasion to terrorize Okinawan citizens (or drop out of the sky onto their shores or their farmland). A "seawall," supposedly the first step in reclamation, slowly snakes out into Oura Bay.

The lines of conflict were already clear as we were writing in 2012. The opposition to the base construction project welled up following the government of Japan's 1996 decision that reversion of Futenma Marine Corps base had to be matched by construction of a replacement, and that that FRF (Futenma Replacement Facility) could not be built anywhere but in northern Okinawa (Nago City). Okinawa rejected that decision from the outset, commencing with the Nago City plebiscite in 1997. By the end of 2011, the "No" movement rejecting base construction was prefecture-wide. Thus our title: *Resistant Islands*.

In late 2012, after we had put down our pens, Abe Shinzo resumed office as prime minister (following his earlier stint in 2006–2007) and set about determinedly implementing the regional US military "reorganization" according to the agenda set in 2005, confirmed by the Guam International Agreement of 2009 (see pp. 102-106), and then expanded during 2012. Japan's role was strengthened, although the number of marines to be transferred from Okinawa to Guam was reduced from 8,000 to 4,700 (other contingents going to Australia, Hawaii, and the Philippines). Japan accepted the new arrangement in a late 2013 "Protocol," reiterated its base construction commitments on Henoko and Guam, and added the pledge to cooperate in a new joint military project on the Northern Marianas (Tinian). It also promised to move toward construction of two new bases, an "International Emergency Center" on Shimoji Island (part of the Miyako Island group in southern Okinawa) and a possible night takeoff and landing site for US carrier-based planes on Mage Island in the Osumi island group just south of Kagoshima (see p. 192).

Devoting itself to alliance service, the Abe government in 2014 then went on to adopt a revised interpretation of its constitution that eviscerated Article 9 so as to allow "collective self-defense" and a consequent package of security legislation in the summer of 2015 that opened the way for Japan's Self-Defense Forces to go to the aid of its ally under certain circumstances, i.e., to join it in war.

Abe has spoken repeatedly of "Futenma return," but always only on condition that there be a Futenma substitute, the substitute had to be in Okinawa, and in Okinawa it had to be at Henoko. By 2017, not only was his government taking determined steps toward construction of substitute facilities for the US military on Okinawa Island, but it was also deepening overall "interoperability" (merger of US and Japanese military training, command, and intelligence under US direction) and moving to militarize the frontier Japanese islands. In the name of "defense" and "security," life for Okinawans was becoming increasingly intolerable. Confrontation was steadily deepening between the Abe government and Trump administration on the one hand and the people of Okinawa on the other.

## NOTE

The first edition of this book covered the period to 2012. Both authors have written a good deal since then, essays now accessible in the *Asia-Pacific Journal*, http://apjjf.org//, and (Norimatsu) in Peace Philosophy Centre, http://peacephilosophy.com. See also McCormack, "Ryukyu/Okinawa's Trajectory—From Periphery to Center, 1600–2015," in *Routledge Handbook of Modern Japanese History*, ed. Sven Saaler and Christopher W.A. Szpilman (London: Routledge, 2018).

# Note on Names

In all Japanese publications, Japanese names are given in the traditional order of family name followed by personal name(s), and, in principle, that is how they are cited in this text. Thus Hatoyama Yukio and Ota Masahide are the full names of former Prime Minister Mr. Hatoyama and former Okinawa Governor Mr. Ota.

However, Western media reporting and popular writing about Japan commonly reverses, that is, Westernizes, the name order, so that, for example, the above become Yukio Hatoyama and Masahide Ota. Also, some Japanese writers, especially those residing in English-speaking countries, choose to be known in their writings in English by their names in Western order, coauthor of this book, Satoko Oka Norimatsu—Ms Norimatsu—among them.

Our rule is to retain Japanese name order for all authors whose work is cited from Japanese sources and for major Japanese figures featured in the text, but to follow the Westernized name order for those who follow the Western convention when they publish in English or in citing materials about them in which their names are Westernized. It is therefore possible for the same author to be cited in our text according to Japanese name order when we cite from Japanese sources and in Westernized name order when we cite English language sources. Doubts may be resolved by reference to the index, where all individuals listed in the text are cited under family name and personal name (the Japanese convention) or family name followed by comma and personal name (when following the Western convention).

# Chronology

## *Japan versus Okinawa, 1995–2017*

| | |
|---|---|
| 4 September 1995 | 12-year-old Okinawan girl raped by three US servicemen. |
| April 1996 | The US and Japanese governments promise return of Futenma marine base "in five to seven years." |
| December 1996 | Futenma replacement to be on "east coast of the main island of Okinawa" (Special Action Committee on Okinawa Final Report). |
| December 1997 | Nago City plebiscite: majority reject base replacement plan, but mayor accepts and resigns. |
| December 1999 | City and prefecture accept substitution project but subject to three conditions: joint civil-military, fifteen-year limit, and no adverse environmental impact. |
| December 1999 | Obuchi government adopts Henoko construction project, subject to conditions. |
| August 2004 | Marine helicopter crash on Okinawa International University. |
| October 2005 | Agreement on "realignment" of US forces in Japan (*Beigun Saihen*). |
| May 2006 | Roadmap for Realignment Implementation. |
| 30 August 2009 | Election of Hatoyama as prime minister, promising Futenma substitution "at least outside Okinawa." |

| | |
|---|---|
| May 2010 | Hatoyama reverses himself, agrees to Henoko project, and resigns. |
| December 2013 | Governor Nakaima issues license for reclamation of Oura Bay for Futenma Replacement Facility construction. |
| 10 December 2014 | Onaga Takeshi replaces Nakaima as governor of Okinawa. |
| 16 July 2015 | Okinawan Third Party [Experts] Commission advises that Oura Bay reclamation license issued in December 2013 by (former) Governor Nakaima is "flawed." |
| 13 October 2015 | Governor Onaga cancels Oura Bay reclamation license. |
| 27 October 2015 | Government (Ministry of Land, Infrastructure, Transport and Tourism [MLITT] minister) "suspends" Onaga order. |
| 2 November 2015 | Okinawa prefecture complains to Disputes Council (Central and Local Government Disputes Management Council). |
| 17 November 2015 | National government (Ishii, MLITT) launches malfeasance suit under Administrative Appeals Act in Naha court (Fukuoka High Court, Naha branch) against Okinawa seeking "proxy execution." |
| 24 December 2015 | Disputes Council refuses to act on prefectural complaint. |
| 25 December 2015 | Prefecture launches suit in Naha court against government. |
| 29 January 2016 | Naha court advises government and prefecture to settle. |
| 4 March 2016 | *Wakai* (out-of-court) court-recommended settlement. Works stop. |
| 7 March 2016 | State (MLITT) demands Onaga retract his cancellation order. |
| 14 March 2016 | Onaga (prefecture) refuses MLITT request (an "illegal intervention by the state"). |
| April 2016 | Rape/murder of a 20-year-old Okinawan woman by a US military base worker. |
| 17 June 2016 | Disputes Council refuses to rule, urging "sincere discussions" to resolve "continuing undesirable" relations between state and prefecture. |

| 22 July 2016 | State launches new suit against prefecture in Naha court. |
| 16 September 2016 | Naha court verdict upholds state. Okinawa prefecture appeal to Supreme Court. |
| 13 December 2016 | Marine Corps Osprey crashes off the coast of Nago City. |
| 20 December 2016 | Supreme Court dismisses prefectural appeal. |
| 22 December 2016 | Half (ca. 4,000 hectares) of Marine Corps' Northern Training Area in Yambaru forest returned to Japan. |
| 26 December 2016 | Governor Onaga cancels his October 2015 cancellation order (thus reviving the reclamation permit). |
| April 2017 | Seawall construction works begin at Henoko. |
| 24 July 2017 | Okinawa prefecture launches Naha court suit seeking stoppage of reclamation works because rock and coral crushing license issued by previous governor Nakaima has expired. |

# 1

# Ryukyu / Okinawa

## *From Disposal to Resistance*

### ISLANDS OF AMBIGUITY

In May 1972, following twenty-seven years of direct American military rule, the Ryukyu Islands reverted to being a Japanese prefecture under the name "Okinawa." The year 2012 therefore marks its fortieth anniversary. These islands have a complex history and every year is punctuated by anniversaries, many with painful associations. Okinawa today looks back upon a history as an independent kingdom, enjoying close affiliation with Ming and then Qing dynasty China (1372–1874); a semi-independent kingdom affiliated with both China and Japan but effectively ruled from Satsuma in southern Japan (1609–1874); a modern Japanese prefecture (1872–1945); a US military colony, first as conquered territory and from 1952 subject to the determination of the San Francisco treaty (1945–1972); and then, from 1972 to today, once again as a Japanese prefecture but still occupied by US forces. Before the recent and contemporary disputes that are at the center of the US-Japan relationship can be understood, something of this checkered history as a region alternately in and out of "Japan" has to be recounted.

Okinawa's chain of islands—around sixty of them inhabited and many more not—stretch for 1,100 kilometers (683 miles) along the Western Pacific between Japan's Kagoshima prefecture and Taiwan. The largest and most populated island is about one hundred kilometers long and between four and twenty-eight kilometers wide, and the islands as a whole are about one-seventh the area of Hawaii. Linked to the Asian continental landmass until a million or so years ago, the islands have long been

1

separated from it by a gulf sufficiently deep and dangerous to have allowed the emergence in relative isolation of a rich and distinctive human as well as botanical and zoological environment. Today its people are both "Japanese," speaking more-or-less standard Japanese and constituting part of the Japanese nation-state, but also "non-Japanese," whose ancestors a century ago spoke languages distinct from Japanese, that is, separate languages rather than dialects, and five of which, still spoken today, especially on the outlying islands, are recognized by UNESCO as either "endangered" or "severely endangered."[1]

In 2008, the UN's Committee on Civil and Political Rights recognized the Okinawan people as indigenous inhabitants and called on the government of Japan to recognize them as such and "to adopt special measures to protect, preserve and promote their cultural heritage and traditional way of life, and recognize their land rights."[2] It also called for adequate opportunities to be provided for "Ryukyu/Okinawa children to receive instruction in or of their language and about their culture . . . in the regular curriculum." Three years later, neither had been taken seriously by the government of Japan, and, as detailed below, at the heart of the so-called Okinawa problem is the struggle by Okinawans to regain their land compulsorily and often forcefully acquired for US military purposes more than six decades ago.

The islands enjoy a mild subtropical climate and good rainfall with a rich marine reef environment. From the fifteenth century a flourishing autonomous state, the Ryukyuan Kingdom, trading along the China coast and as far south as Vietnam and Siam, formed part of the East Asian "tribute" world centering on Ming China. Though virtually obliterated from conventional historical memory, premodern Okinawa was a vigorous, independent economic, cultural, and political system, flourishing on the frontiers of the early modern Asia-Pacific. Its music and performing arts and its crafts, including lacquerware, dyed textiles, and pottery, were widely known and appreciated. However, the island kingdom that flourished in the fifteenth and sixteenth centuries was profoundly affected by major shifts in the global geopolitical balance starting in the late sixteenth century and continuing into the mid-twentieth century.

Both the early and then the mature phases of European maritime expansion, in the seventeenth and nineteenth centuries, opened new routes of commerce, spread new ideas and technologies, and helped dissolve and reform states. In the seventeenth century, as European capitalism and nationalism, underpinned by war and its technologies, despoiled Africa, colonized the Americas, and encroached on Asia. Japan, emerging from a long period of chronic civil war and failed attempts (in the 1590s) to subject Asia to Japanese rule, retreated to concentrate on developing its so-called closed country (*sakoku*) polity. But it first launched in 1609 one last expansionary thrust: an invasion force of three thousand musket-bearing samurai to conquer the Ryukyu Kingdom, punishing it for its recalcitrant attitude toward Hideyoshi's grand continental invasion plan. Within days, the court submitted and King Sho Nei (1564–1620) and his entourage were carried off to Kagoshima.[3]

The new order that was imposed was more "modern," rationalized, and bureaucratic than the shamanistic, ritual court world it displaced. It was also often harsh, with basic policy decided from Kagoshima (capital of the Satsuma domain), 660 kilometers away. The king and court continued, but the kings were no longer sovereign.

Okinawa/Ryukyu became a Potemkin-like theater state: Okinawans had to hide the fact that they were incorporated into the Japanese system in order to sustain the tribute relationship to China, those involved in missions to and from China were ordered to hide all things Japanese, and those on embassies to Edo (Tokyo) were required to wear distinctive, non-Japanese clothing. Thus the façade of independence was preserved, a trading window between Japan and China kept open through Japanese-controlled Ryukyuan tributary missions to China, and the prestige of the Bakufu heightened by the appearance of a foreign mission pledging fealty to it.

Ryukyu became in effect Japan's colony, its kings tied to the Japanese domain of Satsuma, and through it to the Edo Japanese state, while maintaining all the appearances of continuing attachment to the Chinese court in Beijing. Dual vassalage characterized the next several centuries. It meant that Okinawan officials were required to perform theater designed to conceal the locus and nature of political authority, and Shuri Castle, the site of the Ryukyu kings, was a carefully constructed stage.

The curtain did not ring down on this peculiar state till the mid-nineteenth century. For a brief period then, the omens for Ryukyu seemed good. Left more than usual to its own devices as the crisis in the Japanese Edo order deepened, Ryukyu courts negotiated modern "opening" treaties, as an independent kingdom, with the Americans, French, and Dutch (in 1854, 1855, and 1859).[4] Visitors were impressed. When the US Navy's Commodore Perry sailed into what was known as the Loochoos on his Black Ships en route to open Japan in 1853, his scientific advisers reported on a fertile, friendly, and prosperous state, a "most rich and highly cultivated rural landscape," with an agriculture more akin to horticulture, in a "system which could scarcely be improved" and its villages "quite romantic, and more beautiful than any of like pretensions I have ever seen."[5] The French missionary Furé, who spent the years 1858–1861 in Naha, described the villages as "resembling the beautiful gardens of England." It was by then diminished from its flourishing sixteenth-century peak and maintaining a precarious autonomy through judicious expressions of respect toward its two powerful and sensitive neighbors: the kingdom of Satsuma (one of the domains, centering on Kagoshima, making up the loosely linked Japanese state structure) to the north, and the Qing court in Beijing to the west. The Okinawan kings relied on their remoteness and their diplomatic skills to preserve the relative autonomy they enjoyed within their dual dependence on two powerful neighbors.

However, Ryukyu's ambiguous, dual-sovereignty status was incompatible with the "new world order" of expansive, rapacious, and militarized modern states and competing empires. It was of this state without weapons and ignorant of war that Napoleon Bonaparte (1769–1821) was said to have been told by passing sailors in his St. Helena exile, exclaiming that it was unbelievable. While the island elite debated possible responses to Commodore Perry on his 1853 visit and struggled to explain their island's status as a dual attachment, to China as mother and Japan as father, and their wish to maintain things as they were, the governing elite of the new modern Japanese nation-state in Tokyo adopted a strict modern, legalist view of the world, in which sovereignty was absolute and indivisible and frontiers had to be secured. The Japanese flag was first raised over the main island of the Ryukyus in 1872 and in 1873 over the outlying islands of Kume, Ishigaki, Miyako, Iriomote, and Yonaguni.

The Ryukyu court faced an impossible dilemma. The dual fiefdom status quo was unsustainable however much they clung to it, and the Qing court could not come to their aid with the Chinese "world order" under siege from central Asia to Indochina and Korea and much of the country only slowly recovering from the calamity of the Taiping rebellion and civil war. Beijing viewed Ryukyu as of relatively minor significance, just a "small kingdom in the sea."[6] The Shuri court, after much agonizing, ended its feeble resistance in 1879.[7] Submitting to the "punishment" from Tokyo over its lukewarm response to the new Meiji state order, in the first of the series of modern *shobun* or "disposals," it handed over the castle and sent the king, Sho Tai (1843–1901), into exile. Its incorporation into the modern Japanese state is unique in having been accomplished as part of a punishment (*shobun*), "unilaterally and by force," thus becoming an "unrecognized colony," and its subsequent status within the state was marked by persistent suspicion, discrimination, and forced assimilation.[8]

According to one story, probably apocryphal, as King Sho Tai in 1879 surrendered Shuri Castle to the superior force of the Meiji government, he uttered the words "Life is precious" (*Nuchi du takara*). These words later came to be understood as a core statement of Okinawan moral value, and the catastrophe that swept over the islands in the 1945 Battle of Okinawa was taken as confirmation of their wisdom. In the face of oppression, militarism, and colonialism the Okinawan people struggled to preserve the ideal of the supremacy of life over death, peace over war, the *sanshin* (samisen) over the gun.

## THE WEIGHT OF THE NATION-STATE

Thus Okinawa was incorporated in a subordinate status within the Japanese state. The new national government in Tokyo regarded the islands as crucial to state defense rather than as integral elements of any national community. This was clear from the readiness they showed, in negotiations with China from 1879, to split the islands either into two, ceding the farthest islands, Miyako and Yaeyama, to China in return for the grant of "most favored nation" trading rights within China itself. China in response, proposed a three-way split, south to China, north to Japan, with a reinstated Ryukyu Kingdom in the main island. In the end, no agreement was reached.[9] China only formally acknowledged Japanese sovereignty over the Ryukyu Islands under the Treaty of Shimonoseki in 1895, as part of the settlement of the Sino-Japanese War, which also ceded Taiwan to Japan.[10]

The historian Nishizato Kiko offers this judicious assessment:

> Had those Ryukyuans who evolved a "Ryukyuan Salvation Movement," instead of treating the tribute order as absolute been able to respond to the dawning of the new era, taking account of the proposals of Ueki Emori and Guo Songtao[11] as possible ways forward and forging links with the kingdoms of Korea and Hawaii[12] or with Vietnam, they might have been able to find a new way forward. But the Ryukyuans who plunged into the Salvation Movement treated the traditional tribute order as absolute and just sought the help of the Qing authorities to restore the Ryukyu kingdom. That was their historical limitation.[13]

Though this history is today largely forgotten, it is instructive. Again in early twenty-first-century East Asia, Okinawans, now living in a prefecture of the Japanese state that is closer to China (and Taiwan) than to the rest of Japan, seek a way to coexist peacefully and to cooperate with both in the formation of some kind of East Asian commonwealth. Where the dominant paradigms of the international system were tragically incompatible with Ryukyuan aspirations in the seventeenth and nineteenth centuries, in the post–Cold War twenty-first (in the context of partial US eclipse and the rise of China), the prospects might be better of reducing the iron grip of US military power or of the US-Japan condominium as nation-states perforce yield more of their authority to supranational institutions and the movement for regional and global cooperation grows.

Belatedly incorporated within the modern Japanese state, Okinawans were pressed to follow a path of self-negation, casting aside their distinctive language and culture, their "Okinawan-ness," in order to become "Japanese." Punished for speaking their own language, they were required to reorient their identity around service to the Japanese emperor and to participate in mainland myths and rituals. Less than seven decades after being launched on this process of identity change, in 1945 Okinawa was to be sacrificed in order to stave off attack on the "mainland" and preserve the "national polity"—meaning the emperor system. Japan's war on Asia came "home" in the cataclysmic Battle of Okinawa, when more than 120,000 Okinawans, between one-quarter and one-third of the population, died. These months, March to June 1945, marked the islands as nothing before or since has. Beneath the surface of contemporary Okinawa, the memory of its horror remains fresh, and it constitutes a wellspring of thinking about the present and future.

From the onset of the Battle of Okinawa in late March 1945, Okinawa and the surrounding (Nansei) islands were severed from Japan by order of the commander of the US Pacific Fleet, Admiral C. W. Nimitz.[14] Months later, the thirtieth parallel was defined as the dividing line.[15] Separated, when the catastrophe of the war ended, Okinawa was transformed into the American "Keystone of the Pacific." The Japanese emperor himself, Hirohito (1901–1989), gave his blessing to the separation and long-term military occupation. While publicly endorsing the May 1947 constitution under which all political authority was stripped from his office, Hirohito told the occupation commander, General Douglas MacArthur, that he believed Japan's security depended on "initiatives taken by the United States, representing the Anglo-Saxons," and in September 1947, Hirohito said the US military occupation of Okinawa "should be based upon the fiction of a long-term lease—25 to 50 years or more—with sovereignty retained in Japan."[16] His message must have confirmed to US authorities the wisdom of their decision to retain him in office rather than put him in the dock for trial as a war criminal during the Tokyo International War Crimes Tribunal.

Although the new constitution abjured the "threat or use of force" in international affairs, the emperor plainly believed that only the massive force at General MacArthur's disposal could assure Japan of its security, while for MacArthur, the fact that US military control of Okinawa would be acceptable to Japan for the long term gave him confidence to order the demilitarization of mainland Japan. However much that "25 to 50 years or more" stretches into "more," that imperial pledge to General MacArthur is not forgotten.

In an arrangement thus blessed at the highest level, mainland Japan became a constitutional "peace state" and Okinawa a "war state," both tied symbiotically within the US Pacific and Asian Cold War empire of bases. In mainland Japan, the US occupation ended in 1952; in Amami, the most northerly of the major Ryukyu Islands in December of the following year; but in Okinawa itself and its adjacent islands, and in Miyako and Yaeyama Islands, US occupation lasted until 1972.

In 1972, as the islands reverted from direct American military control to Japanese administration, switching in the process from the Sinic name Ryukyu (Liuqiu) to the Japanese Okinawa, the curtain rose over a different kind of "theater state." Nothing on stage was quite what it seemed. First, the reversion was not so much a "handing back," as implied by the words, but actually a "purchase" (discussed in detail below). Second, the "return" was a "nonreturn" since the US military continued to occupy and enjoy free use of much of the most fertile agricultural lands and to control the seas and skies. And third, following this strange transaction in which roles of buyer and seller were reversed, Japan adopted as national policy the retention of a substantial US military presence in Okinawa. To prevent any significant reduction of US forces ever taking place, it began to pay a sum that steadily increased over the years. The price that Japan paid to *avoid* reversion thus rose steadily. Japan also took steps to ensure that the truth of the reversion transaction be concealed and pursued mercilessly those who would venture to lift the curtain on it.

Okinawans had sought a reversion that would release them from the parameters of force, return their most fertile lands, and restore something of their ancient ideal of demilitarized, peaceful islands. The 1972 terms thus disappointed and angered many. On the actual day of the reversion ceremony, none of Okinawa's seven recently elected members of the national diet attended the Tokyo ceremony, and in Naha far more gathered in Yogi Park to protest the terms of reversion than attended the official ceremony. For them, May 15 was a day of humiliation. Yara Chobyo (1902–1997), long a major proponent of reversion and Okinawa's first elected governor, referred to the terms of reversion as "not necessarily what we had so earnestly striven for." He nevertheless tried to project a hope "to overcome the history in which Okinawa has always been a means and become a prefecture in which it would be possible to hope."[17]

The formal documents and instruments of power were therefore as deceptive and misleading as the Ryukyu expressions of tribute fealty to China and Japan in the seventeenth and eighteenth centuries. Post-1972 Okinawa performed Japanese sovereignty, constitutional pacifism, prefectural self-government, and regional autonomy while in reality sovereignty was only partially returned (the bases and American military sovereignty retained intact). The US-Japan security treaty continued to serve as Okinawa's key charter, in effect transcending and negating the constitution, and all important decisions were reserved to Tokyo and

Washington. Despite nominal incorporation in the constitutional pacifist Japanese state, therefore, the American military colony of Okinawa became the militarized, dual-colonial dependency of Japan and the United States.

For the Japanese state to impose a "priority to the military" polity on Okinawa and secure its compliance to an agenda whose core was priority to the US alliance over the constitution, to military over civil or democratic principle, and to the interests of the nation-state over those of the Okinawan people, Okinawan opposition had to be neutralized. Reversion, therefore, was built on deception and trumpery, bribery and lies. The Japanese state used smoke and mirrors to try to create a theater capable of deceiving and persuading the Okinawan people on a mass scale.

Two decades after "reversion," the Cold War ended. The enemy against whom the base structure had been directed collapsed, but the base complex remained. The bases did not just remain, but to the bitter disappointment of Okinawans, both governments insisted they be reinforced. In the Gulf, Iraq, and Afghan wars, the United States called on Japan to play a stepped-up military role, and governments in Tokyo did their best to comply, with Okinawa pivotal. "Deepening the alliance" meant reinforcing Japan's subservience and, therefore, its irresponsibility. As of 2012, nearly 20 percent of the total area of Okinawa Island is occupied by US bases. Okinawa prefecture, which is only 0.6 percent of the total area of Japan, hosts 75 percent of the US military bases in Japan. This means that the density of US bases in Okinawa is about five hundred times that of the mainland.

Okinawans who aspired to a reversion that would transform their islands from the militarism of war and occupation to the peace-centered values of the constitution of Japan found that the role assigned them in the post–Cold War order was to be that of bastion for the projection of force to maintain a US-dictated order from the Western Pacific to Central Asia. As after the reversion in 1972 and after the end of the Cold War in 1990, the military relationship with the United States, not the constitution, was to be Okinawa's key charter.

When mass discontent at these arrangements threatened to boil over, especially following the rape of a schoolgirl by three US servicemen in 1995 (discussed below), a new round of "reversion" was promised; but again deception was the keynote. Where "reversion" in 1972 meant retention (and purchase), so in 1996 it came to mean substitution, modernization, and expansion of US military bases. Of the dense web of bases across the main island of Okinawa, the return of none was more urgently sought than that of Futenma Marine Air Station, which sat uncomfortably in the midst of the bustling city of Ginowan. While the two governments sought to contain the 1995 crisis by promising Futenma's return, they did so only by attaching the condition that an alternative facility would first be constructed. They assumed it would be possible to impose such a solution on the people of Okinawa. As the nature of the process was obfuscated by calling it reversion, so its scale too was concealed by calling the projected new base a "heliport" and by using the expression *seiri shukusho* (base reduction) to try to convey the impression that *overall* that was what was happening.

The post–Cold War reorganization called for Japan to move from being a dependent and semisovereign state to become a full *zokkoku* or "client state."[18] For the most part, clientelism and the Japanese state priority to military ties to the United States could be ignored by people in mainland Japan because it impinged little on their everyday lives; but in Okinawa it weighed heavily and was felt intolerable. While protest elsewhere was scattered and easily contained, in Okinawa it grew steadily. Okinawans were also able to see what mainlanders only rarely could: that the US insistence on Japan's submission and support for its hegemonic order rose even as US credibility shrank on all fronts: economic, political, and especially—with the launch in the early twenty-first century of illegal, aggressive wars and the adoption of tactics such as torture and assassination—moral.

Today, as in the late sixteenth to early seventeenth and nineteenth centuries, the old order is again breaking down. The global coalition of US-led, militarized, and alliance-supported neoliberal states confront uneasily the crumbling of an order that once they believed to be unshakable. For Okinawa, geopolitical and economic flux constitutes threat and opportunity: to be swallowed again into an exploited and manipulated status, or to assert a distinctive role as a historical actor. Alternately "in" and "out" of Japan over four centuries, and an integral member of the China-centered "tribute world" for a similar period before that (and partly coinciding with it), Okinawans sense the opportunity encased in the present crisis: to formulate a way beyond nation-states and military blocs and to reconstitute itself at the center of the process of evolution of an East Asian or Northeast Asian community, as a bridge linking Japan, China, Korea, and the Asia-Pacific.

## RESISTANCE

Okinawans tend to look back and see the four hundred years of their troubled premodern and modern history in terms of successive *shobun*, or "disposals," by superior, external forces depriving them of their subjectivity, with militarism their peculiar bane—under Satsuma from 1609, the modern Japanese state from 1879 to 1945, direct US military rule from 1945 to 1972, and nominal Japanese rule after 1972. Though helpless to avoid or resist past disposals, from 1996 the balance shifted. Okinawa gradually has come to play a major, if rarely acknowledged, role in the regional and global system. It became a *state of resistance.*

Nothing in its historical circumstances or long record of being victimized can account for what today has become Okinawa's most distinctive feature: its deep-rooted, sustained resistance. Almost in proportion to the denial of their aspirations and their autonomy, Okinawans challenge not only their own island fate but also the pillars on which the Japanese "client state" and the US-imposed regional and global order itself rests. This book is an attempt to elucidate the process by which disposal, oppression, and alienation become resistance.

The contest over the Marine Corps base at Futenma and the plan to replace it, commonly represented as a struggle over the question of construction of a single base, is therefore much more. It pits the Okinawan community against the nation-states of both Japan and the United States. As detailed in the following pages, we believe that Okinawa as of 2012, fiercely insisting on the constitutional principle of popular sovereignty (*shuken zaimin*), astonishingly holds the advantage. It deserves to be understood in the context of the global democratic movements of the early twenty-first century.

As the Japanese nation-state replicated its own dependence on the United States in the regional order it imposed within Japan, it evolved mechanisms by which to distribute largesse to buy off opposition and win consent. The state design was one in which Okinawa was to be locked into dependence by several conditions: first because it was seen (and saw itself) to be backward in that its per capita GDP and other economic indexes were below the rest of Japan, so that it therefore had to "catch up"; and second because "development" funds were seen by state bureaucrats as the best device to foster the sort of mendicant mentality in which the antibase and environmental movements would lose momentum. "Development" therefore tended to be concentrated on infrastructural public works projects that often were economically retrogressive, ecologically damaging, and debt and dependence building (the same strategy that was followed by the state in order to impose nuclear power on reluctant local communities elsewhere in Japan). Nature came to be seen as something to be "fixed" (by *seibi*) in a process that had virtually no limit, with the result that the natural environment was subject to siege, even as public works–led *doken kokka* (construction state) development came to be discredited elsewhere in Japan.[19]

Today no spectacle is sadder to the regular visitor to Okinawa than to see, in the north, the steady pressure designed to impose a huge new military complex on the quasi-pristine waters and reef of Oura Bay (and associated helipads throughout the Yambaru forest), and in the south, the gradual reclamation of the Awase tidal wetlands (Okinawa's "rain forest") to create an artificial beach.[20] Base-dependent development replicated two decades later than mainland Japan the worst features of the "construction state," with devastating consequences for the prefecture's economy and ecology. In 2010, however, as we detail below, the people of Nago City demonstrated that they had seen through this manipulative device and decisively rejected it.

In the centuries before 1609, Okinawa's smallness of scale and its relative geographic isolation from major powers were its strengths. After 1609, in the Westphalian era of nation-states contesting and prevailing by force, they became its weaknesses. The Japanese nation-state (and its American patron) continue today to see Okinawa's location as crucial for the defense of "Japan proper" and for the regional and global projection of military force to advance their interests. Okinawans know from their history that armies do not defend people and that security in real terms depends on the forging of close, friendly, and cooperative ties with neighbor countries. To attain such security, Okinawa's "war preparation" functions designed to secure American power throughout the Asia-Pacific have to be converted into "peace-building" functions. Okinawa's geographical location and multicultural history suit it well to serve in the future as a peace center, a Sino-Japanese bridge, and an obvious candidate to house some of the core institutions of a Northeast Asian concert of states, as an Asian Luxembourg or Brussels.

So in a sense this is a book about relations between two great and powerful countries from the perspective of a relatively remote and peripheral region and within that region an even more remote village and bay. We believe, however, that much is to be learned by shifting the focus away from the capitals and the centers of state power in this way. Beyond the immediate issues of the future of Okinawa, Henoko, and Oura Bay, the struggles under way highlight some large questions: if, as seems the case, the Japanese constitution's guarantees of popular sovereignty, basic human rights, and peace do not apply to Okinawa, what does that mean for the rest of the country?[21] In the context of relations between major states, especially those in "alliance" relationships, how should the confrontation centered on the Okinawan base issue that occurred between the United States and Japan in 2009–2010, in which abuse and intimidation led to the fall of a government, be understood? And through the lens of Japanese history, what does it mean that an entire prefecture unites, as does Okinawa today, in saying "no" to the central state authorities and the world's military colossus? Can that incompatibility be resolved within the existing state system, or is Okinawa headed toward semi- or even full detachment from the Japanese state?

These are all matters of large import not only for scholars specializing in modern Japan, the United States, and the Asia-Pacific but for concerned citizens everywhere. We make no claim to have resolved them in this book, but we hope we have provided enough material for readers to make better-informed judgments about them.

Above all, this is a story of the process by which, for the first time in Japan's history, grassroots democratic forces seized the initiative and over a sustained period became the key subject in determining the course of history. That struggle is of far-reaching significance. Their immediate message to the governments of Japan and the United States is simple: "No!" to the new base project. But it is a negative that holds within it a positive vision of a different future, a message addressed to all its surrounding countries, not just Japan and the United States. And to which the "*nuchi du takara*" principle is central.

## NOTES

1. Kunigami, Miyako, Okinawa, Yaeyama, and Yonaguni. Christopher Moseley (ed.), *Atlas of the World's Languages in Danger.* 3rd ed. (Paris: UNESCO Publishing, 2010), http://www.unesco.org/culture/en/endangeredlanguages/atlas.

2. United Nations Human Rights Committee, "International Covenant on Civil and Political Rights" (Geneva: United Nations, 2008).

3. The Ryukyu resistance was overwhelmed by superior force, especially forearms. Gregory Smits, "Examining the Myth of Ryukyuan Pacifism," *Asia-Pacific Journal: Japan Focus* (September 13, 2010), http://japanfocus.org/-Gregory-Smits/3409. After the initial hostilities and surrender, resistance ceased, but one prominent member of the Ryukyu nobility, Jana Teido (a.k.a. Jana Uekata Rizan) (1549–1611), was summarily executed in Kagoshima because of his refusal to swear allegiance to the new Satsuma overlord.

4. Nishizato Kiko, "Higashi Ajia shi ni okeru Ryukyu shobun," *Keizaishi Kenkyu* no. 13 (February 2010): 74.

5. J. Morrow, "Observations on the Agriculture, Etc, of Lew Chew," in *Narrative of the Expedition of an American Squadron to the China Seas and Japan, Performed in the Years 1852, 1853, and 1854, under the Command of Commodore M. C. Perry, United States Navy* (Washington: A.O.P. Nicholson, 1856), 15; and D. S. Green, "Report on the Medical Topography and Agriculture of the Island of Great Lew Chew," in *Narrative of the Expedition of an American Squadron to the China Seas and Japan, Performed in the Years 1852, 1853, and 1854, under the Command of Commodore M. C. Perry, United States Navy* (Washington: A.O.P. Nicholson, 1856), 26, 36.

6. Li Hongzhang, quoted in Nishizato, "Higashi Ajia," 99.

7. One Ryukyuan scholar-official, Rin Seiko (1842–1880), who had been active in the "Salvation Movement," sought refuge in Beijing in 1876 and committed suicide there in despair and protest at the new order in 1880.

8. Hideaki Uemura, "The Colonial Annexation of Okinawa and the Logic of International Law: The Formation of an Indigenous People," *Japanese Studies* 23, no. 2 (September 2003): 107–124: 122.

9. Nishizato, "Higashi Ajia," 107–8.

10. Ishii Akira, "Chugoku no Ryukyu/Okinawa seisaku: Ryukyu/Okinawa no kizoku mondai o chushin ni," *Kyokai Kenkyu* no. 1 (2010): 73.

11. Ueki, a prominent figure in the "Liberty and People's Rights Movement" in Japan of the 1880s, and Guo Songtao, an official and prominent member of the Chinese "Self-Strengthening Movement" in the 1870s, both favored independence for Ryukyu/Okinawa.

12. Hawaiian king, King Kalākaua, visiting China in 1880 or 1881, expressed a desire to mediate a Sino-Japanese agreement on Ryukyu/Okinawa, in the context of promoting Asian unity, resisting European-American pressure and promoting Asia's rise (Nishizato, "Higashi Ajia," 120).

13. Nishizato, "Higashi Ajia," 120.

14. "Proclamation No. 1 (The Nimitz Proclamation), 5 April 1945," Gekkan Okinawa Sha, *Laws and Regulations during the U.S. Administration of Okinawa, 1945–1972* (Naha: Ikemiya Shokai, 1983), 38.

15. "Navy Military Government Proclamation No. 1-A, 26 November 1945," Gekkan Okinawa Sha, *Laws and Regulations*, 41–42.

16. For the former, the emperor's view as stated just three days after the new constitution came into force on May 3, 1947, Toyoshita Narahiko, *Anpo joyaku no seiritsu: Yoshida gaiko to tenno Gaiko* (Tokyo: Iwanami shoten, 1996), 144, and Toyoshita interviewed in Narusawa Muneo, "Showa tenno to Anpo joyaku," *Shukan Kinyobi* (May 1, 2009): 11–17; for the latter, Shindo Eiichi, "Bunkatsu sareta ryodo," *Sekai* (April 1979): 45–50. (The "emperor's letter" discussed in the latter was penned by Hirohito's aide, Terasaki Hidenari, but emanated from the emperor.)

17. Arasaki Moriteru, *Okinawa gendaishi*, 2nd ed. (Tokyo: Iwanami shoten, 2005), 34.

18. See Gavan McCormack, *Client State: Japan in the American Embrace* (New York: Verso, 2007).

19. For further discussion, see Gavan McCormack, "Okinawa and the Structure of Dependence," in *Japan and Okinawa: Structure and Subjectivity*, ed. Glenn D. Hook and Richard Siddle (London, New York: RoutledgeCurzon, 2003).

20. According to Okinawa University's Sakurai Kunitoshi, Okinawa has thirty-eight artificial beaches and is planning ten more while its natural ones shrink. Sakurai Kunitoshi, "COP 10 Igo No Okinawa," in *Okinawa wa doko e mukau no ka* (Okinawa University, December 19, 2010).

21. Editorial, "Okinawa no min-i—Kennai isetsu 'No' ga senmei da shusho wa omoku uketome eidan o," *Ryukyu Shimpo*, November 3, 2009.

# 2

*~~*

# War, Memory, and Commemoration

No prefecture contributed so little to the preparation for war and its prosecution through the years, but none suffered as much in widespread misery, in loss of human lives and property, and in ultimate subservience to military occupation.

—George H. Kerr[1]

Nothing about contemporary Okinawa can be understood without first confronting the events that took place there more than sixty-five years ago: the shock and horror of the Battle of Okinawa (March 26–September 7, 1945). In this book directed primarily at understanding recent and contemporary Okinawa, we therefore devote this chapter to clarifying the events, their context, and the way they have been remembered and commemorated. If Okinawans today overwhelmingly hate war, distrust the military (whether Japanese or American), and refuse to be persuaded by "national defense" agendas (whether of Tokyo or of Washington), it is above all because of what happened then. As Miyume Tanji states, the direct experiences in the battle have been "an ideological resource" for the postwar opposition to military bases.[2] Mobilized, manipulated, tricked, and then abandoned, Okinawans suffered an outcome that was an unimaginable catastrophe. What they were forced to "defend" then were not their lives and property but mainland Japan, in particular the imperial institution. In place of gratitude for their sacrifice in a hopeless cause, they were abandoned once again, and once "reverted" to Japan two and a half decades later were told that, yet again, they must sacrifice for the sake of the "national" defense.

Today, while Okinawans struggle against the imposition of any new base on their island, they struggle with at least as much passion and determination against any attempt to deny or distort the cataclysmic horror that they remember as the Battle of Okinawa.


# WAR

## Imperial Subjects

Mobilization for the imperial cause began in the 1870s with incorporation into the modern Japanese state as Okinawa prefecture, followed soon afterward by severance of its long and close ties with the Chinese court and the stationing of mainland troops, a garrison force from Kumamoto in southwestern Japan. The word by which the process was known was *Ryukyu shobun*, disposition or punishment, and the first military base was part of the design to intimidate and subdue Okinawans. As Okinawa's former governor and Battle of Okinawa survivor, Ota Masahide, recounts,

> Indeed, this was the beginning of transforming of the Ryukyus into a military base by the Japanese Government, and later on was followed suit by the U.S. Government. Needless to say, it was also the real cause of Okinawa's tragedy in the Pacific War.[3]

*Komin-ka* policies designed to indoctrinate and assimilate Okinawans as imperial subjects followed. Like colonial subjects in Korea and elsewhere, Okinawans were obliged to learn and speak Japanese, that is, the newly established national language, in place of the Okinawan languages used in everyday life. Those caught speaking Okinawan at school were shamed by being made to wear a wooden "dialect placard" (*hogen fuda*) around their necks. Okinawans were encouraged to substitute mainstream Japanese names for distinctively Okinawan names, and emperor-centered State Shintoism was introduced, with shrines erected in front of Okinawa's sacred *utaki* groves while schools constructed stone shrines (*hoanden*) to enshrine photographs of the emperor, who was worshipped as a living god. Teachers and students were obliged to learn and to recite on special occasions the Imperial Rescript on Education as a ritual designed to instill and enforce emperor-centered education principles.

## The "Bloodiest" Battle

The Battle of Okinawa (Operation Iceberg in US military history) is often referred to as one of the bloodiest battles fought in the Pacific War. The story may be summarized in its grim statistics. The battle was fought between

548,000 US troops (183,000 mainly infantry and marines in assault phases, and the rest support units) and more than 110,000 Japanese troops (of which about 25,000 were Okinawan home-guards and high school students), but it also involved in various ways more than 400,000 local civilians pressed into service. Indiscriminate and relentless bombing and shelling from sea, air, and land—the "Typhoon of Steel"—lasted three months, involved firing as many as fifty shells on average for each Okinawan resident,[4] and killed civilians, babies, women, children, and elderly alike. The Battle of Okinawa killed over 210,000, including over 120,000 Okinawans out of the population of 460,000.[5] Noncombatant Okinawan casualties (approximately 94,000) far exceeded those of Okinawan members of Japanese defense forces (28,228). The Battle of Okinawa also killed 65,908 soldiers from other prefectures of Japan and 12,520 Americans, along with smaller numbers of other nationalities.[6] Some thousands of Koreans (perhaps 10,000), including men who had been mobilized to work for the Japanese military and women who were made into military sex slaves, were also killed.

### War Crosses the Pacific

Okinawan civilians had suffered serious consequences even before the bombardment and invasion of Okinawa itself began, as many Okinawans—mostly those who had emigrated because of poverty in the 1920s and 1930s—had settled on South Pacific islands and in other parts of the world. By 1940, over 57,000 Okinawans lived outside the Japanese border.[7] There were 25,772 Okinawans on Saipan, 4,799 on Palau, and 1,145 on Ponape.[8]

In February 1944, US forces began the aerial bombing of Truk Island, followed by attacks on Saipan and Tinian. It was an unmistakable signal of the war's advance toward Japan itself. Non-Okinawan residents in Okinawa evacuated to the mainland, and on March 22, 1944, the Thirty-Second Army was established for defense of Okinawa. As the South Pacific islands became battlegrounds, many local residents, including emigrants from Okinawa and Japan, were trapped in the fighting and killed. The fall of Saipan in July 1944 was a foretaste of what lay ahead for Okinawa. Thirteen thousand of the fifteen thousand Japanese emigrants who died were Okinawans, and many were forced to kill themselves in what was known as *gyokusai*, literally "shattering the jewel," the term used to describe suicide for the sake of the emperor.

In September 1943, the Imperial Headquarters decided to reinforce defense of the Nansei Islands (from the south of Kyushu to the east of Taiwan, including Okinawa Island) in order to protect the Japanese mainland. All local Okinawan residents who "were able to stand up and move were conscripted in a 'root-and-branch' (*nekosogi*) mobilization"[9] to build airfields throughout the prefecture.

After April 1944, battle units started to arrive in Okinawa from China and from mainland Japan. Since there were too few barracks, school buildings and other community buildings in villages were used as barracks, military supply storage, and "comfort stations"—places of military sex slavery for the Imperial Japanese forces. This mixing of military personnel and civilians was one cause of the later high casualty rate; also, as military secrets were exposed to the eyes of civilians, especially Okinawan civilians, whom Japanese military men were instructed not to trust, it led to the killing of Okinawans by Japanese soldiers.

## Evacuation and the Sinking of the *Tsushima maru*

In July 1944, as the Joint Chiefs of Staff began to prepare for the Allied landing, orders were issued to evacuate women, children, and the elderly from the Ryukyu and surrounding islands. The plan did not proceed smoothly as families resisted being separated, and anxiety rose over the safety of crossing the ocean in the possible path of enemy submarines.[10] On August 22, 1944, the *Tsushima maru* was en route to Kagoshima, the southernmost port of mainland Japan, with 1,788 on board (834 school children, 827 teachers and other adults, 127 crew). Torpedoed by the *USS Bowfin*, it sank. Confirmed dead were 1,418, including 775 children, 29 teachers and caregivers, 569 other adults, and 21 crew members. In Okinawan memory, this is remembered as a case of civilian mass killing. Before the Battle of Okinawa began, only 100,000 Okinawans evacuated, leaving 490,000 confined on the island with no way to escape.[11]

On October 10, 1944, the US aerial bombing on Okinawa destroyed 90 percent of the capital city (Naha), killing 668 (military and civilians combined). As the land battle loomed, the Japanese military concentrated on indoctrinating Okinawans with the principle of "military, government, and civilians, living and dying together." This principle is a key to understanding how civilians suffered so much as victims in the Battle of Okinawa.[12]

## Imperial Directive

In February 1945, former prime minister and imperial aide Konoe Fumimaro advised the emperor that defeat was "inevitable" and Japan should seek terms to end the war. Defeat carried the risk of a communist revolution that might endanger the national polity (*kokutai*), the emperor system. Emperor Hirohito disagreed, saying that negotiations should not be sought without first achieving one more military success.

Where public discourse beyond Okinawa concentrates on the emperor's so-called sacred judgment (*seidan*) to accept the Potsdam Declaration and surrender on August 15, 1945, thus ending the war, in Okinawa it tends to concentrate on this decision to continue to fight when the war was already lost. It was not only Okinawans who paid the price of this imperial decision. Most of mainland Japan's civilian war casualties (estimated at about 500,000, including Hiroshima and Nagasaki)[13] occurred after the rejection of Konoe's advice. Sociologist Hayashi Hirofumi argues that Okinawans developed the foundation for independent thinking and action through their experience of war, while mainlanders lagged behind, particularly where the emperor's war responsibility is concerned.[14]

## Kerama Islands

Following air raids on March 23 and naval bombardment the following day, US forces landed on the Kerama Islands, about forty kilometers west of Naha, on March 26, 1945. As the battle began, the isolated and terrified islanders were summoned by Japanese military officers and coerced into forced mass suicides; in other words, they were ordered to kill themselves and their family members instead of surrendering. The Japanese military feared that Okinawans might become spies for the Americans and intimidated them into believing that surrender was shameful and would be followed by slaughter for men and rape followed by killing for women. Hand grenades were distributed, and when grenades were not available, ropes, knives, sickles, razors, and rocks were used. These "forced mass suicides," or *gyokusai*, have come to be known as *shudan jiketsu* (collective suicide) or *kyosei shudanshi* (forced collective deaths). Hundreds died such deaths on the Kerama Islands on March 26 and March 28.[15]

## Okinawa Island

On April 1, 1945, US forces landed on the west coast of the main island of Okinawa, between Yomitan and Chatan, and split into two forces, one heading north and the other south. Since the Japanese strategy was to delay the US land invasion to the mainland, it allowed the US to land unchallenged (*muketsu joriku*, or "bloodless landing") while concentrating its remaining offensive power on two thousand suicide plane attacks on US warships by *kamikaze tokkotai* (special attack units) from bases in Taiwan and Kyushu. The United States had mobilized 1,400 to 1,500 warships and about 548,000 troops in all (including 183,000 land troops and members of the supply convoy). By contrast, Japan had a force of some 100,000 troops (estimates of the army troops range from about 69,000 to about 86,400 and navy from about 8,000 to about 10,000). When locals between age thirteen and seventy conscripted as Defense Corps (*boei-tai*), Patriotic Brigades (*giyu-tai*), male and female secondary-school students, women's

**Figure 2.1.    Civilian victims of the Battle of Okinawa.** *Source:* US National Archives.

relief teams, and cooking teams are included, it might have been between 110,000 and 120,000.[16] The US forces not only outnumbered the Japanese, but they were also overwhelmingly better armed, with a near total command of the sea and air.

The main US forces reached the Japanese front lines on April 8. With the fierce resistance of the Japanese army, it took the Americans fifty days to break through and commence an all-out offensive around Shuri (the Japanese headquarters) on May 11. Despite desperate resistance at Sugar Loaf Hill in Asato and in the Untamamui woods, by the end of May the Thirty-Second Army, having lost 70 percent of its forces, abandoned its Shuri headquarters and fled south. Commanding General Ushijima set up a new headquarters at Mabuni Hill in the south, where he planned to gather the remaining thirty thousand troops and continue fighting. For Japan, Okinawa was to serve as a "breakwater"—or "sacrifice stone" (*sute ishi*)—for the defense of the mainland, allowing mainland Japan to buy time and try to negotiate a peace deal that would permit the preservation of the emperor system.[17] On April 20, 1945, the Imperial Headquarters Army Department issued a "Directive for the Decisive Homeland Battle," saying,

Even when the enemy advances by using local residents and women as their shields and tries to weaken our morale, do not hesitate to annihilate the enemy, and believe that they will wish for victory of our imperial nation more than they wish for their own long life.[18]

For the Imperial Army, Okinawans' lives were disposable.

The Japanese army in southern Okinawa followed this directive between Shuri and Mabuni, on the southward retreat route, where many women, children, and the elderly had evacuated, and the military used them as shields in fighting the last desperate stage of the battle. Okinawans learned that the military, far from protecting local residents, made them targets of attack, coerced them to commit suicide, and often even directly killed them. Civilian murders and mass suicides occurred only in places where the Japanese military was present.

In the south of the island, local civilians had taken refuge in naturally occurring limestone caves called *gama*. The Japanese troops who fled from the mid-island took possession of these caves, evicting the local residents and exposing them to danger and often death outside. Some were killed by the Japanese military on allegations of spying. The south became a chaotic battlefield, with Japanese troops and civilians fleeing from Naha, Shuri, and central Okinawa while being subjected to artillery barrages, bombing raids, and flamethrower attacks. Using what were called "horse-rider tactics," the American troops would straddle the entrance holes of the caves and throw in explosives and flames, killing civilians and soldiers alike.

With the suicide of General Ushijima and his chief of staff, Cho Isamu, on June 22,[19] the organized operations of the Japanese military ended.[20] Ushijima's last order, however, was to continue to fight to the end, and therefore many soldiers and civilians died after him. The formal surrender of the Thirty-Second Army was signed on September 7, 1945, three weeks after the emperor announced surrender and five days after the surrender ceremony in Tokyo Bay.

General Ota Minoru, commander of the Japanese naval forces, which defended the Oroku Peninsula in southern Okinawa, also committed suicide earlier, on June 13, 1945, in the naval underground headquarters. In his last cabled message, one week before his death, he commended Okinawans for their dedication in fighting the battle and concluded, "This is how the Okinawan people have fought the war. And for this reason, I ask that from now on the Okinawan people are given special consideration."[21] For his recognition of Okinawan suffering and his request for "special consideration" for them, Ota tends to be remembered more favorably than Ushijima.[22]

Figure 2.2. *The Battle of Okinawa*, by Maruki Iri and Maruki Toshi. *Source:* Sakima Art Museum.

## THE PEOPLE UNDER THE WAR

### Betrayal

The Battle of Okinawa was hopeless from the start, simply a bloody design to postpone the Allied landing on the Japanese mainland. Since Okinawa was not regarded as really being part of Japan, little consideration was paid to protecting its people. The Okinawan memory is more of the neglect, abuse, deprivation, and even killing suffered at the hands of Japan's own forces than of the civilian casualties caused by the US attacks. The experience was so much the more traumatic since they had been taught to become Japanese and loyal subjects of the emperor, and indeed, many had tried to be even more Japanese than the Japanese in order to be treated as equals. The internalization of Japanese values aggravated the sense of betrayal caused by the Japanese military's behavior.

### Total Mobilization

Under the "total mobilization system" adopted following the entry into full-scale war against China in 1937, wartime measures were imposed on every aspect of people's lives, and all cultural, social, economic, and human resources were strictly regulated under imperial and ministerial orders. Okinawa was required to provide soldiers, labor, and food. Men were conscripted for military, and women for labor (often in mainland factories). With the deployment of the Thirty-Second Army in 1944, all-out mobilization and exploitation of local civilians occurred, and after the air raids of October 1944 civilian mobilization accelerated. Men between seventeen and forty-five years of age were conscripted first to build airfields, and after January 1945 to supplement military forces.

### Children

The Thirty-Second Army mobilized all middle-school students as soldiers or for paramilitary service in late March 1945. At least 1,787 junior-high boys across the island, mostly from age fourteen to nineteen, were drafted as members of the "Blood and Iron Student Corps" (*Tekketsu Kinnotai*). More than half (at least 921) died.[23] Middle-school girls were organized into "Army Nursing Corps" and required to work around the clock in field army hospitals or makeshift cave hospitals, looking after injured soldiers, attending surgery, and disposing of amputated limbs. Of 717 known girls mobilized as military nurses, 283 are known to have died in the Battle of Okinawa. Student casualties were only a small proportion of overall casualties of infants and children. One military report estimated that 11,483 children under fourteen years of age died in the battle, more than 10 percent of the total civilian casualties. Nearly 90 percent of the deaths occurred because the children were evicted from their cave shelters in order to make space for Japanese soldiers, at a time when that meant exposure to immediate high risk of death. Others died doing chores for the military such as cooking, rescue work, and transportation of food and other supplies. Three hundred children were victims of "forced mass suicides," that is, they were killed by family members made to believe that it was imperative in order to protect their loved ones from becoming the prey of the enemy. Fourteen were shot by the Japanese military. In summary, the overwhelming majority of child deaths were due to the Japanese military's failure to protect them or its direct violence against them. Out of 11,483 recorded child deaths, 5,296, or just above 50 percent, were children under five years of age.[24]

## Military Murder of Civilians

As tens of thousands of Japanese troops arrived on the island, where there was an obvious shortage of food and weapons, they often took what they wanted from Okinawans. As soldiers and civilians "lived and died together" on the same battlefields, the army feared that military information would leak out through them, especially if they surrendered. An order was issued, "Anybody speaking in the Okinawan language will be punished as a spy."[25] Those who possessed American leaflets encouraging surrender or who tried to convince others to surrender were often executed on the spot. Also, not a few murders of POWs and rape by US soldiers happened throughout the battle.[26]

## The Kumejima Massacre

On June 13, 1945, when the battle on the main island headed toward Japan's inevitable defeat, the US military kidnapped three locals on Kumejima Island, about 100 kilometers west of Naha. The Kumejima navy garrison commander directed the community leaders to turn in the abductees as soon as they were returned and also to turn in any leaflets dropped from enemy planes. Disobedience was to be punished by execution for spying. On June 26, US forces landed on the island, and two of the abductees were returned. Because of the chaotic situation of the battle, and because the villagers did not know the location of the garrison commander, the return went unreported. When eventually the navy garrison members found the men, they bayoneted and killed them, their family members, and two community leaders, and set fire to their houses. By that time, the organized battle was over, but Ushijima's final order to "keep fighting until the last remaining soldier" meant that Japanese resistance and violence against local civilians continued. Other atrocities continued on Kumejima, even days after the emperor's announcement of surrender on August 15, including the brutal killing of a Korean resident and his entire family on suspicion of spying. [27]

### Forced Mass Suicides

On the Kerama Islands, after hundreds died in forced mass suicides, the biggest fear for the residents after the cessation of US bombing and shelling was "spy hunting" by the remaining Japanese military in hiding.[28] Forced mass suicides often stand out in Battle of Okinawa narratives, but they occurred in the context of military violence against Okinawan civilians in general, such as civilian massacres like that at Kumejima. Ultimately, as Ishihara Masaie insists, the murder of local residents and the forced mass suicides served the same purpose of thwarting surrender and information leakage:

> The military had implanted strong fear in the minds of Okinawans, threatening that those who would try to put up their hands and surrender would be shot, and the captives, if they were men, would be torn limb from limb, and if they were women, would be raped then killed. The local residents had already been overwhelmed, psychologically, beforehand. The government explains *"shudan jiketu* (mass suicide)" as "residents willing to die for the sake of the emperor and the country," but in reality, in order to prevent leakage of military secrets, the military ordered, coerced, directed, guided, and convinced the residents to kill each other rather than become enemy captives.[29]

Forced mass suicides in Okinawa occurred between March 26 and June 21, at thirty known sites. The scale of each incident varies from a few to a few hundred. Large-scale incidents include the Kerama Islands (329 on Tokashiki; 234 on Zamami; 53 on Geruma) between March 26 and 28, Chibichiri-gama in Yomitan Village (83) on April 1, and Ahaja-gama on Ie Island (about 100) on April 22, all shortly after US forces landed nearby.[30] Here are two stories.

### Tokashiki Island

Many survivors of the forced suicides did not speak about their experience for a long time. Kinjo Shigeaki, age sixteen at the time, is among the few who did. When the US troops landed on his island, the young boy thought death was inescapable. The Japanese military had already given hand grenades to village leaders, saying the residents had to die when they encountered the enemy. On the enemy's landing, the people were gathered, and with the mayor's shout of "Long Live the Emperor!" began killing each other.[31] Since there were not enough hand grenades for everyone, and many did not detonate, people used whatever came to hand. Kinjo saw one man take a tree branch and beat his wife and children to death. Others used razors and sickles to cut throats and ropes to strangle and hang themselves.[32] Kinjo and his elder brother used their mother's kimono belt to strangle their little brother, little sister, and mother. They used a rock, too.[33] Kinjo writes, "When I assisted my mother, I burst into tears from sadness."[34] Kinjo recounts, "Taking their own lives before the weaker family members would have meant that they would leave their loved ones in the devilish hands of the enemy."[35] When Kinjo and his brother were about to kill themselves, someone rushed in and urged them to kill at least one enemy before they died, so he and his brother followed. When they discovered, astonished, that some of the Japanese troops and local residents were still alive, they felt betrayed. In due course they were captured. Kinjo started his postwar life with an unbearable burden of guilt and trauma. In the depth of despair, he found hope in Christianity and became a minister.

*Chibichiri-gama*

On April 1, the day US forces landed at Yomitan, 140 local people were hiding nearby in Chibichiri-gama cave. When American soldiers urged them to surrender at the entrance of the cave, two men dashed out with sharpened bamboo sticks and were promptly shot. The following day, an unarmed US soldier went into the cave, again counseling surrender. Again residents refused, at the order of a senior member of the community. When the soldier left, tensions rose and suicides started. Eighty-three died, of whom forty-seven were children under age fifteen, four were shot, and fifty-three managed to escape and survive.

At nearby Shimuku-gama cave, one of the residents had lived overseas and was able to persuade the residents that the Americans would not kill those who surrendered. All survived.[36] After the war, shame, shock, and horror kept the local residents silent about the Chibichiri-gama incident for decades. Then writer Shimojima Tetsuro, after years of persuasion, interviewed survivors and their families, and in 1987, families and villagers together built a memorial sculpture at the entrance of the cave, with the support of local sculptor Kinjo Minoru. The sculpture was defaced seven months later by ultranationalists. The residents covered it and became silent again, but after two years, they uncovered it, saying, "We will stand up again, even if we get punched two or three times." The sculpture was later restored.[37]

*Factors behind the Deaths*

Hayashi Hirofumi suggests six intertwined factors behind the forced mass suicides: (1) people were taught that it would be shameful to be captured and that it was virtuous to die bravely in the name of the emperor; (2) people were heavily indoctrinated that men would be brutally killed and women raped and then killed if captured; (3) the Japanese military threatened local residents that they would be killed for becoming or wanting to become captive of the US (actually, many were killed for that reason); (4) the idea of "military, government, and citizens living and dying together" was widely imprinted in Okinawan minds; (5) many residents were handed hand grenades by Japanese soldiers, who ordered, recommended, and suggested using them for suicide in extreme circumstances; and (6) the understanding held by Okinawans that a military order had been issued for suicide.[38] According to the US analysis, based on POW and civilian captive interrogation, the second of these reasons—the fear of being brutally killed once captured—appeared to be the number one reason.[39] This is consistent with many of the testimonies by former Japanese Battle of Okinawa soldiers. Many of them had previously fought in China, where looting, rape, and slaughter of local residents were taken for granted, and they assumed that Americans would behave in the same way.[40]

## Korean Victims

From Korea, then the Japanese colony of Chosen, thousands of men were brought to work for the military as *gunpu* (laborers), building airfields and fortifications, transporting ammunition, and working as stevedores on the docks. Many died under severe working conditions, abuse, and malnutrition. Despite the slogan of *"Naisen ittai"* (Japanese and Koreans as one), Koreans suffered discrimination. One former laborer on Aka Island in the Kerama Island group said, "Because we were hungry, we took rice and potatoes from the field and ate them. My fellow Korean laborers were shot and killed because of that."[41] Twelve were slaughtered on Aka Island. Fed up with the way Japanese treated them, more and more Korean laborers began to surrender.[42]

The Korean Monument in Okinawa Peace Park, build in 1975, states that "as many as ten thousand" Koreans were killed in the battle. As of 2011, however, only 447 Koreans are listed on the Cornerstone of Peace at the Okinawa Prefectural Peace Memorial Park, built in 1995.[43] Much is still to be discovered about this gap. In June 1999, a list of 2,815 Korean laborers brought to Okinawa was discovered in Korea. Only 650 were reported to have survived, 273 were confirmed dead, and 1,872 were "unknown, but most probably died from war-related disease and injuries." In that case, over 70 percent of the laborers died or disappeared during the war.[44]

## "Comfort Stations" and Rape

Wherever the Japanese military went, there were so-called comfort women, or military sex slaves—thousands of women from Korea, Japan, China, Philippines, and beyond who were forced into sex slavery systematically by the Japanese military—and Okinawa was no exception. According to one former Japanese soldier, "When a military unit moved, what the commanding officer first does is to talk to leaders of the village and build a comfort station."[45] Okinawa, including surrounding islands, had over 130 comfort stations with Okinawan, Japanese, and Korean women. Some of the latter were deceived by job posts calling for factory workers and maids.[46] Rape of local women by both Japanese and US soldiers also occurred.[47]

## Malaria on Remote Islands

The scourge of war was rampant not just on the islands where US troops landed, but also on remote islands where they did not land, including the Miyako and Yaeyama island groups, about three hundred to six hundred kilometers southwest of Okinawa Island, and Yonaguni, only one hundred kilometers from Taiwan and the westernmost point of Japanese territory. On Ishigaki Island, the second-largest and most populated island of Yaeyama, residents were mobilized to build airfields—two thousand residents per day on average, plus six hundred Korean laborers—and were forced to offer rice and cattle to the military. Ten thousand Japanese troops came to Yaeyama (population then 31,000), and 30,000 troops came to Miyako (population then 60,000). Apart from the expropriation of farmland for building airfields, the seizure of food, and forced labor, the biggest problem on those islands was malaria.[48] The malaria epidemic was concentrated in populations who were forced to evacuate to mountainous areas. Close to 17,000 (53 percent of the population) fell ill with malaria on Yaeyama islands, of whom 3,647 died. On the southernmost island of Hateruma, almost everyone (1,587 out of the population of 1,590) fell ill, and of them, about one-third (477) died.[49] The reason for forcing so many local residents to evacuate to mountainous, disease-ridden areas is not clear, but apart from the intention to expropriate all the island's food supplies, the Japanese may have wanted to prevent the islanders from being captured by the United States.[50]

## Internment Camps

Upon surrender, Okinawa Island residents were taken to internment camps. US psywar operations, including the distribution of four million leaflets to convince the Japanese military and civilians to surrender, seem to have been effective. From the onset of the Battle of Okinawa on March 27 until the end of June 1945, 10,740 POWs (7,401 soldiers and 3,339 "labor troops" or "unarmed laborers") and 285,272 civilians were taken into custody.[51] The ratio of those taken captive to those who died in the Battle of Okinawa was about 18 percent, much higher than battles of the other Pacific islands, which ranged around 1 to 2 percent.[52] Upon surrender or capture, Okinawans were interrogated, civilians separated from soldiers and placed in civilian refugee camps, and soldiers placed in POW camps. Civilians were provided plots of land where they built temporary huts and put up tents to live in. The US military provided food, clothing, and medication. Still, many died of malaria and malnutrition. Rape by US soldiers frequently happened.[53]

Yoshida Kensei, an Okinawan journalist who was sent to a camp with his family, recalls:

> Just before I turned four years old, we returned from a natural evacuation cave to a shelter in the backyard of our home. Then, at the gunpoint of US soldiers, my family and I were brought to an internment camp. My father, who was a member of a Defense Corps [civilians mobilized to work for the military, conscripted by the Thirty-Second Army], was taken away to Hawaii, and my grandmother and my younger brother died in the internment camp, perhaps from malnutrition. Farms had traces of naval bombardment, and ammunition and human bones lay scattered around. People unceasingly died from explosion of undetonated bombs. I lived my childhood in severe hunger and unsanitary conditions.[54]

## Aftermath

The experience of the battle left incurable scars on many Okinawans. As a member of the Blood and Iron Student Corps, Ota Masahide almost daily saw his classmates bombarded and "die the deaths not of humans, but of worms." Of his 386 schoolmates, 226 died. After spending the last months of the battle hiding among the rocks of Mabuni Beach, surviving hunger, injury, and desperation, he surrendered on October 23, 1945, two months after Japan's formal defeat, and was admitted to the internment camp in Yaka. War still haunts him. When the army left its Shuri headquarters to retreat toward the south of the island in May 1945, an injured soldier begged Ota to take him along, saying, "Gakusei-san!

**Figure 2.3.   Undernourished children being fed at Koza, Okinawa, August 4, 1945.**
*Source:* US National Archives.

Gakusei-san!" ("Student! Student!") More than six decades later, Ota
still hears the soldier's cry every day.[55] "There is so much unfinished
business," says Ota. He spent the early months after the end of hostilities searching for the remains of the dead and returning them to their
families,[56] despite the fears of some of his colleagues that such activity
might seem provocative to the Americans. Eventually, the bones of over
180,000 war victims were gathered,[57] but thousands more remain to be
discovered. Unexploded bombs also abound across the island and are
expected to take forty to fifty years to dispose of.[58]

"The war is far from over in Okinawa," says Ota. "Then why prepare
for more wars?"[59] It is a sentiment widely shared. The islanders' resistance against US military bases is inseparable from their experience of the
indescribable horrors of the war. Not only do they not want to see another
war in Okinawa, many feel responsible for indirectly participating in US
wars in Iraq and Afghanistan since their land is being used for military
bases.

The poem on the tapestry hung inside the Henoko sit-in tent reads as
follows.

At the end of the Battle of Okinawa,
Mountains were burned. Villages were burned. Pigs were burned.
Cows were burned. Chickens were burned.
Everything on the land was burned.
What was left for us to eat then?
It was the gift from the ocean.
How could we return our gratitude to the ocean
By destroying it?

—*Okinawa Uminchu (Fisherman) Yamashiro Yoshikatsu*

## MEMORY

### Forced Mass Suicides

Forced mass suicides may have been a relatively minor cause of death in the total scale of Okinawan Battle casualties,[60] and it was certainly not unique to Okinawa. Such deaths occurred to Okinawan and Japanese civilians in other parts of the Pacific, including Saipan, and in Manchuria. However, in postwar Okinawa and Japan, forced mass suicides have been at the center of contention in historical debates over the battle: most notably, the Ienaga textbook lawsuits (1965–1997), the defamation lawsuit against Iwanami Publishing Company and author Oe Kenzaburo (2005–2011), and the controversy over the Japanese government's advice to remove or tone down accounts of military coercion in the description of those deaths in history textbooks (2006–2007). Although forced mass suicides were part of the Japanese military's aggression on local residents, those intent on reducing or eliminating military responsibility insist that those acts were carried out by the victims alone.

The terms, too, are contested. During the war, people used the word *gyokusai* (jewel shattering), which applied to dying in battle in suicidal ways such as in kamikaze attacks, or to soldiers dashing headlong into attacking enemy forces. The phrase *shudan jiketsu*, "mass suicide," appeared in the media from July 1945 to refer to the suicide of heavily injured soldiers who chose not to burden others,[61] and it was later used in 1950 when it was chosen in preference to the older term, *gyokusai*. However, the word *jiketsu*, literally "self-decision," but with the particular meaning of suicide, later came to be considered problematic because conservative forces stressed precisely that—self-inflicted death—and downplayed or denied the Japanese military's role. The presence of military order became the focus of contention in the Ienaga and Oe/Iwanami lawsuits and in the textbook controversies.[62] To resolve the problem, some use "*shudan jikestu*" in brackets, implying that the reality was different from the one implied by the word,[63] and others use "*kyosei shudanshi*," literally "forced collective deaths," to emphasize the forced quality of the acts.[64] Yakabi Osamu develops the contradictory notion of suicidal acts in a coercive environment and believes that "compulsory group suicides," as described by Norma Field, done under "duress, both in the form of the presence of the two armies and in the long discipline required for the production of Japanese imperial subjects,"[65] best represents the structural complexity behind the acts.[66]

## Textbooks

The pressure to reduce reference to military coercion in the forced mass suicides in the Battle of Okinawa should be understood in the context of the repeated attempts over the past six decades by conservative governments, bureaucracy, and right-wing groups to downplay Japan's war responsibility in textbooks and war narratives in general. Other issues of contention include military sex slavery, the Nanjing Massacre, and the biological warfare Unit 731. Historian and textbook author Ienaga Saburo fought against such pressures of historical distortion in a thirty-two-year-long series of lawsuits.[67] Efforts such as his were instrumental in thwarting rightist control of textbooks and in nurturing an educational environment for learning of Japan as a war perpetrator. Alarmed by such trends, in the mid-1990s the Society for the Making of New School Textbooks in History (*Atarashii Rekishi kyokasho O Tsukuru Kai*), or Tsukuru Kai, was formed and started an aggressive campaign to produce and promote textbooks that downplayed Japan's aggression. The forced mass suicides in the Battle of Okinawa have been one of their major targets, and their pressure intensified between 2005 and the present, both in the public sphere and in educational media (textbooks).[68]

## The Oe/Iwanami Suit

In 2005, another suit was filed, alleging that accounts by author Oe Kenzaburo of the Battle of Okinawa that referred to Japanese commanders on Zamami and Tokashiki islands ordering residents to commit suicide were defamatory. The claim was rejected, first by the Osaka District Court and then later by the Osaka High Court in 2008, and a further appeal was dismissed by the Supreme Court in April 2011. With this decision, the Nobel Prize–winning author and the publisher won the six-year-long lawsuit. This lawsuit was directly connected to the 2006/2007 textbook controversy, discussed below, as the plaintiffs and their supporters were among the forces that promoted reduction of discussion in high-school textbooks about military coercion in the forced mass suicides.[69]

## The MEXT Contest, 2006/2007

In December 2006, the Ministry of Education, Culture, Sports, Science and Technology (MEXT, formally MOE) requested revisions in seven out of the eight high-school history textbooks submitted for review, referring to the passages about military coercion in the residents' mass suicides as likely to "cause misunderstanding on the reality of the Battle of Okinawa."[70] In arguing that there was no evidence of any direct military order, it reproduced essentially the arguments used by the plaintiffs in the Oe/Iwanami suit, only pointing to the absence of direct verbal order in some instances without looking at the larger structural background behind the occurrences of such deaths. The textbook authors were required to modify their descriptions of the mass suicides so as to reduce the suggestion that the military had used coercion. For example, the phrase "There were some who were forced (*kyosei sareta*) by the Japanese military to commit mass suicide" had to be altered to read, "There were some who were cornered into (*oikomareta*) committing mass suicides." Words with a clear and strong connotation of coercion were watered down, and the subject was removed.[71]

The attack on the coercive nature of mass suicides in Okinawa was part of a systematic attempt to revise the record of Japanese aggression during World War II. Contemporary efforts by Japan's leaders to expand the nation's military capabilities and deepen its cooperation with the United States would proceed more smoothly if the Japanese military could be relieved of responsibility for past military crimes against its own and other Asian people. The revisionist campaign concentrated on three pillars of what it described as the "masochistic view of history" that tended to reduce the prestige of the Japanese military—the Nanjing Massacre, the military comfort women system, and mass suicides in the Battle of Okinawa. According to Ishiyama Hisao, author of one of the textbooks subjected to MEXT revisionist pressure, the revisionists had been successful in eliminating the "comfort women" issue almost entirely from textbooks[72] and in eliminating the estimated number of deaths from the description of the Nanjing Massacre in many of them, but the group had yet to touch treatment of Okinawan issues. The 2006/2007 campaign sought to "extinguish from people's consciousness the important lesson of the Battle of Okinawa that 'armies do not protect people,' and by protecting the 'honor' of the emperor's army, to raise a people who will serve country and army and thus mobilize them again for war."[73]

The Okinawan response was swift. Waves of condemnation, led by peace organizations, teachers' unions, and Okinawan newspapers, swept across the islands. Municipal assemblies and the prefectural assembly demanded withdrawal of the revision. A bipartisan, all-Okinawa protest rally on September 29, 2007, drawing 117,000 people, became the biggest on the island since Okinawa's reversion to Japan in 1972.[74]

Many survivors of the mass suicides, who had never previously talked about their traumatic experience, broke their silence and testified at this rally. As one high school student representative put it, "This may be about only one sentence, only one phrase in a thick textbook, but within it are many precious lost lives."[75] The mass rally adopted a resolution stating, "It is an unquestionable fact that the 'mass suicides' could not have happened without the involvement of the Japanese military. To remove or modify this fact in the textbooks is to deny and distort numerous survivor testimonies."[76]

MEXT in due course issued notice that it would respond to such an unprecedented expression of Okinawan opinion and, after a series of negotiations and hearings, at the end of 2007 authorized modifications, although it refused to rescind the original revision advice. It would not accept the reintroduction of the word *kyosei* (forced), although it approved a description that hinted at coercion.[77] Five years after the controversy, the struggle for reversal of the original MEXT revision continues. Even in the wake of the Supreme Court's dismissal of the defamation claim against Oe Kenzaburo and Iwanami Publishing, MEXT still refused to rescind its March 2007 decision. High school students in Okinawa today use textbooks which reflect the MEXT revision requests.

The fact that the Okinawan rally against the revision of textbook references to forced mass suicides drew more people than any previous antibase demonstration suggests that Okinawans feel even more strongly about historical issues than about the bases. The two are, of course, related, but the denial of Japanese military coercion of forced mass suicides is plainly intolerable to Okinawans, especially survivors and families of victims. The strong reactions from across Okinawa also indicate a resistance to the centrally controlled educational curricula and point to an Okinawan determination to own the history to be taught to younger generations of Okinawans.

## Border Islands Targeted

While the 2007 textbook debate remains unresolved, a new textbook dispute erupted in mid-2011. The textbook selection committee of Yaeyama Islands (the southernmost islands of Okinawa) endorsed the civics textbook by Ikuhosha, one of two textbook publishers associated with *Tsukuru-kai*. When *Tsukuru-kai* texts were first approved by MEXT in 2001, countries that had been victimized by Japan during the war were highly critical. However, less than 1 percent of schools in Japan adopted those textbooks during the first few years. By the summer of 2011, the figure for junior high school history and civics textbooks had grown to about 4 percent.[78]

The Yaeyama Islands are divided into three school board jurisdictions—Ishigaki, Taketomi, and Yonaguni—with a combined population of only about 55,000, about 4 percent of Okinawa's total. Yet the textbook selection process on those islands was headline news, the subject of numerous articles and editorials for weeks in the two major Okinawan newspapers. Even mainland media paid attention. It was the first time that a *Tsukuru-kai* textbook was adopted by an Okinawan school board. The *Tsukuru-kai*-affiliated history textbooks made no mention of the Japanese military's involvement in the mass suicides. Ikuhosha, whose cover map of Japan did not even show Okinawa, framed the constitution of Japan as one imposed by the US occupation forces and offered no discussion of the principles of popular sovereignty, peace, and human rights. It also neglected Okinawa's long suffering from the base burden or the Futenma relocation problem.

Although it seemed inconceivable for Okinawan schools to choose such texts, Ikuhosha's civics textbook was adopted under controversial circumstances. According to media reports, the textbook selection by-laws and processes were changed to influence the decision, backed by conservative politicians and *Tsukuru-kai*-affiliated forces in mainland Japan. Previously, a group of experienced teachers had acted as textbook examiners, ranking the textbooks and making recommendations to committee members. For the first time, committee members were empowered to choose from nonrecommended textbooks. Procedures to select committee members and teachers for the review panel were also made less democratic and less transparent.[79]

The Yaeyama textbook issue has to be seen in the light of recent moves to step up Japanese and US military presence and activities on and around these islands that border so closely on China and Taiwan, especially following the 2010 dispute between China and Japan over the Senkaku/Diaoyu Islands (discussed in chapter 11). Textbook controversies, now and in the past, tend to be closely linked to the political climate of the times, whether in the 1980s, when then prime minister Nakasone Yasuhiro called for transforming Japan into America's "unsinkable aircraft carrier" and for revising postwar history education, or in the early 2000s, when Prime Minister Abe Shinzo likewise called for Japan to move away from the principles of its postwar regime, including the peace constitution. In the view of one Okinawan critic,

> This is not just a matter of history revisionism; it is closely related to Japanese defense policy . . . history revisionism emerged as a Japanese government policy to cultivate the people's defense consciousness as Japan remilitarized.[80]

Right after the Self-Defense Force was established in 1954, a cabinet Intelligence and Research Office publication addressed the subject of "People's Defense Consciousness," saying,

> If the memory of wartime victimization in people becomes a peace ideology (*heiwa shiso*), that will thwart cultivation of people's defense consciousness. In order to nurture people's patriotism and defense consciousness, it is necessary to eliminate the memory of wartime victimization, and appeal to the young generations who have no memory of being victims of war.[81]

## Okinawa versus Yasukuni

Sculptor Kinjo Minoru, born 1939, is a native of Hamahiga, a small island just off Okinawa's Katsuren Peninsula. He insists that his father, Kinjo Seisho, who enlisted a year after marrying Kinjo's mother, Akiko, and who died in the battle on Bougainville in March 1944 at age 24, "died in vain," or literally, died a "dog's death (*inujini*)." Only his hair and nails were returned. Kinjo says his attitude used to infuriate his mother, who was proud of her husband's death and took comfort in the fact that he was honored at Yasukuni Shrine. There, in Tokyo, some two and a half million military personnel who died in battle for the emperor are enshrined as heroic gods (*eirei*). As Minoru puts it, "Unless I frame my father's death as a 'dog's death,' I won't be able to truly see what the Battle of Okinawa was."[82]

Kinjo was one of the ninety-four plaintiffs in the "Okinawa Yasukuni Lawsuit" launched in September 2002 to claim that the visits of Prime Minister Koizumi Junichiro to Yasukuni Shrine were in breach of the Constitution's Article 20 requiring the state to "refrain from . . . any religious activity." They also demanded the state compensate for the psychological suffering caused by the prime minister's visit. In five previous Yasukuni-related court rulings on suits filed by mainland groups, claims of violation of rights and demands for compensation had been dismissed, although one had deemed the prime minister's visits to be unconstitutional.[83] For the Okinawan suit, the Naha District Court conducted an on-site visit by judges, attorneys, and plaintiffs, presumably to better understand the suffering of civilians embroiled in the battle in southern Okinawa. Nevertheless, in January 2005 the court dismissed all the plaintiffs' claims.[84]

Okinawa's case was unique in that most of the plaintiffs were survivors or bereaved family members of the Battle of Okinawa. They protested against their family members, war victims, being enshrined as war heroes together with Japanese military personnel who had actively cooperated in the war. Their primary motive was not so much to seek compensation as to educate the public about the emperor's war in which so many Okinawan and Japanese lives were lost in vain and to problematize the visit by a state leader to a religious institution that not only denied the aggressive nature of the war but glorified it.

Kinjo Minoru is also one of five plaintiffs who filed suit against Yasukuni Shrine and the state in March 2008, requesting removal of their bereaved family members from the list of the enshrined. This suit constitutes part of a larger national and international movement to demand removal of those who were enshrined at Yasukuni without approval or knowledge of their families. Plaintiffs in these suits include those from Korea and Taiwan and also those who object on religious grounds to having a member of their family enshrined at an institution that practices a faith they do not accept.

## Enshrining Civilians

Yasukuni in principle enshrines only military personnel who died in battle for the emperor, not, for example, the hundreds of thousands of civilian victims of conventional or atomic bombing. But over 55,000 Okinawan civilians are enshrined there as "combat participants." Civilian victims of the war in Okinawa have been categorized in this way as quasi-military personnel in order to qualify them for compensation under the Law for Relief of War Victims and Survivors.[85] When the law was applied to Okinawan civilians in 1958, the Okinawa prefecture divided the "circumstances of combat" into twenty categories and helped the bereaved families to fit their dead family member into one.[86] Those who were forced out of evacuation caves into enemy fire were placed in the category of "offering [military personnel] shelter in a cave," those who provided food became "donors of food," and even those who committed forced mass suicide and those who were killed as "spies" were deemed to have cooperated with the battle by "preserving military secrets." Once certified as "quasi-military personnel," these were added to the list of those enshrined at Yasukuni. The names were sent to the shrine through the Japanese government office in Okinawa and the Ministry of Welfare, without the knowledge or permission of bereaved families.[87]

In this way 55,000 Okinawan civilians, including children, were enshrined. The relief law and its associated compensation scheme were used to "cover up the Japanese military's crime against Okinawans"[88] and to conceal the truth about the Battle of Okinawa. This falsification also influenced the Japanese Education Ministry's revision of textbooks.[89] The families, many of them impoverished, seem to have had little idea that they were applying for compensation by agreeing that their family members had died because of cooperating with the military. Yet Kinjo and the other plaintiffs did challenge Yasukuni and the state. Yasukuni Shrine, discontinued by the occupation forces as a state-sanctioned war memorial shrine and later revived as a private religious organization, has never agreed to remove any "gods" from its enshrined list. On October 26, 2010, Naha District Court turned down the five plaintiffs' demand, ruling that it could not intervene with Yasukuni Shrine's "freedom of religion." A year later, in September 2011, the Fukuoka High Court upheld that ruling, and Kinjo and his associates appealed to the Supreme Court. For them, the lawsuit is not about compensation but about righting the wrong of enshrining family members killed in war, including a two-year-old boy, as "combat participants."

Kinjo, sculptor of the Chibichiri-gama memorial to victims of the mass suicides, did not always think his father, who had wanted Kinjo to be educated properly as a Japanese citizen in order to be free from discrimination against Okinawans, had died in vain. But no matter how Okinawans strived to "be Japanese," they were driven out of the caves, killed, and forced to kill one another, he concluded. They were tricked into dying. Kinjo's mother, Akiko, eventually came to support her son and joined as a plaintiff in the suit against Koizumi.

It may be said that the Okinawa and Yasukuni issues embody opposite philosophies of life and death, the one celebrating life and denying war, the other celebrating death and promoting war. The struggle between them continues. For Kinjo, activity on the Yasukuni suits and protest against base construction plans constitute two sides of a coin. He remarks that "construction of a 'Futenma relocation facility' in Okinawa is the same as the battle of Okinawa, in which we were told to die rather than be caught by the Americans."[90]

## Public Memory

Japan is an archipelago of peace museums, where artifacts and memories of past wars, particularly World War II, are exhibited. About one-third of approximately two hundred museums for peace around the world are in Japan,[91] although that number also includes many museums, especially in mainland Japan, which emphasize Japan as a victim of war, highlighting the destruction of aerial bombings of Japanese cities, the atomic bombings of Hiroshima and Nagasaki, and wartime poverty while slighting or ignoring Japan's responsibility for war and aggression against Asian neighbors.

In that archipelago, Okinawa stands out as an island of peace memorials and museums, particularly southern Okinawa, where the fiercest battles in the later phase of the overall Battle of Okinawa were fought. Ota Masahide quotes the central "statement" exhibited in the Okinawa

Prefectural Peace Memorial Museum as conveying the perspective on war of the majority of Okinawans:[92]

> Whenever we look at the truth of the Battle of Okinawa
> We think there is nothing as brutal
> Nothing as dishonorable as war.
> In the face of this traumatic experience
> No one will be able to speak out for
> Or idealize war.
> It is human beings who start wars.
> But more than that
> Isn't it we human beings who must also prevent wars?
> We have abhorred all wars
> Long yearning to create a peaceful island.
> To acquire
> This
> Our unwavering principle
> We have paid dearly.[93]

Itoman, a city on the southern edge of Okinawa Island, has two major peace museums[94] and about 250 war memorials and monuments.[95] Okinawa prefecture as a whole, including Yaeyama and Miyako islands, has over 400 monuments to the war dead—including the Cornerstone of Peace, which commemorates all war dead regardless of nationality; *Konpaku no to* (Monument of Souls), the first citizen-oriented monument built in the early postwar years to remember the 35,000 unidentified victims; prefectural monuments remembering soldiers from each prefecture, mostly on Mabuni Hill; other military-oriented ones including those commemorating suicide attack units; Korean monuments; and monuments to the Student Corps, victims of forced mass suicides and malaria, medical professionals, and journalists. Other monuments have been built by towns and villages.[96] Over 14,000 American names are inscribed on the Cornerstone of Peace, and other monuments remember General Simon Buckner of the US Tenth Army, journalist Ernie Pyle, and three US pilots tortured and killed by the Japanese navy after their plane was shot down on Ishigaki Island.

Sakihara Seishu, a plaintiff in the Yasukuni suit, and his family come to *Konpaku no to* each year to mourn for his mother and elder brother. Bridling at their enshrinement in Tokyo, he says, "We have nothing to do with Yasukuni. We just come here."[97] For Sakihara and many like him, *Konpaku no to* is a symbol of citizens' suffering and mourning, the antithesis to Yasukuni.

Ota Masahide worries, nevertheless, that the philosophy of peace is fading as Japanese government, industry, and Self-Defense Force leaders attempt to reshape the memory of the Battle of Okinawa to prepare the way for future wars.

> They do not pay attention to the over 200,000 people killed in the Battle, and when it comes to the Japanese military's responsibility for the loss of some 20 million people in neighboring countries, they do not just neglect the issues, but they even deny the fact itself. Under this environment, the significance of the memorial monuments built all over Okinawa will be lost.[98]

Memory remains fiercely contested. Epigraphs of 37 out of 140 memorials, especially those built from the 1960s, when veterans and bereaved family associations from mainland Japan started to build memorials, include "affirmation and praise of war and dying in war" and "patriotic emotions" but lack expressions of remorse over participation in the war.[99] Of the memorials representing each prefecture, only two mention victimization of Okinawan local residents.[100] Many of the two million visitors each year to Okinawa go to Mabuni Hill, where the prefectural monuments to mourn for the soldiers from each prefecture stand, and to "*Reimei no to* (monument of dawn)," where General Ushijima is honored.[101] Perhaps only a few of the visitors to the latter note the contrast between the pride of position enjoyed by the commander of the Thirty-Second Army on the hilltop, overlooking the ocean, and the students of the "Blood and Iron" Corps, whose monument is to be found down many stairs below it, symbolically preserving across many decades the immense gap in status and power between those responsible for the catastrophe and its victims.

Oshiro Masayasu warns of "Yasukunization" of mourning for and remembering the war dead and criticizes the prevailing narratives by tour guides, who tend to depict the war victims as if they were precious martyrs for the country and who also ignore Japanese military violence against Okinawan civilians.[102]

### Contest over Museum Display

Okinawa's bitter war experience makes for heightened sensitivity to attempts to manipulate its memory or to build up military forces. Issues such as the revision of the Fundamental Law of Education, slow but steady penetration of *Tsukuru-kai* textbooks into classrooms, the reduction in peace education curricula, and the growing coercive use of the *Hinomaru* flag and *Kimigayo* anthem in school ceremonies arouse greater critical response in Okinawa than elsewhere in Japan. For that reason, Okinawa is subjected to intense pressure to remold its thinking.

In 1999, Okinawa was in an uproar over what became known as the "museum display falsification incident." When first established in 1975, the Okinawa Prefectural Peace Memorial Museum in Okinawa Peace

Memorial Park in Mabuni, southern Okinawa, was essentially a central government–planned initiative, with little input from Okinawans. It therefore had the look of a military museum and even resembled the museum attached to Yasukuni shrine. After much criticism, it was redesigned by a new steering committee that included Okinawan scholars. When it reopened in 1978 it highlighted the war experience from Okinawan perspectives.[103]

The 1999 prefecture-wide controversy was thus the second for this museum. The expansion and improvement of the existing museum was part of the three-pillar peace initiative of Ota Masahide (governor, 1990–1998), along with establishment of the "Cornerstone of Peace" and of an Okinawa International Peace Research Institute. The Cornerstone of Peace was completed in 1995, but after Ota lost the election for a third term in office in 1998, the remaining initiatives were significantly altered by the prefectural staff under his successor, Inamine Keiichi. They covertly changed the contents of the projected exhibition while the museum was being renovated. The changes were designed "so that cruelty of the Japanese soldiers would not be overemphasized."[104] A life-size model of the inside of a *gama* was to show civilian evacuees watched by a Japanese soldier and pressured to silence a crying baby by suffocating it. According to the prefectural staff who briefed the governor on the exhibit plan, Governor Inamine found this problematic. Emphasizing that the museum was prefecture funded, he suggested that the exhibit content should not provoke the national government.[105] When the supervising committee members examined the model being made in July 1999, they noticed that the soldier in the *gama* did not have a bayonet in his arms. The prefectural staff acknowledged that it had made two changes—removing both the bayonet and the military medic who coerced suicide with potassium cyanide.[106] Historians and journalists discovered and publicized at least eighteen changes planned by the prefectural staff. The plan was designed to downplay not merely Japanese military violence against Okinawans or just in Okinawa but aggression against the people in neighboring countries as well.[107]

The Inamine administration also made changes to the exhibits at the Okinawa Prefectural Yaeyama Peace Memorial Museum on Ishigaki Island, which had been built on the initiative of the Ota administration and completed in 1998. The debate in this case centered on how to refer to military coercion compelling people to move to mountainous areas, where they caught malaria and suffered heavy casualties. It favored the term "evacuation" over "forced eviction."

From August to October 1999, the "museum exhibit falsification incident" dominated Okinawan newspaper headlines and public discourse. Governor Inamine Keiichi eventually allowed the museum's supervising committees to restore the project to its original design, and the Okinawa Peace Memorial Museum opened in April 2000. The Yaeyama museum reopened in November 2000.[108]

There seems to be no end to controversy over how we remember and record the Battle of Okinawa. In February 2012, the prefecture under Nakaima governorship removed phrases such as "slaughter of local residents" and "comfort women" from the description of the information board that they were planning to install in front of the former shelter of the 32nd Army headquarters in Shuri. Governor Nakaima, upon being questioned at the prefectural assembly on February 24, said he would not rescind those changes. Further, the prefecture eliminated more phrases from the text for translation into English, Chinese, and Korean, including "sacrifice stone" (*sute ishi*), a critical key word to understand the Battle of Okinawa, in which the whole prefecture and its people were sacrificed for defense of the mainland and the emperor. Ishihara Masaie commented that previous debates were about distortion of specific events within the Battle, but this one was distortion of the Battle of Okinawa itself.[109] On March 23, the prefecture hastily set up the board, with typos and grammatical mistakes in the translated texts. As of April 2012, movements by citizens' organizations and experts are continuing to demand that the prefecture rescind the changes.

## The Cornerstone of Peace

The Cornerstone of Peace, recording the names of all who died in the Battle of Okinawa, regardless of nationality or of military or civilian status, was erected in 1995 under the peace policy initiative of then governor Ota. As of June 23, 2011, it carried the names of 241,132 people.[110] But the monument, though often cited as one of the most unbiased, humanistic war-related memorials in the world, has not been free from contention. Some object that although the monument defines itself as free of religious association[111] and a symbol of war renunciation,[112] respecting all who died in the war as equal, to remember victims and perpetrators together is to blur the responsibility of perpetrators and victims. The result, they hold, is to tend toward "Yasukunization" of the monument, that is, glorification of the war perpetrators and the war itself.[113] In this vein, US president Bill Clinton, speaking at the monument when visiting Okinawa for the Kyushu-Okinawa Summit of 2000, said,

> While most monuments remember only those who have fallen from one side, this memorial recognizes those from all sides and those who took no side. Therefore, it is more than a war memorial; it is a monument to the tragedy of

all war reminding us of our common responsibility to prevent such destruction from ever happening again.

However, he then added:

> Over the past 50 years, our two nations have come together in this spirit to meet that responsibility. The strength of our alliance is one of the great stories of the 20th century. Asia is largely at peace today because our alliance has given people throughout the region confidence that peace will be defended and preserved. That is what alliances are for and that is why ours must endure."[114]

In other words, he framed the US-Japan military alliance as the embodiment of the pacifist spirit of the monument. To Ota Masahide, Clinton's true intention was the "maintenance of the US-Japan alliance, affirming and requesting Okinawan's role as host of US military bases."[115] It was far from the poignant sentiment of Okinawans' mourning for the war dead.

## Still at War

One phrase often to be heard from those who experienced the Pacific War in Japan is "now we are in a time of peace." In peace education in mainland Japan it tends to be the case that war is past, and peace is here, guaranteed by Article 9. By contrast, Okinawans lament that mainlanders show no awareness of who pays the price for this "peace" and whose safety and well-being is sacrificed for it. In Okinawa, peace education revolves around war sites and bases. Oshiro Masayasu says, "In Okinawa, if you walk in and around a military base, you stumble upon a war memory site, and if you walk in a war memory site, you stumble upon a military base."[116] They are intertwined. They are not past. They are now.

Okinawan author chinin usii teaches her young children about the Battle of Okinawa, not just because it is important for the younger generation to inherit the history, but also because "the war is not over yet, and attacks on Okinawa are not over yet."

> Right now, we are not in the middle of a battlefield, with neither our bodies injured nor our lives lost. But, no matter how we protest, military bases are strengthened and expanded. The Japanese military come to Okinawa to threaten us and to overcome our resistance against military bases. Interceptor Missiles are being deployed with an assumption that our land will be attacked. Accident-prone military aircraft continue to fly over our heads. The Japanese military has started to use the US military bases jointly and together engage in drills. Sakishima Islands [Yaeyama and Miyako islands] are being

turned into military bases. If the constitution changes into one that directly allows Japan to wage wars, these moves will be intensified.[117]

War for Okinawa is far from being confined to memory.

## NOTES

1. George H. Kerr, *Okinawa: The History of an Island People* (Boston, Tokyo: Tuttle, 2000), 465.

2. Miyume Tanji, *Myth, Protest and Struggle in Okinawa* (New York: Routledge, 2006), 37.

3. Ota Masahide, *This Was the Battle of Okinawa* (Naha: Naha shuppansha, 1981), 2.

4. Okinawa Prefectural Peace Memorial Museum, *Sogo Annai*, ed. Okinawa Prefectural Peace Museum (Itoman: Okinawa kosoku insatsu kabushiki geisha, 2001), 69.

5. Ota, *This Was*, 96.

6. Okinawa Prefectural Peace Memorial Museum, *Sogo Annai*, 90.

7. Arashiro Toshiaki, *Junia ban Ryukyu Okinawa shi* (Itoman: Henshu kobo toyo kikaku, 2008), 209.

8. Okinawa Prefectural Peace Memorial Museum, *Sogo Annai*, 31.

9. Ishihara Masaie, *Okinawa no tabi: Abuchira gama to Todoroki no go* (Tokyo: Shueisha 2007), 199.

10. Tsushima maru Memorial Museum, "Tsushima maru gekichin jiken towa," http://www.tsushimamaru.or.jp/jp/about/about1.html.

11. Oshiro Masayasu, "Okinawa sen no shinjitsu o megutte," in *Soten: Okinawa sen no kioku* (Tokyo: Shakai hyoronsha, 2002), 19.

12. Ishihara, *Okinawa no tabi*, 201.

13. Yoshida Yutaka, *Ajia taiheiyo senso* (Tokyo: Iwanami shoten, 2007), 219–20.

14. "On the basis of having experienced a land battle or not, a big gap separates Okinawa, which has cultivated such collective subjectivity (*shutai*) through the experience of the battle, and the mainland (*Yamato*), which has experienced the defeat of the war without truly liberating itself from the curse of the imperial system and without squarely confronting that fact. Having studied the people who lived through the Battle of Okinawa, and those who wanted to live but were unable to live through the Battle, I cannot but feel that the problem lies in the mainland, not in Okinawa." Hayashi Hirofumi, *Okinawa sen to minshu* (Tokyo: Otsuki shoten, 2001), 365–69.

15. Two hundred thirty-four on Zamami Island, fifty-three on Geruma Island, around ten on Yakabi Island, and three hundred twenty-nine on Tokashiki Island. Ota Peace Research Institute, *Okinawa kanren shiryo—Okinawa sen oyobi kichi mondai* (Naha: Ota Peace Research Institute, 2010), 5–6.

16. According to Ishihara Masaie, historians are still researching for a closer estimate of the number of Japanese troops in the Battle of Okinawa. The estimates of 69,000 army and 8,000 navy troops are according to the Prefectural Peace Me-

morial Museum guide, *Sogo Annai*, 81, and that of 86,400 army and 10,000 navy are according to Ishihara, *Okinawa no tabi*, 202.

17. Arasaki Moriteru, *Okinawa gendaishi*, 2nd ed. (Tokyo: Iwanami shoten, 2005), 2–3.

18. Directive (*kokudo kessen kyorei*) archived in the library of the National Institute for Defense Studies, Ministry of Defense, quoted in Ishihara Masaie, *Okinawa No tabi*, 204.

19. There are mixed records and testimonies on whether Ushijima and Cho committed suicide on June 22 or June 23 and on how they did it. Ota Masahide and Sato Masaru, *Tettei toron Okinawa no mirai* (Tokyo: Fuyo shobo shuppan, 2010), 34–38.

20. The overview of the Battle of Okinawa in this chapter, unless specifically noted, is based on the accounts from Okinawa Prefectural Peace Memorial Museum, *Sogo Annai*; Ota Masahide, *This Was*; Ota Masahide, *The Battle of Okinawa: The Typhoon of Steel and Bombs* (Nagoya: Takeda Printing Company, 1984); Arasaki Moriteru, *Okinawa gendaishi*; Arashiro Toshiaki, *Junia ban Ryukyu Okinawa shi*; Arasaki Moriteru et al., *Kanko kosu de nai Okinawa: Senseki, kichi, sangyo, shizen, sakishima*, 4th ed. (Tokyo: Kobunken, 2008); Ishihara Masaie et al., *Okinawa sen to beigun kichi kara heiwa o kangaeru*, Iwanami DVD Books Peace Archives (Tokyo: Iwanami shoten, 2008); and Ishihara Masaie, *Okinawa no tabi*.

21. The English translation of Ota Minoru's last cable is exhibited at the Former Japanese Naval Underground Headquarters.

22. Much later, Ota's son, Ota Hideo, questioned this tendency, concerned that his father's words and his example of a compassionate military leader might be used by politicians and bureaucrats to promote militarism. Ota Masahide, *Shisha tachi wa imada nemurezu* (Tokyo: Shinsensha, 2006), 30–35.

23. Ota Peace Research Institute, *Okinawa kanren shiryo*, 2.

24. Rikujo jieitai kanbu gakkou (GSDF Officer Candidate School), *Okinawa sakusen kowa kiroku*, 1961. As quoted in Ota Peace Research Institute, *Okinawa kanren shiryo*, 4.

25. Quoted from a newsletter issued by the Okinawa Defense Army Headquarters on April 9, 1945, and on May 5, officially announced in the name of Chief of Staff Cho Isamu. Ota Masahide, *Soshi Okinawa sen* (Tokyo: Iwanami shoten, 1982), 180.

26. Hayashi, *Okinawa sen to minshu*, 356–362.

27. Description of the Kumejima incidents is based on Ota Masahide, *Shisha tachi wa*, 96–108. For a detailed account of the incidents, see Matthew Allen, "Wolves at the Back Door: Remembering the Kumejima Massacres," in *Islands of Discontent: Okinawan Responses to Japanese and American Power*, ed. Laura Hein and Mark Selden (Lanham, MD: Rowman & Littlefield, 2003), 39–64.

28. Janamoto Keifuku, "Guntai ga ita shima: Kerama no shogen" (Naha: Okinawa sen kiroku firumu 1 fito undo no kai, 2009).

29. Ibid.

30. Ota Peace Research Institute, *Okinawa kanren shiryo*, 5–6.

31. Jahana Naomi, *Shogen Okinawa "shudan jiketsu" Kerama shoto de nani ga okita ka* (Tokyo: Iwanami shoten, 2008), i.

32. Kinjo Shigeaki, *"Shudan jiketsu" o kokoro ni kizande* (Tokyo: Kobunken, 1995), 53–54.

33. Kinjo Shigeaki's brother Kinjo Juei's account in Kunimori Yasuhiro, *Okinawa sen no nihon hei: 60 nen no chinmoku o koete* (Tokyo: Iwanami shoten, 2008), 74.

34. Kinjo, *"Shudan jiketsu,"* 54.

35. Ibid., 55.

36. Account of the Chibichiri-gama incident is based on Hayashi Hirofumi, *Okinawa sen: Kyosei sareta "shudan jiketsu,"* Rekishi Bunka Library (Tokyo: Yoshikawa kobunkan, 2009), 53; Shimojima Tetsuro, *Okinawa Chibichiri gama no "shudan jiketsu,"* Iwanami booklet (Tokyo: Iwanami shoten, 1992); and Ishihara et al., *Okinawa sen to beigun kichi kara heiwa o kangaeru,* 42–43.

37. Shimojima Tetsuro, *Chibichiri gama no shudan jiketsu: Kami no kuni no hate ni* (Tokyo: Gaifusha, 2000), 260.

38. Hayashi, *Okinawa sen: Kyosei sareta,* 192–208.

39. Ibid., 194–95.

40. Kunimori, *Okinawa sen no nihonhei,* 119–20.

41. Janamoto, "Guntai ga ita."

42. Jahana Naomi, "Okinawa sen no ato o tadoru," in Arasaki et al., *Kanko kosu de nai Okinawa: Senseki, kichi, sangyo, shizen, sakishima,* 97.

43. Okinawa Prefecture Peace and Gender Equity Promotion Division, "Heiwa no Ishiji kokumei sha su," http://www3.pref.okinawa.jp/site/view/contview.jsp?cateid=11&id=7623&page=1.

44. "Okinawa renko no chosenjin gunpu wa 2815 nin/meibo wo kankoku izokukai ga hakken/honshi nyushu, koseisho wa hikokai," *Ryukyu Shimpo,* June 22, 1999.

45. Kunimori, *Okinawa sen no,* 95–96.

46. Hayashi Hirofumi, *Okinawa Sen ga tou mono* (Tokyo: Otsuki shoten, 2010), 47.

47. Hayashi, *Okinawa sen to minshu,* 61–69, 362–64.

48. Hayashi, *Okinawa sen ga tou mono,* 165–66.

49. Ota Peace Research Institute, *Okinawa kanren shiryo,* 8.

50. Hayashi, *Okinawa sen ga tou mono,* 169–70.

51. HQ Tenth Army, *G2 Report* (RG407/Box2948), 1945, 3.26–6.30, quoted in Hayashi, *Okinawa sen to minshu,* 338–39.

52. Hayashi, *Okinawa sen to minshu,* 334–37.

53. Yoshida Kensei, *Democracy Betrayed: Okinawa under U.S. Occupation* (Bellingham: Center for East Asian Studies, Western Washington University, 2001), 23:12; Hayashi, *Okinawa Sen Ga,* 182.

54. Yoshida Kensei, e-mail message to the authors, June 29, 2011.

55. Ota Masahide and Satoko Norimatsu, "'The World Is Beginning to Know Okinawa': Ota Masahide Reflects on His Life from the Battle of Okinawa to the Struggle for Okinawa," *Asia-Pacific Journal: Japan Focus* (September 20, 2010), http://japanfocus.org/-Norimatsu-Satoko/3415.

56. Ota, *Shisha tachi wa,* 137.

57. Ota Masahide, *Okinawa no irei no to: Okinawa sen no kyokun to irei* (Naha: Naha shuppansha, 2007), 40.

58. An estimated 2,200 tons of unexploded bombs still remain in Okinawa. Okinawa prefecture disposes of about thirty tons each year. At this rate, it will take

about seventy years to complete the job. "Fuhatsudan shori kuni no sekinin de hosho seido tsukure," *Ryukyu Shimpo*, September 12, 2011, http://ryukyushimpo .jp/news/storyid-181533-storytopic-152.html.

59. Ota and Norimatsu, "The World Is Beginning."

60. In Ota Peace Research Institute's *okinawa kanren shiryo*, a total of 1,202 known deaths by forced mass suicides have been recorded.

61. Ishihara Masaie, "Okinawasen o netsuzo shita engoho no shikumi," in *Pisu nau Okinawa sen: Musen no tame no sai teii*, ed. Ishihara Masaie (Kyoto: Horitsu bunkasha, 2011), 25–26.

62. Arashiro Yoneko criticizes the general tendency of Okinawan newspapers to use the term *shudan jiketsu*, no matter how qualified, emphasizing the importance of not accepting definition of such deaths by civilians as self-initiated. Arashiro Yoneko, "Okinawa jimoto shi shasetsu ni miru Okinawa sen ninshiki," in *Pisu nau Okinawa sen: Musen no tame no sai teii*, ed. Ishihara Masaie (Kyoto: Horitsu bunkasha, 2011), 40–63.

63. Hayashi Hirofumi discusses the complexity behind the use of the term *shudan jiketsu* and argues that simply dismissing its use by judging it as accepting of the Yasukuni philosophy is oversimplification and not productive. Hayashi, *Okinawa sen: Kyosei sareta*, 229–32.

64. Yakabi Osamu refers to the contributions of historians such as Aniya Masaaki and Ishihara Masaie in eliminating the term and concept of *jiketsu* and bringing a new term, *shudanshi*, in the 1990s, as a counternarrative to that of the government, which attempted to frame the deaths as self-initiated. Yakabi Osamu, *Okinawa sen, beigun senryo shi o manabi naosu: Kioku o ikani keisho suruka* (Yokohama: Seori shobo, 2009), 28–31.

65. Norma Field, *In the Realm of a Dying Emperor: Japan at the Century's End* (New York: Vintage Books, 1993), 61.

66. Yakabi, *Okinawa sen, beigun*, 50–54.

67. For details on the Ienaga lawsuits and textbook controversy in general, see Yoshiko Nozaki, *War Memory, Nationalism and Education in Postwar Japan, 1945–2007: The Japanese History Textbook Controversy and Ienaga Saburo's Court Challenges* (Florence: Routledge, 2008); Julian Dierkes, *Postwar History Education in Japan and the Germanys—Guilty Lessons* (New York: Routledge, 2010); and Laura Hein and Mark Selden, eds., *Censoring History—Citizenship and Memory in Japan, Germany, and the United States* (New York: Sharpe, 2000).

68. Yoshiko Nozaki and Mark Selden, "Japanese Textbook Controversies, Nationalism, and Historical Memory: Intra- and Inter-National Conflicts," *Asia-Pacific Journal: Japan Focus* (June 15, 2009), http://japanfocus.org/-Yoshiko -Nozaki/3173.

69. Steve Rabson, "Case Dismissed: Osaka Court Upholds Novelist Oe Kenzaburo for Writing That the Japanese Military Ordered "Group Suicides" in the Battle of Okinawa," *Asia-Pacific Journal: Japan Focus* (April 8, 2008), http://japan focus.org/-Steve-Rabson/2716.

70. Ishiyama Hisao, *Kyokasho kentei: Okinawa sen "shudan jiketsu" mondai kara kangaeru* (Tokyo: Iwanami shoten, 2008), 56.

71. Publisher Shimizu Shoin's example in Kurihara Keiko, *Nerawareta shudan jiketsu: Oe Iwanami saiban to jumin no shogen* (Tokyo: Shakai hyoronsha, 2009), 60.

72. Descriptions of the Japanese military's "comfort women" were toned down dramatically in the 2002 revision of junior high history textbooks, and by 2006, the words "comfort women" disappeared altogether. See VAWW-NET Japan, "Kyokasho ni iwanfu ni tsuite no kijutsu o," http://www1.jca.apc.org/vaww -net-japan/history/textbook.html.

73. Ishiyama, *Kyokasho kentei*, 43.

74. Kamata Satoshi, "Shattering Jewels: 110,000 Okinawans Protest Japanese State Censorship of Compulsory Group Suicides," *Asia-Pacific Journal: Japan Focus* (January 3, 2008), http://www.japanfocus.org/-Kamata-Satoshi/2625.

75. Ishiyama, *Kyokasho kentei*, 57.

76. Okinawa Taimusu, ed. *Idomareru Okinawa sen: "Shudan jiketsu" kyokasho kentei mondai hodo tokushu* (Naha: Okinawa Taimusu sha, 2008), 245.

77. For example, in the Shimizu shoin example discussed earlier, "Among residents who were given education and publicity that taught that surrender was shameful and death preferable to becoming a captive of the US with its harrowing consequences, some were cornered into mass suicide using things such as hand grenades distributed with the involvement of the Japanese military." Ishiyama, *Kyokasho kentei*, 34.

78. "Hoshukei kyokasho giron yobu: rainendo kara 4 nenkan no chugaku shakaika kyokasho o kakuchi de saitaku," *Mainichi Shimbun*, September 19, 2011.

79. The two Okinawan newspapers, *Ryukyu Shimpo* and *Okinawa Taimusu*, ran extensive special articles on the Yaeyama textbook controversy from mid-August to the end of September 2011, chronicling and analyzing the complicated allegation of manipulation over the textbook selection process. See the editorial "Rekishi ni kakon nokosanu minaoshi o," *Ryukyu Shimpo*, September 8, 2011; "Shinto suru 9.29 ketsugi," *Ryukyu Shimpo*, September 8, 2011; "Mirai ninau sedai no tameni— Yaeyama kyokasho mondai zadankai," *Ryukyu Shimpo*, September 11, 2011; and Maeda Sawako, "Yureru Yaeyama no kyokasho erabi," Peace Philosophy Centre, September 16, 2011, http://peacephilosophy.blogspot.com/2011/09/blog-post_16.html.

80. Tonaki Morita, in the first of a three-part series, "Haikei ni arumono— Yaeyama kyokasho mondai," *Ryukyu Shimpo*, September 1, 2011.

81. Ibid.

82. "Eirei ka inujini ka" (Ryukyu Asahi Broadcasting, 2010).

83. Fukuoka District Court in April 2004. Later on, in September 2005, the unconstitutionality of Koizumi's visit to Yasukuni was also recognized at Osaka High Court. For details of Yasukuni-related lawsuits, see Tanaka Nobumasa, *Dokyumento Yasukuni sosho: Senshi sha no kioku wa dare no mono ka* (Tokyo: Iwanami shoten, 2007), 122–29.

84. "Weekend Station Q" (Ryukyu Asahi Broadcasting, September 3, 2004); "Weekend Station Q" (Ryukyu Asahi Broadcasting, January 28, 2005).

85. *"Senshobyosha senbotsusha izokuto engoho,"* or *"Engo-ho"* in short. The law was enacted in 1952 for the state to compensate injured military personnel and bereaved families. Since Okinawa was still under US occupation then, the law did not apply to any Okinawan; but in 1953, it was applied to Okinawan military personnel and their families. In 1958, the law was applied to Okinawan civilians. Tanaka, *Dokyumento Yasukuni*, 77–88.

86. Tanaka Nobumasa, "Desecration of the Dead: Bereaved Okinawan Families Sue Yasukuni to End Relatives' Enshrinement," *Asia-Pacific Journal: Japan Focus* (May 7, 2008), http://www.japanfocus.org/-Nobumasa-Tanaka/2744. (This article, originally published in the April 4, 2008, *Shukan Kinyobi*, is slightly abridged and translated by Steve Rabson.)

87. Ishihara, "Okinawa sen o netsuzo," 30.

88. Ishihara interviewed in documentary "Eirei ka inujini ka," *Ryukyu Asahi Broadcasting*, 2010.

89. Tanaka, "Desecration of the Dead."

90. "Eirei ka inujini ka."

91. Yamane Kazuyo, ed. *Museums for Peace Worldwide* (Kyoto: Organizing Committee of the Sixth International Conference of Museums for Peace, 2008), 10–15.

92. Ota, *Shisha tachi wa*, 15–17.

93. Okinawa Prefectural Peace Memorial Museum, *Sogo Annai*, 98–99.

94. Okinawa Prefectural Peace Memorial Museum and Himeyuri Peace Museum (for Army Nursing Corps victims).

95. Ota, *Okinawa no irei*, 12–15.

96. Ibid., 230–39.

97. "Eirei ka inujini ka."

98. Ota, *Shisha tachi aa*, 14–15.

99. Oshiro, "Okinawa sen no shinjitsu," 39–40.

100. Ota, *Okinawa no irei*, 34.

101. Editor Umeda Masaki's note, in Arasaki et al., *Kanko kosu*, 315–16.

102. "The suffering of Okinawans is replaced with decorative depictions of 'Himeyuri Nurse Corps' and the Blood and Iron Student Corps. What happened on the roadsides where these tour buses run today is ignored—mothers fleeing, babies on their backs, under the storm of fire, injured elderly abandoned, babies sucking still on the breasts of mothers already dead, villagers forced out of caves to run the gauntlet of strafing, Japanese soldiers who robbed food from civilian evacuees, military officials brandishing their swords and shouting 'All Okinawans are spies!,' soldiers shooting in the back members of the Defense Corps who tried to run or civilians who tried to surrender, and garrison commanders coercing "mass suicides" by handing out hand grenades. Why do the guides not talk about these facts of war, which every one of the hundreds of thousands of the Battle survivors know? Do they think telling the truth would offend guests from the mainland?" Oshiro, "Okinawa sen no shinjitsu," 34–35. For a detailed discussion of peace monuments and tours in Okinawa, see Gerald Figal, "Waging Peace on Okinawa," in *Islands of Discontent: Okinawan Responses to Japanese and American Power*, ed. Laura Hein and Mark Selden (Lanham, MD: Rowman & Littlefield, 2003), 65–98.

103. Oshiro, "Okinawa sen no shinjitsu," 49–56.

104. Ota, *Shisha tachi wa*, 203.

105. Matsunaga Katsutoshi, "Shin Okinawa heiwa kinen shiryokan mondai to hodo," in *Soten Okinawa sen no kioku* (Tokyo: Shakai hyoronsha, 2002), 141–42.

106. Ibid., 142–44.

107. Ibid., 131–209. The map of "comfort stations" in Okinawa was to be deleted, the term "the 15-Year War" (which included Japan's war against China

between 1931 and 1945) was changed to "the Asia-Pacific War" (which referred primarily to Japan's war against the United States and Allies that started in 1941); and photo displays of Japanese aggression, such as the operation of Unit 731 in Northeast China and slaughters of residents from Korea and Taiwan, were to be cancelled. For detailed accounts of the museum display falsification issue, see Julia Yonetani, "Contested Memories—Struggles over War and Peace in Contemporary Okinawa," in *Japan and Okinawa: Structure and Subjectivity*, ed. Glen Hook and Richard Siddle (London, New York: RoutledgeCurzon, 2003), 188–207.

108. The discussion of the "museum exhibit falsification incident" is based on Matsunaga, "Shin Okinawa," and Ota, *Shisha tachi wa*, 202–4.

109. Ishihara Masaie "Okinawasen sono mono o netsuzo," *Ryukyu Shimpo*, March 17, 2012.

110. A total of 149,233 Okinawans (including those who died in the 15-Year Wars of Japan, 1931–1945), 77,327 from mainland Japan, 14,009 Americans, 447 Koreans, 82 British, and 34 Chinese (Taiwanese).

111. Ishihara Masaie, "Okinawa ken heiwa kinen shiryokan to 'Heiwa no Ishiji' no imi suru mono," in *Soten Okinawa sen no kioku* (Tokyo: Shakai hyoronsha, 2002), 321.

112. Ibid., 321; Ota, *Shisha Tachi Wa*, 189.

113. Ibid., 319.

114. Bill Clinton, "Remarks by the President to the People of Okinawa (July 21, 2000)," Okinawa Prefecture Military Affairs Division, http://www3.pref .okinawa.jp/site/view/contview.jsp?cateid=14&id=681&page=1.

115. Ota, *Shisha tachi wa*, 192–196.

116. Oshiro Masayasu, "Okinawa sen no shinjitsu," 46.

117. chinin usii, *Usii ga yuku: Shokuminchi shugi o tanken shi, watashi o sagasu tabi* (Naha: Okinawa Taimusu sha, 2010), 171–73.

# 3

~~

# Japan's American Embrace and the "Partnership" for Peace and Prosperity

Japan is a puzzling, paradoxical state. After the calamity of war followed by six and a half years of occupation by victorious Allied forces, it resumed its role in the world as a sovereign state in 1952. But through the six decades that have followed, its voice in global affairs has been muted. The occupation, though formally ended, continued, and the United States, though withdrawing, retained multiple levers of influence. We take the view that Japan throughout the Cold War era had been a semisovereign, dependent state but that since the end of the Cold War it has been transmuting into a US "client state," or *zokkoku*—that is, a nominally sovereign state that was structurally designed to attach priority to US over Japanese interests.[1] It seemed a controversial proposition just a few years ago but has become much less so. Much fresh evidence has surfaced in the past several years to support the thesis.

For such to be the case between the world's two most powerful capitalist economies and flag bearers of democracy is deeply incongruous. Until it can be straightened out into something based on equality and mutual respect, Japan's sense of selfhood and identity is diminished and its role in the evolution of a regional East Asian or Asian order distorted or blocked.

In August 2009, the Japanese people, tired of half a century of corrupt and collusive Liberal Democratic Party (LDP) rule, voted to end it. But in the year that followed, their efforts were reversed, renewal and reform blocked, and a compliant US-oriented regime reinstated whose irresponsibility was matched only by its incompetence. This is true whether considering the response to Okinawa base issues (which means the country's dealings in its most important relationship, that with the United States) or the response to the nuclear crisis that erupted following the Tohoku earthquake and tsunami of March 2011. In both cases, the response was marked by evasion, manipulation, and collusion (of bureaucrats, politicians, the media, and, in the nuclear case, the nuclear industry).

Especially since the September 2009 advent of the Hatoyama government, which came to office promising a new regional order in Asia-Pacific, there have been successive revelations of the truncated character of the Japanese state. Created and cultivated under US auspices in the wake of war nearly seven decades ago, that state maintains to this day a submissive orientation toward its distant founding fathers. A consideration of the events of these years, and of the revelations that emerged of the inner workings of the political process, reinforces the conclusion that the notion of democratic responsibility on the part of the Japanese state is illusory. Independence for Japan is not something to be protected, but something still to be won.

Okinawa is embedded in this state and interstate system, so it is necessary to sketch first some key dimensions of that frame. On January 19, 2010, the foreign and defense ministers of the United States and Japan, in a statement to commemorate the fiftieth anniversary of the signing of the mutual treaty on cooperation and security, jointly declared that

> the U.S.-Japan Alliance plays an indispensable role in ensuring the security and prosperity of both the United States and Japan, as well as regional peace and stability. The Alliance is rooted in our shared values, democratic ideals, respect for human rights, rule of law and common interests. The Alliance has served as the foundation of our security and prosperity for the past half century and the Ministers are committed to ensuring that it continues to be effective in meeting the challenges of the twenty-first century.[2]

The Treaty of Mutual Cooperation and Security (commonly known, from the Japanese abbreviation, as Anpo), was adopted in 1960, replacing the 1951 San Francisco Treaty of Peace with Japan, which was the postwar settlement imposed by the conqueror upon its defeated enemy in the wake of cataclysmic war and a six-year occupation. The Eisenhower administration saw that direct, long-term, military colonial rule was impossible. As Dwight Eisenhower himself put it in 1958, "The natives on Okinawa are growing in number and are very anxious to repossess the lands they once owned."[3]

In 1951, independence had been restored on condition of division of the country into "war state" (American-controlled Okinawa) and "peace state" (demilitarized and constitutionally pacifist mainland Japan), both under US military rule. The 1960 treaty upheld that division, confirming the US occupation of Okinawa and its use of bases elsewhere in the country.

The 1960 adoption of Anpo was tumultuous. The Liberal Democratic Party (LDP) government at the time had been set up in part with CIA funds five years earlier and in character and inclination owed much to American patronage. It was headed by Kishi Nobusuke, who had been installed as prime minister in 1957. Kishi rammed the bill through the House of Representatives in the predawn hours on May 20, in the absence of the opposition, as protesters milled about in the streets outside. After passage of the bill, President Eisenhower had to cancel his planned visit for fear of a hostile reception, and Kishi had to resign. The then US ambassador, Douglas MacArthur II, reported to Washington on Japan as a country whose "latent neutralism is fed on anti-militarist sentiments, pacifism, fuzzy-mindedness, nuclear neuroses and Marxist bent of intellectuals and educators."[4] The memory of that 1960 crisis has deterred both governments from submitting the relationship to parliamentary or public review ever since.

Nearly seven decades since its defeat in war, and more than six since it recovered its independence, Japan remains occupied by its former conqueror under the US-Japan security treaty. Yokosuka is home port for the Seventh Fleet and Sasebo a major secondary facility for the US Navy. Misawa in Aomori and Kadena in Okinawa are key assets for the USAir Force, as for the US Marine Corps are Camps Kinser, Foster, Futenma, Schwab in Okinawa, and Iwakuni in Yamaguchi prefecture. Scattered throughout Japan are the housing, hospitals, hotels, golf courses (two in Tokyo alone), and other facilities that combine to make some believe that, "As a strategic base, the Japanese islands buttress half of the globe, from Hawaii to the Cape of Good Hope. If the US were to lose Japan, it could no longer remain a superpower with a leadership position in the world."[5]

Especially in the two decades since the end of the Cold War, the United States pressed Japan to make the relationship into a "mature" alliance by removing barriers to full cooperation, that is, to joining the United States in war as in peace.

## INTERVENTIONS AND SECRET DEALS

Prior to the renewal, during Kishi's term in office, several agreements were struck that determined key aspects of the subsequent relationship. In 1959, the US government intervened to neutralize a Tokyo District Court judgment (the "Sunagawa Incident" case) in which Justice Date Akio held US forces in Japan to be "war potential" and therefore forbidden under the constitution's Article 9 (the peace commitment clause). Had the Date judgment been allowed to stand, the history of the Cold War in East Asia would have had to take a different course. At 8:00 a.m. on the morning immediately following it, however, and just one hour before the cabinet was to meet, US ambassador Douglas MacArthur II held an urgent meeting with Foreign Minister Fujiyama.[6] He is known to have spoken about the possible disturbance of public sentiment that the judgment might cause and the complications that might ensue. Following that meeting, the appeals process was cut short. The matter was referred directly to the Supreme Court, and MacArthur then met with the chief justice to ensure that he, too, understood what was at issue. In due course, in December 1959 the Supreme Court reversed the Tokyo District Court judgment, ruling that the judiciary should not pass judgment on matters pertaining to the security treaty with the United States because such matters were "highly political" and concerned Japan's very existence.

Following the Supreme Court ruling, the not-guilty verdicts in the initial hearings were reversed, and the Sunagawa defendants were convicted of trespass in the course of their protest against compulsory acquisition of their land. The US intervention only became known more than fifty years later from materials discovered in the US archives in April 2008. It was April 2010 before the Japanese foreign ministry released thirty-four pages of material to the surviving defendants of the 1959 action.[7]

The Supreme Court ruling, in effect elevating the security treaty above the Constitution and immunizing it from any challenge at law, entrenched the US base presence and opened the path to the revision of the security treaty (and the accompanying secret understandings) a month later. It also helped remove wind from the sails of the then burgeoning anti-US treaty movement. Denied recourse to the judiciary, the antiwar and antibase struggle was forced into the streets.

In a long-term perspective, however, although the Sunagawa case ended in a victory for the base proponents, the political price of further base expansion was deemed too great. The process of cutting back on and consolidating base land in mainland Japan continued. From 1952 to 1960, the US base lands on the mainland decreased from about 130,000 hectares to about 30,000 hectares, while those on Okinawa doubled.[8] Not only did the planned Tachikawa expansion not go ahead, but the process of winding down and cutting back on mainland bases as a whole gathered strength. What this meant, however, was that Okinawa was slated for further consolidation and expansion. Its great advantage was that base functions were not subject to any constitutional or legal restrictions. Protests in Okinawa, discussed below, were no less intense than those in the mainland, but the military occupation, enjoying unfettered powers, could, and did, either brush them aside or crush them. The US control of Okinawa enabled the dispatch of marines from Okinawa to launch an invasion at Danang in 1965 and, from early 1968, B-52 bombers to be transferred from Guam to Kadena, from which they took off on daily bombing raids over Vietnam and indeed the whole of Indochina for the next decade.

The frame of US-Japan relations of the late twentieth and early twenty-first century was set in a series of secret agreements negotiated in the late 1960s and early 1970s and known therefore by the Japanese word *mitsuyaku*. Two highly sensitive areas of the relationship—US nuclear war preparations and Okinawa—were reserved for secret diplomacy. The key secret agreements covered Japanese covert cooperation in US nuclear war strategy on the one hand and the reversion of Okinawa to Japan that took place in 1972 on the other.

### Secret Deals—Nuclear

Under the secret agreements, *mitsuyaku*, especially in 1958–1960 but also in 1969 and later, Japan agreed to support US war preparations and nuclear strategy. With the memory of Hiroshima and Nagasaki still fresh in people's minds, and with their even fresher memories of the *Daigo Fukuryu-maru* (*Lucky Dragon 5*), when Japanese tuna fishermen in 1954 fell victim to radioactive ash from a US hydrogen bomb test at Bikini Atoll, no Japanese government could have survived if citizens had known how ready they were to embrace nuclear weapons.

From time to time, however, there were revelations about these agreements. The 1960 nuclear agreement was first made public by a retired US Navy admiral, Gene R. LaRocque, in 1974, and a secret pact to allow nuclear-armed US vessels into Japanese waters and ports was confirmed by former ambassador Reischauer in 1981. The relevant documents turned up in the US archives in 1987.[9] Although successive Japanese governments attempted to brush all this aside, their denials became increasingly hollow.

It is no mere matter of historical concern that the government of Japan was secretly complicit in US nuclear war strategy by its consent to the US introduction of nuclear weapons into Japan, negating one of the country's famous "Three Non-nuclear Principles" (nonpossession, nonproduction, nonintroduction), and that the country's nuclear policy has therefore long been based on deliberate deception at the highest level of government. Japan was, at times, superficially faithful to the non-nuclear pledge. Together with Australia, it sponsored a new global nuclear disarmament initiative in 2008, the International Commission on Nuclear Non-proliferation and Disarmament (ICNND), which was followed by President Obama's "Prague Speech" in 2009 on the US moral responsibility to act to bring about a nuclear-free world. However, Japan's national defense policy remained firmly nuclear, that is, based on the umbrella of "extended nuclear deterrence" provided by the United States, and behind the scenes it pressed Washington to maintain it. One well-informed nuclear specialist refers to a "nuclear desiderata" document in which the government of Japan (presumably in the latter phase of the Aso government, 2008–2009) urged Washington to maintain its nuclear arsenal, insisting that it be reliable (modernized), flexible (able to target multiple targets), responsive (able to respond speedily to emergencies), stealthy (including strategic and attack submarines), visible (with nuclear-capable B-2s or B-52s kept at Guam), and adequate (brought to the attention of potential adversaries).[10] The Congressional Commission on the Strategic Posture of the United States (headed by William Perry and James Schlesinger) adopted very similar wording in advising Congress in May 2009 that "the United States requires a stockpile of nuclear weapons that are safe, secure, and reliable, and . . . credible."[11] One sentence in the report (pp. 20–21) read, "One *particularly important ally* has argued to the Commission privately that the credibility of the U.S. extended deterrent depends on its specific capabilities to hold a wide variety of targets at risk, and to deploy forces in a way that is either visible or stealthy, as circumstances may demand" (emphasis added). That "particularly important ally" is generally understood to refer to Japan.[12] Schlesinger also told the *Wall Street Journal* that US nuclear weapons are needed "to provide reassurance to our allies, both in Asia and in Europe."[13]

With Japanese government after government denying the existence of the agreements and blackballing and humiliating those who attempted to expose them, deviousness and deception became keynotes of Japanese politics and diplomacy. In 2008–2009, four former Foreign Ministry vice ministers gave evidence of the existence of the agreements and the deception surrounding them. Under the Democratic Party government that took office in September 2009, Foreign Minister Okada ordered a search of the archives for relevant materials on the *mitsuyaku*, and his committee published its findings in March 2010.[14] The "experts committee" he set up in due course confirmed three main understandings: first, what they called a "tacit agreement" of the government of Japan (January 1960) to turn a blind eye to US nuclear weapons, agreeing that "no prior consultation is required for US military vessels carrying nuclear weapons to enter Japanese ports or sail in Japanese territorial waters";[15] second, a "narrowly defined secret pact" to allow US forces in Japan a free use of the bases in the event of a "contingency" (i.e., war) on the Korean peninsula; and third, a "broadly defined secret pact" for Japan to shoulder costs for restoring some Okinawan base lands for return to their owners.[16]

The committee chose to exclude from its "secret agreements" category other important agreements whose existence was known from US archival sources, notably the 1958 Japanese agreement to surrender jurisdiction over US servicemen accused of crimes in Japan[17] and (with one partial and limited exception) the 1969 secret agreements concerning the Okinawan "reversion" (discussed below).[18]

These findings were notable for what they excluded as well as for what they revealed. The Okada committee did not accept the authenticity of the "Agreed Minute to Joint Communiqué of United States President Nixon and Japanese Prime Minister Sato Issued on November 21, 1969," to allow nuclear weapons into Okinawa "in time of great emergency," even though it was recognized as genuine (for the reason that it did not have binding power beyond the term of the Sato administration).[19] This document too had been long known only from US sources. Prime Minister Sato's special representative to negotiate the agreements with the Nixon administration wrote in his memoirs of the agreement being signed in a special room of the White House in the presence of the two leaders only.[20] Forty years passed before what appears to have been Sato's copy turned up in the home of his son.[21]

In a sense, these agreements were therefore not intrinsically "secret" so much as *kept* secret by the United States at Japan's request. The government of Japan continued up to 2009 to deny that they existed, presumably driven by fear of exposing to the Japanese people its complicity in nuclear war preparations that directly violated its proclaimed "Three Non-nuclear Principles."

Although the term "umbrella" is innocuous, even comforting, it means that nuclear victim Japan became nuclear-dependent Japan, resting its defense on nuclear-weapon-capable B-2 and B-52 bombers stationed at Guam and on cruise-missile-carrying submarines, both ready to inflict nuclear devastation on an enemy just as the United States did to it sixty-seven years ago. And unless US nuclear submarines somehow are scrupulous in unloading their missiles before heading for Japanese ports, the likelihood is that the governments of the two countries continue today to connive, as through the past fifty years, to flout the "Three Non-nuclear Principles" while holding the Japanese people in contempt for their incorrigible "nuclear neuroses."

Furthermore, the Lower House Foreign Affairs Committee in March 2010 heard evidence from Togo Kazuhiko, a former Foreign Ministry official, to the effect that during his term as head of the Treaties Bureau in 1998–1999 he had drawn up and handed to senior ministry officials a set of fifty-eight documents (sixteen of them of high-level significance) on "secret agreements" in five red file boxes. Foreign Minister Okada's commission had discovered evidence relating to only eight (of which it confirmed only three). Togo told the Diet that he "had heard" of a process of deliberate destruction that preceded the introduction of freedom of information legislation in 2001.[22]

According to the *Asahi*, the Ministry of Foreign Affairs had shown particular haste to destroy masses of documents on the eve of the coming into operation of freedom of information laws. It did so at the rate of two tons per
day, much of the material being soaked in water, dried, and then processed
by contractors into toilet paper, some of it for return to the department.
The haste to prevent evidence of the ministry's wrongdoing from leaking
to the public was akin to that in 1945, when the furnaces burned long and
late to destroy evidence of Japan's aggression. It was a signal bureaucratic
response to Japan's inauguration of the freedom of information era.[23]

## Secret Deals—Okinawa

When Okinawa was eventually "returned" to Japan in 1972, Prime Minister Sato proudly declared that Japan had won back the islands on the
basis of their being "nuclear-free and on a par with the rest of Japan"
(*kakunuki hondonami*). Nothing, however, was as it seemed.

First, the United States retained virtually all its bases and the freedom
to use them as it wished. As the war against Vietnam gathered momentum from 1965, the Pentagon, wanting to keep open the option of using
nuclear weapons, feared that any "reversion" of Okinawa to the Japan
that was constitutionally pacifist might mean liquidation of the bases
and removal of the nuclear weapons stored there. Evidently to quell
such fears, and presumably to show that he at least did not suffer from
any nuclear allergy, Prime Minister Sato, visiting Washington in January
1965, pressed Defense Secretary Robert McNamara for an assurance that
the United States would be prepared to use its nuclear weapons to attack
China in the event of any war between Japan and China.[24] Shortly afterward, as was disclosed only recently in declassified documents from the
US archives, then US ambassador Edwin O. Reischauer (*éminence grise* of
Japanese studies in the United States through much of the postwar era),
proposed a formula for managing Okinawa:

> If Japan would accept nuclear weapons on Japanese soil, including Okinawa,
> and if it would provide us with assurances guaranteeing our military com-
> manders effective control of the islands in time of military crisis, then we
> would be able to keep our bases on the islands, even though "full sover-
> eignty" reverted to Japan.[25]

Nuclear (and chemical) weapons were indeed stored at Kadena, Naha,
and Henoko[26] and not removed—or at least not assumed to have been
removed—until 1971. Otherwise, the Reischauer formula has underpinned the Okinawan position within the US-Japan relationship ever
since: free use of the bases under "full sovereignty"—words requiring
quotation marks now as then.

Two years later, shortly after returning from Tokyo to the United States, Reischauer told Japanese officials in Washington that the US military had considered the possibility of withdrawal and concluded that it would be "theoretically possible" to move the bases, lock, stock, and barrel, to Guam, but that it would cost between three and four billion dollars to do so.[27] For cost reasons, Reischauer added, Congress would be reluctant to contemplate this. It was revealed only in 2011 that from the commencement of the "reversion" negotiations, also in 1967, it was Japan, not the United States, that insisted on this crucial qualification.[28] When pressed by a surprised US government as to the reason, Foreign Minister Miki submitted a memorandum saying that his government expected the US forces to remain since they constituted an "effective deterrent." Miki and the Sato government thus gave their assurance that prosecution of the war would not be affected by the kind of "reversion" they had in mind. When they referred to "deterrence," they in fact justified aggression.

So not only was the process one as much of "retention" as of "reversion," but instead of a "giving back," it was actually a "purchase." Once Japan had made clear that it insisted on the bases staying, the United States began to think of the price that could be extracted from such an eager (and at that time economically booming) Japan. It formally demanded the sum of $650 million and insisted the payment be made in a "lump sum."[29]

It was a prodigious amount of money at that time and may be compared, for example, with the sum of $500 million that Japan paid to the government of South Korea upon normalization of relations in 1965, understood to be compensation for four decades of colonial rule. When Japan protested that it might sound too much as though a "price tag" had been put on the "reversion," Washington obligingly offered to help find suitable pretexts to explain it to the Diet.[30] Weeks before the Sato-Nixon meeting and formal agreement on "reversion" in November 1969, the deal was struck. The formally published terms of the bilateral pact gave the figure of $320 million (nominally for the Japanese purchase of US assets on the islands), but the best estimate, based on US sources, is that about $685 million, somewhat more than the United States initially demanded, was actually paid.[31] Included in the payments was one sum of $70 million, supposedly to remove nuclear weapons from Okinawa. Nearly forty years later, however, the chief negotiator on the Japanese side revealed that that had been a groundless figure.

> We decided on the cost to be able to say, "Since Japan paid so much, the nuclear weapons were removed." We did it to cope with opposition parties in the Diet.[32]

In September 2008, a group of citizens demanded the Ministry of Foreign Affairs and the Ministry of Defense disclose documents relating to the Okinawan reversion. In the following month, both ministries rejected disclosure, for the reason of "non-existence" of the documents. Unconvinced by the government's decision, in March 2009, a group of twenty-five people, including scholars and journalists, launched a court action to demand that the government find and release the documents. They argued that it was inherently improbable that significant aspects of the reversion deal, including the amounts Japan would pay, should have left no trace in the Japanese archives while being recorded in precise detail in the American.[33] One of the plaintiff group members was Nishiyama Takichi. It was Nishiyama who, as a journalist for the *Mainichi Shimbun* in 1971, had first published details of one part of the secret deal, a payment of four million dollars supposedly due from the United States for restoration of lands to be returned to Okinawan owners, which secretly and illegally the government of Japan would pay. For that revelation he and the whistle-blowing Foreign Ministry woman who supplied him with the documents suffered arrest and indictment for breach of the public servants secrets law (and public humiliation over the revelation of their personal relationship). Nishiyama lost his job and reputation, and it was nearly forty years before he was at least partially vindicated, although the "radical legal summersaults" adopted by the defenders of state privilege "to prevent the full truth from seeping out" would have the effect of making full vindication for him only likely to come posthumously.[34]

In the immediate wake of the incident, Japanese ambassador to Washington Ushiba Nobuhiko apologized to Secretary of State U. Alexis Johnson for upsetting the United States by allowing a segment of truth to leak out; but Johnson assured him the United States was pleased with the way Tokyo had handled it.[35] The four million dollars on which Nishiyama had focused attention turned out to be only a tiny sum in the context of the huge Japanese payments, and of that four million dollars, it turned out that more than three-quarters did not go to Okinawan landowners but directly to the US military.[36]

The ministry persisted in denying any wrongdoing and insisted that it had handed over everything of relevance. But the court in April 2010 ordered it to search its records again, to locate and hand over other documents concerning the Okinawan reversion, and to pay a nominal sum, approximately one thousand dollars, to Nishiyama and each of the twenty-five-person plaintiff group. It took the unprecedented step of criticizing the ministry's "insincerity" in "neglecting the public's right to know," and noted its suspicion that the ministry might have deliberately destroyed sensitive documents in order to cover up the record.[37] If the documents had indeed been destroyed, the court wanted to know when and on whose instructions.

Half a century after Judge Date in the Sunagawa case, Judge Sugi-hara Norihiko thus took a courageous stand in the same spirit in this Okinawan *mitsuyaku* case, directly challenging the executive branch of government.

Not surprisingly in view of the stakes, the state appealed, protesting that what did not exist could not be produced. The citizen group stood its ground, evidently convinced that the reversion was a key episode in setting the pattern of Japan's government lying to its people and giv-ing priority to US interests over those of its own citizens, especially in Okinawa-related matters.[38] As the *Ryukyu Shimpo* put it in its editorial, the case revealed "the priority attached to 'putting a seal on state lies' in government by bureaucrats for bureaucrats."[39] It is not so much that the plaintiffs are seeking exposure of things unknown, since the US archives have long made the details known, but of exposing Japan's responsibility in choosing to serve Washington even to the extent of deceiving its people and then lying about it for more than thirty years afterward. As the plain-tiff group put it, they sought the documents in order to "enable Japanese citizens to examine the nation's past policies and hand them down to future generations."[40] The issue, in short, was the right of the people, as the bearers of sovereignty under the 1947 constitution, to know what the government had done in their name. Both the bureaucrats in Tokyo and the alliance managers in Washington had good reason to resist exposing the nature of the unequal relationship to public scrutiny.

In September 2011, the Tokyo high court (presiding judge Aoyagi Kaoru) overturned Judge Sugihara. It adopted a strained position that the secret pact had existed and that the government of Japan needed to conceal the process because it did not want the public to think it had "bought back Okinawa." Further, it was "highly likely these papers were kept in an unconventional way . . . and cannot be denied they were secretly abandoned." Yet it ruled that it was credible that the state had conducted a search and "it cannot be said that the state owns these papers." So Sugihara had been wrong to demand their release or to punish the state for cover-up. It was a curious, contradictory judgment, saying essentially that what did not exist did not exist, the state's bona fides had to be trusted, and its responsibility for concealment and/or destruction of important state documents would not be pursued. The plaintiffs described it as "a total joke as it does not give consideration to our right to know."[41] The *Nihon keizai Shimbun* editorialized it as a "hard to accept" decision.[42]

As the high court itself obliquely recognized, however, the Okinawan "reversion" was indeed a "buyback." Even as a buyback it was bizarre in that the Japanese purchaser insisted the American vendor retain control of the assets it was being paid for. An appeal was lodged with the Supreme Court the following month.

The arrangement doubly violated the Japanese constitution because it was premised on a lie and because it violated Article 9 in the most direct way possible. Japan paid the United States while insisting that it *not return* what it was paying for. It created two separate accounts, a secret one with the real figure entered, and a public one, which referred to about half the real sum (and even that public figure was substantially false). University of the Ryukyus professor Gabe Masaaki commented that "the US bases were left in Okinawa [after reversion] in accord with a conspiracy between Japan and the US. The *mitsuyaku* kept the conspiracy covered up."[43] The two governments were content to have Nishiyama bear their shame and to send him to prison for it. Not only were the bases left intact, but, despite the public promise that the "reversion" was "without nuclear weapons," Sato secretly assured the United States that it could continue introducing nuclear weapons into Okinawa in the event of some crisis. Just two years earlier he had announced "Three Non-nuclear Principles" for Japan, but he evidently did so in order to placate and deceive the fiercely antinuclear public opinion since, as he confided to US ambassador Alexis Johnson, he thought the policy was "nonsense."[44] Five years later, he accepted the 1974 Nobel Peace Prize on behalf of his government for having declared those very principles, having covertly agreed to vitiate one of them.

In 2011, the Japanese Ministry of Foreign Affairs released one additional, hitherto unconfirmed document, dating from October 28, 1953. The government of Japan agreed then that it would not exercise its primary right of jurisdiction over US military personnel involved in crimes unless the incidents were of "material importance."[45] The United States had demanded that Japan formally abandon any such right but settled in the end for this vague formula, which nevertheless had the effect of removing US military crimes from the reach of Japanese courts for well over half a century. In effect, it is a concession of extraterritorial right, the classic abrogation of right imposed on colonial territories by their masters. Although the 1953 document was, technically, a unilateral Japanese statement and therefore did not qualify as a *mitsuyaku*, its consequences in stirring anger and resentment at the fundamental inequity of the arrangement and at the relative impunity guaranteed by it to US servicemen continue to this day.

## From Treaty to "Alliance"

With the relationship launched in this shady, duplicitous, and corrupt way, it still took almost a decade before it was described for the first time as an "alliance." The use of the term in the communiqué issued after the return of Prime Minister Suzuki Zenko from a visit to the White House in 1981 caused a furor. When Suzuki explained that he had not meant to suggest any military implications in the relationship, one foreign minister resigned, and his successor issued the lame explanation that communiqués were "not binding." Suzuki was followed, however, by Prime Minister Nakasone, who defined the relationship in his memorable phrase of Japan as the United States' "unsinkable aircraft carrier." Gradually the terms "alliance" and "alliance relationship" became more common, although the term "*Nichibei domei*" (Japan-US Alliance) was used in an official document for the first time only in 1995.[46] So although the treaty is fifty years old, the "alliance" is much younger.

The reservations over thinking of the treaty relationship as an "alliance" stem from its limitations. The treaty is a very narrow agreement for the defense of Japan (in the "Far East" according to Article 6). Although its terms have never been revised, its content and interpretation have been revised repeatedly. Late twentieth-century Japanese governments continually adjusted it by expanding its scope in practice, and early twenty-first-century governments went further, struggling to meet American prescriptions for making it "mature," which meant extending it into a global agreement for the combat against terror.[47] Legal and constitutional inhibitions were set aside.

It means that Japan, whose constitution outlaws "the threat or use of force" in international affairs, is allied to the one country above all others for whom war and the threat of war are key instruments of policy, supporting US wars in every possible way short of actually sending troops, and offering more extensive military facilities and more generous support than any other country. The "reversion" agreement, now in its fifth decade, was thus encased in deception from the outset.

From 2008, as the mandate of the LDP order shrank rapidly and DPJ support grew until in due course it formed a government the following year, details of the interventions and secret deals began to surface, casting a shadow over the anniversary celebrations. The anodyne and celebratory statements issued by official and semiofficial sources on the occasion of the anniversary passed over the humiliating circumstances and near catastrophe of the "alliance's" origin, the web of lies, deception, and surrendered sovereignty that grew around and became inseparable from it, and the deliberate deception of the Japanese people. Instead, they celebrated the "alliance" as an unqualified good, to be deepened and strengthened.

Under the long, almost unbroken era of LDP governments or LDP-centered coalitions, 1955–2009, on only one occasion was serious consideration given to the possibility of a basic change in the US-Japan relationship. When conservative one-party (LDP) government was briefly interrupted in 1993, Prime Minister Hosokawa appointed a commission to advise on Japan's post–Cold War diplomatic posture. Under the chairmanship of the head of Asahi Beer, Higuchi Kotaro, the commission in retrospect was farsighted in predicting the slow decline of US global hegemonic power. Higuchi therefore recommended that Japan revise its exclusively US-oriented and essentially dependent diplomacy to become more multilateral, autonomous, and UN oriented.[48] In Washington, the "Higuchi Report" findings stirred anxiety. A US government commission headed by Joseph Nye (then assistant defense secretary for international security affairs) shortly afterward came to a diametrically opposite conclusion, advising President Clinton that since the peace and security of East Asia were in large part due to the "oxygen" of security provided by US forces based in the region, the existing defense and security arrangements should be maintained, the US military presence in East Asia (Japan and Korea) held at the level of one hundred thousand troops rather than wound down, and allies pressed to contribute more to maintaining them.[49] Higuchi was thereafter forgotten and the Nye prescription applied.[50]

In arguing that East Asian peace, security, and prosperity depended and would continue to depend on the "oxygen" provided by the United States, not only was Nye's frame of thinking paternalistic, but it ignored the problem of how—in countries from Korea, Guatemala, and Iran in the 1950s, through Vietnam in the 1960s, Chile in the 1970s, Iraq and Afghanistan, and now Pakistan, Yemen, Libya, and elsewhere—that "oxygen" has worked to subvert governments, devastate countries, and kill or drive into exile millions of people. In the United States itself, the wisdom and the legality of these wars have been subject to considerable debate, and, famously, former defense secretary Robert McNamara declared the catastrophic Vietnam War a "mistake." But Japan's unconditional support for all US wars remains to this day generally unquestioned.

LDP governments from 1995 to 2009 did their best to accommodate the prescription spelled out in the detailed policy agendas drawn up by Nye in association with Richard Armitage and others in 1995, 2000, and 2007. Not until 2009 was there any serious questioning of the wisdom of the formula.

## Deterrence

The shared refrain on both sides of the Pacific is that the Anpo base system is the indispensable source of the "oxygen," as Joseph Nye put it in 1995, for East Asian, especially Japan's, security and prosperity, and that Okinawa will continue to be the irreplaceable source of that oxygen. The same justification was central to the commemorative statement by the two governments in January 2010 (reiterated in June 2011): the peace and security of East Asia depend on the presence of the marines in Okinawa. The Japanese media took up the theme in generally acclaiming the alliance's accomplishments and agreeing it must be expanded and deepened.

Yet the view of many military analysts is that the security treaty has little to do with the defense of Japan and that the marines in particular are in Japan because the government of Japan provides the bases and pays such generous subsidies for them. Since the end of the Cold War and the collapse of the putative "enemy," the bases have become oriented to global rather than to Japanese or even "Far Eastern" considerations as required by the treaty. Since 1990, the marines have flown from bases in Japan for participation in the Gulf, Afghanistan, and Iraq wars. They are essentially an expeditionary land combat "attack" force, held in readiness to be launched as a ground force into enemy territory or for the defense of US carriers and ships, but not for the defense of Okinawa or Japan as stipulated under the treaty.[51]

The notion that a marine force in Okinawa somehow deters China or North Korea from possible aggression seems especially misconceived. China, if ever it might have been considered a potentially hostile country, is now Japan's largest trading partner, and the governments of Japan and China talk—however sporadically—about formation of an East Asian Community. As for North Korea, if it constitutes a threat, it is the threat of its possible collapse rather than of its launching a suicidal attack on its neighbors.

Even at high levels of the Japanese defense establishment, the illogic of justifying the presence of between ten and twenty thousand members of the US Marine Corps on Okinawa in deterrence terms is not especially controversial, even though it means dismissal of the official stance of successive Japanese governments. According to Yanagisawa Kyoji, former director of the National Institute for Defense Studies, marines are a forward deployment force and their location, whether Guam or Okinawa, is a political choice, not a military one.[52] In a similar vein, Okinawa International University's Sato Manabu rejects the notion that the construction of a new Marine Corps base at Henoko in Northern Okinawa is crucial to Japan's defense: "This is not a replacement of Futenma, whose main function is training. This is a new, different, upgraded facility that U.S. Marines will receive for free and will use as a forward base capable of attacking foreign territories, not just for training."[53] Sato might have had in mind the "simulated cities" constructed at Camp Hansen in central Okinawa, where live-fire training exercises prepared marines for urban combat, such as the assault on the Iraqi city of Fallujah, for which they left Okinawa in November and December 2004.[54]

Second, and perhaps more important, it becomes increasingly likely that the United States has, for its own strategic purposes, decided to transfer core units of the Futenma marines (not just their command) to Guam.[55] Months after the issue of the 2006 "United States-Japan Roadmap for Realignment Implementation," the US Pacific Command released the "Guam Integrated Military Development Plan,"[56] and in November 2009, the US Navy released an eleven-thousand-page environmental impact statement on Guam and the Northern Mariana Islands.[57] In 2010 Guam was identified in the *Quadrennial Defense Review Report* of 2010 as a "hub for security activities in the region."[58] Objection on environmental grounds applied to the Guam project as to that for Henoko. The US Environmental Protection Agency in February 2010 declared that the Department of Defense's nine-volume "Draft Environmental Impact Statement" of the buildup process planned for Guam was "environmentally unsatisfactory," citing a range of serious problems, including the risk to the coral reef, and giving it the lowest possible rating of "EU-3."[59] Nevertheless, as Iha Yoichi, at the time Ginowan mayor, pointed out, it seemed clear that the marine units stationed in Futenma Air Station, helicopter units included, were to be transferred to Guam. In that case, a new base at Henoko would become unnecessary. With Guam's military infrastructure upgraded—Anderson Air Base is four times larger than Kadena, the largest US Air Force base in Asia (or thirteen times larger than Futenma)—and with three nuclear submarines, Guam is to become a military fortress and strategic staging post covering the whole of East Asia and the Western Pacific. In that case, the Henoko project loses its strategic purpose.[60] When spokespersons for both governments today equivocate, saying the future of Guam is "not yet decided" (as US ambassador Roos said to Iha), Iha believes it amounts to deliberate obfuscation. That, he says, means "deceiving the people of Okinawa, deceiving the people of Japan, and deceiving the Japanese Diet."[61]

Even if this analysis is correct, however, and the Pentagon has indeed decided to convert Guam into the core military fortress for the region, that is not to say that the United States would be likely to let Japan off its promise to build and furbish an *additional* base for them, particularly one with a multiservice capability and a deep-sea port such as attached to the Oura Bay design at Henoko.

As the two governments scrambled for a satisfactory explanation of what role the marines might be serving by their Okinawan presence, Pentagon spokesmen began to offer alternative accounts of their role: as a kind of humanitarian force, spending much of their time in disaster relief, given "the increasing frequency of disasters in the Asia-Pacific," including fires, floods, tsunamis, volcanic eruptions, and mudslides,[62] or as a force needed to cope with the possibility of North Korean collapse.[63] In the wake of the Tohoku earthquake-tsunami-nuclear-meltdown catastrophe beginning in March 2011, the two governments advanced a plan for construction of a new base—a shared "US-Japan International Disaster Relief Center" (provisional title—see chapter 11) to be located probably on the island of Miyako.[64]

However worthy such missions may be, there is no warrant for them in the Anpo treaty. Those trained to take life are not necessarily best at protecting it, and the insistence for geographic reasons on locating such facilities in Okinawa makes no sense (Kyushu would be much closer to North Korea).

The legal justification for the bases, in mainland Japan as in Okinawa, is the 1960 Japan-US Security Treaty.[65] That treaty, however, entitles the United States (under Article 6) to station troops in Japan for "the purpose of contributing to the security of Japan and the maintenance of international peace and security *in the Far East.*" The marines, however, as noted above, are not a defensive, Far Eastern force but an expeditionary attack force, dispatched repeatedly since 1990 for participation in the Gulf, Afghanistan, and Iraq wars and held in readiness to be launched as a ground force into enemy territory. As Yanagisawa Kyoji put it, the Third Marine Expeditionary Force is "for deployment at any time to particular regions beyond Japan . . . not for the defense of particular regions."[66] Their presence, supposedly justified by the security treaty, is actually in breach of it. The base project on which the two governments have been intent since 1996 presents large legal and constitutional problems so far not seriously addressed. It is concerned not with a Futenma substitute, or even with the defense of Japan, but with supplying the US Marine Corps with a new, upgraded, multiservice facility to be used as a forward base capable of attacking foreign territories.

## CLIENT STATE

The problems of Japan and East Asia are rooted in the self-abnegation at the heart of the Japanese state. As little as four years ago, publication of a book about Japan under the title *Client State (Zokkoku)* had a certain shock effect.[67] But so much has been revealed of the way the Japanese state functions that the term has steadily become uncontroversial, adopted even by prominent Japanese conservatives. How can it be, we ask ourselves, that such an ignominious status could so long be tolerated by a people for whom in the past nationalism has been so dear? The Japan once troubled by ultranationalism now lapses into negative, or compensatory, nationalism.

Japan, that is, its political, bureaucratic, and business elite, since ordinary people have never been consulted, *chooses* to be a "client" and to be occupied, is determined at all costs to avoid offense to the occupiers, to pay whatever price necessary to be sure that the occupation continue. It pays meticulous attention to adopting and pursuing policies that will satisfy its occupier. As one Japanese scholar puts it, for the bureaucrats who guide the Japanese state, "'servitude' is no longer just a necessary means but is happily embraced and borne. 'Spontaneous freedom' becomes indistinguishable from 'spontaneous servitude.'"[68]

It is a stratagem deeply entrenched in the Japanese state, followed by government after government and by national and opinion leaders. It is not a phenomenon unique to Japan, nor is it necessarily irrational. To gain and keep the favor of the powerful can often seem to offer the best assurance of security for the less powerful. Dependence and subordination during the Cold War brought considerable benefits, especially economic, and (with the important exception of Okinawa) the relationship was at that time subject to certain limits mainly stemming from the peculiarities of the American-imposed constitution (notably the Article 9 expression of commitment to state pacifism).

But as that era ended, instead of then gradually reducing its military footprint in Japan and Okinawa as the "enemy" vanished, the United States ramped it up, demanding a greater "defense" contribution from Japan and pressing for its Self-Defense Forces to cease being "boy scouts" (as Donald Rumsfeld once contemptuously called them) and to become a "normal" army, able to fight alongside, and if necessary instead of, US forces and at US direction, in the "war on terror," specifically in support of US wars in Iraq, Afghanistan, and Pakistan. It wanted Japanese forces to be integrated under US command, and it wanted greater access to Japan's capital, markets, and technology. While "client state" status came to require heavier burdens and much-increased costs in contrast to those borne during the Cold War, it offered greatly reduced benefits, especially as the rate of US decline steepened. Opposition was sharpest where the burden was heaviest: Okinawa.

Even on the part of the LDP governments to 2009, discontent with the Nye prescription was slowly rising. Kyuma Fumio, a core LDP figure who rose to become director-general of the Defense Agency and then Minister of Defense in the Abe government from September 2006, referred in 2003 to Japan as being just "like an American state."[69] Of the Iraq war, he later (2007) remarked that he might have expressed "understanding" of it, but never "support,"[70] and of US base rights in Okinawa, that "we're in the process of telling the United States not to be so bossy and let us do what we should do."[71] Even Aso Taro, when foreign minister in early 2007, referred to Donald Rumsfeld's prosecution of the Iraq war as "extremely childish."[72]

These, however, were occasional blips in the US-Japan relationship, dismissed as annoying gaffes[73] and not affecting Tokyo's continuing commitment to serve. The Democratic Party's ascent to power was an altogether more serious matter, especially after its 2005 manifesto declared a commitment to "do away with the dependent relationship in which Japan ultimately has no alternative but to act in accordance with US wishes, replacing it with a mature alliance based on independence and equality."

That commitment was somewhat watered down as the party came closer to office, but Hatoyama and his team still talked of "equality" and of renegotiating the relationship (while forging a new one with East Asia). Washington therefore subjected them to a ceaseless flow of advice, demand, and intimidation, pressing for the kind of subservience that had become presuppositional.

It was Joseph Nye who, as the credibility of the LDP faded and the star of the opposition Democratic Party of Japan rose in 2008–2009, emerged again at the heart of the Washington mobilization of pressure to neutralize the opposition both before it took power and also after it did so. Nye issued two unmistakable warnings. In a Tokyo conference in December 2008, he spelled out the three acts that Congress would be inclined to see as "anti-American": cancellation of the Maritime Self-Defense Agency's Indian Ocean mission, and any attempt to revise the Status of Forces Agreement or the agreements on relocating US forces in Japan (including the Futenma transfer).[74] He repeated the same basic message when the Democratic Party's Maehara Seiji visited Washington in the early days of the Obama administration to convey his party's wishes to renegotiate these agreements, again warning that to do so would be seen as "antiAmerican."[75]

The truth is that the United States does not admit "equality" in its relations with any other state. The role of Japanese prime minister is to manage a Washington satellite "client state." The "closeness" and "reliability" of allies is measured by their servility. The words of Clare Short, looking back ruefully on her part in the Blair cabinet's role in the war on Iraq, apply equally to Koizumi's Japan: "We ended up humiliating ourselves [with] unconditional, poodle-like adoration" because the "special relationship" meant "we just abjectly go wherever America goes."[76]

The Nye frame of thinking was essentially paternalistic, predicated on US military occupation continuing and based on distrust of Japan. Ota Masahide, who as governor of Okinawa between 1990 and 1998 had occasion to deal with Nye from time to time, notes that Nye spoke of Okinawa as "like American territory" and that he (Ota) felt "inclined to ask him was it not part of the sovereign country, Japan."[77] Despite their overweening attitude and assumption of the prerogative of dictating to Japan, Nye and other "handlers" of the relationship were respected, even revered, as "pro-Japanese." One well-placed Japanese observer recently wrote of the "foul odor" he felt in the air around Washington and Tokyo given off by the activities of the "Japan-expert" and the "pro-Japan" Americans on one side and "slavish" "US-expert" and "pro-American" Japanese on the other, both "living off" the unequal relationship they had helped construct and support.[78] Yet LDP governments, back in power from 1995, did their best to accommodate to it. The Nye prescription was spelled out in detailed policy agendas drawn up in association with Richard Armitage and others in 2000 and 2007. DPJ governments, too, after a brief flurry of confusion on assumption of office in 2009, settled into the pattern set by their predecessors.

In line with such thinking, the Obama administration targeted the Hatoyama desire to renegotiate the relationship with the United States so as to make it equal instead of dependent. For the Obama administration, as for that of George W. Bush, the model and high point of the alliance would seem to be the golden era of "Sergeant-Major Koizumi" (as George W. Bush reportedly referred to the Japanese prime minister) when compliance was assured, annual US policy prescriptions (*"yobosho"*) were received in Tokyo as holy writ, and "slave-faced" expressions were fixed on the faces of Japanese bureaucrats, intellectuals, and media.

Under the Nye doctrine, the United States' East Asian bases, far from being liquidated, as people especially in Okinawa had grown to hope, were to be consolidated and reinforced. The general principles of the doctrine were affirmed in the joint statements and agreements on security adopted between 1996 and 2009. Like arrows one after the other from Joseph Nye's quiver came the legal and institutional reforms adopted to transform the "alliance": the Hashimoto-Clinton "Joint Security Declaration" on the "Alliance for the 21st Century" (1996), the "New Defense Guidelines" (1997), the "Vicinity Contingency Law" (*Shuhen jitaiho*, 1999), the "Law for the Protection of Japanese" (*Kokumin hogoho*, 2004), the Law on Response to an Armed Attack (*Buryoku kogeki jitaiho*, 2003), the "Law to Facilitate Support to US Forces" (*Beigun shien enkatsuka ho*, 2004), the agreement on the alliance's "Transformation and Realignment for the Future" (2005) and "Roadmap for Realignment Implementation" (2006), the "Law to Advance Reorganization of US Bases" (*Beigun kichi saihen sokushinho*, 2007), and the "Special Measures" laws (*Tokusoho*) for dispatch of the Self-Defense Forces to the Indian Ocean (2001), Iraq (2003), and Somalia (2009).[79]

Richard Armitage, a regular visitor to Tokyo during these crucial years, often bringing Washington's orders to Koizumi and later governments, by 2006 expressed himself satisfied that Japan was not "sitting in the stands any more" but had put Japanese "boots on the ground" in Iraq, come out as "a player on the playing field," down to the "baseball diamond," and, by agreeing to the Pentagon's military reorganization plans, elevated the relationship onto a par with the American-British alliance. He gave it high points for its efforts to please.[80]

The second report (issued in February 2007 by Nye, Armitage, and their associates) on the US-Japan alliance through 2020 spelled out the agenda for Japan to lift the alliance to its next phase: strengthen the Japanese state, revise the constitution, pass a permanent law to authorize regular overseas deployment of Japanese forces, step up military spending, and explicitly support the principle of use of force in settling international disputes.[81] Later that year (in November 2007), Defense Secretary Robert Gates instructed Japan to resume operating its Indian Ocean naval station (then hotly debated), maintain and increase its payments for hosting US bases, increase its defense budget, and pass a permanent law to authorize overseas dispatch of the SDF whenever the need arose.[82] It bore all the marks of orders issuing from patron to client.

## NOTES

1. Gavan McCormack, *Client State: Japan in the American Embrace* (New York: Verso, 2007).

2. Minister of Defense Kitazawa, Minister for Foreign Affairs Okada, Secretary of State Clinton, Secretary of Defense Gates, "Joint Statement of the U.S.-Japan Security Consultative Committee Marking the 50th Anniversary of the Signing of the U.S.-Japan Treaty of Mutual Cooperation and Security" (Ministry of Foreign Affairs, January 19, 2010), http://www.mofa.go.jp/region/n-america/us/security/joint1001.html. (Eighteen months later, this time with Okada replaced as Japanese foreign minister by Matsumoto Takeaki, the same principles were again affirmed by the Two plus Two. See p. 191.)

3. Dwight D. Eisenhower, "Memorandum for the Record," *Foreign Relations of the United States, 1958–60* 18 (April 9, 1958): 16.

4. Ambassador MacArthur to Department of State, "Cable No 4393," *Foreign Relations of the United States* 18 (June 24, 1960): 380.

5. Military analyst Ogawa Kazuhisa, quoted in Saito Mitsumasa, "American Base Town in Northern Japan: US and Japanese Air Forces at Misawa Target North Korea," *Asia-Pacific Journal: Japan Focus* (October 4, 2010), http://japanfocus.org/-Saito-Mitsumasa/3421.

6. Odanaka Toshiki, "Sunagawa jiken jokokushin to Amerika no kage: Shiho-ken dokuritsu e no oson kodo," *Sekai* (August 2008). See also "Judicial Independence Infringed," *Japan Times*, May 3, 2008.

7. "Sunagawa jiken no 'Bei kosaku' o itten kaiji, chunichi taishi to gaisho kaidanroku," *Tokyo Shimbun*, April 3, 2010.

8. Arasaki, *Okinawa gendaishi*, 36–37.

9. Richard Halloran, "Sign of Secret U.S.-Japan Pact Found, *New York Times*, April 7, 1987; and on the 2008–2009 confirmation from four former administrative vice foreign ministers, see national media for summer 2009, especially *Akahata*, "Kyosanto ga akiraka ni shita kaku mitsuyaku," June 22, and "Nichibei kaku mitsuyaku no shinso," July 7, 2009. See also Honda Masaru, "Kensho: Kore ga mitsuyaku da," *Sekai* (November 2009): 164–75.

10. Hans M. Kristensen, "Nihon no kaku no himitsu," *Sekai* (December 2009): 180.

11. US Institute of Peace, "Congressional Commission on the Strategic Posture of the United States Issues Final Report" (May 2009), http://www.usip.org/print/newsroom/news/congressional-commission-the-strategic-posture-the-united-states-issues-final-report.

12. A Kyodo report dated July 30 explicitly referred to Japanese pressure. See Narusawa Muneo, "Beigun no kaku haibi to nihon," *Shukan Kinyobi* (March 26, 2010).

13. Melanie Kirkpatrick, "Why We Don't Want a Nuclear-Free World," *Wall Street Journal*, July 13, 2009.

14. Ministry of Foreign Affairs, "Iwayuru 'mitsuyaku' mondai ni kansuru chosa kekka," (March 9, 2010), http://www.mofa.go.jp/mofaj/gaiko/mitsuyaku/kekka.html.

15. Ministry of Foreign Affairs, "Iwayuru 'mitsuyaku' mondai ni kansuru yushikisha iinkai hokokusho," March 9, 2010, p. 22. http://www.mofa.go.jp/mofaj/gaiko/mitsuyaku/pdfs/hokoku_yushiki.pdf.

16. Togo Kazuhiko and Sato Masaru, "Gaimu kanryo ni damasareru Okada gaisho," *Shukan Kinyobi* (March 26, 2010).

17. Kishi-MacArthur Agreement of October 4, 1958. ("Japan 'ceded right to try US forces'—secret accord 'covers off-duty offenses,'" *Yomiuri Shimbun* (April 10, 2010). The Okada Commission did not disclose this document, but it surfaced and was disclosed several weeks later. Professor Sakamoto Kazuya of Osaka University is here cited as authority for the view that, fifty years on, this agreement still holds force.

18. Niihara Shoji, "Anpo joyaku ka no 'mitsuyaku,'" *Shukan Kinyobi* (June 19, 2009).

19. Kitaoka Shinichi, "The Secret Japan-US Security Pacts: Background and Disclosure," *Asia Pacific Review* 17, no. 2 (2010).

20. Kei Wakaizumi, *The Best Course Available: A Personal Account of the Secret US-Japan Okinawa Reversion Negotiations* (Honolulu: University of Hawaii Press, 2002). (Japanese original published in 1994.) See especially chapter 10, "Writing the Script in Collaboration with Henry Kissinger," and p. 236 for text of the secret "Agreed Minute."

21. "Top Secret. Agreed Minute to Joint Communiqué of United States President Nixon and Japanese Prime Minister Sato Issued on November 21, 1969," reproduced in Shunichi Kawabata and Nanae Kurashige, "Secret Japan-U.S. Nuke Deal Uncovered," *Asahi Shimbun*, December 24, 2009.

22. "Mitsuyaku bunsho, doko e kieta," *Asahi Shimbun*, March 20, 2010.

23. "Kimitsu bunsho, tokashite katamete toiretto pepa ni Gaimusho," *Asahi Shimbun*, July 11, 2009.

24. Ishizuka Hiroshi and Inada Shinji, "Bei ni hyomei—Nichusen katei 'kaku hofuku o,'" *Asahi Shimbun*, December 22, 2008.

25. Steve Rabson, "'Secret' 1965 Memo Reveals Plans to Keep US Bases and Nuclear Weapons in Okinawa after Reversion," *Asia-Pacific Journal: Japan Focus* (December 21, 2009), http://japanfocus.org/-Steve-Rabson/3294.

26. According to the top-secret "Agreed Minute" of the Sato-Nixon meeting issued on November 21, 1969, cited above.

27. "Gaiko bunsho kokai—'Guamu iten kano' 67 nen, Raishawa shi meigen," *Ryukyu Shimpo*, February 19, 2011. (Another source, not named in the documents released in 2011, gave the figure of two billion as the estimated cost of a transfer from Okinawa's main island to the smaller island of Iriomote.)

28. "Kichi no sonzoku zentei ni," *Asahi Shimbun*, February 19, 2011.

29. "'Ranpu samu' bunsho," *Ryukyu Shimpo*, February 19, 2011.

30. "US Demanded Japan Pay $650 Million in Okinawa Reversion Costs," *Mainichi Daily News*, February 18, 2011.

31. Gabe Masaaki, *Okinawa henkan wa nan datta no ka* (NHK Bukkusu, 2000), 190–206.

32. "Ex-negotiator: Cost to Remove U.S. Nukes from Okinawa Exaggerated to Dupe Public," *Asahi Shimbun*, November 13, 2009.

33. "Okinawa mitsuyaku kaiji zenmen shoso kichi futan no teiryu tou gaimusho chosa ni gigi," *Ryukyu Shimpo*, April 10, 2010; "Okinawa mitsuyaku hanketsu/'Kokka no uso' juzai ga senmei da towareru rekidai kanyosha no sekinin," *Ryukyu Shimpo*, April 10, 2010.

34. David McNeil, "Implausible Denial: Japanese Court Rules on Secret US-Japan Pact over the Return of Okinawa," *Asia-Pacific Journal: Japan Focus* (October 10, 2011), http://japanfocus.org/-David-McNeill/3613.

35. "Nishyama jiken 'tegiwa yoku shori' Bei ga Nihon no tai-o hyoka," *Tokyo Shimbun*, February 18, 2011.

36. "Okinawa henkan mitsuyaku: kurikaesareta inpei kosaku," editorial, *Ryukyu Shimpo*, May 16, 2007.

37. "State Told to Come Clean on Okinawa," *Asahi Shimbun*, April 10, 2010; Masami Ito, "Court: Disclose Okinawa Papers," *Japan Times*, April 10, 2010.

38. Togo Kazuhiko, testifying to the Diet Committee in 2010 on his role as head of the Treaty Bureau in the Ministry of Foreign Affairs in 1998–1999, "Mitsuyaku bunsho haki—kokumin to rekishi e no hainin da," *Tokyo Shimbun*, March 20, 2010. See also Togo and Sato, "Gaimu kanryo."

39. "Kaiji sosho kesshin, mitsuyaku gaiko no fusaku-i o tate," *Ryukyu Shimpo*, May 19, 2011.

40. "Appeals Trial on Public Disclosure of Okinawa Reversion Papers Concludes," *Japan Times*, May 19, 2011.

41. "High Court Overturns Ruling on Disclosure of Okinawan Reversion Papers," *Mainichi Shimbun*, September 29, 2011.

42. Editorial, "Settokuryoku nai 'mitsuyaku' kososhin hanketsu," *Nihon Keizai Shimbun*, September 30, 2011.

43. "Okinawa henkan, saidai mitsuyaku wa shisetsu kojihi, koen de Nishiyama Takichi shi," Japan Press Network, February 27, 2010.

44. "Peace Prize Winner Sato Called Nonnuclear Policy 'Nonsense,'" *Japan Times*, June 11, 2000.

45. Alex Martin, "1953 Records on Handling U.S. Forces Released," *Japan Times*, August 27, 2011.

46. Maeda Tetsuo, *"Juzoku" kara "jiritsu" e—Nichibei Anpo o kaeru* (Tokyo: Kobunken, 2009), 32.

47. See McCormack, *Client State*.

48. Boei mondai kondankai, *Nihon no anzen hosho to boeiryoku no arikata—21 seiki e mukete no tenbo* (Tokyo: Okura sho insatsu kyoku, 1994). Commonly known as the "Higuchi Report" after its chair, Higuchi Kotaro, the report was presented to Prime Minister Murayama in August 1994.

49. United States Department of Defense, Office of International Security Affairs, *United States Security Strategy in the East Asia-Pacific Region* (1995). Commonly known as "the Nye Report."

50. Magosaki Ukeru, *Nichibei domei no shotai* (Tokyo: Kodansha gendai shinsho, 2009), 107–10.

51. Taoka Shunji, quoted in Taketomi Kaoru, "Amerika ga keikai suru Ozawa dokutorin 'honto no nerai,'" *Sapio*, September 9, 2009, 11–14.

52. Yanagisawa Kyoji (special researcher and former director of the National Institute for Defense Studies), "Futenma no kakushin—kaiheitai no yokushiryoku o kensho seyo," *Asahi Shimbun*, January 28, 2010.

53. Sato Manabu, "Forced to 'Choose' Its Own Subjugation: Okinawa's Place in U.S. Global Military Realignment," *Asia-Pacific Journal: Japan Focus* (August 2, 2006), http://japanfocus.org/-Sato-Manabu/2202.

54. See Furutachi Ichiro and Satoko Norimatsu, "US Marine Training on Okinawa and Its Global Mission: A Birds-Eye View of Bases from the Air," *Asia-Pacific Journal: Japan Focus* (May 2, 2010), http://japanfocus.org/-Satoko-Norimatsu2/3363.

55. See the discussion in Ota Masahide, *Konna Okinawa ni dare ga shita: Futenma isetsu mondai saizen saitan no kaiketsu saku* (Tokyo: Dojidaisha, 2010), 146–69.

56. US Pacific Command, "Guam Integrated Military Development Plan" (July 11, 2006).

57. US Department of the Navy, "Guam and CNMI Military Relocation—Environmental Impact Statement" (November, 2009).

58. US Department of Defense, *Quadrennial Defense Review Report* (February 2010).

59. Clynt Ridgell, "US EPA calls DEIS 'Environmentally Unsatisfactory,'" Pacific News Center, February 25, 2010.

60. Iha Yoichi and Satoko Norimatsu, "Why Build a New Base on Okinawa When the Marines Are Relocating to Guam? Okinawa Mayor Challenges Japan and the US," *Asia-Pacific Journal: Japan Focus* (January 18, 2010), http://japanfocus.org/-Norimatsu-Satoko/3287; Yoshida Kensei, *Okinawa no kaiheitai wa Guamu e iku* (*Marines in Okinawa Are Going to Guam*) (Tokyo: Kobunken, 2010); Yoshida Kensei, "Okinawa and Guam: In the Shadow of U.S. and Japanese 'Global Defense Posture,'" *Asia-Pacific Journal: Japan Focus* (June 28, 2010), http://www.japanfocus.org/-Yoshida-Kensei/3378.

61. Iha Yoichi, "Futenma isetsu to Henoko shin kichi wa kankei nai," *Shukan Kinyobi* (January 15, 2010).

62. Retired marine general Wallace Gregson, currently Pentagon Foreign Office Assistant Secretary for East Asia, addressing the Japan Institute for International Affairs, "U.S. Awaiting Futenma Decision, to Seek Joint Solution: Official," *Kyodo*, February 1, 2010.

63. Lt. General Keith Stalder, Commander of US Marines in Asia. "US Commander Reveals True Purpose of Troops in Okinawa Is to Remove North Korea's Nukes," *Mainichi Shimbun*, April 1, 2010.

64. Secretary of State Hillary Clinton et al., "Joint Statement of the Security Consultative Committee, *Toward a Deeper and Broader U.S.-Japan Alliance: Building on 50 Years of Partnership* (June 21, 2011).

65. Japan and United States, "Treaty of Mutual Cooperation and Security between Japan and the United States of America," *Ministry of Foreign Affairs* (January 1960).

66. Yanagisawa, "Futenma no kakushin," *Asahi*, January 28, 2010.

67. McCormack, *Client State*. The revised Japanese, Korean and Chinese editions of the book offer the following definition: "a state that enjoys the formal trappings of Westphalian sovereignty and independence, and is therefore neither a colony nor a puppet state, but which has internalized the requirement to give preference to 'other' interests over its own."

68. Nishitani Osamu, "Jihatsuteki reiju o koeyo—Jiritsuteki seiji e no ippo," *Sekai* (February 2010): 126.

69. *Asahi Shimbun*, February 19, 2003.

70. "Kyuma: U.S. Invasion of Iraq a Mistake," *Japan Times*, January 25, 2007.

71. "Kyuma Calls for Futenma Review: 'Don't Be So Bossy,' Defense Minister Tells US over Base Relocation," *Yomiuri Shimbun*, January 29, 2007.

72. "Aso gaisho no Bei seiken hihan," *Asahi Shimbun*, February 5, 2007.

73. Ibid.

74. Quoted in Narusawa Muneo, "Shin seiken no gaiko seisaku ga towareru Okinawa kichi mondai," *Shukan Kinyobi*, September 25, 2009.

75. *Asahi Shimbun*, February 25, 2009. See also Maeda, *"Juzoku,"* 17–25.

76. Clare Short, formerly International Development Secretary, "Clare Short: Blair Misled Us and Took UK into an Illegal War," *Guardian*, February 2, 2010.

77. Ota Masahide and Sato Masaru, "Taidan Okinawa wa mirai o do ikiru ka," *Sekai* (August 2010).

78. Terashima Jitsuro, "Noriki no ressun, tokubetsu hen (94), Joshiki ni kaeru ishi to koso—Nichibei domei no saikochiku ni mukete," *Sekai* (February 2010). Terashima refers to Japanese intellectuals by the term "do-gan" (literally "slave face," a term he remembered from a savagely satirical early twentieth-century Chinese story by Lu Hsun). For an English translation of this Terashima text, see Terashima Jitsuro, "The Will and Imagination to Return to Common Sense: Toward a Restructuring of the US-Japan Alliance," *Asia-Pacific Journal: Japan Focus* (March 15, 2010), http://japanfocus.org/-Jitsuro-Terashima/3321.

79. See Maeda, *"Juzoku,"* 90–92.

80. McCormack, *Client State*, chapter 4.

81. Richard L. Armitage and Joseph S. Nye, *The U.S.-Japan Alliance: Getting Asia Right through 2020* (Washington, DC: Center for Strategic and International Studies, February 2007).

82. On the Gates visit: Fumitaka Susami, "Gates Backs Permanent Law to Send SDF," *Japan Times*, November 11, 2007. See also Kaho Shimizu, "Greater Security Role Is in Japan's Interest: Gates," *Japan Times*, November 10, 2007.

# 4

*⌒*

# Okinawa

*Separation and Reversion*

When the typhoon of steel cleared over the devastation of Okinawa in the late summer of 1945, what awaited the shell-shocked people was not liberation from militarism and fascism but the appropriation of their land and livelihood as part of the spoils of war, direct military rule that was to continue for twenty-seven years, and subjection to foreign military prerogative thereafter to this day.

Okinawa's postwar position was peculiar from the outset, since the American occupation was at the express invitation and encouragement of no less a figure than the Showa emperor, Hirohito (see chapter 1). Under direct US military jurisdiction until 1972, Okinawa's raison d'être, for both Washington and Tokyo, was as a center for the cultivation of "war potential" and for preparation for the "threat or use of force"—both forbidden under Article 9 of the Japanese constitution.

The fiftieth anniversary celebrations of the US-Japan alliance in 2010 therefore had a peculiar poignancy for Okinawa. Fifty years earlier the Anpo treaty settlement simply confirmed its exclusion, its status under direct US military rule unchanged. With mainland Japan a constitutional "peace state," Okinawa served as the indispensable base for the prosecution of war in Vietnam (from the early 1960s) and in preparation for world war. The problem of how to reconcile the contradictory roles of mainland Japan and Okinawa confounds both governments to this day.

Because of their distinctive, disadvantaged (and until 1972 excluded) location, Okinawans could understand better than citizens elsewhere the hollowness of Japan's democratic façade and could more clearly see beneath it the system designed and cultivated by means of deep US penetration and manipulation and continuing use of soft power levers to ensure that Japan followed the path deemed correct by Washington rather than any abstract democratic principle.

Though restored to Japanese administration in 1972, and therefore to the realm of constitutional democracy, in practice the interests of the US military were—and still are—accorded priority over Okinawan civilian interests. While it is now clear that the two states that supposedly uphold democracy and the free world used secrecy, lying, intimidation, and bribery to impose on Okinawa their will for continuing priority to US military ends, while Okinawa relied on democratic, constitutional, and (after reversion to Japan in 1972) consistently nonviolent procedures to seek redress. Its people found, however, that political and judicial processes are imperfect instruments for achieving the rights supposedly guaranteed them under the constitution.

As US military colony until 1972, and as joint US-Japan condominium since then, Okinawa's subjection has been rooted in the alienation of its land. That process began as the smoke cleared from the war-ravaged island and has continued through several major stages since then. It has been characterized by breaches of international and national law and of the constitution of Japan.

When Okinawans were released from their detention (in effect, in concentration camps) from late 1945 to 1947, many found that their homes, family graves, and sacred sites had already been demolished. Eighteen thousand hectares, about 8 percent of the land of the prefecture, was requisitioned, forty thousand landowners lost their land, and twelve thousand households their homes.[1] This uncompensated and unilateral appropriation of land on a grand scale was in breach of Article 46 ("private property cannot be confiscated") of the 1907 Hague Convention.

In Okinawan social memory, the process is remembered as the terror of bulldozers and bayonets. The initial appropriation of private land in the years immediately following war's end continued at an accelerated pace during and after the Korean War (1950–1953). Futenma Marine Air Station, with its 2,800-meter runway, slowly emerged on a site a little under 500 hectares in an area at a traditional junction point between the island's north and south, where formerly the villages of Ginowan, Kamiyama, and Aragusuku once stood with tree-lined avenues amid well-watered fields.[2] Though in area a mere 2 percent of US-occupied base land in Okinawa, most controversy in recent decades has concentrated on this camp. On Iejima Island, US forces in 1953 drove the inhabitants to emigrate, requisitioned 63 percent of the island, and bulldozed and burned the homes of thirteen protesters.[3] Today Iejima serves mainly as a site for parachute training and takeoff and landing exercises. Torishima Island, once covered with rich forest, became disfigured as a result of being used as an aircraft firing range, the site for testing depleted uranium weapons in the 1990s and for cluster bomb dropping since then.[4] The US Air Force Kadena Base, which occupies 83 percent of Kadena Township, is twice the size of Japan's biggest civil airport Haneda, and with the adjacent Ammunition Storage Area, has a combined area of 46 square kilometers of prime Okinawan farm and town land. Three other towns lost over 50 percent, and five more over 30 percent, to bases. Not only residential and town, but farmland area also shrank. Camp Hansen came to occupy more than half of the towns of Kin and Ginoza as well as parts of Nago and Onna,[5] growing to be ten times greater in area than Futenma. The thick forests of Camp Hansen contained several "simulated cities" for urban combat preparation. In late 2004, 2,200 marines were dispatched from them to join the assault on Fallujah, in which thousands were killed and the city destroyed.[6] The concentration of military facilities on Okinawa Island in particular became such that, as Ota Masahide put it, it was "almost impossible to live as [decently as] humans should."[7]

In the northeast of the island, Camp Schwab, on Oura Bay, was established in 1959. There as elsewhere, dispossessed and threatened with being cut off and left with nothing, many reluctantly chose to try and negotiate a deal to alleviate their loss. As Kayo Soshin (then eighty-five years old) put it in 2010,

> It wasn't even like, "This place may become a base." It was just going to be a base. There was no consultation. It was the same as the Japanese military (during the war)—suppression from above.

Though fiercely opposed to the base at first, facing the overwhelming might of the military and the choice between being arrested and losing his land or agreeing to give it up, he chose the latter. "There was no way to win," said Kayo. "I shifted to thinking about how we could profit from this situation."[8]

Over time, some landowners, like Kayo, flourished under this dispensation, receiving regular, substantial, and steadily rising incomes. A steady flow of "benefits" was directed to the areas targeted for expansion, including Kayo's village of Henoko.

Farther to the north, straddling the villages of Kunigami and Higashi, from 1957 the US Marine Corps appropriated a huge swath of over 19,300 acres (78 square kilometers) of single- and double-canopy forest as Camp Gonsalves. Until 1998, Gonsalves was known as the "Northern Training Area" and from then explicitly as "Jungle Warfare Training Center," the only one in the world. This same, militarily highly significant Yambaru forest also constitutes one of the richest areas of biodiversity in Japan, home to over one thousand plant species and five thousand species of birds and animals, including many that are indigenous, endemic, and threatened, such as the Yambaru Kuina (Okinawan rail) and Noguchi Gera (Okinawan woodpecker).

During the Kishi administration (1957–1960), negotiations for renewal of the joint Security Treaty proceeded in Tokyo and Washington, and the US forces in Japan undertook a major reorganization. The US military presence in Okinawa doubled, and the density of base presence in Okinawa rose to one hundred times that of mainland Japan.[9] Deprived of land and livelihood, many Okinawans fled to better employment prospects elsewhere in Japan, and some moved overseas.

A further consolidation occurred during the Vietnam War in the 1960s, in part because of facilities being transferred to Okinawa from mainland Japan in the face of the gathering strength of mainland antibase movements. For mainland Japan, it helped shift attention away from the politically sensitive base question. Antibase struggles in mainland Japan gradually lost momentum. From 1969, the First Marine Aircraft Wing's Marine Air Group 36 established its headquarters in Marine Corps Air Station Futenma, which squatted in the middle of Ginowan City. Okinawa was also preferred because it was under direct American military rule. Both the United States and Japan were happy to concentrate warfighting capacity on islands made especially attractive by the absence of democracy and effectively under colonial rule.

Before the reversion of 1972, bases occupied 27,893 hectares of Okinawan land. The figure has since been reduced to 22,923 hectares, but still bases occupy 10 percent of the total area of the prefecture and almost 20 percent of Okinawa Island, including the most fertile, cultivable, nonmountain or forest area.[10]

These decades in which so many Okinawans lost land and homes and experienced the construction of a polity that accorded absolute priority to the interests of the US military created bitter resentments. The formula adopted in March 1954 was for landowners to be compensated by a single lump-sum payment of 16.6 years rental, estimated at 6 percent of land value, conferring on the US military permanent leasehold rights in effect.[11] The House Armed Services Committee report published in 1956, known commonly as the Price Report, confirmed this basic formula for permanently severing Okinawan ownership rights. The report outraged Okinawans by justifying long-term occupation of base land in a site where, as the report put it, "there are no restrictions placed by a foreign government on our rights to store or to employ atomic weapons."[12]

As major new bases were constructed and existing ones significantly upgraded, villages and towns erupted in the mass protest known as the *shimagurumi toso*, or all-island struggle.[13] Denied legal or political redress, between 1953 and 1956 the islands were convulsed by protest over the land seizures (with not the "slightest pretence of due process" on the government side, as Chalmers Johnson put it).[14] It was an Okinawan response to ten years of military occupation, no less determined or less widely supported than protests against base expansion in Tachikawa and other sites elsewhere in Japan, but doomed. Arasaki writes: "Had Okinawa not been cut off from the rest of Japan and placed under American military control, it would not have been possible for the US military bases as they now exist in Okinawa to have been built."[15]

Redolent of the atmosphere of the time was the second University of the Ryukyus incident. In August 1956, the university had to decide what to do about seven students who had participated in the province-wide protests and demonstrations over the Price Report. It first decided to caution them, but the US authorities insisted that that was not enough and threatened that the future of the university itself was at issue. President Asato Genshu felt he had no alternative but to compromise the university's autonomy and the students' rights in order to save the university. Six students were expelled and one cautioned. More than fifty years passed before the university, in 2007, rescinded the decision.[16]

In February 1965 the United States began bombing North Vietnam. In February 1968 it moved up its B-52s from Guam to Okinawa, in order to better conduct massive bombing raids on Indochina. Admiral Ulysses S. Grant Sharp, US Pacific Fleet Commander, maintained in 1965 that "without Okinawa, we cannot carry on the Vietnam War."[17] Freedom of action—to launch bombing raids on Vietnam directly from Kadena in Okinawa and to store nuclear and chemical weapons at other bases there in readiness for expansion of the conflict—became policy imperatives. Negotiations therefore began not long afterward on two fronts: to determine the terms that would be entered into the "secret agreements" (*mitsuyaku*) that would govern reversion, and to cope with burgeoning pressures for democratic rights in Okinawa without actually conceding to them, in other words, to fabricate a façade of democracy. In the same memo cited above, in which American ambassador (1961–1966) Edwin O. Reischauer suggested the formula for a reversion that would allow the United States to retain its bases (and nuclear weapons), he also suggested covert intervention to manipulate the democratic process and ensure that US objectives would be met: bribery. It was not such an uncommon thought at the time. Under President Eisenhower, CIA payoffs to favored Japanese politicians had become routine, and, according to the historian of the CIA, they "flowed for at least fifteen years, under four American presidents."[18] Reischauer was concerned only that it be done with discretion:

[W]e should not incur . . . the danger of exposure. . . . It would be risky to take clandestine political action in Okinawa using direct U.S.-Ryukyuan channels. It would be much safer to use only the Japanese route, permitting the Japanese LDP to handle the money.[19]

Electoral manipulation began shortly afterward, with the very first election in 1968 for the office of Chief Executive of the Ryukyu Government, until then filled by USCAR (US Civil Administration of the Ryukyu Islands) nominees. The US authorities only reluctantly agreed to permit the election, despite the risk involved that an antibase person might actually win. But US Lieutenant General Ferdinand T. Unger thought there was no alternative: the election would be "a palliative [that] might temporarily satisfy Okinawan aspirations and give us more time in putting off the day when our freedom of operations would be circumscribed."[20] According to CIA sources, Prime Minister Sato engaged the services of Kaya Okinori, finance minister in the Tojo wartime cabinet and a well-known "fixer" in the postwar decades once released from prison in December 1948.[21] According to secret cables published by *Ryukyu Shimpo*, two large payments were negotiated during 1968, one for $880,000 in March and another, for $720,000, in August of the same year.[22] The meetings to settle the method and route of payment were conducted at LDP headquarters in Tokyo and involved Fukuda Takeo (prime minister 1976–1978), but the funds were understood to be from the CIA.

In the event, however, and despite the best efforts of the two governments and Kaya's playing a "key role," the progressive, antibase Yara Chobyo, calling for the "immediate, unconditional, complete return of the bases," defeated the CIA's preferred Nishime Junji.[23]

Washington and Tokyo were united in their determination to resist Okinawan democracy, and in that they have been consistent ever since. Under the "LDP Okinawa system," governments in Tokyo served the United States, paid it large subsidies, and gave priority in Okinawa policy in particular to US strategy and planning while exacting compliance from local government authorities in Okinawa by supporting "development" projects and encouraging local governments to avoid discussion of the base issue at elections.

Since resistance against the occupying power was basically futile, and since Okinawans had no democratic rights, they could only protest and then protest again, firmly and by all available means. What is striking is that throughout these years of desperation they maintained a resolutely nonviolent stance. From 1968, B-52s were transferred from Guam to Kadena, whence they began taking off on daily bombing raids to Vietnam. One, loaded with bombs destined for Vietnam, even crashed just after takeoff from Kadena on November 19, 1968. Okinawan anger and distress at thus being dragged willy-nilly into involvement, however indirect, in a war of aggression rose. A general strike, planned for February

4, 1969, was cancelled only at the last minute after Chief Executive Yara Chobyo succumbed to persuasion on the grounds that the strike might delay or even risk the reversion. As Tanji comments, "While his intention was to preserve the 'unity' and effectiveness of the movement, it had precisely the opposite effect. It damaged the cohesion and the confidence of the community of protest."[24]

In July 1969, US media reports of servicemen suffering from exposure to leaked VX gas awakened Okinawans to a new threat: chemical weapons, originally stockpiled in readiness for attack on mainland Japan's cities in the autumn of 1945 that was pre-empted by the nuclear attack on Hiroshima and Nagasaki. Protest and demand for the removal of the materials merged with the movement for the base-free and weapons-free reversion of Okinawa.

On December 20, 1970, with passions high over the poison gas and Vietnam War issues, a melee broke out in Koza City (later Okinawa City) between US military police and angry Okinawans following an accident involving a vehicle driven by an American soldier and an Okinawan civilian. MPs fired warning shots and helicopters sprayed tear gas over the Okinawan crowd, which during that single night destroyed more than eighty US military and private vehicles. These events, known generally as the "Koza riots," might better be described as the "Koza uprising."[25]

Forty years after the events at Koza, a former official of the city lamented:

Fundamentally, nothing has changed . . . in the name of democracy, we have had an occupation, with the same treatment meted out to us as to Iraqis and Afghanis, while both the US and Japan turn a blind eye. The anger that exploded 40 years ago has not abated.[26]

It took nearly two years of struggle and protest before approximately 12,500 metric tons of mustard gas, phosgene, Agent Orange, and sarin were removed from Okinawan bases in 1971 under "Operation Red Hat."[27] Whether they were fully removed, and what impact they may have had or might still be having on the human or physical environment, has today become again a large issue, discussed further in chapter 8.

## 15 MAY 1972—"DAY OF HUMILIATION"

To resolve these many matters, Okinawans came to think reversion to Japan the first and most necessary condition. The constitution adopted in mainland Japan in 1946 entrenched the values of peace, human rights, and democracy, for which all Okinawans surely longed. The focus of their many demands for justice and human rights and their protest at being forced into complicity in an aggressive war therefore became reversion to the constitutional peace state (as they saw it) of Japan. Okinawan social movements coalesced under this single unifying cause.

Their hopes were severely dashed in November 1969, however, by the communiqué issued following the meeting in Washington between Prime Minister Sato Eisaku and President Richard Nixon.[28] The communiqué began by declaring that

> The President and the Prime Minister . . . declared that, guided by their common principles of democracy and liberty, the two countries would maintain and strengthen their fruitful cooperation in the continuing search for world peace and prosperity and in particular for relaxation of world tensions.

By this, they presumably meant that the devastation of Vietnam, in what Defense Secretary Robert McNamara was later to declare a "mistaken" war, would continue, and that although Okinawan reversion to Japan was important, Japan would continue to attach highest priority to advancing the US war aims. Consequently,

> The two governments would fully consult with each other . . . so that reversion would be accomplished without affecting the United States efforts to assure the South Vietnamese people the opportunity to determine their own political future without outside interference.

"Outside" interference, needless to say, meant interference by other outsiders.

The provisions concerning Okinawa were then spelled out as follows:

> The Prime Minister emphasized his view that the time had come to respond to the strong desire of the people of Japan on the basis of the friendly relations between the United States and Japan and thereby to restore Okinawa to its normal status.

However, "normal" was immediately qualified to mean consistent with continuing to fight the war in Vietnam.

> The President and the Prime Minister also recognized the vital role played by United States forces in Okinawa in the present situation in the Far East. As a result of their discussion it was agreed that the mutual security interests of the United States and Japan could be accommodated within arrangements for the return of the administrative rights over Okinawa to Japan. . . . *The President and the Prime Minister agreed also that the United States would retain under the terms of the Treaty of Mutual Cooperation and Security such military*

*facilities and areas in Okinawa as required in the mutual security of both countries.*
(italics added)

The qualification concerning nuclear weapons was also entered in such a way as to assuage Japanese public opinion while retaining American freedom, with the substantive agreement on this head addressed only in the *mitsuyaku*, secret covenants that accompanied the public agreements.

The bases were to stay, and war was to remain Okinawa's priority. It was a devastating blow to the Okinawan reversion movement. Prime Minister Sato's promise to the Japanese Diet in March that the reversion would be *kakunuki hondonami* (without nuclear weapons and on the same basis as mainland Japan) was plainly at odds with his promise to President Nixon that the war would be given priority in any arrangements for the future of Okinawa. Of course, they had no inkling then of the full measure of Sato's duplicity: his secret agreement with Nixon on nuclear cooperation[29] or the financial arrangements that transformed the "reversion" into a Japanese "purchase" (see the discussion on pages 58–62). What they knew from the published communiqué, however, was enough to outrage them. As the date of reversion, May 15, 1972, approached, the Okinawan demand for "real" or "complete" reversion grew.

In May 1971 a general strike paralyzed the bases, and a large crowd gathered for a mass meeting to protest the nonreturn of the base lands. When the deal between the two governments was formally ratified at a Tokyo signing ceremony on June 17, 1971, Ryukyu chief executive Yara Chobyo refused to attend.[30] Four months later, he prepared a petition (*kengisho*) for submission to the special session of the Diet on Okinawan reversion. It began:

> The sentiment of the Okinawan people for reversion is for no other reason than their desire for basic human rights under the peace constitution. For too long Okinawa has been treated as a means, sacrificed to state power and base power. Through the grand transition process of reversion now underway, Okinawa must cast off this status. But I fear that the Okinawan people's demands have not been adequately reflected in the relevant draft laws.

While Yara was still on his way to the Diet to deliver the petition, and before either of the two Okinawan members of the Diet who were scheduled to speak had been allowed to do so, and in the absence of the opposition parties, the LDP railroaded the agreement for Okinawa reversion.[31] Okinawa would be returned to Japan, but the opinions of Okinawans were irrelevant.

Reversion took place on May 15, 1972. It was celebrated at formal events in Tokyo and Naha. But the man who had negotiated it on Prime Minister Sato's behalf, Wakaizumi Kei, felt "general misgivings" about the event and wondered how "this deception" could be justified. He could only reassure himself, following Machiavelli, that states occasionally had to resort to subterfuge, and Plato, who thought rulers of the state "may be allowed to lie for the public good."[32]

In Tokyo, Sato emphasized the "strong bilateral connection" that made the peaceful return of Okinawa possible.[33] In Naha, Chief Executive Yara somberly remarked that

> Okinawa's day of return has undoubtedly come. But return has been carried out with all sorts of issues unresolved, including the problem of the US bases.

In Yogi Park, adjacent to Naha City Hall where the Naha event took place, the "Council for Reversion of Okinawa Prefecture to the Motherland," a coalition of some fifty civic and labor organizations, convened a meeting at which thirty thousand people gathered to protest against what to them was a new Okinawan *shobun* (disposal) and to call for the overthrow of the Sato government. As Fukuchi Hiroaki, one of the organizers of the protest meeting in Naha on the day of reversion, commented thirty-four years later, the reversion that was supposed to be "nuclear free and on the same basis as mainland Japan" was actually "nuclear concealing and base reinforcing" (not *kakunuki hondonami* but *kakukakushi kichikyoka*).[34] Though they could not know then the full measure of deception surrounding the Nixon-Sato deal, of which details still continue to emerge, Fukuchi and his co-organizers knew that reversion was a lie. One of the meeting's slogans was "15 May: Day of Humiliation."

Nearly four decades after its return (or five decades since the adoption of the Anpo treaty), three-quarters of all military facilities in Japan for exclusive US use are concentrated in Okinawa: twenty-five on the main island, taking up one-fifth of its land, and nine more on other islands. In mainland Japan, no new base has been built since the 1950s, and the bases were steadily reduced in two main phases—by about 75 percent from the late 1950s and early 1960s and again by about 25 percent between 1968 and 1974—while the concentration in Okinawa was stepped up. Bases elsewhere, too, have been steadily wound down to about one-third of Cold War levels in Europe and about three-quarters in South Korea.[35] Japan stands out as exceptional, and in Japan, Okinawa.

In the sense that the constitution in Okinawa from 1972 has been subject to the overriding principle of priority to the military, like North Korea, Okinawa has been a *"Songun"* (priority to the military) state (although in the Okinawan case it was an external power imposing the formula). As the peace and war functions, split from 1945 between the peace constitution of mainland Japan and the war-oriented Okinawa, were merged from 1972, the peace constitution, which never had a role in

Okinawa, played a steadily diminished role throughout Japan. Governments and foreign affairs and defense bureaucracies cultivated the belief that submission to the United States (rather than the nominally supreme charter of the constitution) was, and had to be, the first principle of the Japanese polity.

The adoption of the Nye rather than the Higuchi vision for the future of East Asia, following the restoration of LDP governments in 1995 after a short interlude, was especially fateful for Okinawa. Political and intellectual resistance to the Nye agenda crumbled nationally with the return to power in Tokyo of the LDP in 1995, but popular resistance welled in Okinawa, stirred in particular by the infamous rape case of September that year. The rape attack on a twelve-year-old girl by three GIs in 1995 shocked and galvanized the prefecture. As the LDP stumbled again in the late years of the first decade of the century and an alternative government moved to assume power, it was the Okinawan periphery that set the agenda for the national debate on the country's and the region's future.

What becomes clear from the reversion process is that sovereignty, nominally in the hands of the Japanese people under the 1947 constitution, was actually exercised in secret confabs by officials of the two governments. For the forty years to 2009, all Japanese governments persisted in lying to legislators and people by denying the existence of the secret agreements. In 1999, the Japanese government even prevailed upon Washington to withdraw documents released under the Freedom of Information Act in the United States that exposed the secret nuclear deals and therefore also exposed the Japanese government's denial as a lie.[36] Obligingly, the US government withdrew the "open" classification.

The assurance that Ambassador Ushiba gave Secretary of State Johnson in 1972 that the government of Japan would do what it could to ensure that the truth not be exposed by troublemakers such as *Mainichi Shimbun*'s Nishiyama held for thirty-seven years. As the long-suffering Nishiyama put it, the Okinawa handover treaty negotiated by the Sato and Nixon governments was "the prototype of the current alliance," and the problem for the Japanese state is that "admitting to the secret pacts would be to admit that the US-Japan alliance strategy was built on illegal grounds."[37]

## NOTES

1. Japan Communist Party, "Okinawa no beigun kichi mondai o sekai ni uttaemasu," http://www.jcp.or.jp/seisaku/gaiko_anpo/2002117_okinawa_uttae.html.
2. Yoshio Shimoji, "Futenma: Tip of the Iceberg in Okinawa's Agony," *Asia-Pacific Journal: Japan Focus* (October 24, 2011); Yoshida Kensei, "A Voice from

Okinawa (18)—Futenma kichi no kigen," *Meru magajin Oruta* (January 20, 2011), http://www.alter-magazine.jp/backno/backno_85.html#08.

3. For a detailed account of the Iejima struggle: Tanji, *Myth*, 62–70; Jon Mitchell, "Beggars' Belief: The Farmers' Resistance Movement on Iejima Island, Okinawa," *Asia-Pacific Journal: Japan Focus* (June 7, 2010), http://japanfocus.org/-Jon-Mitchell/3370; Ahagon Shoko and Douglas Lummis, "I Lost My Only Son in the War: Prelude to the Okinawan Anti-Base Movement," *Asia-Pacific Journal: Japan Focus* (June 7, 2010), http://japanfocus.org/-Ahagon-Shoko/3369.

4. See Furutachi and Norimatsu, "US Marine Training."

5. Japan Communist Party, "Okinawa no beigun."

6. See Furutachi and Norimatsu, "US Marine Training."

7. Ota Masahide, "Governor Ota at the Supreme Court of Japan," in *Okinawa: Cold War Island*, ed. Chalmers Johnson (Cardiff: Japan Policy Research Institute, 1999), 208.

8. Ryukyu Asahi Broadcasting and Satoko Norimatsu, "Assault on the Sea: A 50-Year U.S. Plan to Build a Military Port on Oura Bay, Okinawa," *Asia-Pacific Journal: Japan Focus* (July 5, 2010), http://japanfocus.org/-Ryukyu_Asahi_Broadcasting-/3381.

9. Arasaki, *Okinawa gendaishi*, 20.

10. Okinawa Prefecture, http://www3.pref.okinawa.jp/kititaisaku/toukeishiryou1.pdf. For a detailed study of the bases, replete with photographs, see Suda Shinichiro, Yabe Koji, and Maedomari Hiromori, *Hondo no ningen wa shiranai ga, Okinawa no hito wa minna shitte iru koto—Okinawa beigun kichi kanko gaido* (Tokyo: Shoseki johosha, 2011).

11. Arasaki, *Okinawa gendaishi*, 14.

12. United States Congress House Committee on Armed Services, *Report of a Special Subcommittee of the Armed Services Committee, House of Representatives: Following an Inspection Tour, October 14 to November 23, 1955*, CIS US Congressional Committee Prints, H1531 (Washington, DC: Government Printing Office, 1956).

13. Tanji, *Myth*, 71.

14. Chalmers Johnson, "The 1995 Rape Incident and the Rekindling of Okinawan Protest against the American Bases," in *Okinawa: Cold War Island*, ed. Chalmers Johnson (Cardiff: Japan Policy Research Institute, 1999), 111.

15. Arasaki, *Okinawa gendaishi*, 19.

16. "Dai ni ji ryudai jiken rekishi no kage ni me o muketai," editorial, *Ryukyu Shimpo*, August 18, 2007; "[Gaiko bunsho kokai] Ryudai jiken kuju no shobun Asato gakucho daigaku sonzoku de handan," *Ryukyu Shimpo*, February 19, 2011.

17. December 1965, quoted in Rabson, "'Secret' 1965 Memo."

18. Tim Weiner, *Legacy of Ashes: The History of the CIA* (New York: Doubleday, 2007), 120–21.

19. "U.S. Policy in the Ryukyu Islands, Memorandum of Conversation" (US National Archives, July 16, 1965, record number 79651). See the discussion in Rabson, "'Secret' 1965 Memo"; George R. Packard, *Edwin O. Reischauer and the American Discovery of Japan* (New York: Columbia University Press, 2010), 171.

20. Quoted in Rabson, "'Secret' 1965 Memo."

21. Weiner, *Legacy*.

22. "Kobunsho no kiroku USCAR jidai, 7, shuseki kosen to Nishime shien, Bei mo kanyo shi shikin teikyo," *Ryukyu Shimpo*, July 16, 2000.

23. See the account by Ota Masahide, in Ota and Norimatsu, "'The World Is Beginning."

24. Tanji, *Myth*, 101.

25. Christopher Aldous, "'Mob Rule' or Popular Activism: The Koza Riot of December 1970 and the Okinawan Search for Citizenship," in *Japan and Okinawa: Structure and Subjectivity*, ed. Glenn D. Hook and Richard Siddle (New York: Routledge, 2003); Wesley Iwao Ueunten, "Rising Up from a Sea of Discontent: The 1970 Koza Uprising in U.S.-Occupied Okinawa," in *Militarized Current: Toward a Decolonized Future in Asia and the Pacific*, ed. Setsu Shigematsu and Keith L. Camacho (Minneapolis: University of Minnesota Press, 2010).

26. *Okinawa Taimusu*, December 17, 2010.

27. Former governor Ota, however, notes that "even now, 60 to 70 percent of Okinawans believe(d) that chemical as well as nuclear weapons are still stored on their island." Ota and Norimatsu, "'The World Is Beginning." Jon Mitchell, "US Military Defoliants on Okinawa: Agent Orange," *Asia-Pacific Journal: Japan Focus* (September 12, 2011), http://japanfocus.org/-Jon-Mitchell/3601.

28. Eisaku Sato and Richard Nixon, "Joint Statement by Japanese Prime Minister Eisaku Sato and U.S. President Richard Nixon" (November 21, 1969).

29. Eisaku Sato and Richard Nixon, "Agreed Minute to Joint Communiqué of United States President Nixon and Japanese Prime Minister Sato Issued on November 21, 1969," reproduced in Shunichi Kawabata and Nanae Kurashige, "Secret Japan-U.S. Nuke Deal Uncovered," *Asahi Shimbun*, December 24, 2009.

30. Fukuchi Hiroaki, "Okinawa no 'Nihon fukki,'" *Shukan Kinyobi* (May 12, 2006): 32.

31. Agreement between Japan and the United States of America Concerning the Ryukyu Islands and the Daito Islands, June 17, 1971. Taira Kamenosuke, "Okinawa fuzai no 'fukki' ni i o tonaeta Yara Chobyo," *Shukan Kinyobi* (July 15, 2011). Taira was a member of the Ryukyu government's reversion office between 1969 and 1972.

32. Wakaizumi, *The Best Course Available*, 315.

33. Arasaki, *Okinawa gendaishi*, 34.

34. Fukuchi, "Okinawa," 33.

35. Oguma Eiji, "Kitokuken ni agurakaku Beigun," *Asahi Shimbun*, December 16, 2010.

36. "99 nen Bei kokai no 'kaku mitsuyaku' bunsho Nihon saikimitsuka o yosei," *Asahi Shimbun*, August 26, 2009.

37. Toko Sekiguchi, "Okinawa-gate: The Unknown Scandal," *Time*, May 1, 2007.

# 5

*~~*

# Henoko

## *The Unwanted Base*

On September 4, 1995, three American servicemen abducted a twelve-year old schoolgirl off the street, shoved her into their rented car, and drove her to a deserted beach where they covered her mouth, bound her hands and feet with duct tape, and took turns raping her.[1] Okinawan rage at the event was further fed by the crass comment from the commander of US forces in the Pacific, Admiral Richard C. Macke, that "[f]or the price that they [the confessed rapists] paid to rent the car, they could have had a girl [i.e., a prostitute]."[2] The incident shook the prefecture so profoundly as to threaten the base presence (and therefore the "alliance") and engrave the date on the memory of all Okinawans. It brought to a head the Futenma base return issue that continues, unresolved, to threaten the US-Japan relationship. For that reason it marks the beginning of a new phase in Okinawan history.

In response to the incident and the fury it aroused, the prime concern of the two nation-states was to counter the threat it posed to them. Rather than seek justice or take steps to protect Okinawan society from such future outrages, they sought a formula that would allow them to maintain the threat, that is, the base presence. Characteristically, they resorted to deception. A year later, they announced (after a series of bilateral talks under the name "Special Action Committee on Okinawa" (SACO) that Futenma Marine Corps Air Station, in the middle of Ginowan City and later dubbed by Donald Rumsfeld the world's most dangerous base, would be returned to Japan. However, the deception of this "reversion" was in the small print. Where in 1972 "reversion" (of Okinawa) had meant "retention," in 1996 "reversion" (of Futenma) meant "substitution": the construction of a new, enlarged, multiservice facility for the obsolescent Futenma. Fifteen years on, that agreement remains unfulfilled.

That December 1996 SACO agreement began the present phase of the "Okinawa problem" and especially the long and continuing agony of Nago City, the preferred site for a "Futenma Replacement Facility" (FRF).[3] Futenma sits incongruously and dangerously amid the bustling city of Ginowan. The gold of its promised return turned to dross as people realized that instead of closing and returning, it was simply to be replaced, that a new base would substitute for the old.

The site for the Futenma replacement was soon narrowed to Henoko, offshore from the fishing port, a site first featured in a 1966 US Navy "master plan," at the height of the Vietnam War, for a large-scale naval and marine facility. Despite many transmutations of the detail, the idea of Henoko as the site for a major new military base has existed for four and a half decades.

From 1996, the Henoko plan was repeatedly either rejected by a citizenry angry at the injustice and unfairness of one more base being built in their already excessively base-concentrated prefecture or accepted by local government authorities under conditions (civil-military joint use, fixed term, etc.) that amounted to rejection. The more the project was rejected or subjected to impossible conditions, the more it returned, the floating, temporary heliport slowly shedding its conditions and expanding its scale.

In the following discussion, we draw in part on the account of this process provided by former governor and distinguished Okinawa historian Ota Masahide.[4]

## HENOKO VERSION 1, 1966–1969

Before the reversion in 1972, neither the Japanese constitution nor the Japan-US Security Treaty applied in Okinawa, so the US military could operate its bases free of any constraint. The Korean and Vietnamese wars could be conducted from Okinawan bases as though they were American territory, and the US authorities were also able to freely rehearse nuclear attacks over Iejima and to import nuclear and chemical weapons to select bases, not removing them until the eve of reversion. From the mid-1960s, however, as the reversion movement and the Okinawan antibase movement gathered strength, the implications of reversion had to be considered. The Joint Chiefs of Staff paid attention to a reorganization that would involve shifting major US force concentrations away from heavily populated areas in the south and center of the island to the more lightly populated—but ecologically sensitive—north. Under that general design, the north of the island would become the center for a major Marine Corps concentration. Early in 1966 a "General Development Plan, Marine Corps" was drawn up for an "all-weather, jet-capable" airfield at Henoko on the reef area between Oura Bay and Kushi Bay. The design shown in figure 5.1 was drawn by consultants at the behest of the US Navy.[5]

The waters of Oura Bay are deep, up to thirty meters, which makes it attractive for its capacity to berth aircraft carriers unable to dock at Naha military port. Consequently, the Oura Bay design included plans for a military port with a gigantic pier. However, any large-scale construction project at that time would have been entirely a US responsibility, since the United States exercised unfettered control over Okinawa. With Vietnam War costs escalating and the dollar in trouble, however, the plan was put on a back burner; and with the announcement in 1969 of the US intention to withdraw from Vietnam, the immediate need for the project faded.[6] Attention focused instead on the grand design to return Okinawa while retaining the bases as a whole—in other words, to simultaneously return and retain.

## HENOKO VERSION 2, 1996–1997

Thirty years after the original US design and sporadic US attempts at that time to get rid of the coral nuisance in Oura Bay by bombing it,[7] attention turned again to Cape Henoko. The Nye report of 1995, discussed in chapter 3, heralded a reconsideration of the base structure in the context of the US post–Cold War determination to retain a 100,000-strong force in Japan and Korea. Okinawa was destined to play a key role in this strategy. Before deliberations could begin to address what that might mean, the 1995 rape case galvanized both the Okinawan people and the strategists in Washington and Tokyo.

Initially, it seemed that the US presence might have to be scaled back, even perhaps drastically, in the face of the fierce anger that swept over the islands, but the resentment was contained. The promised "return within five to seven years" of Futenma marine base astonished Okinawans, and their astonishment only died when they understood, days later, that there was a condition attached: Futenma would first have to be replaced, and that replacement would have to be in Okinawa. In the early talks, the term "heliport" conveyed to some of those involved the idea of a modest site where helicopters could land and take off. One Japanese participant envisaged something of around forty-five meters in length.[8] By the end of 1996, however, SACO (Special Action Committee on Okinawa) in its final report

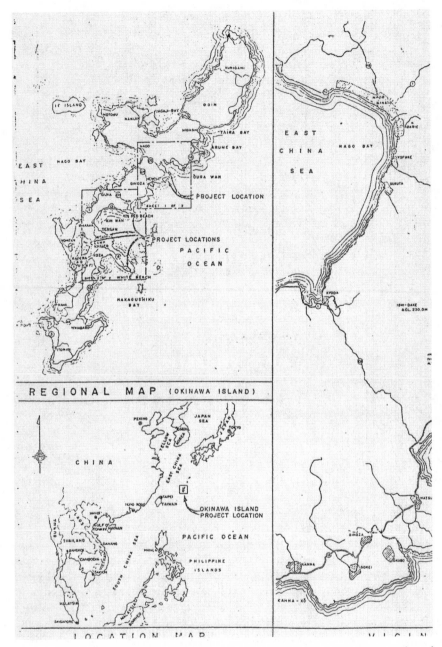

**Figure 5.1.** US plans for a navy military port at Henoko, 1966. *Source:* Master Plan of Navy Facilities Okinawa Ryukyu Islands, Okinawa Prefectural Archives.

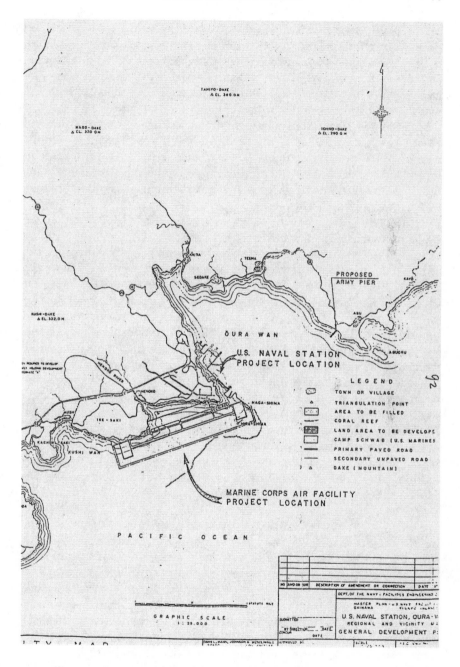

called for a 1,500-meter "sea-based facility" (SBF) with a 1,300-meter main runway to be built by pier, pontoon, or semisubmersible off the east coast of the main island of Okinawa, connected to land by a "pier or causeway" and able to be removed "when no longer necessary."[9] As the reversion of Okinawa in 1972 had been in fact retention, so the reversion of Futenma was to be substitution and expansion.

In 1997, the Hashimoto administration established that the location would be off the coast of Camp Schwab. In other words, Cape Henoko and the initial design (see figure 5.2) was, in essence, a return to US military plans of thirty years earlier, though no one thought to mention the fact since the plan now was represented as part of a design to lighten the Okinawan burden, not increase it.

Residents of Nago, which includes the hamlet of Henoko, organized a plebiscite in 1997, in which a majority adopted an antibase position, despite heavy government pressure and interference. The Japanese government representation of the facility as something temporary that would in due course be removed was belied by the Department of Defense's September 1997 report that specified use for forty years and durability for two hundred years.[10] The US GAO's estimate was for a project that would cost between $2.4 billion and $4.9 billion to construct.[11] Maintenance would add an additional $200 million each year ($8 billion over 40 years), which the US government expected Japan would also pay.[12]

Ota Masahide, governor at the time, gradually came to view the scheme as one to build in Oura Bay a permanent military structure of scale akin to Kansai International Airport.[13] Though he did not learn it until much later, the government in Tokyo decided that Ota would have to be removed from office and began a concerted campaign, culminating in a major, illegal appropriation of funds that was successful in ousting him in the elections of December 1998. (For more on this, see pages 140–41.)

## HENOKO VERSION 3, 2002

With the defeat of Ota late in 1998 and the installation of the conservative Inamine Keiichi as governor, the tide turned towards acceptance, albeit conditional. Inamine insisted that the facility be a joint civil-military one and for fifteen years only: "the limit the people of Okinawa should be asked to tolerate."[14] Nago City's council gave its consent after an all-night debate on December 23, 1999. But Mayor Kishimoto Tateo insisted on seven conditions, including that the construction should be allowed only if it could be guaranteed not to compromise the safety and environment of the surrounding region.[15] When the three parties, national, prefectural,

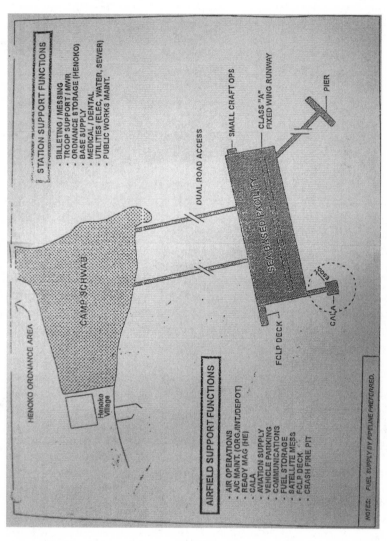

Figure 5.2. The DoD's (Pentagon) "sea-based facility" plan, 1997. *Source:* "DoD Operational Requirement and Concept of Operations for MCAS Futenma Relocation, Okinawa, Japan, Final Draft," Ota, *Konna Okinawa,* 221–23.

and city, reached agreement in 2002 on a FRF plan for a 2,500-meter facility (runway of 2,000 meters) on reclaimed land two kilometers offshore from Henoko, it looked like a return to the 1966 plan (figure 5.1). But the conditions were tough and almost certainly unpalatable to the Pentagon. It would be impossible to combine protection of the delicate marine environment with the large-scale military project.

However, local and international opposition made it more difficult to implement these plans. It was April 19, 2004, before the Naha Defense Facilities Administration Bureau (DFAB, the Defense Facilities Administration's Okinawa branch) moved to undertake preliminary survey works. When it did so, opponents formed a sit-in human barricade to block passage of dump trucks. When the DFAB resorted to working at night, protesters began maintaining the towers around the clock. The "Battle of Henoko" began.[16]

After five months of such tactics, in September the DFAB decided to access the site by going through Camp Schwab, chartering fishing boats from Henoko fishermen (paying them well) and setting out to sea rather than risking further confrontation with the barricade. With this, the battle moved from land to sea. The antibase activists set out in canoes, surrounding the buoy markers an hour before the construction workers started their workday in an effort to stop setup of the scaffolding towers from which the drilling was to be conducted. In November 2004, about twenty neighboring fishing boats joined the protesters, making the drilling more complicated and dangerous (see figure 5.3). Activists in fishing boats and canoes kept their vigil around the scaffold towers from 4 a.m. to 5 p.m. At the height of the struggle, some of them remained on the towers for a fifty-day period, alternating two twelve-hour shifts. During a fiercely contested period of several months in 2004, four towers were completed, prompting some activists, in desperation, to chain themselves to the towers in their attempt to block the works.

As the skirmishes between government-employed surveyors and the peace and environment coalition's opposition continued at sea and on the ocean floor, Prime Minister Koizumi conceded the strength of the opposition. On May 16, 2005, he told a lower house budget committee:

> I think I can well understand the fierce determination and effort of those conducting the sit in to obstruct the works. I am thinking seriously about how to find a compromise solution in consultation with the local people.[17]

In October he declared that the government "was unable to implement the (initial) relocation (plan) because of a lot of opposition."[18] Some 60,000 people had participated in the campaign, including 10,000 who were part

**Figure 5.3.** Struggle between the government survey ship and protesters on canoes, November 2004. *Source:* Toyozato Tomoyuki.

of the protest at sea. It was that exceptionally rare event: a challenge to the authority of the state launched by civic groups that was successful.

## HENOKO VERSION 4, 2005

No sooner was one design dropped than another was adopted in its stead, under the US-Japan "Transformation and Realignment for the Future" Agreement of October 2005.[19] This would be an L-shaped reclamation project centered on the existing Camp Schwab marine base, with an 1,800-meter runway inshore from Henoko (figure 5.4). It would be partially on the peninsula instead of entirely offshore. It came to look, once again, much like the original 1966 plan.

This time even the mayor of Nago and the governor of Okinawa, who had both supported the offshore base, albeit conditionally, opposed the plan, noting that it would be located a mere seven hundred meters from a residential area. The conditions attached to Okinawan consent in December 1999—especially those relating to the joint civil-military character and the fifteen-year term—appear not to have even been raised by the Japanese side in negotiations with the United States.

**Figure 5.4.** Cape Henoko (Camp Schwab) L-shaped plan, October 2005. *Source:* Security Consultive Committee, "Interim Report" (2005), http://www.mofa.go.jp/mofaj/area/usa/hosho/pdfs/gainenzu.pdf.

## HENOKO VERSION 5, 2006

A year later the plan was again revised, this time apparently following discussions between Nukaga Fukushiro, head of the Defense Agency, and Nago mayor Shimabukuro Yoshikazu. Under the "United States–Japan Roadmap for Realignment Implementation" agreement of 2006, the Futenma Replacement Facility would be completed by 2014 as a land-based structure,[20] with dual V-shaped 1,800-meter runways stretching from the existing Camp Schwab US base into Oura Bay, as shown in figure 5.5. The rationale behind the change was to avoid flight over residential areas by using different runways for take-off and landing, and thereby diminishing noise, but many found this unconvincing.

The keywords of the 2005/2006 agreements were "interoperability" and "joint operations posture." Japan was to pay not only for the Henoko construction—expected to cost $2.4–$4.9 billion or possibly more, and to take about ten years to construct (cf. GAO report discussed in page 96)—

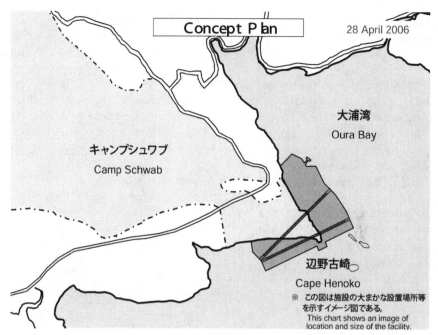

Figure 5.5. The V-shaped runway in the Roadmap Agreement, 2006. *Source:* Secretary of State Rice et al., "United States-Japan Roadmap for Realignment Implementation" (May 1, 2006), http://www.mofa.go.jp/region/n-america/us/security/scc/doc0605.html.

but also to contribute $6.09 billion toward the cost of constructing further US Marine Corps facilities on Guam.

This 2006 Henoko base design called for the reclamation of Oura Bay seas adjacent to the existing Marine Corps Camp Schwab. It amounted to a comprehensive high-tech air, land, and sea base—far larger and more multifunctional than the obsolescent, inconvenient, and dangerous Futenma. A Marine Corps representative spoke of a new base that would not just replace Futenma, but one that would have 20 percent more fire-power.[21] In effect, the agreement de facto transformed the alliance from one limited in scope under Article 6 of the Joint Security Treaty of 1960, for "the defense of Japan and the Far East," into a structural element of the Global War on Terrorism (GWOT) in a process that passed with minimal public or Diet debate or scrutiny but that sidelined the country's constitu-tional pacifism and embedded it in a global military alliance.

For the two governments (Japan and the United States), the 2006 He-noko design had the advantage that the site would be difficult for protest-ers to effectively mobilize against since the Camp Schwab location would be off-limits. For those elements within Okinawa prefecture prepared to cooperate on base construction, a base site stretching as far away from the coast as possible was highly desirable, officially because of desire to minimize noise over residential areas, but really because such construction would much better serve the interests of construction companies, in particular the vested interests of the "gravel industry association." The farther from the coast and the deeper the sea, the more sand or gravel that would be needed, and the greater the potential for profit. Ota Masahide commented in 2010 that Inamine Keiichi, who succeeded him as governor in 1998, Inamine's successor, Nakaima Hirokazu, elected governor in 2006, and Shimabukuro Yoshikazu, Nago City mayor between 2006 and 2010, had all been elected with backing from this group.[22]

While the 2006 agreement passed in mainland Japan with minimal debate or comment, in Okinawa the resistance continued to defy all efforts by the conservative LDP government to persuade, intimidate, divide, or buy it off. On and off the coast of Henoko continued one of the longest political protest sit-ins of modern times, despite the government's escalating intimidation of civil protest, which included the May 2007 dispatch of a Maritime Self Defense Force minesweeper tender at the start of the environmental survey for implementing the Roadmap's V-shape runway construction plan.[23]

Despite the cooperative mien of the Koizumi and subsequent LDP governments and satisfaction on the part of Washington insiders such as Richard Armitage, progress on the agreed agenda was slow, especially on the Futenma Replacement Facility (FRF) issue. By 2008, the survey process still incomplete, the opposition unmoved, and, even more important, the LDP's warrant rapidly running out, Richard Lawless, who as deputy defense secretary had headed the negotiations that culminated in the Roadmap Agreement, told the *Asahi* in May that the alliance was drifting.

> What we really need is a top-down leadership that says, "Let's rededicate ourselves to completing all of these agreements on time; let's make sure that the budgeting of the money is a national priority." . . . Japan has to find a way to change its own tempo of decision-making, deployment, integration and operationalizing this alliance.[24]

The Guam treaty was the embodiment of this "top-down" prescription.


## THE GUAM TREATY

The "Guam International Agreement," signed by Secretary of State Hillary Clinton and Foreign Minister Nakasone Hirofumi in February 2009 and then adopted as a treaty (by the Japanese side only) under special legislation in May 2009,[25] was the device adopted by the incoming Obama administration to extract formal consent from the rapidly declining Aso government in such a way as to bind the prospective Democratic Party of Japan (DPJ) government then waiting in the wings. The US embassy in Tokyo reported to Washington that the Japanese Ministry of Foreign Affairs wanted the 2006 "Roadmap" agreement to be endorsed and reinforced as a treaty, that is, to elevate the agreement into a "treaty-level (on the Japanese side)" agreement that would be "legally binding on the current and future Japanese cabinets."[26]

What distinguished the Guam agreement was not its content—for almost all had been agreed in 2005–2006, but its form, a *treaty*. And because it was binding on one side only (the government of Japan), it was an "unequal treaty." Knowing full well where the opposition DPJ stood—that Futenma should be moved outside of Okinawa[27]—the Obama administration exploited the window of opportunity, while the LDP still enjoyed the two-thirds Lower House majority (delivered by Koizumi's "postal privatization" triumph of 2005), to press the compliant Aso government into adopting the agreement in treaty format and thus tie the hands of the popular forces about to be elected to government. Secretary Clinton made clear that the United States would insist on this point.[28] To successfully block the Japanese democratic will in this way was a perverse early accomplishment for the Obama administration.

The treaty was the culmination of a fifteen-year process of reorganization in accord with the Nye post–Cold War frame. Though widely reported as a US "withdrawal" designed to reduce the burden of post–World War II American military presence in Okinawa, it was actually a design to *increase* the Japanese contribution to the alliance, committing it to the construction of two major US military facilities (at Henoko and on Guam), extracting huge sums in military subsidy in the process. The Japanese government, its credibility rapidly collapsing, pulled out all stops to make sure it could pay $336 million dollars to the US Treasury by May 2009, as an installment, so to speak, on the eventual agreed total of $6.09 billion ($2.8 billion in cash and the rest in credits). The core concern was not national security—which does not appear even to have been discussed—but the determination to prolong the US occupation of Okinawa (and provide whatever service might be possible for the US Afghan and Iraq wars), regardless of the cost.

To better pull the wool over the eyes of the Japanese, and especially the Okinawan people, and enforce the base deal, the bureaucrats on both sides manipulated the figures on the Guam troop transfer and on the proportion of costs that would be met by Japan.[29] The $6.09 billion that Japan was to pay under the Roadmap (2006) and Guam agreements of 2009 on relocation of US forces in Japan included provision for eight thousand Marines and their nine thousand dependents to be relocated from Okinawa to facilities that Japan would construct on Guam, thereby "reducing the burden" on Okinawa. For Japan to pay such a huge sum for construction of facilities (including medical clinic, bachelor enlisted quarters, fire station, etc.) on American soil was unprecedented, although *omoiyari* or "sympathy" payments to help the United States maintain its forces in Japan had become an established budgetary item commencing in 1978 (further discussed in chapter 10).

However, as the embassy dispatch put it, "both the 8,000 and the 9,000 numbers were deliberately maximized to optimize political value in Japan."[30] There were at the time only "on the order of 13,000" marines, and the total number of dependents was "less than 9,000." The US side "regularly briefed" the Japanese government on these numbers, so when government ministers repeatedly used the figures of an Okinawa marine force of 18,000 to be reduced to 10,000, most of whom would transfer to the Futenma Replacement Facility when it was ready, there is no doubt that they did so in bad faith, that is, that they lied. In other words, of the troops supposedly defending Japan under the 1960 security pact, where their role was strictly defined as confined to the defense of Japan and the Far East, a substantial number at any one time were on active service in far-off war zones. Both the supposed eight thousand to be transferred to Guam and the ten thousand to move to Henoko were phantom, groundless figures.[31]

The cost was also inflated by inclusion of an item of one billion dollars for construction of a military road on Guam. This item was nominally to be met by the United States, but the "billion dollar road" was simply "a way to increase the overall cost estimate and thereby reduce the share of total costs borne by Japan."[32] Its inclusion reduced the Japanese proportion of the $10.27 billion overall cost from 66 percent to 59 percent, making it seem slightly more equal. The road was neither necessary nor likely to ever be built.

As haggling over these details continued, distrust between the two parties deepened. The US embassy in Tokyo reported, "The Japanese side . . . registered frustration with over two years of U.S. inability to provide more detailed data on the actual number of dependents . . . that will relocate to Guam, and voiced suspicion that the U.S. intends to hold on to excessive housing in Okinawa and force Tokyo to build more housing in Guam than is required."[33]

The process by which numbers "were deliberately maximized to optimize political value in Japan" was, as the *Asahi* put it, "an unpardonable betrayal of the people."[34] To the *Okinawa Taimusu*, it was another *mitsuyaku*, or "secret treaty."[35] Meanwhile, the two sides quibbled and quarreled over details of numbers to be relocated to Guam.

Signed in Tokyo by Hillary Clinton in February 2009 and ratified in the Diet in May, the Guam International Agreement was the first initiative of the new Obama government toward Japan. It was a design by the two governments to block the democratic will of the Japanese people. The rush to sign the deal reflected the fact that the LDP was on the verge of collapsing at the polls. As McCormack wrote then, the Guam International Agreement (Treaty)

> is likely to be studied by future generations as something crystallizing the defining moment of a relationship, when both parties went *too far*, the US in demanding (hastily, well aware that time was running out to cut a deal with the LDP) and Japan in submitting to something not only unequal but also unconstitutional, illegal, colonial, and deceitful. Excess on both sides was likely to generate resentment and in the long run to make the relationship more difficult to sustain.[36]

That is indeed what happened.

Furthermore, the estimate of Guam transfer costs was soon revised upward. The Government Accountability Office (GAO) in May 2011 noted that no proper, detailed estimates for the associated projects had hitherto been made and estimated that, between them, the United States and Japan faced a staggering total cost of realignment of US forces, including the Guam transfer, of $29.1 billion (2.4 trillion yen), roughly three times the original estimates. It would be shared by the United States ($13.2 billion) and Japan ($15.9 billion). That meant that the total expenditure Japan would be called upon to meet for the realignment would be not $6.1 billion but $15.9 billion.[37]

In addition, the $3.6 billion estimate that Japan put on the Futenma Replacement Facility (as adopted by GAO) was almost certainly far too low; many experts suggested that figure should be doubled or trebled. So Japan's $15.9 billion share ($9.8 billion for the realignment in Japan and $6.1 billion for the Guam move) would certainly rise further. If that rise was proportional with that anticipated for the United States by GAO, it would also treble.

The gradual exposure of the secret deals that surrounded Okinawan reversion and US nuclear strategy and more recently of the multiple layers of deception and deceit shown by the secret and confidential dispatches released in May 2011 have thus far had no apparent effect on general public and media perceptions. The authenticity of the documents has thus far not been seriously challenged. They served to open a devastating window on the inner workings of the relationship.

The government of Japan has studiously avoided comment on the authenticity or significance of the WikiLeaks materials, and the national media, including the *Asahi*, which initially published them, has paid little serious attention to them. No public figure has yet demanded a public or legislative inquiry. To date, the most serious analysis has been that published in the Okinawan daily, *Ryukyu Shimpo*.[38] Consider the assessment of just three of those who contributed essays to it:

Magosaki Ukeru, former director general of the Intelligence and Analysis Bureau of Japan's Ministry of Foreign Affairs:

> The Democratic Party government elected in 2009 planned to revise relations with the US, including concerning the Futenma problem. When the US issued warnings, leading figures in the departments of Foreign Affairs and Defense acted contrary to the intent of the Prime Minister. What they did was contrary to the principles of democracy. What has become of the country Japan? It has lapsed into a chronic ailment of lack of self-hood.

Amaki Naoto, Japanese ambassador to Lebanon, 2001–2003:

> The crime of the authorities is so serious that, if the US has tricked the Government of Japan then the Japanese people must accuse it of deception, and if the Government of Japan has lent a helping hand to the US to deceive the people of Japan and has improperly and unnecessarily handed over the Japanese people's hard-earned tax monies, then the Japanese people must accuse it of betrayal."

Arasaki Moriteru, Okinawa University emeritus professor and author of the authoritative modern history of Okinawa:

> What is exposed, all too vividly and in concrete detail, in the [WikiLeaks] diplomatic cables is just how pathetic and decadent are Japan's political and elite bureaucratic circles. We have seen what we did not want to see: the behaviour of politicians and elite bureaucrats who, while talking all the time of "national interest" and spouting chauvinistic nationalism, were serving the United States and had assimilated to the American "national interest."

## POST-GUAM—OPENING, REPACKING, AND RETYING THE PACKAGE

The 2006 Roadmap Agreement and the 2009 Guam Agreement were followed by the Hatoyama-Obama agreement of 2010 and the "Two plus Two" agreement by the foreign and defense ministers of the United States and Japan in 2011 (see chapter 10); but by early 2012 nothing had been done toward implementing them. The litany of statements that the project was on track signalled that in fact it was not. Yet Japan's national government remained adamant that the project would proceed, insisting to the United States that relocation elsewhere in Japan was out of the question:

it had to be in Okinawa, and it had to be in Henoko. Japanese insistence, not US intransigence, was decisive.[39]

The story of the Futenma Replacement Facility took a remarkable turn early in 2012. The terms of realignment plans stipulated in the 2006–2011 series of agreements (as above), repeatedly declared to be an immutable and indivisible "package," were suddenly reopened and rearranged at American initiative. The key components of the 2006 package—construction of the Futenma Replacement Facility at Henoko and its handover to the United States, the transfer of eight thousand marines from Okinawa to Guam, and the return to Japan of Okinawan base lands in the south part of Okinawa (south of Kadena Base)—would be significantly revised and recombined. The estimated completion date of 2014 originally set in 2006 had already been diluted, in 2011, into "as soon as possible after 2014" (see chapter 10), but now the contents of the package were completely reorganized. *Asahi Shimbun* reported that Tokyo "did not offer a single bold proposal."[40] If that is accurate, then Washington decided on the changes and simply informed Tokyo. And, as US Defense Secretary Leon Panetta put it, "they [the government of Japan] have been very generous in saying that whatever moves that have to be made they'll support, they'll give us a lot of the funds to try to support that."[41] Panetta added, "I'm very pleased with the attitude the Japanese are taking." A more explicit statement of the client state relationship would be hard to find.

The central correction was the separation of the Guam transfer from the Henoko construction. Furthermore, the number of marines to go to Guam would be cut from 8,000 to about 4,700, with 3,300 to be divided into small mobile forces and rotated among bases in the Philippines, Australia (Darwin), Hawaii, and Iwakuni in mainland Japan, according to the principle of a "geographically distributed, operationally resilient and politically sustainable force structure."[42] The reasons appear to have been a combination of growing US abandonment of hope that Japan was ever going to be able to realize its pledges of construction at Henoko, with a comprehensive adjustment of military strategy driven by the need to shrink budgets but simultaneously concentrate force around the perimeter of China. The latter had to be done while at the same time minimizing the risk of Chinese attack by avoiding major force concentrations within the range of its new generation of missiles. Okinawa's location, on the line dividing the first and second Chinese lines of island defense, was too vulnerable to Chinese attack and therefore too close for comfort. By contrast, Australia's Darwin was beyond that range, and the government of Australia was unreservedly positive about hosting the marines, so a base there would be "politically sustainable" in the way that one at Henoko plainly could never be. Initially the Australian deployment would be in the hundreds, but it was expected to build gradually to become a force of around 2,500, including perhaps the command force of the 31st Marine Expeditionary Unit (31 MEU) currently located in Okinawa.[43]

So the Guam transfer would be cut almost in half and become part of a wide regional dispersal, giving the lie to the Japanese insistence that only a major concentration on Okinawa had true deterrence value. And while the Futenma Replacement Facility was still declared "the only viable way forward," that statement sounded increasingly like whistling in the wind. However, the third component of the 2006 package—the return of unneeded base land in the "south of Kadena" zone—would now be accelerated. The land designated for return comprised about one-fifth of all Okinawan base land, and its return might, as the *New York Times* almost wistfully reported, "soften opposition to a new air base by showing Okinawans tangible progress in reducing the American presence."[44]

Okinawans looked at the gradually emerging new strategic doctrine and doubted that the "lessening" of their burden carried weight in either capital. They suspected that the two national governments were intent again on sacrificing Okinawa and that another round of *mitsuyaku* might be in the offing. They noted angrily the response of the government of Japan to the American suggestion that some of the Futenma marines might be relocated to Iwakuni base, in Yamaguchi prefecture in mainland Japan. When the Yamaguchi governor and the Iwakuni City mayor petitioned to oppose any such relocation, Foreign Minister Genba responded, "Relax. We will not be sending any additional marines to Iwakuni."[45] That response stood in marked contrast to the response by Genba and other ministers to identical and repeated protests by Okinawa's governor and the city mayor of Nago. The only conclusion Okinawans could draw was that the government of Japan could, if it wished, say "no" to an American request but that it chose not to in relation to Okinawa, and that Okinawa could be treated with contempt and discrimination while mainland Japanese prefectures and towns could not.[46]

Okinawans noted too that, despite the unresolved state of the environmental assessment process on Henoko (see chapter 8), the national government was proceeding to authorize major construction projects within the Camp Schwab base,[47] as if the outcome were a foregone conclusion. It had ignored the possibility of a negative outcome to the environmental impact process or to various pending lawsuits and had treated the lack of prefectural or city government consent as irrelevant. It had also authorized major renovation works on the Futenma base, despite its public stance that all possible steps should be taken to ensure its earliest return and liquidation of the hugely dangerous site, signifying that it had no expectation that the marine base would be returned any time soon. Okinawans were more inclined to look closely and critically at such national government policies than they were to listen to the protestations of sincerity and burden "lessening."

While emissaries from Tokyo, including Prime Minister Noda, prefaced their messages to Okinawa with apologies and authorized substantial subsidies for Okinawan "development" (293.76 billion yen, or somewhat more than $3 billion in fiscal year 2012), they maintained unrelenting pressure. Determined against all odds to "sincerely persuade" Okinawa, Tokyo appeared to be gearing up for a renewed assault, deploying psychological warfare tactics, financial inducements, and veiled threats. Okinawans girded their loins for new struggle. As the *Okinawa Taimusu* put it, "What is called for is a demonstration of determination from Okinawa on a par with the 'all Okinawa' struggle [of the 1950s]."[48]

## NOTES

1. Carolyn Bowen Francis, "Omen and Military Violence," in *Okinawa: Cold War Island*, ed. Chalmers Johnson (Cardiff: Japan Policy Research Institute, 1999), 189.

2. Johnson, "The 1995 Rape," 116.

3. Minister for Foreign Affairs Ikeda et al., "The SACO Final Report, December, 2, 1996" (1996).

4. For interview with Ota by Satoko Norimatsu on July 20, 2010, see Ota and Norimatsu, "'The World Is."

5. Ota, "*Konna Okinawa*," 197–218. See also Makishi Yoshikazu, "Kushi-wan Henoko kaijo e no shin gunji kuko keikaku," in *Okinawa wa mo damasarenai* (Tokyo: Kobunken, 2000).

6. Makishi, "Kushi-wan Henoko kaijo," 105.

7. Ryukyu Asahi Broadcasting and Satoko Norimatsu, "Assault on the Sea: A 50-Year U.S. Plan to Build a Military Port on Oura Bay, Okinawa," *Asia-Pacific Journal: Japan Focus* (July 5, 2010), http://japanfocus.org/-Ryukyu_Asahi_Broadcasting-/3381.

8. Shimokobe Atsushi, then vice-minister at the National Lands Agency, quoted in Sato Manabu, "Obama seiken no Amerika—Keizai to gaiko seisaku no henka," in *Okinawa 'jiritsu' e no michi o motomete*, ed. Miyazato Seigen, Arasaki Moriteru, and Gabe Masaaki (Tokyo: Kobunken, 2009), 90.

9. Ikeda et al., "The SACO Final Report."

10. "DoD Operational Requirement and Concept of Operations for MCAS Futenma Relocation, Okinawa, Japan, Final Draft," September 29, 1997, Ota, *Konna Okinawa*, 222–25.

11. United States General Accounting Office, *Overseas Presence, Issues Involved in Reducing the Impact of U.S. Military Presence on Okinawa*, March 2, 1998, p. 37, http://www.gao.gov/products/NSIAD-98-66.

12. Ibid., 6, 37.

13. Ota, *Konna Okinawa*, 125–26.

14. Inamine Keiichi, "Okinawa as Pacific Crossroads," *Japan Quarterly* (July–September 2000): 14.

15. Arasaki, *Okinawa gendaishi*, 194.

16. The following account is from Kikuno Yumiko and Satoko Norimatsu, "Henoko, Okinawa: Inside the Sit-In," *Asia-Pacific Journal: Japan Focus* (February 22, 2010), http://japanfocus.org/-Norimatsu-Satoko/3306.

17. *Okinawa Times*, May 16, 2005, quoted in Arasaki, *Okinawa gendaishi*, 225.

18. Kanako Takahara, "Japan, U.S. Agree on New Futenma Site," *Japan Times*, October 27, 2005.

19. Security Consultative Committee, "Transformation and Realignment for the Future, October 29, 2005" (2005).

20. Secretary of State Rice et al., "United States-Japan Roadmap for Realignment Implementation"(May 1, 2006), http://www.mofa.go.jp/region/n-america/us/security/scc/doc0605.html.

21. According to Colonel Thomas R. King, former vice commander of Futenma Air Station, NHK Television News, April 10, 1998.

22. Ota and Norimatsu, "'The World Is Beginning."

23. Kikuno and Norimatsu, "Henoko, Okinawa."

24. Yoichi Kato, "Interview/Richard Lawless: Japan-U.S. Alliance Faces 'Priority Gap,'" *Asahi Shimbun*, May 6, 2008.

25. Hirofumi Nakasone and Hillary Rodham Clinton, "Agreement between the Government of Japan and the Government of the United States of America Concerning the Implementation of the Relocation of III Marine Expeditionary Force Personnel and Their Dependents from Okinawa to Guam" (Tokyo, February 17, 2009).

26. Zumwalt, Cable 08TOKYO03457, Part 1 of 2, "U.S., JAPAN REACH AD REF GUAM," December 19, 2008, *WikiLeaks.* http://wikileaks.ch/cable/2008/12/08TOKYO3457.

27. See the Democratic Party's "Okinawa Vision 2008," http://www.dpj.or.jp/news/files/okinawa(2).pdf.

28. "I think that a responsible nation follows the agreements that have been entered into, and the agreement I signed today with Foreign Minister Nakasone is one between our two nations, regardless of who's in power." ("Clinton Praises Strong U.S.-Japan Ties," *Yomiuri Shimbun*, February 18, 2009.)

29. "The Truth behind Japan-US Ties (3) Numbers Inflated in Marine Relocation Pact to Increase Political Impact," *Asahi Shimbun*, May 4, 2011. See Zumwalt, Cable 08TOKYO03457, Part 1 of 2, ibid.

30. Zumwalt, Cable 08TOKYO03457, Part 1 of 2, ibid.

31. "Tenkanki no Anpo 2010: 'jochu naki Futenma,' shusho 'fukuan' no mikata fujo," *Mainichi Shimbun*, April 8, 2010. English translation in Satoko Norimatsu, "The Myth of 18,000 Marines in Okinawa Admitted by USMC," Peace Philosophy Centre, April 12, 2010, http://peacephilosophy.blogspot.com/2010/04/myth-of-18000-marines-in-okinawa.html.

32. Zumwalt, Cable 08TOKYO03457, Part 1 of 2, ibid.

33. Zumwalt, Cable 08TOKYO03458, "Part 2 of 2—U.S., Japan Reach AD REF GUAM," December 19, 2008, *WikiLeaks.* http://wikileaks.ch/cable/2008/12/08TOKYO3458.

34. "Leaked Documents Reveal Shocking Japan-US Diplomacy," *Asahi Shimbun*, May 5, 2011.

35. "Kichi iten no jittai kakusu 'mitsuyaku,'" *Okinawa Taimusu*, May 5, 2011.

36. Gavan McCormack, "The Battle of Okinawa 2009: Obama vs Hatoyama," *Asia-Pacific Journal: Japan Focus* (November 16, 2009), http://japanfocus.org/-Gavan-McCormack/3250.

37. US Government Accountability Office, "Defense Management—Comprehensive Cost Information and Analysis of Alternatives Needed to Assess Military Posture in Asia" (May 2011), 25; "Bei kansain hokoku de beigun saihenhi 2cho 3000okuen/Bei gikai de keikaku minaoshi mo," *Shimbun Akahata*, May 30, 2011.

38. See the series "'Futenma' koden o toku," *Ryukyu Shimpo*, May 7–11, 2011. Other articles in the series are by Sato Manabu of Okinawa International University and Ota Masahide, former governor of Okinawa.

39. Kurt Campbell, then representing the Department of Defense, dismissed the Japanese claim that it would not be possible on military grounds to replace Futenma anywhere but in Okinawa, saying that the Japanese grounds for saying so were only political, and that the US side was open to suggestions for alternative sites in Kyushu or Shikoku. "Minute of Unofficial Discussion Meeting, March 13, 1998"; "Futenma isetsu hikoshiki kyogi, 98 nen 3 gatsu toji, Bei 'kengai kano' o dentatsu," *Ryukyu Shimpo*, November 15, 2009.

40. "New Okinawa Base Agreement Should Lead to Rethink of Henoko Plan," editorial, *Asahi Shimbun*, February 7, 2012.

41. Quoted in Sabrina Salas Matanane, "Congress Reviewing DoD Plans," *Kuam News*, February 15, 2012.

42. US Department of State, "United States-Japan Joint Statement on Defense Posture" (February 8, 2012), http://www.state.gov/r/pa/prs/ps/2012/02/183542.htm.

43. "Go-ichu, kaiheitai chukaku ka, Bei kaigun toppu shisa," *Okinawa Taimusu*, February 7, 2012.

44. Martin Fackler, "US and Japan Are in Talks to Expedite Exit of 8,000 Marines on Okinawa," *New York Times*, February 8, 2012.

45. "Seifu, Bei kaiheitai Iwakuni iten an o kyohi gaisho boeisho ga meigen," *Chugoku Shimbun*, February 14, 2012.

46. chinin usii, "Shimen hihyo—shinpo o yonde," *Ryukyu Shimpo*, March 10, 2012.

47. A staggering 21.2 billion yen (well over $200 million) was spent on construction works within Camp Schwab between the 2006 realignment agreement and early 2012. "Isetsu koji 'sakidori' bodai na mudazukai wa yameyo," editorial, *Ryukyu Shimpo*, March 12, 2012.

48. "'Beigun saihen minaoshi' shimagurumi no ishi hyoji o," *Okinawa Taimusu*, February 9, 2012.

# 6

*⌒*

# The Hatoyama Revolt

Although the United States experienced regime change from Bush to Obama nine months earlier than did Japan from Aso to Hatoyama, minimal change occurred in its Japan policy or the team responsible for it. With the exception of the new US ambassador, John V. Roos, Obama retained the same figures who had played formative roles in the negotiation of the key agreements since 2005: Kurt Campbell, who had been responsible for the Futenma negotiations under Bush, became Obama's deputy secretary of state for East Asia; Wallace Gregson, marine commander in Okinawa under Bush, became head of the Department of Defense's Asia-Pacific section; and Kevin Maher, consul general in Okinawa under Bush became director of the State Department's Office of Japan affairs.[1] Neither Nye nor Armitage held official posts under Obama, but their influence was scarcely dented.

Concern in Washington over the policy of the DPJ was strong long before it took office in September 2009. When party leader Ozawa began to adumbrate a shift in Japanese foreign and defense policy from a Washington center to a UN (and East Asia) center, ending deployment of the Maritime Self-Defense Forces to the Indian Ocean in service to the US-led war effort in Iraq, prominent US scholar-bureaucrats issued thinly veiled threats about the "damage" that Ozawa was causing to the alliance, and Ambassador J. Thomas Schieffer, who until then had refused to meet him, demanded a meeting.[2] The anxiety rose as Ozawa made clear his dissent from the new president's resolve to expand and intensify the Afghanistan war and went on to raise the possibility of reducing the US presence in Japan to the (Yokosuka-based) US Seventh Fleet, implying that all the

other bases, with their 36,000 officers and military personnel, were unnecessary. Immediately after stating these controversial views, Ozawa was
caught up in a corruption scandal involving staff misuse of funds. In May
2009 he resigned as party chief and was replaced by Hatoyama Yukio. In
January 2011 an indictment was issued against him for fraudulent election accounting, further isolating him and neutralizing any initiative he
might have taken.

During the prolonged one-party state system in Japan between 1955
and 2009, a thoroughly ramified client state system evolved in which priority to US interests was taken for granted, until August 30, 2009, when
Hatoyama Yukio and the DPJ came to power. That triumph signalled a
dramatic shift, and it marked the bankruptcy of the old regime and the
search for a new order.

## PROTECTING LIFE

Hatoyama had a vision for Japan. Like Obama a little earlier, he tapped a
national mood of desire for change, a Japan beyond client state existence
(*zokkoku*). Weeks before his election to power, Hatoyama published an
essay outlining his political thinking, explicitly critical of "unrestrained
market fundamentalism and financial capitalism," in which people
tended to be treated "not as an end but as a means." He remarked on
global trends "away from a unipolar world led by the United States toward an era of multipolarity" of which an East Asian community would
be one sign, and defined his political philosophy as "*Yuai*," literally, "*Fra-
ternité*." He described it as something that was "not tender but rather . . . a
strong, combative concept that is a banner of revolution."[3] For a Japanese
prime minister to use the word "revolution" in such a positive way was
unprecedented.

The United States was deeply suspicious, especially of Hatoyama's
Asian community agenda. Moreover, never contemplating the possibility
of an "equal" relationship with any state, it found particularly absurd that
Japan of all places should propose one. Above all, Washington resolved
to block Hatoyama on the Futenma issue. Because Hatoyama challenged
the deeply embedded structures of the client state system, projecting a
democratic and nationalist vision, Washington saw him as a threat to be
neutralized or crushed.

But it was in particular Hatoyama's immediate and specific agenda of
attempting to renegotiate the agreements adopted by previous, conservative governments to build the new base at Henoko where he crossed a
line. The idea that Futenma should be moved "*saitei demo kengai*" (at the
very least somewhere outside Okinawa, if not outside the country), used

commonly in the campaign including by Hatoyama himself, was seen
as outrageously provocative. The US Departments of State and Defense
delivered ultimatum after ultimatum, telling him that they would not
reopen negotiations and that it would be a "blow to trust" between the
two countries if the existing agreement (on Henoko) could not be implemented.

In January 2010, Hatoyama chose the occasion of his speech opening
the Diet to deliver another elaboration of his core thinking, this time pre-
senting the idea of "protecting life" as his basic philosophical and political
principle.[4] He began with the words:

> I want to protect people's lives.
>   That is my wish: to protect people's lives.
>   I want to protect the lives of those who are born; of those who grow up
> and mature.

Such pronouncements disturbed Washington. Hatoyama was dismissed as a "weirdo." What leader of government ever spoke of an equal
relationship with the United States, something never contemplated and
almost unimaginable; or of "protecting life"? The closeness and reliability
of an ally is commonly a measure of its servility, and Washington reserves
its warmest welcome for those who follow the (Tony) Blair path, even if it
means they become known in their own countries as "poodles."

Hatoyama must have known his words would have special resonance
in Okinawa, either because of the "Association for Protecting Life" that
has long played a central role in the movement for the protection of
Henoko from base development or for the words attributed to the nine-
teenth-century Okinawan king, "*Nuchi du takara*" (life is precious) that are
understood to encapsulate essential Okinawan values. No prime minister
had ever used this occasion to speak so long (fifty-one minutes) or to utter quite such high-minded, philosophical-religious sentiments before (no
less than twenty-four references to "life").

The Obama administration appeared to fear that Hatoyama's picking
at the last crucial knot in the elaborate package of the unequal relationship—the Guam International Agreement—threatened to expose the
inequity and the iniquity of all that had gone before it, including the de-
ceptions and lies that had become intrinsic to the alliance, and that such
exposure might threaten its moral and political credibility. It directed
a barrage of intimidation across the Pacific against Hatoyama and the
Democratic Party, insisting that Japan "honor" the Guam International
Agreement. The Futenma-Henoko issue became the centerpiece in a major confrontation between the two governments. Dismissing Hatoyama's
vision and ignoring his policies and projects, President Obama simply
refused even to meet him.

Earlier, Kurt Campbell told the *Asahi* there could be no change in the Futenma replacement agreement.[5] Michael Green warned that "it would indeed provoke a crisis with the US" if the Democratic Party were to push ahead to try to renegotiate the military agreements around the Okinawa issue.[6] Wallace Gregson, for the Pentagon, added that the United States had no plans to revise the existing agreements.[7] The view at the State Department was reported to be that "the hardest thing right now is not China. It's Japan."[8] Ian Kelly (State Department) stated that there was no intention on its part to allow revision,[9] and Kevin Maher added a day later that there could be no reopening of negotiations on something already agreed between states.[10] A "senior Department of Defense spokesperson" in Washington said it would be a "blow to trust" between the two countries if existing plans could not be implemented.[11]

In October (2009), Defense Secretary Robert Gates and chairman of the Joint Chiefs of Staff Michael Mullen visited Tokyo. Gates minced no words:

> The Futenma relocation facility is the linchpin of the realignment road map. Without the Futenma realignment, the Futenma facility, there will be no relocation to Guam. And without relocation to Guam, there will be no consolidation of forces and the return of land in Okinawa.[12]

He is also reported to have insulted his Japanese hosts, refusing to attend a welcoming ceremony at the Defense Ministry or to dine with senior Japanese defense officials.[13]

In case there remained any shadow of doubt in Japanese minds, Admiral Mullen added that the Henoko base construction was an "absolute requirement."[14]

## "SLAPPING AROUND" THE UNITED STATES

The Washington chorus rose to a crescendo in late 2009. For Michael Green, former special assistant to the president for national security affairs and senior director for Asian affairs at the National Security Council during the George W. Bush administration, Gates had shown that he was a "shrewd judge of his counterparts," and that Hatoyama and his government would not be able to "continue slapping around the United States" or to "play with firecrackers."[15] Menacingly, Green told the *Asahi* that the DPJ would "regret" it if it changed established policy and withdrew Japan's naval forces from the Indian Ocean.[16] He referred to the Obama administration view that the "DPJ-led coalition will eventually moderate its demands, drop campaign rhetoric which clashes with reality, and seek to demonstrate competent management of the US-Japan alliance."[17] One week before the scheduled Obama-Hatoyama meeting in Tokyo in

November, Ian Kelly (State Department) added ominously that "it's for the Government of Japan to decide what kind of relationship that they're going to have with us."[18]

In a similar vein, Richard Armitage remarked scathingly that the Democratic Party of Japan was "speaking a different language" and that he and his colleagues were "shocked by its platform." He regretted the American failure to "spread our network enough," with the result that the "alliance [was] totally adrift." He reserved special venom for Democratic Party Secretary General Ozawa Ichiro, who had not visited Washington for ten years and was known to be a proponent of closer ties with China.[19]

By December 2009, with the United States keeping up a constant refrain that a decision had to be made before the end of the year and with national (as distinct from the Okinawan) media and almost all political figures echoing it, the government seemed on the brink of yielding. Defense Secretary Kitazawa Toshimi and Foreign Minister Okada Katsuya both sounded increasingly like their LDP predecessors reading bureaucratically prepared briefs. Okada had earlier made statements such as, "If Japan just follows what the US says, then I think as a sovereign nation that is very pathetic,"[20] and "I don't think we will act simply by accepting what the U.S. tells us."[21] By October 2009 he had switched to saying that there seemed no alternative but to relocate Futenma within Okinawa.

In January 2010, when Foreign Minister Okada and US Secretary of State Hillary Clinton met in Honolulu,[22] setting aside the ceremonial and celebratory words from the report of their meeting, what remained was the peremptory US message:

> We look to our Japanese allies and friends to follow through on their commitments, including on Futenma.
>
> I have stressed again today, as I have in previous meetings, that it is important to move on Futenma.
>
> We remain of the opinion that the realignment roadmap is the way forward. It is an agreement that was reached between prior governments of each of our countries.

The barrage of Washington interventions (and its abusive and intimidatory tone) prior to and after the advent of the Hatoyama administration would be inconceivable in US relations with any other country, friend or foe, let alone its supposed closest of allies.

But that was not all. The documents released courtesy of WikiLeaks in May 2011 reveal the extent to which Hatoyama was betrayed by his own government. If ever there was a *trahison des clercs*, this was it. From the earliest days of the Hatoyama government, his senior officials had clandestine, one can fairly say conspiratorial, links with US officials, advising the Obama administration to stand firm. They communicated that

Hatoyama was a prime minister "with personality shortcomings," who was "weak when speaking with strong individuals" and "usually voiced his opinion based on the last strong comments he had heard," whose government was "still in the process of organizing itself"[23] and was "inexperienced" and "stupid,"[24] and whose policy process was "chaotic."[25] Hatoyama's senior state officials, like their predecessors in the LDP for over half a century, were loyal to Washington rather than to him or to the Japanese electorate.

The constant refrain from these Tokyo officials was to reassure Washington that provided it stand firm and "refrain from demonstrating flexibility,"[26] they could turn the government around and see to it that the base agreement be implemented. The parliamentary vice minister at the Ministry of Defense spoke of his department's focus as being "finding a quick way to back away from the DPJ's campaign pledge to reopen the realignment pledge," that is, to subvert his government.[27] Okinawans could basically be ignored, because as DPJ Diet affairs chief Yamaoka Kenji put it, "In Okinawa it's all about opposing for its own sake. . . . If Okinawa's will is respected, nothing will ever happen."[28] For that matter, the Japanese people were not much better because, according to Yamaoka, they were "spoiled" and took US protection for granted.[29] Not only that but, as Fukahori Ryo (a former division deputy director at Ministry of Foreign Affairs) put it, "The vast majority of the Japanese public did not understand security issues."[30] And indeed, the prime minister too seemed to fit into this category of hopeless ignorance, such that Vice Foreign Minister Yabunaka Mitoji, over lunch with American ambassador Roos, helpfully suggested that "it would be beneficial for the US to go through the basic fundamentals of security issues with the Prime Minister," that is, explain to him the (political) facts of life.[31]

## SURRENDER

The pressure peaked in October with the overtly intimidatory visit to Tokyo by Defense Secretary Gates and Assistant Secretary of State Kurt Campbell's blunt warning to Hatoyama that "U.S. patience would wear thin if the DPJ government continued to make multiple suggestions to review and adjust extant alliance arrangements."[32]

As Hatoyama vacillated, Ambassador Roos (said to be a close personal friend of President Obama) expostulated to the Japanese defense and foreign ministers on December 4 that trust between Obama and Hatoyama might be grievously damaged if agreement (to construct the Henoko base) was not reached within the year.[33] Visiting Okinawa the following day, ostensibly to "listen to the views of the people," Okada startled his Nago

City audience by seeking the understanding of Okinawans for the "crisis of the alliance" and for the "dilemma" in the negotiations. When he even suggested Okinawans have sympathy for President Obama, "who might not be able to escape criticism for weakness in his dealings with Japan at a time of falling popularity" if the Guam Treaty deal was not implemented, the meeting erupted in catcalls and shouts of anger. The Okinawan daily *Ryukyu Shimpo* described his public identification with the position of the US government as "pathetic."[34]

It later emerged (see below) that while Hatoyama accepted the Henoko location, he hoped to save some face by pursuing a preference for an offshore, pile-resting structure rather than by reclamation and extension from the shore, but when the US (and Japanese) government stood firm in insisting on reclamation, as promised in the Guam Agreement, in due course he simply yielded.

Just over three months into his term of office, Hatoyama crumbled. On December 8, 2009, the government, through DPJ Diet Affairs Chief Yamaoka Kenji, assured the US embassy that although it would have to be patient, "a decision had already been made" and "the government would implement the deal," though "managing the Diet" made it difficult to do so immediately and it might take until the summer of 2010.[35] The following day, Maehara Seiji, who among other things was then state minister for Okinawa, delivered the same message to Ambassador Roos: The government of Japan would explore "alternative options" but "if no alternative options are accepted, then SDP and PNP coalition minority parties [Social Democratic Party and People's New Party] would agree to accept the Henoko option." In other words, if the US did not agree to any alternative (the likelihood of finding any being virtually zero), then the existing plan would go ahead.[36]

With these secret understandings in place, Hatoyama and his government maintained the public façade of searching for a relocation site outside Okinawa (in accordance with his and the party's electoral pledge) for six more months. What was enacted on the Tokyo political and media stage over those months was essentially an elaborate charade. The depth of the deception was not known publicly until a year and a half later.

Playing his part, Hatoyama announced December 15 that he would postpone the crucial decision until May 2010. Despite the secret assurances he had given it, Washington exploded in blustery outrage. Unnamed officials in Washington were quoted as saying of Hatoyama, "We don't trust him."[37] Pentagon press secretary Geoff Morell declared that the United States "did not accept" the Japanese decision.[38] Kurt Campbell, assistant secretary of state for East Asia and the Pacific, said the Japanese public would *have to understand* (italics added) the need to keep US forces in Okinawa.[39] And Joseph Nye referred to the DPJ as "inexperienced, divided and still in the thrall of campaign promises," by which he plainly meant that attempts to renegotiate the Guam Agreement would not be tolerated.[40]

Mainland media for the most part simply relayed the US message, turning a blind eye to the intimidation and blatant interference in Japan's affairs.[41] Only the Okinawan newspapers lambasted the Hatoyama government for its inability to counter the US "intimidatory diplomacy" (as *Ryukyu Shimpo* put it) and for its drift back toward "acceptance of the status quo of following the US." "If this is to be the new government," it concluded, "then the change of government has been a failure."[42]

The rest of the world showed minimal interest. In the United States, officials, pundits, and commentators alike supported the Guam treaty formula and showed neither sympathy nor understanding for Japanese democracy or Okinawan civil society. There was, however, one honorable exception: former Soviet president Mikhail Gorbachev. Gorbachev chided both governments over the continuing impasse, insisting that a 70 percent popular opposition to the base project was something that they should treat very seriously. "Change of government means change of policy, as both governments should recognize. The Hatoyama government talks of political leadership and [should] not allow itself to be manipulated by bureaucratic initiative and intelligence [organs]."[43]

One particular statement on the dispute deserves attention as possibly the single most overbearing and abusive in the history of the relationship. When making these remarks, Richard Lawless was not a serving official. But, as deputy undersecretary of defense for Asian and Pacific security affairs under George W. Bush (2002–2007), he had played a central role in negotiating the 2006 deal and in 2010, out of office, he could give free rein to sentiments that almost certainly were common in official Washington.[44] For Lawless, Japan under Hatoyama and the Democratic Party had been allowed

> to spiral downward into a swamp that is a mixture of mindless revenge directed at the former LDP administration, mixed with internal Minshuto (DPJ) political maneuvering, a wandering dynamic between Minshuto and various Okinawa political groups, all overlaid by ruling coalition calculations keyed to the July Upper House election. If Japan has decided, on its own, that the alliance does not need these capabilities, Japan needs to tell us this new reality and explain what it expects us to do.

Hatoyama and his government were "digging a hole that only gets deeper with time and indecision," forcing the United States to make a decision as to whether to leave Okinawa, and Japan.

The idea that you could move just Futenma somewhere else and plunk it down, like a poker chip in the middle of Kyushu, is an irrational or half-baked idea. All that new government had to do was understand what compromises had been reached, the underlying logic of those arrangements, accept the value of the alliance and the requirements needed to sustain the credibility of the alliance, and then get on with the execution of that agreement.

. . . the Hatoyama government and its political overlords, do not have any sense of the magnitude of the issue with which they are playing. In the greater scheme of things (for) the security of Japan, it almost seems we have a group of boys and girls playing with a box of matches as they sit in a room of dynamite. Long after they have endangered themselves, the real damage will be done to the house of Japan. And the American firemen will not be around once the decision is made to burn down the house. . . . When you have dug yourself a great big hole, it is usually wise to stop digging, or somebody has to take away the shovel. . . . Once the momentum and goodwill move away from Japan, it will be very difficult for Japan to put this problem back in the box.

. . . Mr. Hatoyama as the leader in his party, must accept the consequences of what he and his party leadership has set in motion. . . . There are consequences here far beyond Japan and the self-marginalization that Japan as a nation, and as a security partner, appears to have embarked upon.

Castigation by a prominent and closely policy-connected US figure of any other country by use of terms such as "mindless," "irrational," "half-baked," "boys and girls playing with . . . matches," who have "dug themselves into a great big hole" and caused "self marginalization" would be unimaginable. Yet in regard to Japan, a special license seemed to apply. The condescension of General Douglas MacArthur sixty years earlier grandly and contemptuously referring to Japanese people as "twelve-year-olds" still lived on in Washington. It was as if Japan were "our" creation, and anything other than obedience was outrageous. Lawless's outburst elicited no Japanese anger or protest. Weeks later he referred to Japan's investigation into the "secret agreements" ordered by Foreign Minster Okada as "a preoccupation with the past . . . a fool's journey and a distraction that the alliance cannot afford."[45]

In short, what the US government had to say to the Japanese government as the fiftieth anniversary celebrations of the "alliance" got under way in late 2009 and early 2010 was to order Hatoyama, over and over again, to fulfill a highly controversial, unequal treaty pledge signed and railroaded through the Diet by his predecessor (Aso) in a way reminiscent of Kishi pushing the original Anpo treaty through the Diet in 1960. No other major ally had ever been subjected to the sort of abuse and intimidation that characterized the Hatoyama era. Obama, having risen to power in his own country promising "change," forbade it in Japan.

## CHARADE

From December 2009, when the secret decision by Hatoyama to accept the Henoko location (while saving face by pursuing an offshore structure) was communicated to Washington, Tokyo's bureaucrats orchestrated an elaborate story about the search for an alternative to Henoko, designed to convey the impression of serious intent while concealing the decision already made. Numerous sites were considered: Kadena (merging some marine functions from Futenma with those of the USAF base there); other Okinawan islands such as Shimojishima (where there was a civil airport with a three-thousand-meter runway currently used for pilot training) or Iejima (a smaller airfield used by marines); islands relatively near but outside Okinawan prefectural boundaries, such as Tokunoshima (Tokuno Island, with a little-used two-thousand-meter-runway airport) or Mageshima (Mage Island), both in Kagoshima prefecture;[46] Saga prefecture's Ariake Saga (with its existing two-thousand-meter runway); and various unused or underused airports in mainland Japan itself, from Tokyo's Yokota US base (with its four-thousand-meter runway) to Osaka's Kansai International (suggested by the Osaka governor) or the recently built "white elephant" Shizuoka or Ibaraki airports. Another site, in a somewhat different category because of being foreign territory, was Guam or other US Pacific territories. Assistant Secretary of State Kurt Campbell played his part in the charade by protesting, not unreasonably, "Almost every day someone comes up with a statement or a proposal."[47]

Gradually, Hatoyama's government narrowed the selection process to several main options:[48]

a. Schwab: building either a 500-meter-square helipad at U.S. Marine Corps Camp Schwab (on Cape Henoko) or a 1,500-meter runway, also within the camp but farther inland, needing more time and involving more substantial earthworks.
b. "White Beach": building an 1,800-meter runway in a 200-hectare reclaimed area offshore from a US Navy facility at White Beach, in the shallow seas off the coast of Katsuren Peninsula, in the vicinity of Tsuken Island, or, in a longer-term variant, reclaiming a larger (1,021 hectares) ocean area between Ukibaru and Miyagi Islands and building an artificial island that would be shared by the US Marine Corps, US military port facility (relocating from Naha Port) and Japan's Air Self-Defense Forces (relocating from Naha Airport).

Either of these options would be accompanied by relocation of some of the training drills currently conducted at Futenma to the islands of Tokunoshima or Mageshima, both administratively in Kagoshima prefecture though the former being historically part of the premodern Ryukyu king-dom and culture zone (and south of the 30-degrees line by which the US Navy divided Japan in 1945), or to the Self-Defense Force's Omura Air Base in Nagasaki prefecture or the Nyutabaru Air Base in Miyazaki prefecture.

Washington, even while knowing the emptiness of the charade, must have noted with quiet satisfaction the range of alternatives for base ex-pansion Japan had presented—including not only the militarization of Cape Henoko and Oura Bay by either offshore or onshore construction but also the idea of constructing a massive artificial island off White Beach, a reclamation project six times greater in scale than was being contemplated for Henoko, and of transferring some base functions, that is, extending the Okinawan base complex to neighboring prefectures, especially Kagoshima. Pentagon planners would not unreasonably have anticipated that Hatoyama, in his desperate anxiety to please, might even deliver several of these.

Washington, however, stuck to its core insistence that the Guam agree-ment design had to be implemented; however attractive in themselves, as alternatives they would not work. Most had been considered and ruled out in the years leading to the 2006 and subsequent agreement. Furthermore, adoption of either of the major alternatives—Schwab (inland Henoko) and White Beach/Katsuren—would require a fresh environmental impact as-sessment, something both governments were determined to avoid because it would take years and, if done properly, would be open to possible nega-tive outcome or, in the event of a positive outcome, would be followed by up to ten years for construction. The US government therefore simply con-tinued to insist that Tokyo maintain ("honor") the Guam accord.[49]

On the Okinawan side, the response as the details of the various schemes were revealed was one of anger and incredulity. The governor declared that either plan (Schwab or White Beach/Katsuren) would be "extremely difficult" (read: impossible),[50] and the latter site's artificial island would take "twenty years" to build.[51] The *Ryukyu Shimpo* said that it "would be hard to imagine anything worse" than this plan, with its combination of two "worst" choices.[52] The Katsuren/White Beach site was supposed to present no major environmental problem because the coral was either dead or dying, but when divers from the two Okinawan newspapers investigated the site, they found thriving colonies, a veritable "sea of fertility" as the *Ryukyu Shimpo* put it.[53] Both Uruma City (which includes White Beach) and the Kagoshima prefecture towns and villages that had been mentioned all insisted they would not tolerate any such project. As Naha City's conservative LDP-backed mayor Onaga put it, by reviving plans considered and rejected thirteen or fourteen years earlier, the government "showed lack of concern for the Okinawan people and a lack of any philosophy toward the base problem."[54]

In April, Tokunoshima Island was the scene of the largest assembly of people in its history. Three in five of the island's inhabitants (population 26,000) gathered to send Tokyo a message of defiance and resistance to any base transfer plan.[55] Hatoyama appears to have simply dropped the idea of moving the Futenma base to this island when faced with such opposition. Okinawans could not help feeling outrage that he was not similarly moved by the equally plain evidence of opposition in Okinawa.

Playing its role in the charade, the Pentagon let it be known that there was nothing to negotiate with Japan unless and until its government could show it had secured the consent of residents in the newly chosen sites.[56] Such newfound sensitivity was presumably intended as pressure on Hatoyama to try and strike a deal with the necessary Okinawan power brokers to impose the Henoko plan, assuming that as Tokyo had always been able to impose its will on recalcitrant local governments, it would in this case as well. It cannot have been intended literally since the one unambiguous element in the situation was the hostility of Okinawan residents to any Henoko design.

At the Nuclear Security Summit in Washington on April 12–13, 2010, Hatoyama tried to seize the opportunity of being seated near President Obama at dinner to tell the president that the May deadline would be met. He was, according to reports, rebuffed with the skeptical response: "Can you follow through?"[57] (This is commonly interpreted as a reference to Hatoyama's attempt to reassure Obama on their previous meeting when he said, "Trust me.") The *Washington Post* described Hatoyama as "the biggest loser [among world leaders] . . . , hapless, . . . increasingly loopy,"[58] and reported that Japan was so "taken aback by the toughness of Obama's tone that they did not draw up a written record of the words exchanged."[59] In effect, the US was saying, Japan's prime minister was mad.

Shortly afterward, on April 25, ninety thousand Okinawans gathered at Yomitan Village. The governor, all forty-one town and city mayors or their representatives, members of the Provincial Assembly, Okinawan representatives of all political parties from Communist to Liberal-Democratic, and Okinawan citizens presented a united front of opposition to any new base construction and a demand for the unconditional closure and return of Futenma (see figure 6.1). The Network for Okinawa (NO), a Washington-based citizens' group, organized a rally in front of the Japanese Embassy on the same day, and with a coalition of NGOs in Japan, raised funds to place a full-page notice in *Washington Post* (figure 6.2).

Hatoyama's last attempt to square the circle was an indication of readiness to "broadly accept" the 2006 and 2009 agreements for a Futenma replacement at Henoko, but in the form of a pier-like structure that would rest on thousands of piles (four thousand by some accounts) driven into

Figure 6.1.   All-Okinawa rally, April 25, 2010. *Source: Ryukyu Shimpo.*

the seabed instead of actual reclamation of Oura Bay. This idea was both
new and old. It differed from the land-based Schwab option that had been
favored only weeks earlier, but it was essentially a regurgitation of a plan
considered but rejected in 2000–2002 because of the technical difficulties
it involved.[60] Though the damage a pile-resting structure would cause to
coral and sea life might be less than that caused by reclamation, it seemed
absurd to pretend that the imposition of such a vast structure onto the bay
and the concentration there of intense military activity would not have
serious environmental consequences. The sunlight would be blocked
from the coral, the cost higher, and the risk higher (an extensive breakwater would have to be built because of the rough seas in the vicinity),
and even the benefit of the construction contracts would seem likely to be
appropriated largely by mainland specialist marine construction companies (*maricon*), leaving slim pickings for local Okinawan firms. This plan
also retained a much-reduced "outside Okinawa" element in the form of
transferring some helicopter training units, about a thousand marines, to
Tokunoshima Island.

In any case, whatever the outcome, it was understood that Japan was
to meet all costs of construction and maintenance. The Pentagon could be
expected to return to the range of facilities offered by Tokyo during these
frenzied months at some future date, when further "strengthening" and
"deepening" of the alliance was required.

Figure 6.2. Public notice placed in *Washington Post*, April 28, 2010, by Japan-U.S. Citizens for Okinawa Network (JUCON) and the Network for Okinawa (NO). Designed by Bill Melton Jr.

**Figure 6.3.** Prime Minister Hatoyama Yukio (middle) looking at Futenma Air Station with Ginowan City's mayor Iha Yoichi (right), May 2010. *Source: Ryukyu Shimpo.*

## JAPAN'S "SECOND DEFEAT"

As his self-imposed May 2010 deadline approached, Hatoyama was in the unenviable situation of facing the US ultimatum and the Obama cold shoulder on one side and Okinawan obduracy on the other, all while heading a government that was in virtually open rebellion against him and under unremitting attack from the Japanese press for poisoning the alliance. Bureaucrats of the Departments of Foreign Affairs and Defense launched a "rollback" operation to force his submission,[61] refusing cooperation and conspiring instead to bring him down. Hemmed in by his faithless—if not traitorous—bureaucrats and lacking the courage or clarity of purpose to confront them or to resist the pressures coming from Washington, Hatoyama's political position crumbled. Support for his government fell in just under nine months from around 73 percent at its inception to 19 (or in the last days of his government, 17) percent. The national media blamed him for the deterioration in the country's key relationship, insisting that he cease offending and irritating the United States.[62]

In the last wretched weeks of his government, Hatoyama shifted his public stance to conform with his private one of surrender by making clear that he would meet the US demands, even if it meant alienating Okinawans (who would be offered "compensation").[63] He still attempted to distance himself from previous LDP governments by opposing the "V" design for bay reclamation, that is, the detail rather than the substance. Reclamation, however, was the formula adopted in 2006 and the only one acceptable to the United States.

Hatoyama hinted at the complicated emotions he must have felt as, even after giving his secret consent to Washington, he told a meeting in Gunma, plaintively: "When I stood by the waters of Henoko, I felt very strongly that creating a landfill over those waters would defile nature. The current agreement should not be accepted."[64] Yet he had actually accepted it, even if only for the time being, and by tortuous logic persuaded himself that while a landfill would "defile" nature, a pile-resting structure would not.

While the public was distracted by reports of the "search," Hatoyama declared that at last he had come to understand the importance of the marine presence in Okinawa for "deterrence" purposes. Because of that, it would be inappropriate to relocate them far from Okinawa, and because of that he had decided to accept the Henoko relocation "V" plan.[65] On May 28, 2010, he signed a deal to that effect, and in less than a week, he resigned.

In this last scene of his government's theater of the absurd, as in so many of the strange flourishes that marked the six months of "search" for an alternative base site, Hatoyama was doing no more than reading from the script prepared for him by his bureaucrats, designed to divert attention from the fact that he had already decided in December to yield to Washington's pressure. That became clear half a year later when he confessed that he had simply made up the clinching argument of deterrence. Deterrence, he confessed, was just a pretext, *hoben*, something he himself did not believe but had been persuaded by his advisers to use as an argument to justify betrayal of his own election pledges.Officials in the Departments of Foreign Affairs and Defense had "scornfully dismissed" (he said) his ideas until, eventually, he reached the point where "anything else was futile, I could go no further and I came to doubt my own strength." He spoke of the "overwhelming atmosphere" in his own government that it "would be difficult to relocate Futenma outside of the prefecture." In retrospect he wished he had gone first to talk to Obama, although he remarked that "Mr. Obama himself was probably surrounded by voices that told him the only option was to hew to the status quo."[66]

Together with the revelations from the "secret agreements," Hatoyama's confession opened a rare window into the processes of Japanese government decision making on matters that concerned the relationship with the United States. There is a clear contradiction between Hatoyama's recollection (in his "confession") and the documentary evidence that his government made its key decision at latest by early December the preceding year. But, whatever the case, his government was deeply engaged in the politics of deception and the theater of the absurd. The bitter lesson he had learned was not one about deterrence but about the limits on the power of a prime minister and on the sovereignty of the government of Japan.

Here is not the place for detailed discussion of the fate of Hatoyama's other agendas, including that of an East Asian community. But one recent revelation sheds further light on just how exposed he was in his own cabinet. In February 2010, while Washington's abuse and intimidation rained down upon Hatoyama, his minister of land, infrastructure, and transport (later foreign minister and clear American favorite), Maehara Seiji, met with US Assistant Secretary of State Kurt Campbell to assure him that he (that is, unlike his prime minister) "voiced his support for the alliance at every opportunity, adding that the notion of a U.S.-Japan-China 'equilateral triangle,' a concept suggested by DPJ Diet Affairs Chief Kenji Yamaoka, was 'ridiculous.'"[67] That "ridiculous" concept was also dear to the heart of Hatoyama.

Despite the surface clangor between Washington and Tokyo, the two sides cooperated without qualms in duping the Japanese public, following secret agreement with secret agreement and aiding in the charade designed to distract and deceive the Japanese public during the first six months of 2010. To the *Ryukyu Shimpo* the WikiLeaks revelations showed that "although Japan was supposedly a democratic country, its officials, bowing and scraping before a foreign country and making no effort to carry out the will of the people, lacked any qualification for diplomatic negotiation" and that Japan was destined "to go down in history as in practice America's client state."[68]

The 2009 Hatoyama rhetoric of a close and "equal" relationship had worried Washington. But the flood of abuse, intimidation, and derision wore him down so that in a matter of months he and his ministers came to look like nothing so much as clones of their LDP predecessors. After nine inglorious and confused months, the "Hatoyama rebellion" ended on May 28, 2010, in humiliating surrender and reinstatement of the 2009 Guam International Agreement (or Treaty). In exactly the fecund waters by the shores of the Oura Bay, which weeks earlier he had declared it would "defile nature" to landfill, Hatoyama promised that he would landfill and build the Futenma Replacement Facility on which Washington insisted. Details of the "location, configuration and construction method would be completed . . . no later than the end of August" by a joint committee of specialists.

To satisfy Washington, Hatoyama thus betrayed his electoral pledge to relocate the facility "at least outside Okinawa." The only shred of face saving about his surrender was the pretense that at least in part some marine functions would be transferred outside of the prefecture (even though Tokunoshima Island was barely outside the prefectural boundary and was unquestionably a part of the Ryukyu culture zone).

Hatoyama also protested, plaintively, that his reclamation would be "environmentally sensitive." What was left of the Yambaru forest after construction of the Henoko base and the associated helipads scattered through it (see the discussion in chapter 8) could be declared a "Yambaru National Park," with possible UNESCO recognition as a World Heritage site and with offshore protection for the dugong.[69] The idea of special steps to protect the dugong was in itself strongly supported in Okinawa. But serious formulations rested on recognition of the incompatibility of that goal with militarization of key sections of its forest and coast.

Hatoyama's capitulation has commonly been described as the outcome of his confused and irresolute leadership. It was that, but it was also much more. For Tokyo University political scientist Shinohara Hajime, it was even a pivotal event in modern Japanese history, a surrender of sovereignty of such moment as to warrant being described as "Japan's second defeat" (i.e., alongside the surrender of 1945).[70]

If the Hatoyama government thus abandoned a core policy objective after nine—or as now seems clear, actually just three—months, it did nevertheless have one unintended but profound consequence: it stirred the Okinawan people's widespread but often fragmented *opposition* into a prefecture-wide mass movement of *resistance*. During 2010, spanning the Hatoyama and Kan ministries, by every conceivable democratic means, Okinawans made their views known:

*January*: the election of a Nago City mayor who was determinedly antibase;

*February*: the adoption of a unanimous resolution opposing construction of any new base in the prefecture by the regional parliament, the Prefectural Assembly;

*April*: "All-Okinawa" mass meeting to oppose base construction;

*July*: a second unanimous Prefectural Assembly resolution, this time also declaring the US-Japan Agreement of May 28 (Hatoyama's "surrender") a "violent, democracy-trampling act" that "treated Okinawans as stupid";

*September*: election of a majority of antibase candidates to the Nago City Assembly;

*November*: the election of a Governor who said he would demand the base be relocated elsewhere than in Okinawa.

Despite the clarity of the message, and the democratic and non-violent ways in which it was articulated at the polls and in direct action, neither Tokyo nor Washington was moved. The US, having announced the high-minded principle of requiring all base development to be dependent on local consent, insisted in practice on the implementation of a deal for which there plainly was no such consent.

The May 2010 US-Japan inter-governmental agreement (Hatoyama's "surrender" document) replaced the February 2009 Agreement (formally adopted by the Diet of Japan as a treaty in May), which in turn reiterated the terms of the 2006 "United States-Japan Roadmap for Realignment Implementation," which in turn incorporated a pledge between the two governments that goes back to 1996: Futenma to be returned to Japan "within five to seven years" when an appropriate replacement facility was ready. Sixteen years on, there are fewer signs than ever of this "world's most dangerous base" being returned or liquidated any time soon, or of a new base being constructed at Henoko.

In 2005, Prime Minister Koizumi had given up the attempt to survey and construct a base on the coral of Oura Bay because of what he called "a lot of opposition." Two years later, Abe Shinzo made tentative steps toward involving the Self Defense Forces in compelling base construction, but soon reverted to traditional "persuasion." Governments since then have continued to threaten and cajole, but have thus far held back from using the full force of state power to impose their will. The question governments in both Japan and the US face since the Hatoyama surrender of May 2010 is this: could they really cope, and could the much vaunted US-Japan "alliance" cope, with the political consequences that could be expected if they resorted to force to compel base construction?

## NOTES

1. Maeda Tetsuo, *"Juzoku,"* 15–18.
2. Kurt Campbell and Michael Green, "Ozawa's Bravado May Damage Japan for Years," *Asahi Shimbun*, August 29, 2007.
3. Hatoyama Yukio, "My Political Philosophy," *Voice*, September 2009 (August 13, 2009), and in English in *Financial Times*, available at http://www.ft.com/cms/s/0/99704548-8800-11de-82e4-00144feabdc0.html.
4. Yukio Hatoyama, "Policy Speech by Prime Minister Yukio Hatoyama at the 174th Session of the Diet" (January 29, 2010).
5. Yoichi Kato, "U.S. Warm to Proposal to Reaffirm Security Pact," *Asahi Shimbun*, July 23, 2009.
6. Quoted in Mure Dickie and Daniel Dombey, "Prospect of Power Softens DPJ's Stance," *Financial Times*, July 21, 2009. (Green, formerly George W. Bush's top adviser on East Asia, was at this time at the Center for Strategic and International Studies.)

7. "Futenma hikojo no isetsu, goi minaosazu Bei kokan minshu koyaku meguri hatsugen," *Asahi Shimbum*, September 3, 2009.

8. John Pomfret and Blaine Harden, "US Pressures Japan on Military Package," *Washington Post*, October 22, 2009.

9. Hiroshi Ito, "U.S. on Futenma Revisit: Forget It," *Asahi Shimbun*, September 2, 2009.

10. "'Kokka-kan no goi' kyocho/Zainichi Beigun saihen/Mea Bei bucho minaoshi kensei," *Okinawa Times*, September 4, 2009.

11. "Futenma isetsu dekineba Nichibei kankei ni dageki, Bei kokan ga keikoku," *Asahi Shimbun*, October 18, 2009.

12. Department of Defense, "Joint Press Conference with Japanese Defense Minister Toshimi Kitazawa and Secretary of Defense Robert Gates" (October 21, 2009).

13. John Pomfret and Blaine Harden, "U.S. Pressures Japan on Military Package," *Washington Post*, October 22, 2009.

14. "Joint Chiefs Chairman: Futenma Must Move to Nago," *Yomiuri Shimbun*, October 24, 2009.

15. Michael Green, "Tokyo Smackdown," *Foreign Policy*, October 23, 2009, http://shadow.foreignpolicy.com/posts/2009/10/23/tokyo_smackdown.

16. *Asahi Shimbun*, August 28, 2009, quoted in Miyazato Seigen, "Okinawa kenmin no ishi wa meikaku de aru," *Sekai* (November 2009).

17. Michael Green, "Japan's Confused Revolution," *Washington Quarterly* 33, no. 1 (2009): 12.

18. US Department of State, Ian Kelly, daily press briefing, November 3, 2009, Washington, DC.

19. Richard Armitage in the 16th Japan-US Security Seminar, Pacific Forum CSIS, January 15, 2010, Washington, DC

20. *Guardian*, August 10, 2009.

21. "Japan urges U.S. to Respect 'Democracy' over Base," AFP, October 22, 2009.

22. Hillary Rodham Clinton, "Remarks with Japanese Foreign Minister Katsuya Okada after Their Meeting" (January 12, 2010), http://www.state.gov/secretary/rm/2010/01/135088.htm.

23. Various senior Japanese officials, quoted in Roos, Cable 09TOKYO2377, "A/S Campbell, GOJ Officials Discuss PM Hatoyama's," October 15, 2009, *Wikileaks*. http://wikileaks.ch/cable/2009/10/09TOKYO2377.html.

24. Saiki Akitaka, director general of the Asian and Oceania Affairs Bureau in the Ministry of Foreign Affairs, speaking to Kurt Campbell, assistant secretary of state for East Asian and Pacific Affairs, on September 18, 2009, in Roos, Cable 09TOKYO2197, September 21, 2009, *WikiLeaks*. "Gaimu kanryo 'Nichibei no taito motomeru Minshu seiken wa oroka," *Asahi Shimbun*, May 7, 2011. http://www.asahi.com/special/wikileaks/TKY201105060396.html.

25. Izawa Osamu, foreign policy assistant to Chief Cabinet Secretary Hirano, quoted in Greene, Cable 09NAHA67, "DPJ Senses USG Flexibility on FRF Renegotiation," October 5, 2009, *WikiLeaks*. http://wikileaks.org/cable/2009/10/09NAHA67.html.

26. Takamizawa Nobushige, director general of Defense Policy at Ministry of Defense, over lunch with US officials, October 12, 2009, quoted in Roos, Cable 09TOKYO2378, "A/S Campbell, GOJ Officials Discuss the History of," October 15, 2009, *WikiLeaks*. http://wikileaks.ch/cable/2009/10/09TOKYO2378.html. Greene, Cable 09NAHA67, ibid.

27. Greene, Cable 09NAHA67, ibid.

28. Yamaoka Kenji, quoted in Roos, Cable 09TOKYO2815, December 9, 2009, *WikiLeaks*. http://wikileaks.org/cable/2009/12/09TOKYO2815.html.

29. Ibid.

30. Roos, Cable 09TOKYO2875, "MOFA 'Alliance Hands' Express Frustration at DPJ," December 16, 2009, *WikiLeaks*. http://wikileaks.org/cable/2009/12/09TOKYO2875.html.

31. Roos, Cable 09TOKYO2946, "Ambassador's December 21 Lunch Meeting with Vice," December 30, 2009, *WikiLeaks*. http://wikileaks.org/cable/2009/12/09TOKYO2946.html.

32. On Gates's visit, see Gavan McCormack, "Ampo's Troubled 50th: Hatoyama's Abortive Rebellion, Okinawa's Mounting Resistance and the US-Japan Relationship (Part 2)," Asia-Pacific Journal: Japan Focus (May 31, 2010), http://japanfocus.org/-Gavan-McCormack/3366, and on Campbell, Roos, Cable 09TOKYO2369, "Managing Alliance Issues: A/S Campbell's," October 15, 2009, *WikiLeaks*. http://wikileaks.ch/cable/2009/10/09TOKYO2369.html.

33. "Futenma nao meiso, Bei makikaeshi de kyuchi," *Ryukyu Shimpo*, December 6, 2009.

34. Quoted in "Gaisho no kenmin taiwa Kiki aoru dake de wa nasakenai," editorial, *Ryukyu Shimpo*, December 7, 2009. For a transcript of the meeting, see author Medoruma Shun's blog, "Uminari no shima kara," "Okada gaisho to 'shimin to no taiwa shukai', zenmen kokai," in seven parts, beginning at http://blog.goo.ne.jp/awamori777/e/1863c314ee19f70bd5c5c676e8409ad1.

35. Roos, Cable 09TOKYO2815, ibid.

36. Roos, Cable 09TOKYO2822, "Ambassador Roos's Meeting With Minister Maehara," December 10, 2009, *WikiLeaks*. http://wikileaks.org/cable/2009/12/09TOKYO2822.html.

37. Yoichi Kato, "Hatoyama Must Have Strategic Talks with U.S.," *Asahi Shimbun*, December 29, 2009.

38. "Pentagon Prods Japan on Futenma Deadline," *Japan Times*, January 8, 2010.

39. Ibid.

40. Joseph S. Nye Jr., "An Alliance Larger Than One Issue," *New York Times*, January 6, 2010. After Nye's issue of a public call for US restraint, cautioning of the consequences of a "pyrrhic victory" over Henoko, overt intimidation diminished, but the underlying message was unchanged: Henoko was the "best solution." "Futenma isetsu Bei seifu no shisei imashime Nai shi ga Bei shi kiko," *Ryukyu Shimpo*, January 9, 2009.

41. Even the "liberal" *Asahi* editorially scolded the Hatoyama government, saying, "There is a limit to Washington's patience. . . . It would be very unfortunate for both countries if the Futenma issue became blown out of proportion." "Relocating Futenma Base," *Asahi Shimbun*, October 23, 2009.

42. "Okada gaisho hatsugen—boso suru Hatoyama seiken no genkai, Ampo no Okinawa izon kara dakkyaku o," *Ryukyu Shimpo*, October 25, 2009.

43. "Gorubachofu shi honshi ni kaito, teigen, Futenma isetsu," *Ryukyu Shimpo*, December 21, 2009.

44. Yoichi Kato, "Former U.S. Official: Japan Could Lose Entire Marine Presence if Henoko Plan Scrapped," *Asahi Shimbun*, March 5, 2010, http://www.asahi.com/english/TKY201003040361.html.

45. "Updating the US-Japan Alliance—An Interview with Mike Finnegan, Richard Lawless and Jim Thomas," National Bureau of Asian Research, April 2, 2010, http://www.nbr.org/research/activity.aspx?id=77.

46. "Kagoshima no Mageshima fujo," *Ryukyu Shimpo*, December 5, 2009. On Mage Island, see also Gavan McCormack, "Mage—Japan's Island beyond the Reach of the Law," *Asia-Pacific Journal: Japan Focus* (February 20, 2012), http://www.japanfocus.org/-Gavan-McCormack/3694.

47. "US in the Dark on Final Futenma Decision," *Asahi Shimbun*, February 5, 2010.

48. Media reports, especially "Govt to offer 2 Futenma alternatives," *Yomiuri Shimbun*, March 18, 2010, and "Kennai keizai kankeisha/1020 hekutaru jinko to o teian/Katsuren oki an de Kitazawa shi to mendan," *Ryukyu Shimpo*, March 16, 2010.

49. "US Likely to Nix Futenma Alternatives," *Yomiuri Shimbun*, March 26, 2010.

50. "Chiji, seifu 2 an o konnan shi, Futenma isetsu," *Okinawa Taimusu*, April 3, 2010.

51. "Ken-nai 2 an wa 'mattaku dame,'" *Asahi Shimbun*, April 1, 2010.

52. Editorial, "Futenma seifu an-min-i azamuku wasuto no an da," *Ryukyu Shimpo*, March 27, 2010.

53. "Hojo no umi sango kagayaku—Futenma isetsu kohochi Katsuren oki hirogaru gunraku," *Ryukyu Shimpo*, April 2, 2010.

54. "'Koyaku ihan' ikari hakka Henoko kui-uchi an, seifu shuho o shimin hihan," *Okinawa Taimusu*, April 29, 2009.

55. "'Hantai!' Tokunoshima's Record-Breaking Addition to Ryukuans' Democratic Voices," *Peace Philosophy Centre*, April 19, 2010, http://peacephilosophy.blogspot.com/2010/04/tokunoshimas-record-breaking-addition.html.

56. "Hatoyama's Latest Futenma Tack: Move Choppers to Tokunoshima," *Japan Times*, April 10, 2010.

57. Satoshi Ogawa, "US Distrust of Japan Sharply Accelerating," *Yomiuri Shimbun*, April 19, 2010.

58. Al Kamen, "Among Leaders at Summit, Hu's First," *Washington Post*, April 14, 2010.

59. John Pomfret, "Japan Moves to Settle Dispute with US over Base Relocation," *Washington Post*, April 23, 2010.

60. "Tero kiken, kankyo-men mo kadai . . . isetsu-an QIP koho," *Yomiuri Shimbun*, April 29, 2009.

61. "Interview—Fukushima Mizuho zendaijin ga kataru Hatoyama Yukio Ozawa Ichiro Kan Naoto," *Shukan Kinyobi* (June 18, 2010).

62. Yamaguchi Masanori, "'Media ichigeki Hato o sagi ni saseta' ote media no 'Nichibei domei fukashin' hodo," *Shukan Kinyobi*, June 11, 2010.

63. Defense Vice-Minister Nagashima Akihisa, quoted in John Brinsley and Sachiko Sakamaki, "US base to Stay on Okinawa, Japanese Official Says," *Bloomberg*, March 2, 2010.

64. "Few Futenma Choices Left for Hatoyama," *Asahi Shimbun*, April 26, 2010.

65. "Hatoyama shusho, Okinawa kinrin o mosaku, seiji sekinin ni hatsu genkyu," *Ryukyu Shimpo*, April 22, 2010.

66. Satoko Norimatsu, "Hatoyama's Confession: The Myth of Deterrence and the Failure to Move a Marine Base Outside Okinawa," *Asia-Pacific Journal: Japan Focus* (February 13, 2011), http://www.japanfocus.org/-Norimatsu-Satoko/3495.

67. Roos, Cable 10TOKYO247, "Assistant Secretary Campbell's February 2 Meeting," February 8, 2010, *WikiLeaks*. http://wikileaks.org/cable/2010/02/10TOKYO247.html.

68. "Gaiko koden bakuro—seifu ni kosho no shikaku nashi—taisei isshin shi shikirinaoshi o," *Ryukyu Shimpo*, May 5, 2011.

69. "Hokubu ni kokuritsu koen nado Henoko isetsu de kankyo 3 saku," *Tokyo Shimbun*, evening, May 26, 2010.

70. Shinohara Hajime, "Toranjishon dai ni maku e," *Sekai* (November 2010): 91.

# 7

*⌒*

# Post–Cold War

## *Elections and Democracy*

From the very first Okinawan "democratic" election, for chief executive in 1968, both Washington and Tokyo saw the issues as too important to be entrusted to popular choice. Intervention, as conceived and recommended by Ambassador Reischauer, might be necessary to advance the higher cause of US policy. Elections therefore tended to be contested at two levels: between candidates of different parties and between those in Okinawa struggling to implement democratic principles and those outside it (and their collaborators) intent on denying or subverting them. As in most respects, however, after the reversion, the government of Japan took over from the CIA in picking up the tab. The secrecy that was always crafted around such intervention is such that details of the processes become known only in part or through indirect sources, often years or decades after the fact. A general pattern may, however, be seen, in which interventions become more blatant as the importance of securing at least the appearance of local consent to major reorganization of the base system rises.

Here is not the place for a full history of the Okinawan struggle for electoral democracy. We confine our attention to 2009–2010, when the issues at stake in elections became steadily more important, the tempo of intervention escalated, and (in our view) the balance shifted decisively in favor of the resistance and against the two national governments.

### OTA AND THE "ACTION PROGRAM," 1990–1998

From reversion in 1972, the role of governor, the locally elected senior official who presides over the prefecture's constitutionally guaranteed self-governing institutions, has been paramount. Gubernatorial elections have therefore been fiercely fought. Yara Chobyo, who had been the first elected chief executive in 1968, was re-elected as governor right after the reversion. After six years of progressive governorship (Yara Chobyo and then Taira Koichi), in 1978 Nishime Junji became the first conservative head of Okinawa. Then, after three terms, twelve years of big construction projects and tourism development (with its accompanying environmental destruction), and at the end of the Cold War in 1990, Okinawans opted for change once again. With the collapse of the Soviet Union and thus the sudden elimination of the threat against which the base system was assumed to have been organized, they anticipated a "peace dividend." Reflecting that mood of anticipation, in 1990 Ota Masahide, Battle of Okinawa survivor and its preeminent historian, won the office, promising realization of the "peace constitution" in people's lives and fair governance. His term of office was marked by the "Action Program for Return of the Bases," which in its principal expression in January 1996 called for return of some major bases, including Futenma, by 2001 and of all others, including Kadena, by 2015.[1] He took important steps to commemorate the war dead and to dedicate Okinawa to a future peace identity. Also important was his economic agenda: to have Okinawa made an international (sometimes translated "cosmopolitan") city, meaning a kind of free-market and deregulated Singapore or Hong Kong, enjoying the status of being within Japan but separate from it, as Hong Kong under China's "one state–two systems."

His five visits to the United States in pursuit of a direct Okinawan diplomacy to advance the cause of base return accomplished little.[2] But the September 1995 rape case roused the prefecture to such anger that Ota, too, shifted his stance. With the backdrop of the island-wide fury, and in response to the Nye Initiative earlier in the year that declared a commitment to maintain 100,000 troops in East Asia, Ota declared that "to build an Okinawa in which young people can hold hope, it will be necessary to get rid of the bases that block independent development."[3] In keeping with this sentiment, he adopted a more directly challenging approach. He understood that the question of land was crucial and chose to contest the legality of the process of appropriation of Okinawan land for the bases. Under the Special Measures Law for Land Used by the American Forces, the government of Japan in effect forcibly leased the land required for the US forces from its owners. When landowners refused, and their mayors refused to sign in their stead, it was up to the governor. Ota had affixed his signature in 1991, but in 1995, in protest over Nye's Initiative, and with Okinawans' overwhelming anger over the rape of a schoolgirl earlier in the year, he chose to refuse.[4] The national government (the prime minister) then sued him before the court seeking an order to compel him to sign.[5] The Naha branch of the Fukuoka High Court first ruled against Ota in March 1996, and the Supreme Court confirmed that ruling in August, showing remarkable promptness and equally remarkable contempt for Ota by dismissing his arguments in two curt sentences: "We reject and dismiss the appeal. The court expenses shall be paid by the appellant" (i.e., Ota).[6]

To the dismay of many of those in the Okinawan movement, Ota chose to submit.[7] The alternative would have been for the national government to draft and pass a special law stripping him of authority and possibly to arrest him for contempt, either course likely to provoke a political and constitutional crisis. Relations between Ota and the government in Tokyo, however, never fully recovered. Ota's own standing among the antibase movement suffered a blow, and the focus of Tokyo-Okinawa exchanges shifted in part to economic and "development" matters, where the national government naturally held the advantage and around which it was able to cultivate a spirit of dependence from which it expected would follow compliance in the base agenda.[8]

Just over a year later, a further land-related problem arose. The government of Japan was concerned that investigations into some cases of owners who were refusing their consent to the base leasing arrangements would not be complete before those leases expired and had to be renewed. Were the leases to expire, the US military's continued occupation would become technically illegal. To avoid that happening with the expiration date looming in May 1997, the Diet adopted a revision to the "Special Measures Law for Land Used by the American Forces," under which it simply cancelled the rights of owners to recover their land upon expiration of the leases. The constitutional provisions guaranteeing the "inviolable" right of land ownership (Article 29) and entrenching local self-government by the provision that a law applicable to one local public entity required the "consent of the majority of the voters of the local public entity" (Article 95) were brushed aside in a brisk and almost unanimous vote (90 percent yes in the Lower House and 80 percent yes in the Upper House).[9] The prevailing view in Okinawa was that such treatment would never be meted out to any other prefecture. They saw it as simply discriminatory.

Arasaki, who interprets Ota's submission to the Supreme Court as the occasion for a severe downturn in the Okinawan antibase movement, comments: "The passage of the revised Special Measures Law was a symbolic representation of the structure of Japanese politics crushing Okinawan opinion."[10]

As demand for liquidation of the bases confronted the two governments with a crisis, the focus of the contest between Tokyo and Okinawa shifted to the north. In April 1996, after a meeting between Ambassador

Walter Mondale and Prime Minister Hashimoto, it was announced that Futenma would be "completely returned" within five to seven years, news greeted by Governor Ota as a shining first step toward the twenty-first century.[11] Later, the astonishment and joy evaporated as it became clear that the return was to be conditional and that the condition would be what was initially described as a floating or anchored "sea-based facility" off the east coast of Okinawa, which in turn, it soon became clear, meant offshore from Henoko. Since Henoko is on the eastern section of Nago City, overlooking Oura Bay, the citizens of Nago City called for a referendum to canvas views on the proposal. Despite heavy Tokyo intervention—Japan's Defense Agency sending agents to buy votes by visiting each household, going door to door, delivering alcohol and money (as Ota Masahide recalls)—and the support of local construction-related businesses, a majority (52.85 percent in an 82.45 percent poll) chose to say no to the idea.[12] In a bizarre outcome, city mayor Higa flew to Tokyo to announce the outcome, *rejected* that outcome on behalf of the city (i.e., agreed to the base construction), and announced his resignation.

Months later, however, Ota again challenged the central government, saying (in February 1998) that as governor he was obliged to carry out the view of Okinawan people and he would not therefore allow the Henoko project to proceed against their wishes. This time Tokyo froze him from all official contact, rendering local administration virtually impossible, and the Obuchi government took steps, by pouring in three hundred million yen (roughly three million dollars) in campaign funds, a very substantial sum in Okinawan terms, to ensure his defeat in the November elections of that year. Illegal (and unconstitutional) intervention in that December 1998 election had long been suspected, but not until more than a decade later was it confirmed, in one of the series of Okinawan "shocks" that punctuated 2010.[13] Much of the money went to a slick campaign designed to divert attention from the base issue. Slogans such as "Give us jobs," "Do something about the recession," "Reverse the current," "Change the pitcher," and "Reality, not ideals" cultivated the sense that Ota was out of touch and his fractured relations with Tokyo unnecessarily hurting the prefecture.[14] As Suzuki Muneo, who in 1998 had been deputy chief cabinet secretary, put it in 2010, "We made the judgment we did [to fund the anti-Ota campaign] because we had to win that election."[15]

The Ota-disposing intervention was part of a pattern of secret, discretionary use of public funds in order to ensure the smoothly orchestrated functioning of the LDP machinery of state. The cabinet secretary's *kanbo kimitsuhi*, or "slush fund" (no receipts necessary), was (according to Suzuki) customarily used, *inter alia*, to provide well-known media "intellectuals" and commentators with cash-stuffed envelopes (five million yen for the "Obon" summer festival, a bonus of five to ten million yen monthly to LDP luminaries, and summer and winter presents of ten million each to former prime ministers). After brief media attention, the corrupt and illegal intervention that apparently (it is still denied by Inamine) ended Ota's political career—or for that matter, the various other corrupt expropriations—has yet to be pursued at either legislative or judicial levels or by the national (as distinct from the Okinawan) media.

The final, bizarre twist to this election was that Inamine, the conservative who defeated Ota, himself declared that he opposed the Henoko project, and just days before the vote the government announced that it was reconsidering the sea-based project and would be prepared to negotiate with Okinawa. As for Inamine's pledge to improve Okinawa's economy and reduce its unemployment rate, which played a large role in his success, no notable change occurred in his term.

However, with the Ota problem thus resolved and the "moderate" Inamine Keiichi installed as governor in December 1998, the national government turned its attention to Okinawa. The outbursts over the 1995 rape case had shocked conservative Tokyo circles, as even more so had the 1987 protest burning of the Hinomaru flag at the national athletics meet.[16] A not untypical view of Okinawa was expressed a little later (March 2000) by the then secretary general of the Liberal Democratic Party (soon to become prime minister) Mori Yoshiro, when he complained that Kimigayo, the national anthem, was not being taught at schools in Okinawa, and the Communist Party ruled the teachers' union and the newspapers in Okinawa.[17]

Tokyo therefore turned its attention to trying to reframe the political relationship with Okinawa, especially to "soften" and co-opt the Okinawan opposition. It had two prongs: financial and ideological.

In financial terms, the blessings bestowed by Tokyo on the Inamine administration were considerable: resumption of the Okinawa program (the joint consultative Tokyo-Okinawa body suspended in the last ten months of Ota's office); the special ten billion yen Okinawa Development Fund (twice what had been available to Ota); and a one hundred billion yen "Northern Districts Development Fund" to be concentrated on projects in the vicinity of the planned new base. The decisions to issue a new two thousand yen note featuring the Shureimon gate of Okinawa's Shuri castle in its design and to host the 2000 G7 "Kyushu-Okinawa Summit" in Nago were further elements of the effort to placate, entice, and co-opt Okinawan communities, "candy" to distract attention from the base problem, as Okinawan author Medoruma Shun put it.[18]

The campaign also had a strongly ideological dimension, first articulated in 1999 by the Okinawan historian Takara Kurayoshi in speaking to the Prime Minister's Commission on Japan's Goals in the 21st Century, and then further developed in the presence of Prime Minster Obuchi Keizo at the "Asia Pacific Agenda Project" on March 25–26, 2000. It was then labeled "Okinawa Initiative."[19] Takara and his colleagues argued that although Japan's wartime policies had been prejudicial toward Okinawans and the terms of the San Francisco Treaty of 1951 and the "reversion" agreements of 1969–1972 had been deeply unfair, the historic sentiments of the Okinawan people regarding the Battle of Okinawa and the subsequent military incorporation of the islands into the US Asian strategy amounted to a form of "victim consciousness" that impeded their positive engagement with the rest of Japan. It was time, they argued, to look to the future, and to understand and take pride in maintaining their island's contribution to the peace and security of East Asia.[20] Within those parameters, Okinawa could adopt a positive regional and world outlook and play a significant regional role mediating and linking the rest of Japan with the Asia-Pacific region. In similar vein, the Inamine prefectural administration moved to alter exhibits in the new Prefectural Peace Museum so as not to offend visitors with their "anti-Japanese stance."[21] Exhibits with "anti-Japanese" stance were those that showed Japanese soldiers menacing or killing Okinawan people. But since such incidents form a core part of the Okinawan memory and its sense of morality and identity, the authorities had to yield quickly.[22]

Both the financial inducements and the ideological barrage aroused fierce criticism. Other Okinawan intellectuals pointed to the Okinawa Initiative's implicit negation of the Okinawan experience, its assumption that a new Japan-Asia relationship could and should be predicated on indefinite Japanese hosting of US military bases and subordination to US geopolitical agendas, and that the twenty-first-century regional order, like that of the twentieth, would be built on the use of force. One scholar referred to it as an attempted "internal colonization . . . of Okinawa *kokoro*, its heart and spirit."[23]

Under these multiple pressures and inducements, and given the straitened economic circumstances of the islands at the time, with high unemployment and structural dependence on the bases, the inducements and the ideological campaign had some effect. Conservative candidates were elected one after the other to local office, and so blatant was the bribery that local governments around Okinawa began an unseemly rush to volunteer their localities as sites for the relocation of various US military facilities, something unimaginable earlier. Higashi Village, Okinawa City, and Katsuren Town (on Tsuken Island) vied with Henoko (Nago City) for the right to house the relocated Futenma Marine Air Station; Kin City sought the Sobe Communications Facility if or when its present site was returned to Yomitan Village; Ie Village volunteered to host parachute training exercises; and Urasoe's Chamber of Commerce and Industry urged that the military port facilities be moved there from Naha.[24]

In the febrile atmosphere of these contentious developments, a December 1999 newspaper poll showed opposition to a new base still running at high levels, 59 percent in Nago City and 45 percent in Okinawa as a whole.[25] Both the prefectural governor and the Nago City mayor agreed at this time to allow the base project to proceed, but only under the strictest of conditions, amounting, if they were taken seriously (see chapter 5), to impossible obstacles.

Shortly after these highly conditional consents were registered, in the face of unprecedented political, economic, and psychological pressure in April 2000, and on the eve of the summit, 27,000 people encircled the seventeen-kilometer perimeter of Kadena in a human chain to press their call for closure of the bases, and a coalition of Okinawan civic groups issued an "Okinawan People's Peace Declaration" to press their vision for an Okinawa initiative counter to that of Takara and his colleagues and the government in Tokyo. Though Tokyo was satisfied to see the "consent" of the governor and city, despite the qualifications, as a wedge that could be further manipulated as needed to accomplish its objectives, subsequent events were to show that that optimism was unwarranted.

## THE THREE ELECTIONS OF 2010

While disillusion with the benefits from Tokyo's base-promoting Okinawan "development" plans mounted through the decade, the mood in Okinawa changed decisively following the Hatoyama victory in the national elections of August 2009. Okinawan DPJ (and associated opposition party) candidates who explicitly opposed any Futenma replacement project swept the polls, recording a higher vote than ever before in the proportional section. Where opinion in Okinawa had once (1999) been almost evenly divided between those who opposed relocation within Okinawa and those prepared to accept it, ten years later antibase sentiment had hardened and opinion was running consistently at around 70 percent against the Guam formula (for Henoko construction).[26] In May 2009, one survey found a paltry 18 percent in favor of the Henoko option on which Washington and Tokyo were adamant, and by November that figure had fallen to 5 percent.[27] Both Okinawan newspapers and prominent figures in Okinawan civil society maintained a strong antibase stance.[28] The signals of anger and discontent rose to their peak with the adoption by the Okinawan parliament (the Prefectural Assembly, elected in 2008) in February 2010 of an extraordinary resolution, unanimously demanding that Futenma be moved "overseas or elsewhere in Japan."[29] In March 2010, all of Okinawa's forty-one local town mayors declared themselves of the same view, and in April the Association of City Mayors, made up of the mayors of the eleven Okinawan cities, unanimously adopted a resolution calling for the closure and return of Futenma and opposing any replacement.[30]

It meant that while Tokyo struggled desperately to find a way to implement the Guam Treaty, Okinawa moved toward unanimously rejecting it. There was no longer a progressive-conservative divide in Okinawan politics on this question. The mayor of Okinawa's capital, Naha, who in the past served as president of the Liberal Democratic Party of Okinawa, even made clear that as a prominent Okinawan conservative, he was disappointed by the Hatoyama government's reluctance to redeem its electoral pledge on Futenma and hoped the Okinawan people would remain united "like a rugby scrum" to accomplish its closure and return (i.e., not replacement).[31] No local government or Japanese prefecture had ever been at such odds with the national government. The elections of 2010 put the seal on this process.

## (a) January: Nago City Mayor

Months after the triumph of the Democratic Party in the August 2009 national elections, in which it promised *inter alia* to see that Futenma was replaced somewhere outside Okinawa, the citizens of Nago (population: 60,000; 45,000 eligible voters) went to the polls on January 24, 2010, to elect a new mayor. No small-town election in modern Japanese history has ever been subject to such widespread and intense interest, nationally and even internationally. This was undoubtedly a consequential mayoral election, with large implications for the alliance relationship, the military equation in East Asia, and even Japanese democracy.

This town, more than any other in modern Japan has resisted the will of the central government, blocking the best efforts of that government and its global superpower ally from 1996. It is true that following the Nago plebiscite of 1997, mayors inclined to do deals with Tokyo were elected in 1998, 2002, and 2006, but their amenability was always hedged by complex conditions. Base-compliant forces developed a formidable framework of equivocation, obfuscation, and conditionality, in a politics of deception similar to that of secret diplomacy and lies that served the alliance at the national level. LDP-supported mayors and city governments in Nago did what they could to divert attention from the base issue and to concentrate it instead on the jobs, fees, and other economic benefits that were supposed to flow from cooperation with Tokyo. The series of local government election victories during the decade initiated by Higa's betrayal gave LDP governments in Tokyo confidence that they could continue to pursue base construction while dividing and buying off the opposition. Insofar as the base was mentioned at election time, it was always in terms of qualified, conditional acceptance. Nobody would agree to a permanent, substantial US military facility, and so nobody could ever say, "What this city needs is a new US base." It was therefore initially called a "heliport," or a temporary offshore structure. The consent that Nago City and Okinawa prefecture gave in 1999 was hedged by such strict conditions as to have been tantamount to rejection. Chameleonlike, however, the project kept changing, with each change growing larger, more permanent, and more threatening.

With the victory of the Democratic Party in the Lower House elections of August 2009, the tide changed. When the government of Japan that had tried unsuccessfully by every means to weaken, split, buy off, and intimidate those opposed to the construction of the new base was itself thrown from office, the Nago opposition, though tired by apparently endless struggle in its resolutely nonviolent contest against the state, took heart.

Challenger Inamine Susumu, supported by the Democratic Party and its coalition partners together with labor and civic organizations, defeated incumbent Shimabukuro Yoshikazu, supported by the LDP (and its Komeito partner) and construction-related business interests, by 17,950 to 16,362 (in a 77 percent poll). The election was not a plebiscite, but Inamine's pledge to stop the base construction was featured so prominently that his victory served as an unambiguous Nago statement to Tokyo and Washington, confirming the evidence of opinion polls that had found a 70 percent level of Nago City opposition to the Henoko project.[32] By rejecting the agreement that had been negotiated over its head to militarize the Oura Bay, Nago City not only chose a new mayor but served notice demanding major adjustments to the diplomatic and security stance of the Anpo allies.

The election shook governments in Tokyo and Washington, compelling them to reconsider the 2005–2006 agreements on reorganization of US forces in Japan and the 2009 Guam Treaty. For Nago itself, the Inamine victory put an end to thirteen years of bitterness and division.[33]

Shimabukuro, guided and helped by his mentor, Higa, fought a desperate campaign. During election week, his camp took advantage of the provision in the election system for early voting to mobilize local businesses (promising them lucrative construction contracts) and press them to muster advance votes collectively, business by business.[34] Though he was the best hope of the probase cause, his votes could not be classified as "probase" because he avoided any mention of it other than to say it was something for the national government to decide, painting himself as a critic of the Guam Treaty plan and as one who favored the offshore option that had been under consideration in 1998–2005. By Nago election day, even local business seemed to have lost faith in the Higa-Shimabukuro model. Dependence on national government handouts dished out for compliance on base matters had served only to deepen the city's economic doldrums. From the outcome, it must be concluded that many of those dragooned by Shimabukuro went along as far as the polling station but did not cast their votes as expected.[35]

The outcome showed that the tide had indeed changed. Inamine pledged to prevent the seas of Henoko being made the site for a new military base, to put an end to the special interests tied up with the base that had destroyed the city's finances and demoralized its citizens, and to give priority to economic policies geared to locally sustainable jobs in harmony with the environment.[36] Beyond the specific promises, however, what Nago City electors were asking of him was that he reverse the betrayal of the city's wishes by his predecessor thirteen years earlier.

However, the Nago election outcome did nothing to shake the insistence in Tokyo on the absolute priority to alliance obligations. Chief Cabinet Secretary Hirano Hirofumi commented that he saw no need for the city's views to be taken into consideration in making the base decision, adding that appropriate legal steps could, if necessary, be taken to compel submission.[37] In this sentiment, the Democratic Party government intimated a readiness to go further than previous LDP governments had ever gone and to resort to force to bring Okinawa to heel. Such statements reminded Okinawans of the way their lands in the 1950s had been seized "in accordance with the law" by US forces with bayonets and bulldozers.[38] The hope and trust that Okinawans had placed in the Democratic Party in 2009 evaporated.

## (b) September: Nago City Assembly

Inamine's January victory was part of a prefecture-wide surge in anti-base mobilization. It was followed by a unanimous resolution of the Prefectural Assembly in February, the "all-Okinawa" mass meeting that declared opposition to the project in April, the unanimous resolution of the Prefectural Assembly in April, and the continuing evidence of opinion polls following the advent of the Kan government in June showing continuing high levels of opposition to any new base construction. Nago City had a long history of alternating progressive and conservative governments and of relentless external pressures. As Nago City resident and prize-winning novelist Medoruma Shun put it on the eve of the election,

Nago people were "fed up to the back teeth" with the base and the incessant outside pressure that for so long had divided families and sown bitterness and hostility in their city.[39]

Urashima Etsuko, key member (and also historian) of the Okinawan northern districts antibase coalition, comments bitterly, writing in 2006,

> So, for these past nine years, the base problem has been cause of unbroken anguish for us, setting parents and children, brothers and sisters, relatives and neighbors, at each other's throats. The base problem, and the "money" that goes with it, have torn to shreds human relations based on cooperation and mutual help, relationships that used to be so rich even though we were poor, or rather, because we were so poor.[40]

The advent of an antibase mayor was a blow to Tokyo and Washington, but it was seen as not in itself decisive provided he could be blocked from obtaining a majority in the city assembly elections, scheduled for September 12, 2010. No city in Japan had been cultivated more assiduously and for so long (since 1999) as Nago. Many had benefited, construction-related special interest groups above all, and if base-induced dependency and compliance was to work anywhere, it should have been here in Nago. Under a "Northern Districts Development" formula (tied to submission to the base project), eighty billion yen had flowed into Nago City and surrounding districts between 2000 and 2009, filling the coffers of construction and public works–related groups and easing the fiscal crisis of local governments. At elections, the LDP made every effort to avoid focus on the base issue while stressing its ability to provide jobs and money. "Conservative" (probase) groups insisted that they could be relied on to handle economic problems better and to produce better outcomes in terms of jobs and services than antibase forces because they enjoyed better "pipelines" of connection to the national government and to national business. Over time, the system of subsidy-induced regional compliance in base siting cultivated cynicism and corruption and blocked development rooted in local needs.

Particular attention focused on the three hamlets of Henoko, Toyohara, and Kushi, the so-called Kube districts on the eastern side of Nago City and closest to the projected base construction site. Henoko (population approximately 2,100 or 450 households) is separated by a narrow strip of beach from the US Marine Corps base at Camp Schwab. It receives a base-related income each year of around two hundred million yen, and at least half of its residents are recipients of rental income (in the range of several hundred thousand to several million yen annually) based on their family's share of the village commons that were handed over to the US military half a century ago.[41] The sweetness of such largesse, once tasted,

is difficult to quit. Historian Arasaki Moriteru refers to Tokyo's persuasion not as candy and whip but opium and whip.[42]

One symbol of Henoko's "prosperity" is its annual "Hari," or dragon
boat festival in June. For the 2010 event, the hamlet displayed four splendid boats, each costing roughly $10,000 (900,000 yen). Sixty teams, includ-
ing some from the adjacent Camp Schwab base, competed.[43] Henoko's Exchange Plaza, completed in 2007 at a cost of just under one billion yen and
featuring a six-hundred-person hall, library, computer facilities, lavishly
equipped sports facilities, and massage equipment, was another symbol
of the fruits of compliance. Supposedly designed for the invigoration of
the village, like so many other local developments this too was part of the
price paid by Tokyo to ensure dependence and complicity.

In apparent seriousness, local organizations in the Kube districts discussed lodging a demand with the government for a three hundred million yen payment per household in return for their consent to construction of the base, and were reportedly in favor of a formula for reclamation
under which they would own the offshore island, once it was constructed,
and lease it in perpetuity to the state for five hundred million yen per
year.[44] The benefits tended to be concentrated in a few hands, however,
and the demeaning character of the exchanges was not lost on local
people. By 2010, the implicit contempt on Tokyo's part for those whose
consent was assumed to be simply a matter of finding the right price bred
resentment and humiliation on the part of Henoko and its adjacent hamlets. In June 2010, the district of Kushi signalled the growing disgust with
the decade of chosen dependence by adopting a unanimous resolution
of support for Nago mayor Inamine's antibase stance. Base opponents
set up an "all Kube" organization to carry Inamine's campaign into the
heartland of Henoko.[45] The tide was turning.

City elections are commonly tied closely to local family and business interests, and apart from the base, Nago, for all its high-profile white elephant
trophies, faced unemployment running at around double the national figure, stressed services, including medical, and a business center lined with
boarded-up shops.[46] Tamaki Yoshikazu, vice president of the prefectural
assembly, said in the lead-up to the election, "It is utter nonsense to think
that a national problem such as the base issue should be affected by a local
election."[47] While the Inamine camp was resolutely antibase—no new base,
declared Inamine, would be built either on land or on sea in Nago City—
the Shimabukuro group candidates refused to answer a local newspaper
opinion survey on the base question, focusing their campaign entirely on
local issues.[48] It was no secret, however, that the Kan government desperately hoped for the antibase forces to be defeated, and senior cabinet ministers campaigned actively for Shimabukuro, something virtually without
precedent in local, small-town elections.[49]

The level of domestic (national) and foreign interest and intervention in this election was also without precedent. The US consul general in Okinawa and senior Japanese government officials met secretly with local probase officials and business leaders to discuss ways to assist their campaign.[50] To Kan and his government, Nago City was akin to enemy territory that had to be reconquered. To win favor, they hammered out a program of livelihood benefits—sewerage, education and welfare, kindergartens—that they wanted Nago City people to realize would be conditional on their adopting the "right" attitude on September 12.[51]

As antibase elements sought to align Henoko with the rest of Okinawa and with Nago City, prominent local authority and head of the Nago fishing cooperative, Kohagura Hiroshi, presented a clinching argument: "What are you [opponents of the project] talking about? There is no way the Americans are going to do this anywhere but Henoko. Before the government carries out its plan over our heads, we have to get in to struggle over conditions."[52] Earlier, Kohagura had played a key role in persuading villagers to refuse cooperation with the scheme for the new base to be constructed within the confines of Camp Schwab, that is, without reclamation. But with the reclamation project back on the table, he changed his tune. For him, it was a "preemptive punch" at the government and the only chance for the local community to cash in on the deal. If the government did not cooperate, then Henoko would resist.

Yet in the end, the best efforts of the local and national probase elements went unrewarded. The balance of seats in the Nago Assembly shifted decisively in favor of antibase Mayor Inamine and against probase former mayor Shimabukuro. Rejecting Tokyo's "opium" of inducement, the city chose a solidly antibase majority. Tokyo's response, as Cabinet Secretary Sengoku Yoshito put it, was that the government would "stick to our basic stance of seeking the understanding [of Nago residents], sincerely explaining the transfer plan."[53] As a token of its sincerity, the Kan government froze its contacts with Inamine, and its senior government figures refused to meet with him. The treatment that had worked against Ota in 1998 was expected to work again against Inamine, even though it might take longer.

### (c) November: Governor of Okinawa

The climactic event of 2010 was the third major election of that year, for governor, which took place on November 28. Its significance rose as the Nago City votes in January and September went decisively against the Henoko project. For the election, conservative incumbent Nakaima Hirokazu faced Ginowan City mayor Iha Yoichi.

Nakaima, an Okinawa business leader and before that senior official in MITI (Ministry of International Trade and Industry), who took office in

2006 with the support of the LDP and Komeito, had earlier supported the Henoko base. Nevertheless, in recent years, he had protested on countless occasions at the way Tokyo ignored him in its deliberations on the base issue, stating that it was "meaningless for the two governments to think that just because they were in agreement the project would go ahead."[54] In April he told the "all Okinawa mass antibase meeting" that he had the feeling Okinawa was being subjected to "something akin to discrimination." Later he told the Kan government that he would not enter any negotiations over a Futenma transfer or any putative new base construction, and he described the August 31 "experts" report as a "worthless scrap of paper" that would be "impossible to implement."[55] Eventually, he fought the election on the platform of moving Futenma outside of Okinawa, though leaving ambiguity by never expressing opposition against construction of a replacement base within Okinawa. Nakaima was supported by both ruling and opposition national parties (Democratic Party [DPJ] and Liberal Democratic Party [LDP]) and Komeito.

Iha Yoichi, Nakaima's challenger, campaigned on a platform of return of Futenma without construction of any substitute base within Okinawa. As mayor of Ginowan City between 2003 and 2010, he had based his public career on the demand for reversion of Futenma and on opposition to any proposal to construct a substitute for it in Okinawa. Air Station Futenma, the "world's most dangerous," sat in the middle of his town. He was backed by the Social Democratic, Communist, and Okinawan Social Mass Parties.[56]

For any reclamation of the sea to allow base construction to proceed, the governor's authorization was a legal requirement, so the outcome of this election was of high interest to the governments of Japan and the United States. Tokyo's hope rested on the slender thread that in all his bitter and angry comment, Nakaima had not declared outright opposition to the base project and had not said he would absolutely forbid it. The Kan government had to interpret Nakaima's formulation of "difficult" and "extremely difficult" as implying openness to negotiation. The best it could hope was that once reelected, Nakaima would be "reasonable," meaning that he would be open to persuasion and, given suitable incentives would betray his electors. In other words, Kan and his closest advisers believed that once elected, Nakaima would betray his Okinawan constituents and cooperate with Tokyo. Whether it would be done by buying or by threatening was immaterial.

The stakes in 2010 were plainly higher than they had been in 1998 when the national government launched its covert campaign to unseat Governor Ota. The atmosphere, however, was similar. As one commentator put it,

Now as in 1998, in Okinawa a feeling of hemmed-in-ness floats in the air. But what is decisively different now is that the majority of Okinawan people share a suspicion that the reason there is no way out of the oppressiveness is because the DPJ government clings to the idea of transferring [Futenma base] to Henoko and because the mainland is relaxed about imposing the burden of Ampo on Okinawa.[57]

When pressed to deny that his government would resort to the kind of secret (and illegal) interventions the Obuchi government had pursued against Ota Masahide in 1998, the cabinet secretary refused to answer,[58] and Prime Minister Kan declined to order that the practice be stopped or to launch an investigation with a view to launching criminal proceedings. Other, no less scandalous, discretionary funds were certainly maintained under the Kan government.[59] Obviously, the stakes were higher in 2010 than they had been in 1998. Whether and what kind of interventions might have been secretly authorized to ensure Iha's defeat remains to be seen.

In due course, Nakaima was indeed returned to office, with a substantial margin (roughly 52 percent to 46 percent). But hopes in Washington that Nakaima, once reelected, would adopt a more realistic approach to the Henoko question were quickly dampened. In his victory statement, Nakaima was clear:

> Originally, I'd thought it would be inevitable to accept the Henoko plan with certain conditions. But the people of Nago clearly said no to the plan when they voted for an anti-base mayor. Therefore, there is no place in Okinawa to move Futenma.[60]

The one candidate who explicitly endorsed the national government's position for implementation of the May 2010 agreement to relocate Futenma to Henoko was dismissed with a derisory 2 percent of the vote. As for the victorious Nakaima, in his second term as governor he began to sound more and more like his most feared predecessor, Ota Masahide.

## 2011: IRREVOCABLE CHANGE?

What the three elections of 2010 showed was that the carrot system of incentive persuasion no longer worked. The political credibility of the Liberal Democratic Party–based system that ran national, prefectural, and city governments had been fatally weakened in the minds of Okinawan electors: it had simply failed to deliver.

It used to be said of the base presence in Okinawa that it brought to local communities economic benefits of such magnitude as to outweigh the negatives. It is true that US and Japanese base policy created and cultivated a rentier class who prefers to enjoy land rental income that has risen steadily since reversion (and has even generated a speculative exchange that offers investment in such lands), but the benefits to the community as a whole have steadily shrunk. Base-related income that constituted 15 percent of the Okinawan economy at reversion now amounts to only about 5 percent. While the years of state largesse saw dependence deepen and those local governments dependent on it sink into chronic fiscal crisis, towns and villages without bases (and therefore not "enjoying" special subsidies) in general fared much better than those with them, and those that had managed to recover parcels of base land found that productivity and income tended to shoot up, by as much as twenty, thirty, or even forty times, after reversion from military to civilian use.[61] *Ryukyu Shimpo*'s deputy chief editor referred to the bases as "a parasite sucking out Okinawa's vitality" and rotting its economy.[62]

The militarization of Oura Bay, a Pentagon dream since 1966 and a much favored Japanese bureaucratic project since the late 1990s, came close to realization under bilateral agreements in 1996, 2006, and 2009 but was blocked through the terms of nine prime ministers (Hashimoto to Kan) and seventeen defense ministers (Kyuma to Kitazawa) by one of the most remarkable nonviolent political movements in modern Japanese (or world) history. By 2010, the outcome of these three elections was such that the movement was stronger, enjoyed more widespread support, and was more solidly embedded in the democratic process than ever before.

## FUTENMA REPLACEMENT FACILITY (FRF), 1996–2011

*1996–1998:* "Heliport," initially 45 meters, offshore, Northern Okinawa; rejected by Nago City plebiscite in 1997 (then endorsed by mayor but rejected by governor).

*1999–2001:* Henoko offshore, removable, floating pontoon, 1,500-meter runway, 75–90 hectares in area, conditional (joint civil-military, fifteen-year limited, etc.) accepted by city and prefecture; cabinet go-ahead December 1999. US side was open to relocation elsewhere in Japan, but government of Japan insisted on Henoko.

*2002:* Henoko offshore construction plan settled, reef reclamation, 1,500-meter runway, approximately 184 hectares, civil-military, pontoon based. Environmental survey and protest sit-in begin 2004.

*2005:* Koizumi cancels the Henoko plan because of "a lot of opposition." A shore-based, L-shaped, 1,600-meter single runway, one kilometer offshore, is adopted but soon morphs into:

*2006:* Cape Henoko, shore-based, dual V-shaped, 1800-meter runways stretching into Oura Bay from Camp Schwab, plus naval port, plus Yambaru forest helipads. Projected completion date: 2014. Endorsed by both governments in "Beigun saihen" 2006 and adopted in binding form by Japan in Guam Treaty, 2009.

*2010 (March):* Hatoyama passes over the V-shaped Schwab plan of 2006 and substitutes a three-part composite plan:

a. a land-based Cape Henoko helicopter runway, either 500 meters or 1600 meters, within Camp Schwab, or

b. a 1,020-hectare artificial island with 10,200 meters of runway (two runways of 3,600 meters and one of 3,000 meters) offshore from Katsuren Peninsula, in Uruma City (central Okinawa, near existing US White Beach Base), or

c. construction of new facilities on Tokunoshima Island, in Kagoshima prefecture, two hundred kilometers north of Okinawa main island and just outside Okinawan prefectural boundary, or

d. some combination or perhaps all of these.

*2010 (April):* A "final proposal" to the US government, in the form of "broad acceptance" of the Guam Treaty terms, which, however, were significantly altered to

a. a Futenma Replacement Facility at Henoko, comprising a sea-based single runway resting on pillars (perhaps four thousand of them) driven into the seabed, and

b. transfer of some helicopter training units from Futenma to Tokunoshima island.

*2010 (May):* Hatoyama suddenly surrenders, abandoning his various alternative schemes and agreeing to accept the Henoko base construction (and the Yambaru forest helipads), resigning immediately after signing the May 28 agreement.

*2011 (June):* "Two plus Two" foreign and defense ministers of United States and Japan reaffirm intent to proceed with Henoko plan, though postponing completion date to "earliest possible after 2014." Japan pledges to construct military facilities also on Mage and Miyako Islands.

*2011 (September):* Inauguration of Noda government and renewal of Henoko commitment to US President Obama.

## FUTENMA REPLACEMENT FACILITY, POLITICAL DEVELOPMENTS, 2009–2011

*2009 (August):* The Democratic Party of Japan (DPJ), promising a new deal for Japan in its relationships with the United States and China and promising the people of Okinawa that Futenma would be "at very least relocated to outside Okinawa," is swept to power in national elections and forms a new government, headed by Hatoyama Yukio.

*2010 (January):* Nago City elects a mayor who declares that "no new base will be built in this city, whether on land or on sea."

*2010 (February):* The Okinawa Prefectural Assembly adopts a unanimous resolution calling for swift closure of Futenma base and opposing construction within Okinawa of any substitute facility.

*2010 (April):* An "all-Okinawan" mass meeting (some ninety thousand people), including the governor and heads of all local governing authorities, adopts a resolution calling for the same.

*2010 (May):* Prime Minister Hatoyama, under overwhelming American and Japanese bureaucratic and media pressure, signs agreement with Washington to construct Futenma Replacement Facility "in the Camp Schwab–Cape Henoko area and adjacent waters," and immediately resigns.

*2010 (June):* Kan Naoto, succeeding Hatoyama as prime minister, makes it his priority to "restore" relations with Washington, proceeding with the construction of the base for the Marine Corps. He apologizes to Okinawans for reneging on the party's preelection pledge but insists that there is no alternative and that the matter is closed.

*2010 (July):* Okinawa's Prefectural Assembly (July 9) adopts a fresh resolution demanding cancellation of the May 28 agreement, which it terms "a violent, democracy-trampling act" that "treated Okinawans as stupid." The DPJ, facing outrage from Okinawa over its abandonment of the pledge to block any new base construction, is unable to field a single candidate in the Upper House elections.

*2010 (September):* Antibase forces victorious in Nago City assembly elections, crushing probase forces backed by Tokyo.

*2010 (November):* In the Okinawa gubernatorial election, incumbent Nakaima Hirokazu, who pledges to seek relocation of the new base somewhere outside Okinawa, defeats challenger Iha Yoichi, who calls for the closure of Futenma and promises to block any attempt to construct a base within Okinawa. The one candidate who explicitly calls for construction to proceed in accordance with the May 2010 US-Japan agreement secures a mere 2 percent of the vote.

*2011 (June):* Foreign and defense ministers of United States and Japan abandon the 2014 deadline but confirm the intent to proceed with the V-shaped Henoko base project (and to construct bases on other islands); Governor Nakaima declares it "outrageous."

*2011 (September):* Prime Minister Noda promises President Obama that the base construction will proceed, but Governor Nakaima says that could happen only by force and demands that the two governments "stop doing deals and return the bases promptly."[63]

## NOTES

1. Ota, *Konna Okinawa*, 119–29; Makishi Yoshikazu, "SACO goi no karakuri o abaku," in *Okinawa wa mo damasarenai* (Tokyo: Kobunken, 2000), 53.

2. In retrospect, they did accomplish one highly significant thing: Ota invited the well-known—and generally conservative—American political scientist Chalmers Johnson to visit Okinawa late in 1995, and that visit helped precipitate in Johnson a reconsideration of the American role in Okinawa and the global base system that formed the subject of his last, best-selling series of books.

3. Quoted in Arasaki, *Okinawa gendaishi*, 156.

4. Ibid., 78–81, 109–14, 123–28, 148–51, 155–82.

5. Koji Taira, "The Okinawan Charade: The United States, Japan and Okinawa: Conflict and Compromise, 1995–96" working paper, Japan Policy Research Institute, University of San Francisco Center for the Pacific Rim, January 1997, http://www.jpri.org/publications/workingpapers/wp28.html.

6. For Ota's statement to the Supreme Court (and the judgment), see Ota Masahide, "Governor Ota at the Supreme Court of Japan," in *Okinawa: Cold War Island*, ed. Chalmers Johnson (Cardiff: Japan Policy Research Institute, 1999).

7. For a judicious analysis of the complex of reasons involved, see Julia Yonetani, "Making History from Japan's Margins—Ota Masahide and Okinawa," dissertation, Australian National University, 2002.

8. In November 1997, Okinawa prefecture formally asked Tokyo to declare the prefecture a free trade zone by 2005. (See the discussion in Arasaki, *Okinawa gendaishi*, 171–82.)

9. Koji Taira, "Okinawa's Choice: Independence or Subordination," in *Okinawa: Cold War Island*, 175.

10. Arasaki, *Okinawa gendaishi*, 181.

11. "Futenma kichi o zenmen henkan," *Okinawa Taimusu*, April 13, 1996.

12. Chalmers Johnson, "The Heliport, Nago, and the End of the Ota Era," in *Okinawa: Cold War Island*, 219–20.

13. "'Okinawa chijisen ni kanbo kimitsuhi 3 oku en' hatsu shogen," TBS, News 23 Kurosu, July 21, 2010; "Chijisen ni kimitsuhi? soho nattoku iku setsumei o," *Okinawa Taimusu*, July 23, 2010.

14. Ida Hiroyuki, "Kambo kimitsuhi yaku san oku en ga Okinawa chijisen ni nagarekonda shoko," *Shukan Kinyobi*, October 22, 2010.

15. TBS, News 23 Kurosu, July 21, 2010.

16. On this incident, see Field, *In the Realm*, 33–104.

17. "'Okinawa no sensei wa kyosan shihai,' mori jimin kanjicho ga hihan," *Ryukyu Shimpo*, March 23, 2000.

18. Medoruma Shun, "2000 en satsu—naze Okinawa 'Shuri no mon'?" *Asahi Shimbun*, November 4, 1999.

19. Arakawa Akira, *Okinawa: Togo to hangyaku* (Tokyo: Chikuma shobo, 2000).

20. "Prime Minister's Commission on Japan's Goals in the 21st Century," First Sub-Committee, "Japan's Place in the World," July 28, 1999. On Takara's position, see "Kichi no sonzai sekkyoku hyoka," *Asahi Shimbun*, May 15, 2000, and the articles by Takara in the *Okinawa Taimusu*, two-part series, Takara Kurayoshi, "Okinawa Inititiative no kangae kata," May 23–24, 2000.

21. See Yonetani, *Making History*; Yonetani, "Contested Memories"; and Julia Yonetani, "Future 'Assets' but What Price? The Okinawa Initiative Debate," in *Islands of Discontent: Okinawan Responses to Japanese and American Power*, ed. Laura Hein and Mark Selden (Lanham, MD: Rowman & Littlefield, 2003).

22. Arasaki, *Okinawa gendaishi*, 199.

23. Julia Yonetani, "Playing Base Politics in a Global Strategic Theater: Futenma Relocation, the G-8 Summit, and Okinawa," *Critical Asian Studies* 33, no.1 (2001): 84.

24. Osawa Masachi, "Fuhenteki na kokyosei wa ika ni shite kanoka," *Sekai* (August 2000): 151, 158.

25. *Asahi Shimbun* and *Okinawa Taimusu* survey of opinion, published in *Okinawa Taimusu*, December 19, 1999.

26. "Futenma hikojo daitai, kennai isetsu hantai 68%," *Okinawa Taimusu*, May 14, 2009. In the Northern districts (including Nago City), opposition was even higher, at 76 percent.

27. "Futenma iten: Genko keikaku ni 'hantai' 67%, Okinawa yoron chosa," *Mainichi Shimbun*, November 2, 2009; for a partial English account, see "Poll: 70 percent of Okinawans want Futenma moved out of prefecture, Japan," *Mainichi Daily News*, November 3, 2009.

28. The "Open Letter" to Secretary Clinton at the time of her February 2009 visit to Tokyo demanded cancellation of the Henoko plan, immediate and unconditional return of Futenma, and further reductions in the US military presence. "Hirari R. Kurinton Beikokumu chokan e no shokan" ("Open Letter to Secretary of State Clinton"), by Miyazato Seigen and thirteen other representative figures of Okinawa's civil society, February 14, 2009. "Henoko kichi kensetsu chushi o: Bei kokumu chokan rainichi de seimei/kennai gakushikisha 'shinseiken no taio kitai,'" *Okinawa Taimusu*, February 17, 2009.

29. "Kengikai, Futenma 'kokugai kengai isetsu motomeru' iensho kaketsu," *Okinawa Taimusu*, February 24, 2010. A resolution to the same effect had been passed by a majority in July 2008.

30. "Zen shucho kennai kyohi, Futenma kengai tekkyo no shiodoki," editorial, *Ryukyu Shimpo*, March 1, 2010; "Ken shicho kaigi kennai hantai ketsugi zenkai itchi kuni ni chokusetsu yosei e," *Okinawa Taimusu*, April 6, 2010.

31. Onaga Takeshi, "Okinawa wa 'yuai' no soto na no ka," *Sekai* (February 2010).

32. Surveys by *Yomiuri Shimbun, Okinawa Taimusu* and *Asahi Shimbun,* and *Ryukyu Shimpo* and Okinawa TV, published January 19, 2010, found 73, 65, and 69 percent, respectively, wanting the Futenma base relocated outside Okinawa. See Urashima Etsuko and Gavan McCormack, "Electing a Town Mayor in Okinawa: Report from the Nago Trenches," *Asia-Pacific Journal: Japan Focus* (January 25, 2010), http://japanfocus.org/-Gavan-McCormack/3291.

33. Shimabukuro's campaign manager in 2010 was that same former mayor, Higa Tetsuya.

34. Because 31.7 percent of the electorate cast advance votes, citizen groups supporting Inamine lodged a complaint on January 19 with the election commission, arguing that the mobilization of advance votes was in breach of the Public Office Election Law and the antithesis of free voting. Because of Inamine's victory, the matter was not pursued.

35. We are indebted to Urashima Etsuko for this observation.

36. For a discussion by Mayor Inamine, see Miyagi Yasuhiro and Inamine Susumu, "'Unacceptable and Unendurable': Local Okinawa Mayor Says No to US Marine Base Plan," *Asia-Pacific Journal: Japan Focus* (October 17, 2011), http://japanfocus.org/-Miyagi-Yasuhiro/3618.

37. "'Hirano chokan hatsugen' kenmin no kokoro moteasobuna," editorial, *Okinawa Taimusu,* January 28, 2010.

38. Ibid.

39. Medoruma Shun, "Nago shigikai senkyo," *Uminari no shima kara,* September 6, 2010, http://blog.goo.ne.jp/awamori777/e/763baeb3560503c4f1f5f7181352be7a.

40. Gavan McCormack, Sato Manabu, and Urashima Etsuko, "The Nago Mayoral Election and Okinawa's Search for a Way beyond Bases and Dependence," *Asia-Pacific Journal: Japan Focus* (February 16, 2006), http://japanfocus.org/-Etsuko-Urashima/1592.

41. "Bunshukin no eikyo," and "'Mokunin' no haikei," parts 11 and 12 of "Zoku 'Ame to muchi' no kozu," *Okinawa Taimusu,* August 1 and 2, 2010.

42. "Kokusaku no kajitsu," part 21 of "Zoku 'Ame to muchi' no kozu," *Okinawa Taimusu,* August 20, 2010.

43. Ibid.

44. "Kadena hoshiki," part 16 of "Zoku 'Ame to muchi' no kozu," *Okinawa Taimusu,* August 9, 2010.

45. "Sanpi ryoha," part 9 of "Zoku 'Ame to muchi' no kozu," *Okinawa Taimusu,* July 30, 2010.

46. As much as 19.5 percent of businesses in Nago were reported closed (shuttered) as of 2008. Chinen Kiyoharu, "Nago shicho sen hitotsu ni natta min-i," *Sekai* (March 2010): 22.

47. Quoted in "Ippyo no butaiura—2010 nen no toitsu chiho sen," *Okinawa Taimusu,* August 26, 2010.

48. "'Ken-nai' hantai seron han'ei Nago shigisen rikkohosha anketo," *Okinawa Taimusu,* September 6, 2010.

49. Peter Ennis, "Seiji Maehara and Unrealistic Expectations in Washington," *Dispatch Japan,* September 17, 2010, http://www.dispatchjapan.com/blog/2010/09/seiji-maehara-and-unrealistic-expectations-in-washington.html.

50. "'2 homen kosho' ni hihan isetsu yoninha to mikkai kasaneru Maehara shi," *Ryukyu Shimpo*, August 19, 2010.

51. "Chatozu," part 23 of "Zoku 'Ame to muchi' no kozu," *Okinawa Taimusu*, August 22, 2010.

52. "Hanpatsu fuji joken toso—yonin ketsugi isoida ku gyosei-i," part 1 of "Zoku 'Ame to muchi' no kozu," *Okinawa Taimusu*, July 16, 2010.

53. The pre-election balance was 12:12:3 (Inamine supporters, Shimabukuro supporters, and independents). In the election, the Inamine camp won sixteen seats and the Shimabukuro camp, eleven. "Nago Voters Pick Anti-base City Assembly," *Yomiuri Shimbun*, September 14, 2010.

54. "Okinawa fukureru seifu fushin," *Asahi Shimbun*, August 8, 2010.

55. "Henoko hokokusho/jitsugen funo na kara shomon Nichibei goi no hatan akiraka," *Ryukyu Shimpo*, September 2, 2010.

56. In a concession designed to win support of the local Communist Party, Iha's campaign adopted the slogan "Withdraw the Marines" (*Kaiheitai tettai*), which was broader than that of simply a return of Futenma without replacement. This risked exposing him to charges of anti-Americanism that the mainstream Okinawan movement had been at pains to avoid.

57. Watanabe Tsuyoshi, "'Jihatsuteki reiju' no jubaku o tachikiru Okinawa," *Sekai* (December 2010): 51.

58. "Seifu, Kimitsuhi tonyu hitei sezu jiki chijisen, nago shigi sen de," *Ryukyu Shimpo*, August 21, 2010.

59. In July 2010 the Kan government hosted a state visit—charter flight, helicopter tour around Mt. Fuji, and "additional remuneration"—to Japan by the convicted terrorist bomber Kim Hyon-hui. Debito Arudou, "The Victim Complex and Kim's Killer Con," *Japan Times*, August 3, 2010.

60. Eric Johnston, "Nakaima Victory Helps Kan, US," *Japan Times*, November 30, 2010.

61. Figures from a study conducted by the prefecture quoted in Maedomari Hiromori, "'Kichi izon keizai' to iu shinwa," *Sekai* (February, 2010): 207.

62. Ibid., 203.

63. "Okinawan Governor Denies a Japan-US Deal on US Military Realignment Package," *Ryukyu Shimpo*, September 26, 2011.

# 8

*≈*

# Environment

## *The "Nonassessment"*

Setting aside the diplomatic, political, and military considerations, on ecological grounds alone the idea that a huge new military installation should be constructed at Nago is implausible. The Henoko site is commonly described as sparsely populated, as if that made it an obvious and almost unproblematic choice to replace the overcrowded Futenma. However, quite apart from the rights of the people who do undoubtedly live in the area and its vicinity, such discussion passes over the qualities that make Henoko and the surrounding regions not just of regional or national but global significance: its unique and precious marine and forest environment. To impose a large military base on this location would be akin to designating the American Grand Canyon or Australia's Kakadu a military base.

The coastal areas of Henoko are classified under the Okinawa prefectural government's guidelines for environmental protection as rank 1, warranting the highest level of protection. The International Union for the Conservation of Nature (IUCN) has called repeatedly for priority to attach to preservation of the Henoko area's endangered species.[1] In and around Oura Bay and Cape Henoko, the internationally protected dugong graze on sea grasses, turtles come to rest and lay their eggs, and multiple rare birds, insects, and animals thrive. A colony of blue coral was discovered only in 2007 (and in 2008 placed on the IUCN's "red," or critically endangered, list, joining the dugong). A 2009 World Wildlife Fund study found an astonishing thirty-six *new* species of crabs and shrimps,[2] and in March-April 2010 Tokyo marine science researchers found an equally astonishing rain forest–like variety of 182 different species of sea grasses and marine plants, four of which were probably new species, in Oura Bay.[3] The Nature Conservation Society of Japan in 2010 found 362 species of conchs in those same waters, 186 of them in one fifty-centimeter-square area.[4] The discovery of the blue coral, new species of shrimps and crabs, and sea grass came after the EI survey and thus formed no part of it.

The Japanese government announced during the Conference of the Parties to the United Nations Convention on Biodiversity (COP10) in Nagoya in 2010 (the "International Year of Biodiversity") its intention to designate this region as a national park, and the Okinawa prefectural government promoted its adoption as the core of a Ryukyu Islands submission for recognition as a UNESCO World Natural Heritage site. But can high-level nature conservation be combined with the development of a major US Marine war-fighting facility?

In creating the giant, combined-forces military base (misleadingly described as the "Futenma Replacement Facility" when it was to combine, *inter alia*, a deep-sea port facility for docking nuclear submarines as well as two long runways and various ancillary facilities), the coral, dugong, turtles, and other creatures were simply a nuisance. The same must be said regarding the "helipads" that under the 2006 and 2009 agreements were to be constructed in the Yambaru forest of northern Okinawa (discussed below).

When the Marine Corps first developed its plans for militarizing Oura Bay in 1962, it began, as noted above, to deal with the coral by bombing it. Such a course is not open to the marines today, but the scale of militarization envisaged could be expected to have the same effect over the longer term. As with Guam, however, the Henoko (and Takae) projects can proceed only when the necessary legal requirements for environmental protection (national and international) are addressed (whether by compliance or by evasion).

Japan overcame its deep-seated bureaucratic and corporate hostility and adopted (in 1997) an Environmental Impact Assessment Law (*Asesuho*), based on the system in operation in the United States since 1970. However, between thirty thousand and fifty thousand EIAs are conducted each year in the United States while in Japan the figure is about twenty or, with those under local ordinances included, no more than seventy. Furthermore, the law simply mandates the party proposing works to consider their impact and take appropriate steps to protect the environment.[5] It does not stipulate an impartial, scientific process and includes no provision to stop a project from going ahead on environmental grounds. The process involves three stages: the scoping document (defining the scope and methodology of the assessment); the preliminary assessment; and the final impact statement. Citizen input is supposedly guaranteed at the first and second stages, but the only party entitled to comment on the third and final stage is the governor, the party that would have to approve the landfill of publicly owned seafront for the project to proceed.

In April 2007, the government decided that Naha Defense Facilities Administration Bureau (DFAB), part of what was then the Defense Agency and is now the Ministry of Defense, would begin an environmental assessment of the area where the V-shaped runway would be constructed. Civic activists pointed out that such a procedure was in violation of the Environment Impact Assessment Law. The law requires that an actual construction schedule for a major project, which undoubtedly the Henoko base would be, be decided only after assessment, whereas in this case a completion date of 2014 had already been set by international agreement, prejudging a process yet to be undertaken. Furthermore, although the legislation was clear that the scoping document, signalling the opening of the project to citizen participation, was the first step, in this case months of intensive "presurvey" activity, also implicitly forbidden by the law, was carried out. Some 120 pieces of equipment were set in the water, including thirty passive sonars, fourteen underwater video cameras, and machines used to check the adherence of coral eggs and ocean currents. On May 18, the Japanese government sent the Maritime Self-Defense Force minesweeper tender *Bungo* to Henoko to participate and, without doubt, also to intimidate the protesters. Such introduction of the Self-Defense Force against a civil protest was unprecedented.

Then Defense Agency Chief Kyuma Fumio ordered that working ships be reinforced and increased Japan Coast Guard officer-bodyguards from thirty to one hundred. He was reported as saying, "I don't want to repeat that frustrating experience of 2005 when we had to give up the construction of an airbase offshore Henoko."[6] As a result, four Japanese Coast Guard vessels, thirty working ships and sixteen rafts, were anchored offshore from Henoko, reminiscent of the participants in the protest struggle against the US fleets that surrounded Okinawa Island during the Battle of Okinawa. Against such an armada, there was little the protesters could do. From August 2007 to April 2009, the EIA was carried out. Given the government's commitment to the project, its outcome was never in doubt.

With the change of government in 2009 and the prolonged political and diplomatic crisis over the Henoko issue, the EIA process was suspended, its final statement shelved for over two years. From early in 2011, however, US pressure mounted. Defense Secretary Gates pressed Japan to show some progress on the base construction task by "later this Spring."[7] Before anything could be done, however, the disaster of March 11 struck. In June, Kan declared that he would resign once the special legislation called for by the crisis passed. Once the baton passed to Noda at the beginning of September, however, the pressure resumed. When in October Gates's successor, Leon Panetta, declared that it would be very important for the EIS to be completed before the end of the year, that was taken as an ultimatum. Noda's government assured Washington that that deadline would be met. Cabinet ministers one after the other made their "pilgrimages" to Naha to offer their distinctive blend of apology and demand. At all costs, they wanted to be able to present a message of "alliance deepening."

In Naha, however, anger and alarm spread. What Okinawans wanted was a "deepening" of their constitutional democratic rights and of measures for the protection of their natural environment. The Okinawan prefectural assembly adopted a unanimous resolution on November 14 demanding abandonment of the EIA, and a panel of eminent citizens, including two recent governors, Ota Masahide and Inamine Keiichi (one "progressive" and the other "conservative"), lent their weight to it.[8] *Ryukyu Shimpo* referred to Defense Minister Ichikawa as "bowing and scraping" (*ii dakudaku*) and "taking orders" (*goyo kiki*) from the United States. As for the presumed US pressure to make the project move forward before year's end, *Ryukyu Shimpo* speculated darkly that it was "entirely possible that behind the scenes running dog bureaucrats had been putting ideas into the heads of the US Government" (i.e., as they had done when betraying Hatoyama in 2009–2010).[9]

As the clock ticked down toward delivery of the crucial document, neither governor Nakaima nor Nago mayor Inamine was prepared to bow. Inamine spoke of the plan for his city as "unacceptable and unendurable."[10] He would stick to his electoral pledge to allow no new base construction in his city, whether on land or on sea. There was, he insisted, "nothing to negotiate."[11] For his part, Nakaima responded by saying that political circumstances had hugely changed in the two years since the issue of the Interim Report (to which he had raised serious objections anyway) and reiterated his demand for the Futenma base to be relocated outside Okinawa, saying, "I have made a political commitment on this and the Okinawan people's anger has not abated." He also pointed out that it was the DPJ government that had caused the problem by first saying the base would be relocated outside the prefecture and then reneging on its promise.[12] Japan's Department of Defense intimated that it intended to proceed, irrespective of the governor's response.[13] It would, in short, treat the process as a formality.

Knowing that the statement, and the procedure it was based on, was the cause of widespread outrage at all levels of Okinawan society, the government adopted the extraordinary measure of delivering it to the prefectural office in Okinawa at four o'clock in the morning on December 28, 2011, the very last working day of the year. The document, in sixteen copies (rather than the twenty required by law) was lengthy (seven thousand pages), but its bottom line was the terse sentence: "The project, when carried out, will not create particular obstacles to the protection of the environment." The questions and the objections raised by Okinawans to the Interim Report, issued in April 2009 in a 5,400 page version, were mostly passed over. The choice of dead of night for delivery was dictated by fear of the hostile reception that could be expected from citizens (including many members of prefectural and town and village elected assemblies) gathered around the prefectural office. The national government's decision to act in this way, under cover of night, when it could expect that the attention of many would be distracted by New Year preparations and at an hour when witnesses could least be expected, showed its desperation to meet the American-imposed deadline and its fear of an angry citizenry.

The scientific verdict was also terse, that the Henoko EIA had to rank as "the very worst in Japanese experience," if not the very worst anywhere.[14] Okinawa's leading environmental law authority, former Okinawa University president Sakurai Kunitoshi, was unequivocal: this could only serve to "undermine the environmental impact assessment system, which is essential to building a sustainable society. To reduce this system to an empty shell is to rob Japan of its very future."[15] Sakurai had earlier characterized the 2009 version of the assessment as "unscientific" and fatally flawed [16] and described as bizarre the decision by the government of Japan in the International Year of Biodiversity (2010), even while hosting COP10, to go to such lengths and spend such amounts of taxpayer money to push through a thoroughly unscientific justification for the destruction of such a precious concentration of biodiversity.[17] Yoshikawa Hideki commented on the final outcome, "Once envisaged as a democratic and scientific means of creating consensus among stakeholders, the Japanese EIA has been hijacked and turned into a political vehicle with which the Okinawa Defense Bureau (ODB) has forced the base construction plan forward."[18]

The Okinawa Prefecture Environmental Impact Committee found multiple faults in the assessment, both at its preliminary and final stages. At the former, it sought supplementary examination of 412 items in fifty-nine categories (including dugong numbers). At the latter, its advice to the governor early in 2012 was uncompromising: it listed a total of 150 cases of "insufficient and understated adverse effects on the environment."[19] Endorsing their report, Governor Nakaima went even further, declaring that it was "a practical impossibility to go ahead with it without securing local consent," and that it would be "impossible, by the environmental protection measures spelled out in the EI, to maintain completely the preservation of people's livelihood and the natural environment in the vicinity of the project works."[20] He listed 175 specific problems. A prefectural official commented the EIS was "unsound and lacked a scientific foundation."[21] There was no precedent for any such confrontation in the history of environmental assessment in Japan, and no sign of any way by which the confrontation might be resolved.

Supposedly scientific, open, and centering on maximum civic partici-pation, the entire process was conducted under the weight of intense US diplomatic pressure to get the necessary formalities done and produce the go-ahead for construction. In principle, the arrangement was one in which the government of Japan was to construct the facility but then hand it over to be used at the total discretion of the US Marine Corps; so details on the nature of the facility to be built, the kinds or numbers of aircraft that would use it, and the materials that would be stored there or used, were not made available. In that sense, the assessment was an absurdity, an assessment of an unknown, undefined impact.

The EI was problematic in multiple ways. Crucial information was withheld and what Sakurai calls a "dummy" strategy (insertion in the survey of a detail that was intended to be changed at the last minute and so evade scrutiny) adopted.[22] A crucial detail (the MV-22 Osprey) was revealed only after the end of the consultation process. This flaw alone was sufficient—in the view of at least one senior figure in the DPJ gov-ernment (see p. 170)—to necessitate a new environmental assessment. It was problematic in the way it treated the base construction project's likely impact on endangered and protected species (the dugong) and its likely social impact (especially with respect to noise). It neglected entirely the possible risks associated with typhoon (because none happened during the time span of the EI) and the environmental implications of the mas-sive landfill requirement. According to the January 2008 plan, a total of 21 million cubic meters of landfill would be required, of which initially 17 million would be sea sand. That would mean a staggering 3.4 million dump truck loads of sand, more than twelve times the current volume of sand extracted in a year from throughout Okinawa. How this alone could be done without having significant impact on Okinawa's fragile land and sea environment, not to speak of its roads, defies the imagination.[23]

As for the dugong, the preliminary assessment in April 2009 stated that three dugong had been identified (though not in the immediate Henoko vicinity), and that they were not observed to eat the sea grasses of Henoko. The assessment ignored citizens' concerns that it might be precisely because of the survey, which involved large-scale installation of equipment and drilling on the Henoko beach, that dugong had not been sighted there. Even following dugong sightings on May 12, 2010, just four kilometers north of the Henoko construction site, the final assessment in 2011 still concluded that "the loss of sea surface due to the construction of the facility would result in virtually no reduction in the dugong's habitat" because dugong did not live or eat sea grasses in the areas slated for base construction. The assessment paid no attention to the fact that sightings of the dugong had once been numerous in the area (see figure 8.1 for a sight-ing of a dugong and a sea turtle swimming together) or to the possibility

Figure 8.1.   Dugong and sea turtle in Oura Bay. *Source:* Higashionna Takuma.

that the pre-assessment process, which involved the fixing of hundreds of devices to the sea floor, might have served to drive the dugong away from the rich sea-grass beds off Henoko. The fierce struggles that took place in these seas between Okinawa Defense Bureau staff and protestors (discussed in chapter 5) well before the EI process must also have intimidated the notoriously timid dugong.

Court actions challenging the project on environmental grounds are under way in both the United States and Japan, and, as noted below, a tentative process has also been launched with the United Nations in Geneva.[24] In San Francisco a federal court judge in 2008, hearing a suit against the Pentagon on behalf of the Okinawan dugong and their marine habitat, issued a ruling that the US Department of Defense (DoD) had violated the National Historic Preservation Act (NHPA) by failing to "take into account" in planning the construction of a US military base in Henoko and Oura Bays the effects of the construction on the dugong (*Dugong dugon*), a Japanese "natural monument." She ordered the DoD to comply with the act by generating and taking information into account

Figure 8.2.  High-school students from the mainland visit Henoko protest tent, November 11, 2011.  As of the end of 2011, the sit-in has continued more than 2,800 days. *Source:* Conference Opposing Heliport Construction.

"for the purpose of avoiding or mitigating adverse effects" on the dugong.[25] In Japan, 344 (later increased to 622) Okinawans launched a suit in the Naha District Court in August 2009 to have the assessment declared invalid. Both actions were continuing as of 2012. Separate proceedings, not confined to but including environmental matters, were filed with the United Nations in Geneva in March 2012. In the name of Okinawans as an indigenous people, three Okinawan NGOs called on the UN Committee on the Elimination of Racial Discrimination to protest, among other things, the way the EI process had been pushed forward in breach of their rights.[26] Other grassroots protests continue as well (figure 8.2).

The EI process in retrospect seems also to have shared those qualities of bid rigging and featherbedding associated with publicly funded projects that the DPJ committed to rooting out when it came to power in 2009. The assessment process cost 3.4 billion yen (approximately $40 million) over three years, and of the twelve survey items that were contracted out by tender, eight were let to parties whose tender bids were in the 99 percent range of the preliminary (and "secret") estimates, some at 99.97 or 99.86 percent. The successful subcontracting companies included retired senior Defense Department officials on their staff.[27] Despite the whiff of scandal over this, as of the time of this writing there was little sign of parliamentary or media interest outside of Okinawa itself.

## TAKAE AND THE OSPREY HELIPADS

The string of helipads (helicopter takeoff and landing strips) to be built through the ecologically sensitive Yambaru forest area in northern Okinawa has not received as much attention as the Henoko project, but it too has been fiercely contested. Since 1957, the US Marine Corps has used the large swath of forest known to it as Camp Gonsalves and from 1998 as its Jungle Warfare Training Center and has operated twenty-two helipads.[28] During the Vietnam War, villagers here were occasionally mobilized as black pajama-wearing "Vietcong" to convey a sense of realism for marines about to depart for the war zone. Under the 1996 SACO Final Report, six new helipads (75-meter diameter, clear-felled and concreted zones, with access to the ocean) were to be built, in return for which about half of the forest training area was to be returned to Japan. Critics view the US demand for the construction of the helipads as a pretext for reinforcing US military capabilities in Okinawa, much the same way as they see the relocation of Futenma.[29]

The construction of the helipads, though obviously smaller in scale than the Futenma Replacement Facility projected for Henoko, is a major concern for the village of Higashi and, within it, especially the hamlet of Takae (160 households), which sits at the center of the area designated for construction. The Takae struggle reflects the same considerations as the Henoko struggle, save that its threatened ecology is mountain and forest rather than marine and coral. There is, however, a difference with respect to public awareness and support. Where Governor Nakaima followed the all-Okinawa mass meeting of April 2010 by switching to a negative stance on Henoko, he has yet to distance himself from the helipad plans for Takae.

From 2007, complaining of lack of consultation, noise, the risk of crashes, and the loss of their chosen close-to-nature lifestyle, Takae villagers have been sitting in, protesting around the clock, by the side of Prefectural Road 70 to protect not only their own livelihoods and peaceful environment but also the riches of animal, bird, and plant life that drew them to live there (see figure 8.3). Because of the greater distance and difficulty of access, the Takae sit-in (now in its fifth year) is a harder, lonelier struggle than the Henoko sit-in (now in its eighth year).

In November 2008, the Okinawa Defense Bureau (ODB) prosecuted fifteen of the protesters for obstructing traffic. Those prosecuted initially thought they must have become part of some elaborate practical joke since it was well known that there was virtually no traffic in Takae.[30] In due course the suit was dropped for thirteen of the protestors but was merely suspended against the two assumed to be "ringleaders." The court ordered the Okinawa Defense Bureau to enter out-of-court negotiations

**Figure 8.3.    Takae protest tent, July 2010.** *Source:* Satoko Oka Norimatsu.

with local residents to try to reach a settlement.[31] The ODB paid no attention to the court order, and the sit-in continued at the roadside tent. Early in 2012, the ODB tried to literally blast the protesters out of their way by resorting to seventy-five- to eighty-decibel bullhorns designed to test human tolerance levels. The protesters stuffed their ears and sat unmoved.[32]

Apart from the local abhorrence for the imposition of military priorities and war preparations on their peaceful natural environs, the villagers of Takae (and residents of all Okinawan areas in which the marines operate) are also deeply concerned over the type of aircraft the Pentagon has in mind for them. The CH-46 currently used by the marines is large and noisy, but unmistakably it is a helicopter in structure and function. From the earliest discussions over realignment of US forces in Okinawa, however, the United States made clear that it intended to replace the CH-46 with the MV-22 Osprey VTOL (vertical takeoff and landing) aircraft, which is not, strictly speaking, a helicopter at all but a medium-range, heavy-haul aircraft. Because it functions in flight as a fixed-wing aircraft, its flight path tends to be much wider than a helicopter, and it is capable, with refueling, of a range of 3,700 kilometers, around five times that of the CH-46. It is also sometimes known as the "widow maker" because of its propensity to crash.[33]

The Osprey question was regularly discussed during high-level joint meetings in Washington and Tokyo. It was mentioned in the draft version of the December 1996 SACO Final Report ("The SBF [Sea-based Facility] will be designed to support basing of helicopters and MV-22 (Osprey) units") although deleted in the final version.[34] A senior official of the Japanese Defense Agency, Takamizawa Nobushige, even sought US advice on how to handle questions about the Osprey, posing a "Q and A" set of questions, including kind of aircraft, noise levels, and traffic patterns. Takamizawa even provided the Japanese Defense Agency's own preferred answer: "The SBF is assumed as a relocation site of the helicopters currently deployed in MCAS [Marine Corps Air Station] Futenma. From this perspective, the SBF is a heliport."[35]

The projected deployment and operation of the Osprey both at Futenma (and the replacement to be built at Henoko) and at Takae thus had major implications for the levels of noise and risk that adjacent communities could expect to experience. Since the US side had desired "a release of this information soonest,"[36] it is clear that Tokyo, in denying in Diet interpellations and elsewhere that it had information on the matter[37] or insisting that no decision on it had been made, ensured that it would not be the subject of consideration during the environmental impact study. Calculating that Okinawans would not accept the Henoko (and Takae) projects if it meant bringing the MV-22 Osprey, as in the case of the *mitsuyaku*, the government repeatedly denied all knowledge of something about which it had full knowledge and in which it had keen interest, presumably because it wished to conceal it from the Japanese, and especially the Okinawan, people.

The Japanese Defense Agency (as it was then called) in 2006 explained to the residents in the vicinity of the Henoko site that helicopters from the projected base would adopt a trapezoidal flight pattern, avoiding settled areas in order to minimize noise nuisance, and on that basis the local residents and the city of Nago consented.[38] This proved to have been misleading, however, since the eventually adopted pattern was one in which US military flights were going to pass much closer than originally stated, in an elliptical rather than trapezoidal pattern, causing much greater noise disturbance than Nago people had been told to expect.

From May 2011, with Defense Secretary Gates stating that the United States intended to deploy the Osprey to Futenma (and Takae) starting October 2012, the government in Tokyo could no longer plead ignorance. On June 6, Okinawa Defense Bureau sent a cursory one-page fax to the governor of Okinawa and the heads of relevant city and town administrations, including Ginowan City, advising that the Osprey would be coming. Noise and nuisance effect would indeed be felt, and the explanation that had been given to local inhabitants and used as a basis for the environmental impact calculations no longer stood. The Kan government offered no explanation for abandoning the flight path supposedly designed to minimize noise and danger over residential areas around Henoko, and no explanation for suddenly recognizing that Henoko and Takae were to be unwilling hosts to the Osprey. Such irregularities occasioned minimal interest beyond Okinawa itself, reinforcing the Okinawan understanding that the prefecture was the subject of systematic discrimination on the part of mainlanders, especially the national government.

Governor Nakaima's initial response was to dismiss the notification of the Osprey deployment as a "pipe dream" (*esoragoto*), a decision akin to saying that Tokyo's Hibiya Park would be set aside for Ospreys.[39] But if so, it was a pipe dream from which there would be no happy awakening.

When the DPJ formed a government in September 2009, some of its senior figures appear to have become aware of the deception concerning the Osprey. At a meeting with Assistant Secretary of State Kurt Campbell in October, Foreign Minister Maehara Seiji expressed concern that

> U.S. plans to introduce MV-22 (Osprey) aircraft into Camp Schwab would also impact the acceptability of FRF [Futenma Replacement Facility] plans among local residents, due to noise concerns and the fact that the current environmental impact survey (EIS) did not include consideration of the deployment of MV-22 aircraft.[40]

Campbell's response was not recorded, but the concerns were quickly brushed aside by Japan's top defense official, Defense Policy Bureau Director General Takamizawa Nobushige, who contradicted the minister and assured Campbell, separately, that the environmental impact process in Japan did not require reference to aircraft that might in future use the facility.[41] Whether he advised Maehara of the high-level deception in relation to the Osprey that had been practiced by LDP governments since 1996 is not recorded. It was this same Mr. Takamizawa who advised the US government to "refrain from demonstrating flexibility" to the Hatoyama government, that is, to maintain pressure until it submitted. And it was he who in 1996 had sought US advice on how to handle questions about the Osprey.

Whether or not Takamizawa also assured Maehara, Maehara was evidently not convinced. Weeks later, on December 4, 2009, he told a press conference that if the Osprey were to be deployed a new environmental assessment process would become necessary.[42] Defense Minister Kitazawa was also concerned over the legality of the environmental assessment process, though in his case for a different reason: adoption of the US-favored V-shaped dual-runway structure rather than the single-runway I-shaped Japanese design. If that were done, according to Kitazawa in 2010, the environmental assessment study would have to be reopened and that, he added, would take up to three years.[43] A year later, however, Kitazawa submitted without quibble to American insistence and set about attempting to persuade Okinawan authorities to do likewise. Maehara too overcame his scruples on the Osprey.

By 2011, come what may, a positive and early conclusion to the EI process was a policy priority. The Kan government was well aware that with the inclusion of the Osprey, any reopening of the environmental process would be much more likely to result in a negative overall finding than the one carried out from 2007 to 2009.

In February 2012, a Naha district court, hearing the claim by six hundred Okinawan citizens that the EI process was flawed and should be reopened, summoned "Mister Takamizawa" to explain his apparent 1996 deception and to investigate the claim that the government of Japan had in 1996 deliberately withheld from the final SACO agreement (and from all subsequent procedures of the environmental and public consultation process) evidence that the facility to be constructed was designed for use by the Osprey. The case had explosive potential because of the possibility of the court accepting the plaintiffs' claim that the EI process was illegal and invalid. That would be tantamount to a judicial order for the reopening of the EI, and it would sound a death knell on the Henoko project since by 2012 it was clear that it could not withstand serious scientific investigation. Takamizawa in court merely argued that as of 1996 there had been no firm decision on the Osprey and so there was no deception, and he avoided any comment on the WikiLeaks-based questions.[44] However, his court appearance, though brief and revealing little, nevertheless drew attention, especially in Okinawa, to the dark processes that had surrounded the downfall of the Hatoyama government and to the ongoing structure of *mitsuyaku*—deception and deceit—at the heart of the US-Japan relationship.[45]

From the governor down, Okinawans were furious that the national government should be so insensitive to the plain, repeated, and unambiguous expressions of their wishes and aghast that the world's most dangerous airport and Japan's greatest wilderness forest were about to host what they saw as the world's most dangerous plane. Okinawa University's Sakurai Kunitoshi insisted that the Okinawan environmental impact assessment would have to be reopened to take into account the Osprey factor. Otherwise, he insisted, the government was acting illegally.[46] The prefectural assembly, as already noted, took the same view. Ginowan mayor Asato Takeshi and Higashi Village head Iju Morihisa both declared their opposition and insisted that the introduction of a major new factor, the Osprey, meant that the environmental assessment process would have to be reopened.[47] Furthermore, Okinawans pointed out that the question of deployment of the Osprey had been the subject of extensive environmental investigations in the United States lasting nine years, involving ten public hearings and the production of thousands of pages of documentation, and resulting in the elimination of thirteen of the proposed fifteen sites. For Japan to dispense with any environmental consideration was clearly to adopt a double standard. Defense Minister Kitazawa could only protest, hollowly, that different countries had different laws.[48]

The unprecedented confrontation between national and prefectural governments, complicated by the challenges to the legality of the government of Japan's procedures, boded ill for the US-Japan relationship as it faced in 2012 the sixtieth anniversary of the San Francisco Treaty system that provided the basis of the subsequent US-Japan relationship and the fortieth anniversary of Okinawa's reversion to Japan.

## CRIME, ACCIDENTS, NUISANCE, NOISE

From the crash of a fighter jet into Miyamori Primary School in June 1959 (killing eleven schoolchildren and six local residents and injuring 156 children and fifty-four local residents) to the crash of a helicopter onto the campus of Okinawa International University in 2004, Okinawans have lived in insecurity, suffering unending nuisance and danger. The burden of accidents, crime, and general nuisance from virtually all of the US bases in Okinawa weigh heavily. In 2009, setting aside the 179 traffic accidents, there were 59 base-related accidents, ranging from forced landings of planes to oil waste leakages and forest fires, and 50 other criminal cases.[49]

Because the US under the Status of Forces Agreement exercises total control over its bases and their personnel, with extraterritorial jurisdiction on acts committed within the bases and semijudicial exemption on acts outside them under the secret agreement of 1953 noted earlier (see p. 62), many Okinawans doubt that nuclear and chemical weapons were really removed before reversion in 1972 and worry over what base ammunition bunkers might contain or what might be buried on or around the bases. Agent Orange and napalm are two substances of special concern. Large quantities of the former, the highly carcinogenic chemical warfare weapon used to devastate Vietnam's forests between 1962 and 1971, were stored in Okinawa; according to recent accounts given by former US servicemen, the drums occasionally broke open, and a large quantity of the substance was simply buried in a trench in the vicinity of the town of Chatan.[50] It may also have been used for weed control on or around bases, and the Yambaru jungle may have served as a testing site for later large-scale use in Southeast Asia.[51] As for napalm, whose production and use is forbidden under international law, two FA-18 Hornet fighter planes were photographed taking off from Kadena on August 31, 2011, with "improved" model napalm shells attached. An hour or so later, the planes returned, the weapons no longer attached. They had presumably been fired into adjacent waters or one or another of the Okinawan US firing ranges.[52]

From 1972 (reversion) to 2010, Okinawa experienced—even counting only those officially recorded—nearly 10,000 US military–related crimes and accidents, including 2,588 traffic accidents (recorded only from 1981), 1,545 military accidents (506 caused by military aircraft), and 5,705 crimes (10 percent of them serious ones such as murder, rape, robbery, and arson).[53]

Cooperation by base authorities in investigating crimes, handing over suspects, and so on is sporadic and often reluctant. Many crimes go unreported, and the rate of indictment for military-related crime is less than half that in Japan as a whole, where military privilege does not apply.[54] Violence against women and girls frequently occurs and arouses special anger. The 1995 rape attack by three US servicemen on a twelve-year-old schoolgirl is simply the most horrific of many crimes of violence.

Noise is a serious social and health problem. The US Air Force occupies around 80 percent of the land of Kadena Town,[55] and its F-15s (one hundred of them permanently stationed and others often visiting) impose a particularly heavy noise burden on surrounding neighborhoods. Residents suffer sleeplessness and other health problems from the 110- to 120-decibel blasts of aircraft engines. Japan's high court on two occasions, in 1982 and 2000, rejected the call for a flight ban, saying it was a third-party (US military) operation beyond the control of the Japanese government.[56] Despite promises from the two governments concerned that they were doing everything to "lessen" the burden of the bases, incidents of late night or early morning base-generated noise nuisance (in excess of seventy decibels) rose steadily. The number of plaintiffs was around one thousand for the first suit and over five thousand for the second, described then as a "mammoth suit."[57]

In April 2011, some 22,000 residents in the vicinity of the base joined to launch a fresh suit against the government. This plaintiff group, the largest of any civil action in Japanese judicial history, included one in three of the residents of Kadena City. They demanded a nighttime flight ban and compensation for disturbed sleep, physical (hearing) disorders, and psychological disorders.[58]

To Takara Tetsumi, constitutional law specialist at the University of Ryukyus, such large-scale popular suits, based on the constitutional principle of the right to a peaceful existence, are comparable to the movement for Okinawan reversion to Japan prior to 1972. The Okinawan daily

*Ryukyu Shimpo* calls the current suit "a modern-day popular uprising."[59] What Okinawans are saying is that bases in themselves are incompatible with the life to which they feel they are constitutionally entitled. Among their basic rights is the right to sleep. Such actions have to be seen alongside the better-known actions to secure the return of Futenma or to block the construction of a new base at Henoko.

In this, as in other Okinawa-related matters, the government of Japan showed consistent will to prioritize the interests and demands of the Pentagon over those of its Okinawan citizens, a readiness to lie and conceal inconvenient facts, and a carelessness of its own environmental protection laws. Rather than allow informed, public, democratic debate, it sought desperately to satisfy the Pentagon by construction of a new marine base at Henoko and the string of airstrips, under the sobriquet of "helipads," through the Yambaru forest.

## NOTES

1. For details, see Citizens' Network for Biological Diversity in Okinawa, *Call for Your Attention and Action: Protect Yanbaru Forest and Local Community from Helipad Construction*, February 16, 2011, http://okinawabd.ti-da.net/e3264329 .html.

2. "Oura-wan ni 36 shinshu, ebi kani-rui, ken ni hozon hatarakikake e," *Ryukyu Shimpo*, November 25, 2009.

3. "Henoko ni shinshu? Kaiso 4 shu 'umetatereba zetsumetsu no osore," *Asahi Shimbun*, July 16, 2010 (English text: "4 new types of seaweed found at Henoko," *Peace Philosophy Centre*, July 19, 2010, http://peacephilosophy.blogspot .com/2010/07/4-new-types-of-seaweed-found-at-henoko.html).

4. Tomoyuki Yamamoto, "Conservationists Say Futenma Move Threatens Rich Marine Life," *Asahi Shimbun*, September 30, 2010.

5. "'Iho' to 344 nin teiso Futenma asesu yarinaoshi sosho," *Ryukyu Shimpo*, August 20, 2009.

6. Kikuno and Norimatsu, "Henoko, Okinawa."

7. "Gates Hopes for Japan-US Base Progress in Months," Agence France Presse, February 16, 2011.

8. Gavan McCormack, Sakurai Kunitoshi, and Urashima Etsuko, "Okinawa, New Year 2012: Tokyo's Year End Surprise Attack," *Asia-Pacific Journal: Japan Focus* (January 7, 2012), http://japanfocus.org/-Urashima-Etsuko/3673. (This followed an earlier, similarly unanimous resolution on June 14, 2011, calling on Tokyo and Washington to cancel the Henoko plan, saying it "goes against the effort to eliminate dangers" at Futenma and accusing Tokyo of "ignoring human rights and lives of Okinawa locals.")

9. "Chiji boeisho kaidan, daijin wa Beikoku no goyokiki ka," editorial, *Ryukyu Shimpo*, October 18, 2011.

10. Miyagi, "Unacceptable and Unendurable."

11. "'Yakusoku tsuranuku' Nago shicho, senkyo koyaku age Henoko isetsu hantai, gaisho to kaidan," *Ryukyu Shimpo*, October 19, 2011.

12. "Hyokasho nennai teishutsu to dentatsu Henoko asesu de boeisho," *Ryukyu Shimpo*, October 18, 2011.

13. "Henoko hantai de mo asesu shinko, boeisho," *Okinawa Taimusu*, October 22, 2011.

14. Shimazu Yasuo, chairman of the Japan Society for Impact Assessment, quoted in Sakurai Kunitoshi, "Japan's Illegal Environmental Impact Assessment of the Henoko Base," *Asia-Pacific Journal: Japan Focus* (February 27, 2012), http://japanfocus.org/-John-Junkerman/3701.

15. Sakurai, "Japan's Illegal Environmental Impact Assessment."

16. Sakurai Kunitoshi, "Ronsho ketsujo surikae mo—tayosei nen ni towareru shinka," *Ryukyu Shimpo*, August 23, 2010; Sakurai Kunitoshi, "Nokoso! subarashii okinawa no shizen o mirai sedai ni," in *Shinpojiumu: Okinawa no seibutsu tayosei no genjo to kadai* (Naha: Okinawa University Institute of Regional Studies, 2010), 55–67.

17. Sakurai, "Ronsho ketsujo."

18. "Notes on Okinawa Defense Bureau's Sneaky Delivery of EIA," *Okinawa Outreach*, January 3, 2012.

19. "Okinawa Finds Gov't. Report on US Base Relocation Problematic," *Mainichi Daily News*, February 1, 2012.

20. Quoted in Sakurai Kunitoshi, "The Henoko Assessment Does Not Pass," *Asia-Pacific Journal: Japan Focus* (March 5, 2012), http://japanfocus.org/events/view/131.

21. "Asesu chiji iken, Henoko no wa fukagyakuteki da," *Ryukyu Shimpo*, February 21, 2012.

22. Sakurai, "Japan's Illegal Environmental Impact Assessment."

23. World Wildlife Fund, Japan, "Futenma hikojo daitai shisetsu jigyo ni kakawaru kankyo eikyo hyoka junbisho ni taisuru ikensho," May 13, 2009, http://www.wwf.or.jp/activities/2009/05/611813.html; Urashima Etsuko, "Okinawa Yanbaru, kaze no tayori (10) ikusa yo wa tsuzuku," *Impaction* 170 (August 2009): 137.

24. Sakurai Kunitoshi, "The Guam Treaty as a Modern 'Disposal' of Ryukyus," *Asia-Pacific Journal: Japan Focus* (September 21, 2009), http://japanfocus.org/-Sakurai-Kunitoshi/3223.

25. Hideki Yoshikawa, "Dugong Swimming in Uncharted Waters: US Judicial Intervention to Protect Okinawa's "Natural Monuments" and Halt Base Construction," *Asia-Pacific Journal: Japan Focus* (February 7, 2009), http://www.japanfocus.org/-Hideki-YOSHIKAWA/3044.

26. "Racism Panel Asked to Review Futenma Plan," *Japan Times*, February 14, 2012; "Zainichi Beigun saihen: Futenma isetsu wa 'joyaju ihan' 'jinken' de Nichibei yusaburi kokuren sanka NGO, heisoku dakai no kokoromi," *Mainichi Shimbun*, February 12, 2012.

27. "Asesu gyosha ni boeisho OB ga amakudari," *Okinawa Taimusu*, January 24, 2012; "Fukakai asesu kokkai no ba de jijitsu kyumei o," *Okinawa Taimusu*, January 26, 2012.

28. Okinawa Prefecture, "Beigun no shisetsu betsu jokyo." http://www.pref.okinawa.jp/kititaisaku/8kaiheitai.pdf.

29. See architect Makishi Yoshikazu's analysis of the connection between Henoko and Takae through deployment and operation of the p MV-22 Osprey. http://www.ryukyu.ne.jp/~maxi/sub6.html.

30. Mark Driscoll, "When Pentagon 'Kill Machines' Came to an Okinawan Paradise," *Counterpunch*, November 2, 2010.

31. Citizens' Network for Biological Diversity in Okinawa, *Call for Your Attention and Action: Protect Yanbaru Forest and Local Community from Helipad Construction*, February 16, 2011, http://okinawabd.ti-da.net/e3264329.html.

32. "Heripaddo hantai jumin ni daionryo kakuseiki," *Okinawa Taimusu*, January 26, 2012.

33. For a table of Osprey-related accidents up to and including that of April 2010 that took four lives in Afghanistan, see "Osupurei dentatsu nihon seifu, oikomare shisei tenkan," *Ryukyu Shimpo*, June 7, 2011.

34. See "SACO Process, October 1996," and "SACO Process, November 1996," University of the Ryukyus Repository, http://ir.lib.u-ryukyu.ac.jp/bitstream/123456789/6967/19/gabe2_09.pdf.

35. Lt. R. Y. Jelescheff, US Navy, to Commander of Marine Corps and US Embassy, etc., November 27, 1996, University of the Ryukyus Repository, p. 449, http://ir.lib.u-ryukyu.ac.jp/bitstream/123456789/6967/19/gabe2_09.pdf.

36. "SACO Process, October 1996."

37. Nukaga Fukushiro, head of the (then) Defense Agency, responding to a question in the Diet on April 18, 2006. See Makishi Yoshikazu, "Kakusareta Osupurei haibi," *Okinawa Taimusu*, July 25–27, 2011.

38. "Menboku yusen, jimoto hairyo nashi Henoko hiko keiro," *Ryukyu Shimpo*, August 24, 2010.

39. "'Esoragoto da' Chiji, Henoko hoshin ni fukai kan," *Okinawa Taimusu*, June 13, 2011.

40. Roos, Cable 09TOKYO2369, "Managing Alliance Issues: A/S Campbell's," October 15, 2009, *WikiLeaks*. http://wikileaks.ch/cable/2009/10/09TOKYO2369.html.

41. Quoted in ibid.

42. Makishi, "Kakusareta Osupurei haibi," July 27, 2011.

43. "Nihongawa ruto kyohi—Henoko hiko keiro," *Ryukyu Shimpo*, August 25, 2010.

44. "Henoko asesu sosho shonin jinmon, boeisho no Takamizawa shi, gutaiteki kaito sakeru," *Ryukyu Shimpo*, March 5, 2012.

45. Ryukyu Asahi Broadcasting, "Q Ripoto, kankyo asesu to osupurei," December 14, 2011.

46. "Osupurei haibi nara, Henoko asesu yarinaoshi o," *Ryukyu Shimpo*, June 8, 2011.

47. "Osupurei haibi: kankei shucho ra issei hanpatsu," *Okinawa Taimusu*, June 10, 2011.

48. "Osupurei haibi: Bei hondo to niju kijun," *Okinawa Taimusu*, June 9, 2011.

49. Takayuki Maeda, "Okinawa Says No," *Okinawa Taimusu*, April 27, 2011.

50. Mitchell, "US Military Defoliants."

51. Jon Mitchell, "Agent Orange Revelations Raise Futenma Stakes," *Japan Times*, October 18, 2011.

52. "FA18, Napamu dan kairyo gata o tosai 2ki ga Kadena kara hiko," *Ryukyu Shimpo*, September 1, 2011.

53. Okinawa Prefectural Government Military Affairs Division, "US Military Base Issues in Okinawa," 12-15. http://www3.pref.okinawa.jp/site/contents/attach/24600/2011.6%20Eng.pdf

54. Takahashi Tetsuro, Okinawa Beigun kichi deta bukku (Okinawa tanken sha, 2011), 38.

55. "Kadena bakuon sosho—kuni no iinogare yurusarenu," *Ryukyu Shimpo*, April 28, 2011.

56. "Kokunai saidai genkoku 2man cho—Kadena bakuon 3ji sosho, 2ji no 4bai," *Ryukyu Shimpo*, January 1, 2011, and "Genkoku 2man cho gendai no minshu hoki da hiko sashitome ni fumikome," *Ryukyu Shimpo*, January 3, 2011.

57. Ibid.; "So-on gekika no itto, kichi no kujo, kako saita 189 ken," *Ryukyu Shimpo*, June 12, 2011.

58. "22,000 File Suit over Kadena Night Flights," *Japan Times*, April 29, 2011; "Kokunai saidai," *Ryukyu Shimpo*, January 1, 2011.

59. "Kokunai saidai"; "Genkoku 2man cho gendai no minshu hoki da hiko sashitome ni fumikome," *Ryukyu Shimpo*, January 3, 2011.

# 9

⁓

# "Deepening" the Alliance
## The Kan Agenda

When Kan Naoto took the reins of government in early June 2010, the national media defined his key task as being to heal the "wounds" that Hatoyama had caused to the alliance, restore Washington's trust and confidence in Japan, and resolve the Okinawa problem by "persuading" Okinawa to accept the new base. Kan's first act as prime minister was to telephone President Obama to assure him he would do what was required. When in his introductory policy speech to the Diet he pledged the "steady deepening of the alliance relationship," that was what he meant.

Like Hatoyama, Kan found that the deepening process was not easy. It proved impossible to agree on the terms of a joint statement on how the alliance would be deepened for the "golden anniversary" year of 2010. It also proved impossible to agree on the details of implementation of the May agreement on Henoko. Both sides, while maintaining the façade of proceeding toward implementation, stepped back from the agreement, each blaming the other, while looking fearfully forward to the late November Okinawan gubernatorial election, a democratic decision that weighed heavily on both. Both feared a democratic intervention—rejection by the Okinawan people.

In the interim, when Kan defended his party leadership (and the prime ministership) in a September 14 contest with challenger Ozawa Ichiro (see chapter 6 for more on Ozawa), Futenma was a major issue. Both Kan and Ozawa stressed the importance of the US relationship and were at pains to avoid anything that might be construed as serious doubt about the alliance. Kan insisted the May international agreement had to be honored (and therefore the Henoko base constructed) and accused Ozawa of causing "confusion" by wanting to revisit it.[1] But he also declared that he would "not make a decision over the heads of local residents,"[2] even saying, "I am fully aware that the agreement is unacceptable for the Okinawan people."[3] Ozawa, who earlier had been silent on the Okinawan base issue save an enigmatic rhetorical question late in 2009 ("Is it permissible to bury that beautiful, blue sea?"), struck a similarly ambiguous note, saying that the agreement had to be revisited because "we cannot carry out the current plan as it is due to opposition from Okinawa residents." He admitted, however, that he had no clear idea of how to revisit it.

Ambiguity was the keynote for both. They would do what the agreement with the US required to be done, but they would not do it forcibly. This could only mean that it would not be done at all under either, though neither had the courage to say so.

Kan was, however, the clear US favorite. Having reversed his predecessor's policies in an attempt to bring Japan back to unequivocal support for the US relationship and for the neoliberal policies that went with it, his efforts were rewarded by the restoration of Washington's confidence. By contrast, Ozawa's view of the security relationship with the United States tended to fill Washington with foreboding, as when he reiterated his controversial 2009 position that the US Seventh Fleet home based at Yokosuka should be sufficient for any Western Pacific security purpose, in which case not only Futenma but all other bases would presumably be returned to Japan (and Okinawa) as redundant. Washington's "Japan handlers" could not tolerate this. They were presumably also less than happy when Ozawa made an offhanded comment that he "liked" Americans though he found them *tansaibo*, or "unicellular," a gentle way of saying "rather stupid."[4] When Ozawa took five planeloads of Japanese parliamentary and business leaders on a mission to Beijing shortly after the DPJ took office in 2009, Richard Armitage scathingly referred to "the Japanese People's Liberation Army descending on Beijing."[5]

Neither Kan nor Ozawa, however, could openly admit that the series of agreements between the two countries on the Henoko construction dating back to 1996 no longer made sense. Not only was it impossible to impose an unwanted base (or bases, if the Takae sites were included) on Okinawa, but the idea that the marines played a crucial "deterrent" role, such that the peace and prosperity of East Asia somehow depended on them, when many of them were actually absent fighting wars in Iraq and Afghanistan, made little sense. The Pentagon itself had decided to build its core marine concentration for the Western Pacific and East Asia on Guam.

Ozawa is undoubtedly a paradoxical figure, but over the past decade he has seemed to be the one political leader in Japan who grasped the ignominy of clientelism and the urgency of renegotiating the US relationship and forging closer regional links to balance it. It was this that gave offense to the elites of Tokyo and Washington, rather than the possible peccadillos rooted in Ozawa's career as the disciple of Japan's classic "old-style" interest-manipulating prime minister, Tanaka Kakuei. Washington's hostility to Ozawa was mirrored throughout almost the entirety of the Japanese national media. An Ozawa victory, likely to precipitate some return, possibly in a more focused and coordinated way, to the policy orientation articulated by Hatoyama in his early days, would have been intolerable to the elites of Tokyo and Washington. The media campaign against him gathered momentum, and Kan was in due course victorious.

Under Kan, however, agreement followed agreement, postponement followed postponement. The pattern of fourteen years continued. Neither side could admit that Okinawa's resistance constituted a brick wall they could neither ignore nor breach. The failure of the two governments over so many years to solve their "Okinawa problem" left both frustrated and increasingly at odds with each other. As the Kan government struggled vainly to find a way forward, the same magma of resentment that was constantly threatening to burst its Okinawan banks affected the US-Japan relationship as well. The two governments contested each other's interpretation of the agreements, breaching one or another section of them. What "deepened," in fact, was disagreement, bred of the long continuing series of agreements that were not, and could not, be implemented.

## HENOKO VERSUS GUAM

Despite the abjectness of the surrender, disagreement persisted over the details of the bargain: Guam and Henoko. In August 2010, Pentagon sources made an astonishing announcement: the government of Guam—a semicolonial US territory long burdened, like Okinawa, by the base presence—was reneging on a promise to repay approximately $435 million in credit advanced by the Japan Bank for International Cooperation, the official government finance institute, for Guam infrastructural development (water, sewerage, power), saying it could not afford repayment.[6] For such a breach of contract, it would seem that the government of Japan would be fully entitled to seek appropriate legal remedy from the government of the United States, but the planned JBIC loan was structured to "have the Japanese government cover" it if it went sour. To avoid a long delay in the transfer, the Japanese government was reported to have "not ruled out the possibility of shouldering the infrastructure-building costs," a move that would amount to a write-off of the sum on which Guam/the United States had announced the intention to renege.[7]

As for the original agreed date for transfer to Guam of US Marines, 2014, both saw this as impossible. The problems of infrastructure—water, power, and other necessities on the scale necessary for the massive Guam expansion envisaged by Pentagon plans—were formidable and the labor force inadequate. The earliest possible date for a transfer from Futenma to Guam would be 2017, and one Pentagon official told the *Yomiuri Shimbun* it might take until 2020, a delay of six years.[8] The Pentagon message was clear: it would take steps to meet its obligations only if Japan contributed more than the billions it had originally agreed to pay.

## HENOKO—FLIGHT PATH AND RUNWAY DESIGN

The difficulties surrounding the Henoko project were similarly sharp. Under the agreement that Hatoyama signed on May 28 and Kan then affirmed, the details of the new base construction were to be settled by the end of August, but by then only the most general outline had been settled—that the sea would be reclaimed. Beyond that, dispute deepened over the shape and detail of the new base ("V" or "I"), where exactly it would be built, mode of construction, flight path for its aircraft, and whether Japan's Self-Defense Forces could share its use. It was not until June 2011 that these matters were settled.[9]

As far as basic design was concerned, the United States insisted on the V-shaped design originally adopted in the 2006 Roadmap agreement (the "only viable way" according to Ambassador Roos),[10] while Japan preferred an I-shaped single-runway design. The two designs would be different in their impact on coral, sea grasses, and marine life, as well as in terms of noise levels and safety to settlements around the bay. The US-favored design would occupy 205 hectares, of which 160 hectares would be reclaimed from the sea, and the Japanese government's pre-ferred design would occupy 150 hectares, of which 120 hectares would be reclaimed from the sea.[11] The question of approach routes, on which the two governments were far apart, was not mentioned in the August report. Both plans outlined there were simply variants of a design to impose a huge military installation on Henoko and Oura Bay. Whether the single-runway "I" design might take nine months longer, cost 3 percent less, and destroy 1.4 hectares less coral than the dual-runway "V" design (as stated in the report) was neither here nor there in that context.

The experts' report conveyed little sense of the fact that the two sides were at loggerheads on the what, the when, and the where, and almost none of the fundamental contradiction that either plan posed: that the majority of Okinawans were determined not to allow any base to be built. Foreign Minister Okada continued to hold to the view that "what is important is to gain the understanding of Okinawans—without it, we cannot move forward,"[12] even though it was plain that the prefecture had accomplished an unprecedented consensus to say no to the project in whatever variant it was offered and that the fury at the Japanese government for consistently ignoring its sentiment was widespread. The mayor of Nago insisted no base would ever be build in his city, on land or sea, and the Prefectural Assembly had passed a unanimous resolution on July 9 demanding that the May 28 agreement be cancelled.[13]

## HENOKO—TO SHARE?

Aside from the many other problems and disputes that plagued the Henoko project, the two governments were also at odds over a Japanese request to have its Self-Defense Forces share the projected Henoko facilities. This the US government and the Marine Corps absolutely refused, pointing out that the May 28 agreement merely stipulated "increase opportunities for joint use." While to the Japanese side that meant joint operational usage, to the US side it meant an occasional permit for SDF to undertake weekend training camps or their equivalent.[14]

These differences over the details of the project were wrangles that the *Ryukyu Shimpo* saw as exposing the "unchanged character" of the two governments—both ready to conceal or manipulate the truth in order to try to overcome the hostility of Okinawan society to their plans.[15]

## FROM PERSUASION TO COMPULSION

Following the clear expression of prefectural opinion in the November 2010 governor election, and with the prospect of a backroom deal to resolve matters gone, Prime Minister Kan seems to have felt he had no option but to resort to pressure to compel compliance. His government had already tightened the screws on Nago City for its refusal to permit the Okinawa Defense Bureau to conduct a further assessment of the Henoko site by suspending the part of its budget known as the "realignment subsidy" (1.6 billion yen, or approximately 20 million US dollars), as the "realignment subsidy" is provided with the condition that the base construction plan progresses as planned. On December 22, at a predawn hour when it must have expected the people's defenses might be low, Kan's government launched an assault at what it presumed was one of the weakest points of the Okinawan resistance movement, the Takae tent sit-in deep in the forest. One hundred members of the Okinawa Defense Bureau (ODB) charged past the protesters' tent into the site to restart construction. The next night, a US helicopter hovering just fifteen meters above the sit-in tent blew it down in an apparently deliberate act of intimidation. Residents, accompanied by Okinawan members of the Diet and Prefectural Assembly, protested to the ODB over the assault but were told only that the US military had not confirmed any such incident. And in January work began on construction of a wall to replace the existing barbed-wire fence barrier separating the fishing port of Henoko from the Camp Schwab (Henoko) base construction site. Protesters looked on in horror as a phalanx of tanks appeared across the fence from them early in January (see figure 9.1).[16] In late January, moreover, the Ministry of Defense stepped up the pressure by filing a complaint against Nago City for its refusal to allow the preliminary survey works at Henoko.[17]

While steadily building pressure against the geographically peripheral but politically central Takae and Nago, the Kan government also threatened Governor Nakaima, and through him the Okinawan people, by intimating that unless Okinawa surrendered, the dangerous and disruptive Futenma marine base would remain indefinitely. When Cabinet Secretary Sengoku Yoshito told a Tokyo press conference that Okinawans would have to "grin and bear" (*kanju*) the new base, public outrage forced him to withdraw his words. In December 2010, Prime Minister Kan flew into Okinawa and expressed his "unbearable shame as a Japanese" at the way the prefecture had been treated only to go on to say that relocation of

**Figure 9.1.   Tanks on Henoko Beach, October 2010.** *Source:* Conference Opposing Heliport Construction.

the Futenma base to Henoko "may not be the best choice for the people of Okinawa but in practical terms it is the better choice."[18] Governor Nakaima countered that the prime minister had got it wrong and that any relocation within the prefecture would be "bad."[19]

So apparently fearful was the prime minister of the reception he could expect from Okinawans that on this December visit, he met no one but the governor. Avoiding even the members of his own party, he presented a forlorn spectacle, surveying his rebellious prefecture from the safety of an SDF helicopter (see figure 9.2). It is hard to think of any prime minister in modern times received with such unconcealed hostility in any part of Japan.

Days later, Foreign Minister Maehara Seiji followed Kan to Okinawa. When he offered to address the dangers posed by the Futenma base by saying that he would relocate the schools and hospitals of the densely populated Ginowan, local people were incredulous. It signalled to them that the government of Japan gave preference to serving US interests even to the point of removing the people of Ginowan City and their social institutions from the base surrounds rather than remove the base that eroded and threatened their city. Governor Nakaima denounced as "the utmost degeneracy" any suggestion that Futenma air base might become permanent. "The basic problem," he said, "is to advance by even one day the removal of the dangers of Futenma, and it is turning things upside

**Figure 9.2.** Prime Minister Kan inspecting Henoko from the air, December 2010. *Source:* Kyodo News.

down to start extrapolating from the assumption that it is going to be permanent."[20]

One immediate consequence of Japan's "March 11" catastrophe was the shift of the attention of the nation almost exclusively to the northeast and therefore away from Okinawa. Had it occurred even a single day later, Kan might have already resigned, since on that very morning he had been forced to admit to receiving illegal campaign funding (an offense for which Foreign Minister Maehara had resigned only weeks earlier). The disaster that struck that same afternoon, however, relieved him from pressure to follow Maehara, while of course it subjected him to the immense pressure of addressing the country's greatest peacetime disaster.

After March 11, any resolute action was impossible to expect from the Kan government. Its support levels fell steadily, from 60-plus percent in June 2010 to around 20 percent in the early months of 2011 and to 15.8 percent by August 2011, on the eve of Kan's resignation.[21]

## NOTES

1. On the Kan-Ozawa debate, see Kentaro Kawaguchi, Kiichi Kaneko, and Hiroshi Ito, "Futenma Relocation Plan Stuck between a Rock and a Hard Place," *Asahi Shimbun*, September 2, 2010.

2. Quoted in "Futenma Relocation Plan," editorial, *Asahi Shimbun*, August 4, 2010.

3. "Kan and Ozawa Lock Horns on Key Policy Issues," *Asahi Shimbun*, September 4, 2010.

4. "Americans 'Simple-Minded,'" *Japan Times*, August 26, 2010.

5. Center for Strategic and International Studies, "The Japan-U.S. Alliance at Fifty—Where We Have Been; Where We Are Heading," in Pacific Forum CSIS Conference: The Japan-U.S. Alliance at Fifty (Washington, DC, January 15, 2010).

6. "Guamu iten hiyo, keikaku to mo muri ga aru," editorial, *Ryukyu Shimpo*, August 29, 2010.

7. "As a long delay in the transfer could adversely affect the bilateral alliance, the Japanese government has not ruled out the possibility of shouldering the infrastructure-building costs." "US Says It Can't Repay Japan Loan to Build Infrastructures in Guam," Associated Press, August 27, 2010.

8. "Zai Okinawa Bei kaiheitai iten sokushin e 'Futenma' no zenshin o," editorial, *Yomiuri Shimbun*, August 4, 2010.

9. "Henoko Futenma daitai hiko keiro wa 'daen' Bei shucho ukeire," *Ryukyu Shimpo*, June 17, 2011.

10. "[Meiso 'Futenma']/Bei no tankan tomadou seifu/hiko keiro no henko yokyu/Guamu iten enki kenen," *Okinawa Taimusu*, August 25, 2010.

11. US Department of Defense, "Futenma Replacement Facility Bilateral Experts Study Group Report" (August 31, 2010), at http://www.defense.gov/news/d20100831Futenma.pdf.

12. Quoted in Masami Ito, "Futenma Replacement Report Leaves Runway Question Open," *Japan Times*, September 1, 2010.

13. Inamine Susumu, "Yokoso shicho shitsu e shunin no aisatsu," Nago City Office website, http://www.city.nago.okinawa.jp/4/3647.html; "Kengikai, Nichibei kyodo seimei minaoshi motome ketsugi giin futari ga taiseki," *Ryukyu Shimpo*, July 9, 2010. (English version in "Okinawa's Prefectural Assembly Calls for Revision of Japan-U.S. Agreement to Build a New Base in Okinawa," *Peace Philosophy Centre*, July 9, 2010, http://peacephilosophy.blogspot.com/2010/07/okinawas-prefectural-assembly-calls-for.html.)

14. "Henoko ni jieitai jochu Futenma daitai shisetsu," *Ryukyu Shimpo*, August 26, 2010.

15. "Henoko hiko keiro de tairitsu Nihon, hanpatsu osore 'inpei,'" *Ryukyu Shimpo*, August 25, 2010.

16. See Gavan McCormack, Satoko Norimatsu, and Mark Selden, "Okinawa and the Future of East Asia," *Asia-Pacific Journal: Japan Focus* 9, no. 2 (2011), http://japanfocus.org/-Satoko-NORIMATSU2/3468.

17. "Boeisho, Nago shi ni igi moshitate Futenma isetsu genkyo chosa kyohi de," *Ryukyu Shimpo*, January 29, 2011.

18. "Kan shusho—Nakaima chiji kaidan yaritori (yoshi)," *Ryukyu Shimpo*, December 18, 2011.

19. "Kennai wa 'Zenbu baddo' Nakaima chiji, kengai koyaku kenji o kyocho," *Ryukyu Shimpo*, December 18, 2011.

20. "Kengai isetsu e jikko keikaku chiji, nendo nai nimo sakusei Futenma hikojo shuhen itenron o hihan," *Okinawa Taimusu*, December 29, 2010.

21. "Cabinet Polls at New Record Low of 15.8%," *Japan Times*, August 22, 2011. (Under Hatoyama, support had similarly collapsed, from 70-plus percent in September 2009 to around 20 percent in May 2010.)

# 10

___

# "Deepening" the Alliance
## Washington Agendas

Washington's long-term agenda, in accord with the recommendations of Joseph Nye and his colleagues a decade and a half ago, has been to "deepen" the alliance relationship with Japan so as to tie it more tightly to Washington and enhance military coordination between the Japanese Self-Defense Forces and US forces. "Interoperability" has been a key Pentagon-ese word. Under the Obama era reforms (see the Security Consultative Committee document "Progress on the Realignment of U.S. Forces in Japan" issued on June 21, 2011), the US Army Command and Control and the Japan Ground Self Defense Forces have further coordinated command and control capabilities at Camp Zama, and the Bilateral Joint Operations Coordination Center (BJOCC) was going to commence its operation by the end of JFY 2011 at Yokota Air Base, thereby "strengthening bilateral command and control operation." At Yokosuka, home port of the US Seventh Fleet, the Maritime SDF is already essentially a part of the US Navy. However, for that to be matched by full incorporation of Japan's 240,000-strong military forces into the US global force projection capability so that the two can actually stand, fight, and, if need be, die side by side, constitutional revision or reinterpretation is still necessary.

Under such circumstances, it is far-fetched to suggest that Japan retains autonomy of "defense" planning and policy. A more apt description would be that Japan was steadily furthering its client-state agenda by submitting its 240,000-strong military to Pentagon direction. As Defense Secretary Gates began to speak of an end to US land forces' involvement in distant wars, the advantages of substituting Japanese for American forces in regional (or perhaps global) interventions must seem attractive in Washington. One influential academic commentator calls for a shift in US policy under which it should support the eventual elimination of stand-alone military bases in Japan for American forces in favor of maintaining the American military presence in Japan on bases of the Japanese Self Defense Forces. Such a sharing arrangement is the best way to ensure the political viability of an American military presence in Japan.[1] The Hatoyama interregnum was, of course, a Washington nightmare, threatening the unraveling of Washington's East Asian design, even though, as we now know—thanks in part to WikiLeaks—Hatoyama was more a dilettante than a serious, much less a radical, politician. Still, when he passed from the scene in June 2010 and the Kan government took over, Washington breathed a collective sigh of relief that its agenda was back on course. At Kan's meeting with Obama in New York in late September 2010, the two sides reaffirmed the importance of the alliance and agreed on the need for "deepening" it through global security economic, cultural, and human exchange dimensions. Kan also made sure with Obama that the United States would be included in any East Asian Community such as Hatoyama had proposed.

On December 17, 2010, the Japanese cabinet approved the new "National Defense Program Guidelines," which identified the threat of the military modernization of China as part of the "security environment surrounding Japan" and called for enhancing existing security links with the United States, proposed a "dynamic defense force" to substitute for the existing "basic defense force" concept, and outlined the plan to substantially reinforce the Self-Defense Force presence in the outlying Okinawan islands in the East China Sea (Ishigaki, Miyako, and Yonaguni).[2] Adding "China threat" to the existing "North Korea threat" helped advance a security agenda that had been unthinkable under previous, LDP governments.

Military critic Maeda Tetsuo read the 2010 Defense Guidelines as the agenda of a renascent military great power, free from the restraints of the constitution's "peace" clause (Article 9), which would, in effect, be revised or cancelled,[3] and as a contradiction of the Democratic Party's own defense principles. He wrote:

> The substitution of "dynamic defense force" for "basic defense force" means in effect abandonment of exclusive defense and transformation (of the defense forces) to a "fighting SDF."[4]

During the crisis that followed the March 11 Fukushima catastrophe, the link between events in the northeast and questions of alliance and defense policy was provided by the dispatch of marines, including those from Futenma, to assist in relief operations. Kan's government made much of the US forces' relief operations, called "Operation Tomodachi" (Tomodachi meaning "friend"), and mainland Japan was receptive to the claim that the quick and substantial US response demonstrated the true worth of the "alliance" and therefore justification for proceeding with the Okinawa base plans. As the *Yomiuri* put it, "the relief efforts reflect mutual trust both countries have forged over many years."[5]

Operation Tomodachi involved nineteen US Navy warships (including the nuclear aircraft carrier *Ronald Reagan*), 140 aircraft (including Marine Corps helicopters from Futenma), over 18,000 soldiers,[6] and emergency supplies, including 500,000 gallons of fresh water for cooling the Fukushima reactors.[7] US forces played a conspicuous role in helping restore infrastructure such as Sendai Airport and in searching for bodies of victims in Ishinomaki City and elsewhere. The scale of the operation greatly overshadowed that provided by all other nations, and a Marine Corps spokesman referred to it as exemplifying the "oxygen" that the United States provided for its allies.[8]

## TWO PLUS TWO, 2011

Security, however, was never far from the top of official minds on both sides. A security deal was struck in late June, confirmed over the signatures of the foreign and defense ministers of the two countries and therefore known as the "Two plus Two" agreement.[9] Titled "Toward a Deeper and Broader U.S.-Japan Alliance: Building on 50 Years of Partnership," it was designed to mend and reinforce the bilateral relationship from the prolonged tensions and conflicts over the proposed relocation of Marine Corps Air Station Futenma.

Much of the statement simply confirmed well-established principles: "shared values, democratic ideals, common interests," the US commitment to "the defense of Japan and the peace and security of the region, including the full range of U.S. military capabilities, both nuclear and conventional," and the Japanese commitment to continue providing the facilities and areas necessary for US use and paying the major necessary costs. Beyond the rhetoric and the general principles, however, were several significant new commitments and steps toward widening the geographic scope and deepening the process into full-force integration.

Common strategic objectives included for the first time the strengthening of trilateral defense cooperation with Australia and South Korea; the encouragement of a "responsible and constructive role" by China and of "constructive engagement" in the region by Russia; the welcoming of India "as a strong and enduring Asia-Pacific partner" and of "trilateral dialogue" between it, the United States, and Japan; and the strengthening of US-Japan cooperation in humanitarian and peacekeeping operations, disaster prevention and relief, space, and cyberspace. The problematic Futenma Replacement Facility would proceed, the four ministers agreed, at the Camp Schwab Henoko area and adjacent waters, with reclamation the primary method to construct two 1,800-meter runways in a "V" plan, by "the earliest possible date after 2014" (thereby abandoning the 2014 target date set in 2006); the relocation of "approximately 8,000 III MEF personnel and their approximately 9,000 dependents from Okinawa to Guam" would proceed. Reiteration, of course, carried no guarantee of implementation and, as noted below, there was deep skepticism in Washington that it ever could or would be.

Three new commitments stood out: first, to "expanded bilateral access to US and Japanese facilities located in Japan . . . closer bilateral coordination, improved interoperability, and stronger relations with local communities"; second, to "establish a regional HA/DR [humanitarian assistance and disaster relief] logistics hub in Japan," on which the ministers agreed; and third, to construct a new Self-Defense Force base—that would incorporate a "permanent field carrier landing practice site" for the US forces on Mage Island (something that the Government of Japan would now "explain" to local authorities).[10]

Apart from reiteration of the commitment to do the impossible and construct the base that all Okinawa said would not be constructed, the government of Japan entered a series of fresh commitments. It would advance the process of merger of its military forces under US intelligence and command, and it would not only press ahead with the Henoko project, but it would construct *two* additional new military bases in the southwestern islands: one at Mage, which had been briefly considered in 2010 as a possibility for Futenma relocation, and the other (the disaster relief facility) at Shimoji, a small island with an existing 3,000-meter civil runway adjacent to Miyako Island. Of these designs, not only was resistance to the Henoko project already virtually total (and there had been no advance consultation with the localities concerned), but the June 2011 agreement and the idea of making Shimoji an international disaster relief center signalled new fronts of antibase struggle almost certain to open now at Mage and Miyako. Indeed, citizens of the Miyako region soon organized to prevent the Shimoji Island civil airport being turned to military ends.

The *Ryukyu Shimpo* commented editorially that the DPJ government, nominally democratic, had lost any claim to call itself so and was doing what in Okinawan language was known as "*iraranmii*" (choosing to proceed headlong deeper into a hopeless situation).[11] The "Two plus Two" agreement, it went on, was nothing but state violence run rampant and cut loose from democratic oversight. For a project with no prospect of implementation to be carried forward to the detailed engineering and design stage, it added, was "wasteful, insensitive, irresponsible."[12] Okinawa International University's Sato Manabu described it as "meaningless" and a "bad joke."[13] For the mayor of Nago, it was "nothing but intimidation."[14] For Governor Nakaima, it was "incomprehensible," and the suggestion that Okinawa had to choose between having Futenma become permanent and accepting the new Henoko base was "outrageous" (*tondemonai*).[15] The *Asahi* commented that Japan would undoubtedly "pay dearly for the result of this ministerial meeting."[16] Defense Secretary Gates followed the "Two plus Two" agreement with the statement that he expected "concrete steps" to follow within the space of a year. For the government of Japan, that was tantamount to a command.

## OMOIYARI—"CONSIDERATION" OF CLIENT FOR PATRON

While the terms of the reversion were such that the United States retained virtually all its military assets, pocketed a huge sum, and secured a secret agreement to reintroduce nuclear weapons if ever it felt the need, it also established the principle under which Japan would henceforth continue to pay to ensure that US forces not think of withdrawing.

No country matched Japan's generosity in encouraging US forces to continue occupying its prime real estate, allowing free use of roads and harbors, constructing for it barracks, officer housing, training facilities, schools, hospitals, sporting and leisure facilities, providing water, power, gas, and sewerage, and allowing live shell training over its highways and parachute jumps and night takeoff and landing exercises adjacent to its cities. It meant, for example, that Japanese taxpayers (as of 2008) were paying the wages of "76 bartenders, 48 vending machine operators, 47 golf club maintenance personnel, 25 club managers, 20 commercial artists, 9 leisure boat operators, 6 theatre directors, 5 cake decorators, 4 bowling alley clerks, 3 tour guides, and 1 animal caretaker."[17]

The principle that had underpinned the relationship between Japan and its former puppet state of Manchukuo in the period 1932–1945 would be applied to the US-Japan relationship as part of the post–Okinawa reversion redefinition of the relationship: that is, the occupied territory in the interests of "common defense" would pay the costs of its occupier, from 1932 in the case of Manchukuo, and from 1978—initially, as a "provisional, limited, temporary measure"—as Japan undertook to contribute toward the costs of the US base complex in Japan.

As a combination of "reverse rental" (by landlord to tenant) and comprehensive subsidy, the payments grew steadily, reaching over 275.6 billion yen in its peak year of 1999, forty-four times the initial 6.2 billion yen of 1978.[18] Commonly *omoiyari* meant only the "direct" payment, or "cost sharing for the stationing of US forces in Japan," as the Japanese government put it, but the overall sum was also inflated by indirect subsidies. In 2003 the US Department of Defense published a table showing Japan's contribution at $4.6 billion ($3.45 billion in direct and $1.15 billion in indirect payments), which was about five times as much as the next countries in the list of US allies' contributions (Germany and South Korea) and more than 60 percent of subsidies received from all countries in the world together.[19] For the US government, the Pentagon has not published any such table since then, but from the Japanese government's (Ministry of Defense) annual figures, the situation as of 2011 can be seen in table 10.1.

The Democratic Party promised in the lead-up to the 2009 election that once elected it would review the subsidy system (which was universally taken to mean reduce or eliminate it). Since Hatoyama's term of office coincided with the third year of the agreement that ran from 2008, and because his attention was focused so sharply on the question of Futenma replacement, the subsidy system remained unchanged. When Kan took over in June 2010, however, renegotiation became urgent because the ex-

**Table 10.1.   Government of Japan Subsidies for US Japan-Based Forces (2011) (in billion yen)**

| | |
|---|---|
| Expenditure for Basing of US Forces in Japan (Department of Defense Budget) | 359.7 |
| "Cost Sharing for the Stationing of US forces in Japan": so-called *omoiyari yosan* (Facility Improvement Program, salaries and benefits of base workers, utility fees, night landing practice) | 185.8 |
| Locality measures | 55.3 |
| Facilities rent | 93.4 |
| Relocation | 0.2 |
| Other (fisheries compensation, etc) | 25.1 |
| SACO-related (from 1996)[a] | 10.1 |
| "Reorganization" (from 2006)[b] | 116.1 |
| Departments other than Department of Defense (Base hosting localities subsidy, etc.) | 39.4 |
| Facilities rental | 165.8 |
| **Total** | **691.1 (approximately $8.6 billion, at US$1 = ¥80)** |

*Source*: Compiled from Boeisho, *Zainichi Beigun kankei keihi* (Heisei 23 nendo yosan), http://www.mod .go.jp/j/approach/zaibeigun/us_keihi/keihi.html.
[a] Implementation of measures included in the Special Action Committee on Okinawa Final Report of December 2, 1996 (the "Clinton-Hashimoto" agreement).
[b] Implementation of measures for the Realignment of US Forces in Japan in accordance with 2006 agreement, including funding for projected relocation of Marine Corps to Guam and for return of land south of Kadena Air base, etc.

isting agreement was close to expiring. Pressure was applied to ensure that Japan not reduce its payments. Wallace Gregson, Assistant Secretary of Defense for Asia and Pacific Security Affairs, submitted a statement to the House Armed Services Committee on July 27 in which he pointed out that host nation support (HNS) was "a strategic pillar of the [Japan-U.S.] alliance," that any reduction would signal both to allies and to potentially hostile countries alike that Japan was not serious about its defense, and therefore that HNS should be raised, not lowered.[20] Kan lost little time in promising that there would be no reduction. The only item reviewed was that for salaries of base-employed Japanese workers. The 23,055-strong workforce would be reduced (by 430) to 22,625.[21] Furthermore, by building into the agreement components for payment of SACO (starting in 1996) and "Reorganization of US Forces in Japan" (starting in 2006) bilateral agreements, the effect was to entrench a second and third *omoiyari* category, thereby much inflating the basic subsidy sum.

For a cash-strapped Pentagon, the sweetness of an annual subsidy of over $8 billion, along with other ancillary benefits, is immeasurable. Paradoxically, "peace constitution" Japan was the most generous and enthusiastic supporter of US wars, famously supporting the Gulf War with a $13 billion contribution and making similar, if smaller, contributions for subsequent wars down to the Hatoyama 2009 pledge of 500 billion yen (about $5.5 billion) over five years for civilian reconstruction works in Afghanistan. As noted in chapter 5, the cost to Japan of the "realignment" of US forces in Japan was in the multibillion dollar range. With Japan's public debt the highest of all countries in the OECD, and facing a huge bill for reconstruction following the Tohoku disaster of 2011, it is uncertain how much longer these sums can be shielded from public or parliamentary debate. Such generosity, coupled with virtual *carte blanche* on how the bases should be used, is unimaginable elsewhere in the world, and not surprisingly, the Pentagon is determined not to see the *omoiyari* and other payments reduced, much less ended.

It is impossible to be sure exactly how much in total Japan has paid to support the base system, but under the "Cost Sharing for the Stationing of US Forces in Japan" (*omoiyari*) program since its launch in 1978, Japan has paid around six trillion yen (approximately $75 billion).[22] The GAO puts a figure of $22 billion on the value of construction provided under the heading of "Japanese Facilities Improvement Program" between 1978 and 2010.[23] Where other countries "permitted" US bases, often extracting substantial sums for doing so, Japan paid handsomely, insisting that the United States continue, and not reduce, its occupation.

In the wake of Tohoku earthquake/tsunami and the positive attention that focused on the US troop role in Operation Tomodachi, public criticism of the *omoiyari* system ceased. The DPJ, which had voted against it when the arrangements were last confirmed in the Diet in 2008, agreed on March 31, 2011, to continue the payments with only minor adjustments for another five years. When the State Department's Japan section head, Kevin Maher, told an American student group late in 2010, "The high host nation support the Japanese government currently pays is beneficial to the US. We've got a *very good deal* in Japan" (italics added), it was this system he had in mind. The cost of the Tomodachi operation was estimated to be around $80 million,[24] but in the context of the subsidies Japan has been paying to the Pentagon for decades, this was a relatively trivial sum. With the Japanese pledge to maintain for the next five years the amount of *omoiyari* budget (at the 2010 level of 188.1 billion yen, over 2.3 billion dollars), which had been on the decrease in recent years, the United States may easily recoup the cost of the operation.

## "MASTERS OF MANIPULATION" AND "OPERATION TOMODACHI"

The contradictions of the US-Japan relationship were vividly encapsulated in two almost simultaneous events early in 2011: the revelations of the abusive, contemptuous, anti-Japanese and especially anti-Okinawan sentiments made explicit at the highest level of the US Department of State, and the carefully orchestrated campaign of "friendship" that was undertaken when the Tohoku disaster struck.

In December 2010 the Department of State's senior Japan specialist and therefore adviser on Japan to Hillary Clinton, Kevin Maher, met to brief a group of American University students on the eve of their visit to Japan. What he then said is contested, but according to the talk as reconstructed from the notes of the students who heard him, in an apparently relaxed mood Maher set aside diplomatic niceties and spoke his mind. He described Okinawans as lazy (too lazy even to grow goya, the Okinawan staple bitter melon) and as "masters of 'manipulation' and 'extortion' of Tokyo."[25] They also had "darker skin," were "shorter," and had an accent; they were "like Puerto Ricans."[26] Okinawans cared more than anything for money, so the base relocation could easily be accomplished, he said, if only the national government would tell the Governor of Okinawa, "If you want money, sign it." Japanese culture too was similarly contemptible, "based on consensus," by which is meant, he explained, "extortion," and "by pretending to seek consensus, people try to get as much money as possible."

Maher's comments, reported early in March 2011, hit Okinawa like a bombshell. The *Okinawa Taimusu* commented editorially that "those responsible for the Futenma base transfers seem, deep in their hearts, to despise Okinawa and make light of the base problem."[27] It added two days later,

The more one understands Okinawa's post-war history and the circumstances surrounding the base problem, the more one understands that the Henoko base construction plan is impossible and outrageous. The Japanese and US governments have exhausted all and every means to get an impossible project endorsed locally by dangling money in front of people.[28]

Okinawan anger at the insult would not be assuaged by perfunctory expressions from Washington of "Sorry."[29] *Ryukyu Shimpo* agreed. Maher had given, "unintentionally, a revelation of real US thinking,"[30] adding, days later,

At the heart of the Okinawa base problem is the structure of confrontation between the Okinawan people who are always protesting over the US-Japan security treaty and the US bases, and the governments of Japan and the US that are always striving to maintain and reinforce them. Throughout the post-war era the two governments have cleverly used policies of carrot and stick to divide Okinawan society and people and gain "free use of the bases" come what may.[31]

The uproar was such that Maher was quickly shunted aside from his post, but the apologies, by Assistant Secretary of State Kurt Campbell in Tokyo and Ambassador Roos in Okinawa, did indeed seem perfunctory. Maher was not dismissed, however, but merely retired, apparently with full honors. From the moment the earthquake struck on March 11, for both Washington and Tokyo, the Maher affair receded from attention. Indeed, his retirement was postponed to allow him to accept an appointment as a coordinator of US government disaster relief operations (Operation Tomodachi), working with Japanese and other governments and agencies. This appointment made clear that official Washington found nothing untoward in his remarks.

According to Maher's colleague, Michael Green, "Maher is a veteran Japan hand who knows the politics of Okinawa better than just about anyone."[32] The furthest that criticism of Maher went was to suggest that his comments showed a "lack of professionalism" and were "inane" and "shrill," even though he was "knowledgeable" and "speaks Japanese well."[33] The absence of regret on the one side and of anger on the other suggested that many in both capitals shared his contemptuous sentiments.

Maher's defense, not mounted until some weeks later, was blanket denial. He simply accused the students of lying, and in an interview (in Japanese, with the *Wall Street Journal* on April 14) of distorting their evi-

dence "in relation to the antibase movement."[34] He also insisted that he
was going to retire with his own will, but postponed it in order to do what
he could to assist when Japan was struck by disaster. His explanation was
disingenuous in not referring to him being removed from the position of
the director of Japan desk. For those who were ashamed or angered over
his anti-Okinawan diatribe his appointment to "Tomodachi" must have
been embarrassing, and to Okinawans, a slap in the face.

Although the US government, and especially the Pentagon, presented
the events as a demonstration of humanitarianism inspired by the closeness of the two countries, US self-interest alone dictated an urgent response. The disaster, quickly realized in Washington to be of a Chernobyl
scale, not only threatened to paralyze US regional and global military
capabilities but also threatened the Obama government's priority on
nuclear energy promotion as a key economic policy. However, the Pentagon also seized upon the disaster as offering opportunities: in public
relations terms, to soften the image of US forces in Japan (especially the
Okinawa-based marines) by the daily media focus on their bravery and
generosity; and to set a precedent for direct communication and cooperation between US forces and local government authorities—including
ports, highways, and airports—something US authorities were quick to
develop in months following the initial disaster.[35] Months later, the Two
plus Two Inter-Governmental Security Consultative Committee devoted
a special document to commemorating the Tomodachi cooperation as an
expression of the alliance relationship, something that "validated years of
bilateral training, exercises, and planning"—almost as if this had been the
purpose of the base presence.[36] The four ministers agreed that cooperation
would continue. It signalled a ratcheting up of moral pressure on Japan
to deliver on its base promises and a deepening of the engagement of
US forces in Japan at the local government level. Henceforth they would
participate in "disaster drills conducted by local authorities." Perhaps
of greatest military significance, however, the disaster provided Washington an opportunity to rehearse joint operations in a possible future
nuclear-contaminated battlefield.[37]

No exercise could have matched the conditions presented by the crisis
and meltdown. In the early hours of the crisis the *Ronald Reagan* was
ordered to retreat offshore as it and at least seventeen of its crew suffered from radiation exposure. From March 16, an 80-kilometer exclusion
zone was applied. Specialist units, such as the Marine Corps' 150-strong
Chemical Biological Incident Response Force (CBIRF), although rushed
to Japan from their US home bases, remained at Yokota Air Base in Tokyo for their three-week Japan visit without even visiting the disaster
zone.

Despite the highly publicized involvement of US forces, cooperation may have been more fitful and less to Washington's satisfaction than the media releases would have it. The White House was rebuffed when it sought to place its experts in the prime minister's office to supervise the disaster operations, and it threatened that unless Tokyo showed a more cooperative attitude, it might order the evacuation of all US nationals from the country. Far from the relationship being deepened, therefore, one Japanese expert (former parliamentary secretary of the Ministry of Defense and as of 2011 a member of the Diet's Lower House) remarked that there was a risk that the "Japan-US alliance could collapse."[38] In the multiple stresses of the catastrophe, and despite the substantial Pentagon satisfaction over securing a five-year extension of the Japanese subsidy payments, Japanese resentment came close to boiling over at its subordinate status and at the assumption on the part of the United States of the prerogative of overlord.

Overall, however, both Washington and Tokyo had cause for satisfaction at how well the cooperation played in the media in both countries, and both expected that it would help them overcome Okinawan resistance to their base reorganization plans. Defense Minister Kitazawa and Prime Minister Kan both went out of their way to praise Operation Tomodachi. Kitazawa, visiting the *Ronald Reagan* on April 4 especially to convey his thanks, saw it as evidence of the alliance's "deepening," and Kan wrote in the *Washington Post* on April 15 that "the attitude that Americans have displayed during this operation has deeply touched the hearts and minds of Japanese."[39]

For a coldly critical eye on these events, one must turn to the Okinawan media. On March 18, the *Ryukyu Shimpo* editorialized that "disaster relief is not a publicity stunt," adding that there should be no expectation of any payoff and that it was incomprehensible that the US operations should be headed by a man (Kevin Maher) who had just uttered the most egregious insults and slanders of Japan and especially Okinawa. No matter what rhetoric was used to dress up the operation, it insisted that Okinawa would not relent from its refusal to host any replacement for Futenma marine base.[40] Days later, the *Okinawa Taimusu* added that any suggestion that dispatch of the marines on a relief mission might be used to justify the Futenma marine base replacement would be an insult to the soldiers on the mission and akin to involving them in "robbery at the scene of a fire."[41]

National government officials in Tokyo hoped for some softening of Okinawan hostility to any Futenma replacement facility in the prefecture following the positive feedback that greeted the marines' Tomodachi operation. However, an April survey of Okinawa's forty-one heads of municipalities and villages found unanimous opposition to any Futenma substitution in Okinawa (i.e., the Henoko formula on which both Tokyo and Washington insisted). One, mayor of the island of Yonaguni, suggested the Futenma base be relocated to Tokyo.[42] Governor Nakaima continued to insist that construction of any new base in Okinawa would be extremely difficult.

As for Maher, upon his eventual, delayed retirement (April 6) from government, he almost immediately transferred, in the fashion that Japanese would describe as *amakudari*—floating down on a silken parachute from the public sector to a lucrative post in the private sector—to becoming a senior adviser and consultant (specialist on Japan) to a high-powered international consortium, with responsibility in particular for resolving the problem of disposal of the radioactive wastes.[43] The company he joined had been founded by Richard Lawless, who as a senior official had conducted the negotiations over the Futenma replacement in the 1990s and whose views on the alliance are discussed earlier. One month into his new job, in that capacity he was welcomed at the prime minister's residence for a ninety-minute meeting, a rare event for any private businessperson whose behavior the US government has issued high-level apologies, surely unprecedented.[44]

For the governments of the United States and Japan to pass over the abuse Maher had heaped on Japan, especially Okinawa, and the apologies that had been proffered and accepted for them in this way, was to expose the depths of contempt for Japan in official Washington and the corresponding depths of self-abnegation in official Tokyo. No sooner had the *Ronald Reagan* and other US forces been withdrawn from the disaster zone than US pressure to settle once and for all the long-frozen Futenma replacement issue resumed.

In August 2011, Maher published an apologia (in Japanese) in which he gave his account of the American University exchanges, repeating his denials and blaming Ambassador Roos for failing to support him (and thereby allowing the story to gain credibility).[45] He ruled out legal action to clear his name, however, dismissing it with the contemptuous comment, "Never enter a mud-fight with a pig. You'll both get dirty but the pig likes it."[46]

As it happened, however, at around the same time as the apologia, WikiLeaks released a secret dispatch Maher had written when consul general in Naha in 2007.[47] In June of that year, two US mine countermeasures ships, the USS *Guardian* and the USS *Patriot*, visited Sonai port in Yonaguni Island, Japan's westernmost point, located roughly one hundred kilometers from the coast of Taiwan, the first such military visit to an Okinawan civilian port since reversion. Maher reported with satisfaction that the "operationally significant" event set an important "precedent," which he urged be followed with a similar visit to Ishigaki island in the near future. He observed that Sonai port was deep enough to accommodate four "USN mine countermeasures ships" at one time, while its commercial airfield was close by and could be used by support helicopters "in the event of a contingency in the Taiwan Straits." The Pentagon use of the pretext of a port visit for "crew rest" to collect intelligence and advance a US design to militarize Japan's China frontier and embroil Japan in the China-Taiwan confrontation, here reported with enthusiasm by Maher, was, strictly speaking, both mendacious and duplicitous. Such terms aptly describe the treatment the governments of Japan and the United States have meted out to the Okinawan people for four decades.

## THE WEBB-LEVIN-MCCAIN SHOCK

While the Kan government girded its loins for a renewed assault on Henoko and Takae (the base complex and the helipads), official Washington confronted a soaring deficit, two (by some counts three or even four) failed, deadlocked, and prodigiously expensive wars, a rising China, and spreading social and economic crisis and political gridlock over the budget and social programs. Chairman of the Joint Chiefs of Staff Mike Mullen stated on June 4, 2010, that "our national debt is our biggest national security threat."[48] A nonpartisan congressional committee was set up in May 2010 to identify defense spending cuts. It was headed by Democrat Barney Frank and Republican Ron Paul. Frank had unambiguously stated, "We don't need marines in Okinawa. They're a hangover from a war that ended sixty-five years ago." He and Paul agreed that military spending had to be drastically cut and that one way to do it was by reducing US forces based overseas.[49] According to Republican Ron Paul, "It's time for Japan to assume all of its own responsibilities. What if China wanted a base in New York City? We'd be furious."[50] In these circumstances, a high-level congressional "razor gang" (the NCFRR, or National Commission on Fiscal Responsibility and Reform) examined commitments and sought areas in which to rein in expenditure, including reduction of US troops at bases in Europe and Asia by one-third and ending procurement of the MV-22 Osprey, which is projected to be deployed in Okinawa. The NCFRR's final report struck an uncompromising note: "No exceptions. We must end redundant, wasteful, and ineffective federal spending—including defense."[51]

In April 2011, the senate team of Carl Levin (chair of the Armed Services Committee) and Jim Webb (former secretary of the Navy and current chair of the Foreign Relations Subcommittee on East Asia and the Pacific) visited Tokyo and Okinawa (and Korea) to study the situation. In Tokyo, Kan's government assured them that the project, despite delays, would go ahead. In Okinawa, however, the message they had received was very different. The governor—using a formula that had become almost a signature tune for him—told them it would be "extremely difficult" to proceed, and the Okinawan daily *Ryukyu Shimpo* addressed them (and through them the US Senate) with an "Open Letter" asking that the facilities at Futenma be removed "altogether" from Okinawa and expressing hope and anxiety as to how "American democracy handles this test."[52]

Do we want a situation in which every time the United States sneezes, Japan follows; in which if the United States orders Japan to turn to the right that is exactly what happens? Or do we want a situation in which both parties respect each other's opinions and do not hesitate to state their position on matters, however difficult that may be. Which kind of U.S.-Japan relations would you prefer?

. . . Okinawa faced many trials and tribulations during the reign of the U.S. military government, which took control of Okinawan people's land at the point of a bayonet and used bulldozers to build military bases. They blatantly violated the basic human rights of the local people with outrageous behavior and placed limitations on Okinawa's autonomy.

. . . In April 1996, the Japanese and U.S. governments agreed that the United States would return the land used by Futenma Air Station, which is located in a densely populated area, to Okinawa on the basis that the facilities would be moved to an alternative location within the prefecture. However, local Okinawans have consistently opposed the construction of such replacement facilities.

The Governor of Okinawa Nakaima Hirokazu and all the heads of the various municipalities of Okinawa are opposed to the agreement reached by the Japanese and U.S. governments by which the U.S. military would relocate the Futenma Air Station facilities to a coastal area of Nago City. Okinawa's prefectural assembly passed a resolution calling for the Futenma Air Station to be relocated out of the prefecture or out of Japan altogether, and in the national election, all politicians who accepted the option of relocation of the air station within the prefecture lost their seats.

. . . The U.S. government . . . should feel guilty for neglecting what is clearly a dangerous situation. . . . Okinawan people feel that they were sacrificed in the name of defense of the main islands of Japan during the Battle of Okinawa and that the same occurred after the war in the Japan-U.S. Security Treaty.

. . . We consider that the closure and removal of the facilities at Futenma is necessary to rebuild good neighborly relations between the U.S. and Okinawa and we hope that you sense and accept the sincerity of the "spirit of Okinawa."

To respect the will of the people of Okinawa, please show us the true worth of American democracy.

Senators Levin and Webb undoubtedly read this appeal. When, weeks later, they issued their report, it was a bombshell. Senators Levin and Webb, joined for the occasion by former Republican presidential candidate and ranking Republican on the Armed Services Committee, John McCain, issued a joint statement declaring the realignment plans "unrealistic, unworkable, and unaffordable."[53]

It was, as Webb put it in his longer statement of their thinking,

a massive, multi-billion dollar undertaking, requiring extensive landfill, destruction and relocation of many existing facilities, and in a best-case scenario, several years of effort—some estimate that the process could take as long as ten years.[54]

Collectively, the three proposed that the Pentagon set about

Revising the Marine Corps force realignment implementation plan for Guam to consist of a presence with a permanently-assigned headquarters element bolstered by deployed, rotating combat units that are home-based elsewhere, and consideration of off-island training sites.

Examining the feasibility of moving Marine Corps assets at MCAS Futenma, Okinawa, to Kadena Air Base, Okinawa, rather than building an expensive replacement facility at Camp Schwab—while dispersing a part of Air Force assets now at Kadena to Andersen Air Base in Guam and/or other locations in Japan."[55]

The proposals, they insisted, would "save billions in taxpayer dollars, keep US military forces in the region, greatly reduce the timing of sensitive political issues surrounding MCAS Futemna, and reduce the American footprint on Okinawa."

Naturally, in the minds of these Washington power brokers was the steady deepening of US financial crisis. They, perhaps better than most, were aware of the implications of the $14 trillion dollars (as of July 2011) debt, the ongoing costs of multiple wars and of a military budget running at close to half of the entire world's military spending, and the costs of maintaining some one thousand military bases around the world. They would also have digested the sobering report from the Government Accountability Office (GAO) finding that the planned transfer of Marine Corps units to Guam was going to cost the United States not $4.2 billion, as estimated in the 2006 "Roadmap" agreement with Japan, but $11.3 billion.[56]

These views were supported in broad outline by other high-level Washington insiders, most prominently Marine Corps General James Jones, who until October 2010 had been Obama's national security adviser. In one respect, Jones went even further, saying that "it really did not matter where the Marines were,"[57] thus utterly negating the widely repeated view that Okinawa was crucial to their functioning in the regional and global frame of deterrence.

The Kan government was profoundly shocked that such views should be adopted by some at the highest levels of power in Washington. Kan and Cabinet Secretary Edano insisted, rather forlornly, that Levin and his colleagues were not the American government and that what counted were government-to-government agreements. The fact is, however, that the Levin group concentrated enormous power, and its recommendations would be hard to resist.

Indeed in December 2011, the political strength of the Webb-Levin-McCain position became plain when the armed services committees of the two houses of Congress swept aside pleas from the government of Japan and slashed the entire $150 million sum earmarked for Guam transfer costs in the 2012 budget.[58] The hollowness and inequality of the deal made in early 2009 between the incoming Obama administration and the collapsing LDP government, designed to tie the hands of any democratically elected subsequent Japanese government, now returned to haunt Tokyo. Tokyo was manipulated by its own bureaucrats in collaboration with their Washington counterparts into adopting the Guam International Agreement as a binding treaty; but for Washington it was merely an agreement, and plainly by late 2011 the considerations raised by Senators Webb, Levin, and McCain were paramount in rethinking it. In the deepening fiscal crisis, the US government would follow its own logic. The slashing of the 2012 item for Guam was likely to be merely the first of cuts made inevitable by the failure of Congress to agree on voluntary cuts by the November 2011 deadline the president had set.[59] More cuts, at least 2.4 trillion dollars over ten years, would come, and overseas military bases were an obvious candidate for some of them. The marine presence in Okinawa began to be described as a factor that had "destabilized" Japan's politics,[60] and the possibility of withdrawal of marine units to the American homeland began to be publicly canvassed.[61]

The trump card Japan had played from time to time over four decades to ensure that the marines not leave Okinawa—the payment of substantial sums of money—became more difficult to play as Japan, itself broke, bowed under the heaviest debt burden of all OECD countries and faced huge reconstruction costs for its devastated northeast. All that could be said for certain is that its bureaucrats, following their past record, would pull out all stops to try to put together a sufficiently attractive package to entice the congressional leaders back to the Henoko and Guam proposals.

## NOTES

1. Gerald Curtis, "Future Directions in US-Japan Relations," background paper for the "New Shimoda Conference—Revitalizing Japan-US Strategic Partnership for a Changing World, February 2011, http://www.jcie.org/researchpdfs/newshimoda/Bkgd_Curtis.pdf.

2. Ministry of Defense, *National Defense Program Guidelines*, December 17, 2010.

3. Maeda Tetsuo, "Minshuto seiken wa senshu boei o homuru no ka," *Sekai* (November 2010).

4. "Chugokugun zokyo kinpaku no umi/boei taiko ni taichu senryaku/katsudo han-i, taiheiyo ni/shuhen shokoku to no masatsu zoka," *Okinawa Taimusu*, December 18, 2010.

5. "Japan, US Take Step towards Boosting Alliance," *Daily Yomiuri Online*, April 10, 2011.

6. "Beigun kyuen katsudo ni micchaku inochigake 'Tomodachi sakusen,'" *Sankei Shimbun*, March 27, 2011.

7. Ryan Zielonka, "Chronology of Operation Tomodachi," *National Bureau of Asian Research*, http://www.nbr.org/research/activity.aspx?id=121.

8. Robert D. Eldridge (deputy assistant chief of staff at the community policy, planning and liaison office, G-5, of USMC *Okinawa*), "Quake Relief Effort Highlights a Vital US Military Function," *Japan Times*, March 31, 2011.

9. Ministry of Foreign Affairs of Japan, "Japan-U.S. Security Consultative Committee (2 + 2)" (2011), http://www.mofa.go.jp/region/n-america/us/security/scc/index.html.

10. The *Asahi* commented editorially ("More talks needed on bilateral defense alliance," *Asahi Shimbun*, June 25, 2011) on the Mageshima project, "The locals are resisting vehemently, and Tokyo has certainly created a new source of strife."

11. "Boeisho no tsukoku, munashii min-i mushi no gusaku," *Ryukyu Shimpo*, June 14, 2011.

12. "2 purasu 2, minshu seiji mushibamu rekishiteki oten," *Ryukyu Shimpo*, June 22, 2011.

13. Quoted in Urashima Etsuko, "Okinawa Yanbaru, kaze no tayori (21) 'Kokusaku' ni honro sareru ikari," *Impaction* 161 (2011): 123.

14. "Ikidoru Nago shicho 'odoshi to shika kikoenu,'" *Okinawa Taimusu*, June 22, 2011.

15. "Chiji, 'Henoko' 'Futenma' nitaku ron o hihan," *Okinawa Taimusu*, June 24, 2011.

16. "More Talks Needed," *Asahi*, June 25, 2011.

17. George R. Packard, "Some Thoughts on the 50th Anniversary of the US-Japan Security Treaty," *Asia-Pacific Review* 17, no. 2 (2010): 2.

18. Ministry of Defense, "Zainichi Beigun churyu keihi futan no suii," http://www.mod.go.jp/j/approach/zaibeigun/us_keihi/suii_table_53-60.html.

19. Department of Defense, "US Stationed Military Personnel and Bilateral Cost Sharing 2001 Dollars in Millions—2001 Exchange Rates" (July 2003), http://www.defense.gov/pubs/allied_contrib2003/chart_II-4.html.; Yoshida Kensei, "Anpo kichi no shima Okinawa," *Gekkan Oruta* (December 20, 2009), http://www.alter-magazine.jp/backno/backno_72.html.

20. "US Wants Additional Sympathy Budget," *Japan Press Weekly*, July 28–August 3, 2010; "Beigun omoiyari sogaku iji, tokubetsu kyotei 5 nen ni encho," *Akahata*, December 15, 2010.

21. Hana Kusumoto, "US, Japan Sign New Five Year 'Host Nation Support' Agreement," *Stars and Stripes*, January 21, 2011.

22. Ministry of Defense, "Zainichi Beigun churyu keihi futan no suii," 1978–2011, http://www.mod.go.jp/j/approach/zaibeigun/us_keihi/suii_table_53-60.html.

23. US Government Accountability Office, "Defense Management—Comprehensive Cost Information and Analysis of Alternatives Needed to Assess Military Posture in Asia," 40.

24. The US Defense Department's estimate was $80 million as of 29 March. Roxana Tiron, "US Defense Department Will Spend as Much as $80 million on Aid to Japan," *Bloomberg News*, March 29, 2011.

25. For the text of Maher's December 3 talk, see "Mea shi kogi memo zenbun," *Ryukyu Shimpo*, March 8, 2011, http://ryukyushimpo.jp/news/storyid-174372-storytopic-231.html, and "Anger Spreads over Kevin Maher's Derogatory Comments on Okinawans," *Peace Philosophy Centre*, March 8, 2011, http://peacephilosophy.blogspot.com/2011/03/anger-spreads-over-kevin-mahers.html.

26. The Puerto Rican references were added in an account given later by David Vine, the American University faculty member who arranged and attended the fateful Maher briefing. David Vine, "Smearing Japan," *Foreign Policy in Focus* (April 20, 2011), http://www.fpif.org/articles/smearing_japan.

27. "'Mea shi zekka' shinjirarenai bujoku hatsugen," *Okinawa Taimusu*, March 7, 2011.

28. "'Nichibei kyokucho kyu kaigi' konna toki ni 'Henoko' ka," *Okinawa Taimusu*, March 10, 2011.

29. "'Mea shi kotetsu'—ikken rakuchaku ni wa naranai," *Okinawa Taimusu*, March 11, 2011.

30. "Mea shi sabetsu hatsugen, kainin shi Bei no ninshiki aratameyo, yuganda Okinawa kan o toei," *Ryukyu Shimpo*, March 8, 2011.

31. "Mea shi kotetsu, Futenma tekkyo e no tenki da, tsuyo senu ame to muchi," *Ryukyu Shimpo*, March 11, 2011.

32. Josh Rogan, "State Department Japan Hand Loses Post as Campbell Goes on Tokyo Apology Tour," *Foreign Policy*, March 9, 2011, http://thecable.foreignpolicy.com/posts/2011/03/09/state_department_japan_hand_loses_post_as_campbell_goes_on_tokyo_apology_tour.

33. Peter Ennis, "The Roots of the Kevin Maher-Okinawa Commotion," *Dispatch Japan*, March 11, 2011, http://www.dispatchjapan.com/blog/2011/03/the-roots-of-the-kevin-maher-okinawa-commotion.html.

34. Japan Real Time, "Exclusive Video: U.S.'s Ex-Japan Head," *Wall Street Journal*, April 14, 2011, http://blogs.wsj.com/japanrealtime/2011/04/14/exclusive-video-u-s-s-ex-japan-head.

35. "Beigun to jichitai kyoryoku, kokkai mushi shita kanryo no sakibashiri," *Ryukyu Shimpo*, June 16, 2011.

36. Japan-U.S. Security Consultative Committee (2 + 2), "Cooperation in Response to the Great East Japan Earthquake"(June 21, 2011), http://www.mofa.go.jp/mofaj/area/usa/hosho/pdfs/joint1106_03.pdf.

37. Nathan Hodge, "US Military Finds Lessons in Japan's Crisis," *Wall Street Journal*, June 21, 2011.

38. "US Frustrated over Japan's Lack of N-Info," *Yomiuri Shimbun*, April 11, 2011.

39. Naoto Kan, "Japan's Road to Recovery and Rebirth," *Washington Post*, April 15, 2011.

40. "Beigun no saigai shien, sore de mo Futenma wa iranai," *Ryukyu Shimpo*, March 18, 2011.

41. "'Shinsai de Futenma PR' seiji riyo ni kenshiki o utagau," *Okinawa Taimusu*, March 22, 2011.

42. "Futenma isetsu kenmin taikai 1 nen, zen shucho 'kengai kokugai' nozomu," *Ryukyu Shimpo*, April 24, 2011.

43. The board of New Magellan Venture Partners, NMV Consulting (nmvconsulting.com), originally headed by Richard Lawless, former deputy minister for defense, includes other retired senior military and bureaucratic figures and offers "deep expertise in the defense and aerospace; transportation; energy; mineral resource; property development and high-technology sectors."

44. "Mea shi, minkan de kaku nenryo mondai o tanto, sabetsuteki hatsugen de kotetsu," *Tokyo Shimbun*, May 12, 2011.

45. Kevin Maher, *Ketsudan dekinai Nippon* (*The Japan That Can't Decide*) (Tokyo: Bunshun shinsho, 2011).

46. "Buta to tatakaeba ryoho to mo yogore, buta ga yorokobu, Mea shi kakugen mochii sosho hitei," *Ryukyu Shimpo*, August 19, 2011.

47. Maher, Cable 07NAHA89, "First USN Civilian Port Call in Okinawa a Success," June 27, 2007, *WikiLeaks*. http://www.wikileaks.ch/cable/2007/06/07NAHA89.html.

48. "Adm. Mike Mullen: 'National Debt Is Our Biggest Security Threat'," *Huffington Post*, June 24, 2010, http://www.huffingtonpost.com/2010/06/24/adm-mike-mullen-national_n_624096.html.

49. Yonamine Michiyo, "Economic Crisis Shakes US Forces Overseas: The Price of Base Expansion in Okinawa and Guam," *Asia-Pacific Journal: Japan Focus* (February 28, 2011), http://www.japanfocus.org/-Yonamine-Michiyo/3494.

50. "2 Congressmen Call for Pullout of US Forces from Japan," *Japan Today*, February 16, 2011.

51. The National Commission on Fiscal Responsibility and Reform, "The Moment of Truth," December 20, 2010, http://www.fiscalcommission.gov/sites/fiscalcommission.gov/files/documents/TheMomentofTruth12_1_2010.pdf.

52. Editorial, "Open letter, to Mr. Carl Levin, Chairman of the Senate Armed Services Committee," *Ryukyu Shimpo*, April 27, 2011.

53. Carl Levin, John McCain, and Jim Webb, "Senators Levin, McCain, Webb Call for Re-examination of Military Basing Plans in East Asia," May 11, 2011, http://webb.senate.gov/newsroom/pressreleases/05-11-2011-01.cfm.

54. Senator Jim Webb, "Observations and Recommendations on US Military Basing in East Asia, May 2011," http://webb.senate.gov/issuesandlegislation/foreignpolicy/Observations_basing_east_asia.cfm. Note that the "Kadena merger" idea seems to stem from a suggestion made by Shimoji Mikio, People's New Party Okinawan Diet representative. Shimoji, the sole Okinawan Diet member prepared

to contemplate a Futenma replacement facility in the prefecture, exercises considerable influence among Japanese and American officials who want to believe that he represents a "realist" strain of thinking. "Futenma isetsu Bei ni 'san nen kigen' teigen Shimoji shi, Nihon e no dentatsu yobo," *Ryukyu Shimpo*, May 7, 2011.

55. Levin, McCain, Webb, "Senators."

56. US Government Accountability Office, "Defense Management—Comprehensive Cost Information and Analysis of Alternatives Needed to Assess Military Posture in Asia," 25.

57. "Zen Bei daitoryo hosakan ga Henoko isetsu o konnanshi," *Okinawa taimusu*, May 8, 2011.

58. "U.S. Congress to Nix Funding for Relocating Okinawa Marines to Guam," *Kyodo News*, December 13, 2011.

59. Sato Manabu, "Gaiko, anpo tadaseru no wa Okinawa," *Ryukyu Shimpo*, December 14, 2011.

60. Barney Frank, quoted in "We Could Remove the Marines from Okinawa, Suggests US Congressman Frank," *Ryukyu Shimpo* (English web page), December 6, 2011, http://english.ryukyushimpo.jp/2011/12/15/4216/.

61. Mike Mochizuki and Michael O'Hanlon, "Rethink US Military Base Plans for Japan," special to CNN, November 4, 2011.

# 11

⌒

# Senkaku/Diaoyu

## Okinawa as Militarized Outpost or as Bridge of Nations?

### "SENKAKU ISLANDS DAY"

On January 14, 2011, the Okinawan city of Ishigaki celebrated for the first time what it called "Senkaku Islands Colonization Day," commemorating the incorporation into Japan 116 years earlier of the tiny outcrops known in Japan as Senkaku and in China as Diaoyu. The islands today are under effective Japanese control but are claimed also by China and Taiwan. Ishigaki was following the model of the Shimane Prefectural Assembly, which in 2005 declared a "Takeshima Day" in commemoration of the Japanese state's incorporation one hundred years earlier of the islands known in Japan as Takeshima but in South Korea as Tokdo. The Shimane decision prompted fierce protests in South Korea, and the Ishigaki decision stirred comparable passions in China.

East Asia remains troubled by questions of sovereignty over such tiny island outcrops as Tokdo/Takeshima and Senkaku/Diaoyu (see figure 11.1). Both are rooted in the history of Japanese colonialism and the US-imposed post-1945 Cold War East Asian order. Japan took control of Senkaku/Diaoyu in 1895, at the height of the Sino-Japanese War, and of Tokdo/Takeshima in 1905, during the Russo-Japanese War. With the collapse of the Japanese empire, control over the latter passed to South Korea and over the former to Japan (following two and a half decades of US military control), but the ambiguous formula by which sovereignty was addressed preserved the seeds of subsequent dispute. In the twenty-first century, the ability of the countries of the region to reach peaceful and just resolutions of such disputes will be a litmus test of how well

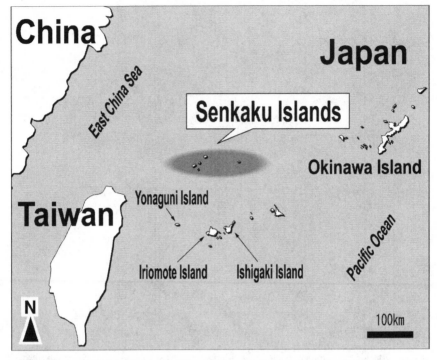

Figure 11.1.  Senkaku/Diaoyu Islands and surrounding. *Source:* Kyodo News.

they have transcended the eras of Japanese imperialism and US Cold War hegemony.

## THE INCIDENT

On the morning of September 7, 2010, the Chinese fishing trawler *Min-jinyu 5179* collided, twice, with Japanese Coast Guard vessels in the vicinity of the islands (figure 11.2).[1] Zhan Qixiong, captain of the Chinese vessel, refused to obey the Japanese orders to withdraw. By Japanese accounts, he deliberately rammed his ship into the Coast Guard vessels and was therefore apprehended and sent to prosecutors.

The Japanese government stated that there was "no room for doubt" that the islands were an integral part of Japanese territory (*wagakuni no koyu no ryodo*), that there was no territorial dispute or diplomatic issue, and that the Chinese captain was simply being investigated for breaches of Japanese law (interfering with officials conducting their duties).

The formal Japanese position—that there was no dispute—rang hollow from the outset. China (both the People's Republic and the Republic, or

**Figure 11.2.** Senkaku/Diaoyu Islands. *Source:* Kyodo News.

Taiwan) disputes the Japanese claim to sovereignty. The United States, which occupied the islands between 1945 and 1972, was carefully agnostic about their sovereignty when returning to Japan "administrative rights" over them, and it has reiterated that stance on many subsequent occasions.[2] As restated in the context of the 2010 clash, the US position is that sovereignty is something to be settled between the claimant parties. Furthermore, while Japan has exercised "administrative rights" and thus effective control since 1972,[3] it has blocked all activities on the islands, by its own or other nationals, thereby acting as if sovereignty were indeed contested. With two Chinese governments denying it and the United States refusing to endorse it, it is surely whistling in the wind for Japan to insist there is "no dispute" over ownership.

Japan handled the crisis in a characteristic and revealing way, by seeking first to escalate it from a bilateral dispute over borders to a security matter involving the United States. Following a meeting on September 23, Foreign Minister Maehara declared that Secretary of State Hillary Clinton had given him the assurance that the Senkakus were "subject to Article 5 of the US-Japan Security Treaty," the clause of the treaty that authorizes the United States to protect Japan in the case of an armed attack "in territories under the administration of Japan."

What Clinton actually said, however, is not clear. Only weeks earlier, the United States had communicated its reluctance to back Japan's Senkaku claims.[4] Not only did the State Department account of the September meeting not mention the pledge claimed by Maehara, but its spokesman repeated the formal US government position urging the two countries to resolve the dispute, and stated, "We don't take a position on the sovereignty of the Senkakus."[5] Weeks later, however, at a joint press conference in Honolulu with Foreign Minister Maehara, Clinton did take such a position, specifically affirming the applicability of Article 5 to the Senkakus.[6] It thus reversed its position in the space of just over a month, evidently under keen Japanese pressure, committing itself to the possible use of force, that is, war, in defense of islands on whose legal ownership it previously had taken no position.

However, despite extracting the ambiguous US backing, the Japanese resolve quickly crumbled. On September 24, the Kan government suddenly released the offending Chinese captain. When it declared that it was following an "autonomous decision of local prosecutors," everyone took it for granted that the opposite was true: the decision had been made at the highest levels of government in Tokyo.

It was widely reported in Japan that the "international community" supported Japan's position, and, in East and Southeast Asia, anxiety about China's dramatic rise evidently fed into support for the reassertion of US alliance-based "containment." Weeks after the incident, the *New York Times* quoted with approval the view of China as "increasingly narrow-minded, self-interested, truculent, hyper-nationalist."[7] Adjectives such as "truculent" and "arrogant" began to attach almost as a matter of course to "China" in mainstream Western media.

However, when Defense Minister Kitazawa talked to regional defense ministers in an attempt to drum up diplomatic support, he failed to find a single defense minister ready to offer it.[8] When Foreign Minister Maehara filed a complaint against Google, demanding it remove the Chinese names from its maps of the islands, Google refused, and Japan's blatant attempt to muzzle the media rebounded to its discredit.[9] Furthermore, Japan's "humiliating retreat" (as the *New York Times* put it on September 24) by release of the Chinese captain signalled to the region that it was actually lacking in the sovereignty it so loudly declared.

Nationalistic passions and fears, once stirred, however, were not easily settled. Demonstrations in both countries continued after the Chinese captain was released. The tabloid daily *Fuji* in Tokyo denounced what it called Japan's "appeasement" (*dogeza*) diplomacy.[10] Widely syndicated pundits thundered that "China's attitude is utterly despicable" (Sakurai Yoshiko in *Shukan Posuto*, October 8, 2010) or that "what China's doing is no different from gangsters. If Japan does nothing, it will suffer the same fate as Tibet" (Tokyo governor Ishihara Shintaro in *Shukan Bunshun*, October 7, 2010). Tamogami Toshio, former chief of staff of the Air Self-Defense Forces and now president of the "Ganbare Nippon! [Go for it Japan!] All-Japan Action Committee" also stressed the threat to Okinawa: "China is clearly aiming to annex Okinawa. So we need to put a stop to it."[11]

In general, the left-right political divide in Japan dissolved into an "all-Japan" media front on this issue. A broad national media consensus supported the Japanese official story of its Senkaku rights, protested China's threat to Japan's sovereign territory, and insisted on the importance of the security alliance with the US in order to cope with China's challenge.

The doyen of Japan's liberal media, the *Asahi*'s editor in chief (and former Beijing correspondent) Funabashi Yoichi, lamented that while Japan had been "clumsy," China was to be blamed for its "diplomatic shock and awe" campaign that had brought the two giant neighbor countries to "ground zero, [so that] the landscape is a bleak, vast nothingness."[12] Though couching his message in the measured tones of the liberal intellectual seeking China's understanding, the insistence that China was solely to blame for reducing the relationship to "ground zero" reflected a widespread Japanese resentment of China's dramatic economic growth and increased international standing.

Japan's leading financial daily declared that Japan had to cooperate with the United States and Europe in putting pressure on China to become a "responsible power."[13] When the chairman of the Japanese Communist Party Shii Kazuo joined the chorus declaring the islands to be Japan's sovereign territory that must be defended, the chief cabinet secretary Sengoku Yoshito received it favorably, saying he would pass it on to the Prime Minister. The widely syndicated Sato Masaru lamented the blows Japan's "national interest" had suffered because of amateurish diplomacy and called for a firm Japanese response in kind, "as an imperialist country" to "China's imperialism."[14]

Sato's role merits attention because of his unique stance as a former Ministry of Foreign Affairs researcher and self-proclaimed rightist embraced also by the "liberal" media and intelligentsia. As of 2010, he was the most prominent advocate of the Okinawan antibase cause in mainland Japan, with regular columns in *Sekai*, *Shukan Kinyobi*, and *Ryukyu Shimpo*. Yet Sato's agenda of opposition to any new marine base construction in Okinawa did not fit well with his insistence on confronting China as one imperialist power to another. Sato's bottom line appeared to be reinforcement of the Japanese national interest, with the Henoko antibase struggle essentially a means to that end.[15] He objected to the way Tokyo was proceeding to foist the new base on Okinawa, but not to enhanced US-Japan military cooperation *per se*. For Japan to adopt, as he urged, a resolutely "imperialist" stance in opposing China required that it reinforce military positions (whether US, Japanese, or some combination) in Okinawa, especially in the Okinawan islands closest to China.

Okinawa itself showed a certain vulnerability to such "national interest" logic. To the extent that "China threat" perceptions spread, Okinawa's antibase movement would surely weaken. In the wake of the September incident, as prominent Okinawan figures wavered, it became possible to imagine that Senkaku/Diaoyu might even serve as the axis of Okinawan conversion to greater understanding of the national government's defense and security agenda. The abandonment of the Henoko project might be tolerable to the defense bureaucracy in Tokyo and Washington if it was combined with readiness to reinforce US-Japanese military presence and containment of China. Hatoyama's 2009 project to turn the East China Sea into a "Sea of Fraternity" looked in 2010 more likely to degenerate into a DPJ project for building confrontation and tension.

As the justice or legality of Japan's claims went unchallenged and, as for the first time in the post-1945 era anti-China sentiment began to spread at the mass level, the political dividing lines between left and right were swallowed by a wave of chauvinism. Japanese elites seemed to have lost the capacity to appreciate the Chinese position or to achieve a self-critical awareness of their own.

## THE HISTORY

The near universal conviction in Japan with which the islands today are declared an "integral part of Japan's territory" is remarkable for its disingenuousness. These are islands unknown in Japan till the late nineteenth century (when they were first identified from British naval references), not declared Japanese until 1895, not named until 1900, and that name not revealed publicly until 1950.[16]

The historical record is only one factor relevant to determining contemporary legal entitlement, but the early modern record is clear: Chinese documents from the Ming Dynasty (1368–1644) record and name the islands as important reference points on the ancient maritime trading and tribute route between coastal China (Foochow) and Okinawa. The Japanese geographer Hayashi Shihei follows the Chinese convention, including the islands, with their Chinese names, as Chinese territory, in the map attached to his 1785 work, *Sangoku tsuran zusetsu*.

The determination in 2010 not to yield one inch on the Senkaku issue may have owed something to the nagging Japanese fear that if China's claim were admitted on Senkaku, it might quickly extend to Okinawa. Japan's claim to the Senkakus followed shortly after it had established its claim over Okinawa by detaching the Ryukyu kingdom, tied to the court in Beijing by a four-century-long "tribute" relationship, from its place in the tribute order. The dispatch of a Japanese naval expedition to Taiwan in 1874 to "protest" the killing of Ryukyuan (Miyako Island) fishermen, passing without effective protest from China, was taken by Japanese authorities to signal for international law purposes that it acquiesced in Japan's claims and was followed, in 1879, by extinction of the kingdom. The years of the rise of the modern Japanese state were years of crisis and decline for the Chinese imperial state, which was subject to internal disintegration, imperialist encroachment, catastrophic wars, and internal rebellions. The revolutionary modern Japanese state, founded in 1868, exploited China's weakness and its multifaceted crises to join the ranks of imperialists, expanding at imperial China's cost by wresting from it first the Ryukyu Islands, then Taiwan and the Senkakus, Korea, and Northeast China, until eventually it plunged the region into full-scale war.

On the largest island of the Senkaku group, a Japanese businessman began to make a living from 1884, collecting albatross feathers and tortoise shells.[17] However, his requests to the government in Tokyo for a formal leasehold grant of the territory were refused for over a decade, until war between Japan and China starting in 1894 and the series of Japanese victories that defined it persuaded the Japanese cabinet in January 1895 to declare them Japanese territory, part of Yaeyama County, Okinawa prefecture.

The Japanese claim rested on the doctrine of *terra nullius*—the presumption that the islands were uninhabited and not claimed or controlled by any other country. However, it stretches common sense to see the absence of Chinese protest or counterclaim as decisive under the circumstance of war, the more so as the appropriation of the Senkakus was followed only three months later by the acquisition of Taiwan under the Treaty of Shimonoseki.

Nearly forty years have passed since Kyoto University's Inoue Kiyoshi reached this conclusion: "Even though the [Senkaku] islands were not wrested from China under a treaty, they were grabbed from it by stealth, without treaty or negotiations, taking advantage of victory in war."[18] In general, however, Japanese scholars today unite in declaring the appropriation of the islands legitimate and in accord with international law, dismissing as irrelevant the circumstances under which Japan made its claim and (with few exceptions) expressing outrage that China does not agree with their reading of law or history.

After its defeat in the Asia-Pacific War, Japan was obliged by the Potsdam Declaration to surrender all territories occupied since the beginning of World War I, and those stolen from China, but sovereignty of Senkaku/Diaoyu islands was neither made clear nor contended. The difficulty with this is that they plainly were not part of Ryukyu's "thirty-six islands" in premodern times nor when the prefecture was established in 1879, but were only tacked onto it sixteen years later when Japan incorporated them.

From 1945, the US military took effective control, and international attention only focused again on the islands from 1968, when a UN (ECAFE) survey mission reported likely oil and gas reserves in their adjacent waters, and 1969, when the US agreed to return sovereignty over Okinawa to Japan.

As Kimie Hara of Canada's Waterloo University points out, the United States played a significant role in the creation and manipulation of the "Senkaku problem," first in 1951 and then again in 1972:

> First, under the 1951 San Francisco Treaty post-war settlement, it planted the seeds of territorial dispute between Japan and its neighbours: Japan and 90 percent communist China over Okinawa/Senkaku, Japan and 100 percent communist USSR over the "Northern territories," Japan and 50 percent communist Korea over the island of Takeshima (Korean: Tokdo). These disputed territories served "as 'wedges' securing Japan in the Western bloc, or 'walls' dividing it from the communist sphere of influence."[19]

Again in 1972, by leaving unresolved the question of ownership of the Senkaku islands when returning Okinawa to Japanese administration, US Cold War planners anticipated that Senkaku would function as a "wedge of containment" of China. They understood that a "territorial dispute between Japan and China, especially over islands near Okinawa, would render the US military presence in Okinawa more acceptable to Japan."[20] The events of 2010 proved them right.

On the eve of the reversion of Okinawa (Senkaku included) to Japanese administration, both the People's Republic of China and the Republic of China laid their counterclaims. Dispute flared, only cooling when, in 1978, Chinese leader Deng Xiaoping made his circuit-breaking offer:

> It does not matter if this question is shelved for some time, say ten years. Our generation is not wise enough to find a common language on this question. Our next generation will certainly be wiser. They will surely find a solution acceptable to all.[21]

Despite occasional lapses, that "gentleman's agreement" held until September 2010, when Japan apparently repudiated it by arresting the Chinese captain, insisting there was no dispute and refusing to listen to China's protests.

## THE CONSEQUENCES

In the brouhaha of 2010, Kan Naoto's government gave priority to extracting an American promise to "protect" the Senkakus in the general frame of insistence on closer integration of Japanese and US military planning and operations in the Western Pacific and East Asia and cooperation in grand regional war games that were plainly intended to intimidate China. The initiatives of his predecessor, Hatoyama Yukio, for closer Japan-China cooperation in the formation of an East Asian community, were a thing of the past. Post-Hatoyama, and for that matter post-Ozawa, Japan would strengthen its "client state" status.[22] The new National Defense Program Guidelines were a significant step in that direction.

In 2011, Yonaguni Island was split between proponents and opponents of an SDF presence while Miyako Island seemed to be firmly opposed to the idea of turning its civilian airstrip at Shimoji over to joint US-Japan military control—even if under the high-sounding name of an "International Disaster Relief" base. The fierce struggles (discussed in chapter 2) over revisionist attempts to rewrite the history of the war have to be seen in this context.

The idea that a Japanese military presence might be acceptable in Okinawa where an American was not had a certain superficial attraction. The principle of "interoperability" proclaimed in recent joint government documents certainly implies closer integration of the two forces—and at least partial replacement of American by Japanese forces—is consistent with the process of merger of command and intelligence being steadily advanced at military installations throughout Japan (see chapter 10).

Such a prescription must sound attractive both in the Pentagon and in the corridors of Japan's defense and foreign affairs establishment. However, the shift from primarily US to primarily Japanese uniforms would not alter the military quality of the process or its "China-confronting" character (in accordance with the Defense Guidelines articulated in December 2010; see chapter 10). Yet it is far from clear that Okinawa could be persuaded to buy into such an agenda. The memory of peaceful coexistence over many centuries means it has little, if any, of the mainland sense of "China threat," while the memory of being exploited and betrayed by the Japanese military in 1945 is seared deep in the Okinawan soul.

After the September events, the Kan government hardened its determination to build in Northern Okinawa a new base for the US Marine Corps, whose major role would clearly be to "deter" China (and North Korea). By involving Okinawa in the nationwide mood of fear and hostility to China post-September 2010, Tokyo might reasonably expect that opposition to the marine base project would weaken. It could only have taken heart when the Okinawan Prefectural Assembly and the city assemblies of Miyako and Ishigaki (geographically closest to Senkaku) adopted unanimous resolutions affirming that the Senkaku islands did indeed "belong to Japan" and calling for Japan to be resolute (*kizentaru*) in defending them, and when prominent antibase figures in Okinawa either supported or else demanded that Tokyo take a stronger stance in defense of that official Japanese position. The Kan government stepped up the rhetoric again on August 10, 2011, when Chief Cabinet Secretary Edano Yukio told the Diet, "Japan would repel aggression against the Senkakus whatever the price," that is, it would go to war over them if necessary.[23]

Despite the evidence of a partial convergence of Okinawan and mainland thinking in insistence on Japanese sovereignty over the islands, there were nevertheless significant differences. First, Okinawans had learned from their experience of 1945 that armies do not defend people; so many tended to believe that any defense of the Senkakus that rested on militarizing them and embedding them in hostile confrontation between Japan and China would expose Okinawa to greater threat rather than improve its security. It is also the case, as Iha Yoichi (defeated 2010 gubernatorial candidate) pointed out, that Okinawans have a long historical memory of friendly relations with China, and in contrast to mainland fears and anxieties, they rather feel "close" to it.[24] Second, for Okinawans, the Senkaku issue is not so much one of national security as one of livelihood.[25] It is the fishing grounds around the islands that are precious, rather than national security or seabed oil and gas reserves. Whoever might profit from any oil and gas, it is unlikely to be the Okinawans. As Okinawa International University's Sato Manabu put it, "It is obvious that Okinawa has to find a future as an 'open' border land. Okinawa has to make every effort to build stronger ties with neighbouring nations, otherwise we will be cornered."[26]

## THE PROSPECT

Though uninhabited, the Senkaku/Diaoyu islands hold considerable strategic and probably also economic significance. At the heart of the Northeast Asia region, exclusive economic rights to the resources of hundreds of square kilometers of the East China Sea presumably attach to them. Confrontation, progressively militarized and in a zero-sum approach to territorial and resource matters, would be a recipe for disaster for both Japan and China. It would mean mega-disaster for Okinawa.

While the Japanese media united in projecting a picture of China as threatening and "other," it paid minimal attention either to the circumstances surrounding the Japanese claim to the islands or to the reasons for the recrudescence of suspicion of Japan in China. Taking it for granted that Japan "owned" the islands, it concentrated its attention only on whether or not the Chinese captain had deliberately rammed the Coast Guard vessels and who might have leaked the apparent film footage of the events occurring. Few expressed any hesitation over Japan's trashing the Deng "freeze" agreement of 1978 or over the contempt with which the government met China's claims by denying they existed. Nor was there any sign of dissent when respected opinion leaders accused China of truculence or diplomatic "shock and awe." It goes without saying that the incident, and the hard-line Japanese response to it, stirred a comparably hard-line response in China.

Virtually nowhere were there discussions of the possible "blowback" aspect of the events—that is, that they might simply have brought to the surface unassuaged Chinese suspicions over Japan's long-neglected or insufficiently resolved war responsibility, the high-level denials of Nanjing, the periodic right-wing attempts to sanitize history texts, the refusal to accept formal legal responsibility for the victims of the Asia-wide "comfort women" slavery system issue, and the periodic visits by prime ministers (notably Koizumi, annually 2001–2006) to Yasukuni.

Peace and security in East Asia depend on the governments and peoples of the region taking the initiative to remove the "wedges of containment" that US planners left ambiguously and threateningly embedded in the state system they designed more than half a century ago. In January 2011, a White House spokesman reiterated that the United States "does not have a position on the question of sovereignty regarding the issue of the Diaoyu islands." His remarks, in which he used the Chinese rather than the Japanese name for the islands, almost certainly for the first time in official discourse, must have deeply disconcerted the government in Tokyo.[27]

For Okinawa, the Senkaku/Diaoyu events serve as a message to think again about the history of the islands' links with (mainland) Japan, China, and Korea. Once the flourishing independent kingdom of Ryukyu, whose aspiration was to serve as the bridge linking the neighboring states and peoples, Okinawa was subjected twice to forceful appropriation by mainland Japan, first in 1609 and then, decisively, in 1879, when its long and friendly links with China were finally severed. Modern history did not deal kindly to Okinawa, and today, as waves of chauvinism and militarism again wash on its shores, only by returning to the vision of the islands as uniquely close to China, Korea, and mainland Japan (as written on the great "World Bridging" *Bankoku shinryo* bell, cast in the year 1458 and now on display in the prefectural museum), can it hope to calm and survive the gathering storms.

## NOTES

1. References in the following text to "Senkaku" carry no implication as to sovereignty or "proper" name.

2. Kimie Hara, *Cold War Frontiers in the Asia-Pacific: Divided Territories in the San Francisco System* (Abingdon: Taylor & Francis, 2006), especially chapter 7, "The Ryukyus: Okinawa and the Senkaku/Diaoyu Disputes."

3. See Ministry of Foreign Affairs, "The Basic View on the Sovereignty over the Senkaku Islands," http://www.mofa.go.jp/region/asia-paci/senkaku/senkaku.html.

4. "US Fudges Senkaku Security Pact Status," *Japan Times*, August 17, 2010.

5. Peter Lee, "High Stakes Gamble as Japan, China and the U.S. Spar in the East and South China Seas," *Asia-Pacific Journal: Japan Focus* (October 25, 2010), http://japanfocus.org/-Peter-Lee/3431/.

6. Hillary Clinton and Seiji Maehara, "Joint Press Availability with Japanese Foreign Minister Seiji Maehara," Department of State (October 27, 2010), http://www.state.gov/secretary/rm/2010/10/150110.htm.

7. "Taking Harder Stance toward China, Obama Lines Up Allies," *New York Times*, October 25, 2010.

8. Mo Banfu, "Nitchu shototsu no yoha o kakudai sasete wa naranai," *Sekai* (December 2010).

9. "Gaimusho, Guguru ni hyoki sakujo yosei Senkaku no Chugoku gawa kosho," *Kyodo News*, October 14, 2010.

10. Quoted in Mark Schreiber, "Weeklies, Tabloids Hawkish over China," *Japan Times*, October 10, 2010.

11. Yuka Hayashi, "China Row Fuels Japan's Right," *Wall Street Journal*, September 28, 2010.

12. Funabashi Yoichi, "Chugoku no tomo e . . . ippitsu keijo," *Asahi Shimbun*, October 6, 2010.

13. "Bei-O to kyocho shi, chugoku o sekinin taikoku e michibike," editorial, *Nihon Keizai Shimbun*, October 1, 2010.

14. Sato Masaru, "Chugoku teikokushugi ni taiko suru ni wa," *Chuo Koron* (November 2010).

15. For general reflections on Sato Masaru, see Gavan McCormack, "Ideas, Identity and Ideology in Contemporary Japan: The Sato Masaru Phenomenon," *Asia-Pacific Journal: Japan Focus* (November 1, 2010), http://japanfocus.org/-Gavan-McCormack/3435.

16. Unryu Suganuma, *Sovereign Rights and Territorial Space in Sino-Japanese Relations: Irredentism and the Diaoyu/Senkaku Islands* (Honolulu: University of Hawaii Press, 2000), 88–99.

17. Inoue Kiyoshi, *"Senkaku" retto—Tsuriuo shoto no shiteki kaimei* (Tokyo: Daisan shokan, 1996; originally published by Gendai hyoransha, 1972).

18. Ibid., 123.

19. Hara, *Cold War*, 188.

20. Kimie Hara, "The Post-War Japanese Peace Treaties and China's Ocean Frontier Problems," *American Journal of Chinese Studies* 11, no. 1 (April 2004): 23.

21. "Sino-Japanese Relations: Vice-Premier Teng Hsiao-Ping's Press Conference in Tokyo 25 October 1978," *Survival* 21, no. 1 (1979).

22. For further discussion, see McCormack, *Client State*.

23. "Senkaku e no shinryaku 'jieiken o koshi' kanbo chokan," *Yomiuri Shimbun*, August 11, 2011.

24. "Okinawa kaiheitai wa Guamu iten o Iha shi intabyu yoshi," *Yomiuri Shimbun*, October 22, 2010.

25. Arasaki Moriteru, "Senkaku mondai ni Okinawa no shiten o," *Ryukyu Shimpo*, October 4, 2010.

26. In personal communication with Gavan McCormack, October 10, 2010.

27. "U.S. Neutral over 'Diaoyu' Sovereignty," *Japan Times*, January 22, 2011.

# 12

⟿

# Turning History Around
## History as Lived Experience

### OKINAWAN VOICES

Who are the people who have been conducting the extraordinarily unequal and prolonged opposition to two of the greatest powers of our era?

In the belief that the personal is the political and vice versa, we have invited a small sample of the Okinawan movement community to share their reflections on the nature of their struggle, their engagement in it, and their hopes for it. Of necessity, we include here only a tiny sample, including both Okinawan born and mainland born, women and men, across several generations. We asked them to reflect on the following questions:

- When and under what circumstances did you get involved in the "Okinawan movement"? And how does it affect your personal and/or professional life? What is the objective of the movement?
- Is the problem now closer to resolution than when you first became involved in the struggle?
- Do you identify yourself primarily as Okinawan, Japanese, and/or something else? What role does identity play in your participation in the movement?
- What do you think of Tokyo's handling of the Okinawan situation?
- What questions or what core message do you think Okinawa poses to mainland Japanese? And to the United States?
- Will you describe how the experience or memory (knowledge) of the Battle of Okinawa has impacted your movement?

- What is your view of the constitution of Japan? Is there a generally "Okinawan" understanding of Articles 1–8 (the emperor) or Article 9 (war renunciation) of the constitution?
- Is there any document or text that, above all others, you insist as the charter of a just and proper resolution of Okinawan problems? Any single essay or text that offers you continuing inspiration? Why?
- In the history of Ryukyu/Okinawa, are there particular individuals who seem to you best to embody the moral essence of Okinawa?

### YONAMINE MICHIYO

b. 1976, Naha City, Okinawa, journalist (*Ryukyu Shimpo*).

For me as an Okinawan newspaper reporter, the issue of US military bases is inescapably the greatest issue. I started to follow the base problem at

**Figure 12.1.   Yonamine Michiyo with her son.**

the time of the US Marine helicopter crash onto the campus of Okinawa International University, adjacent to the Futenma Marine Base, in August 2004. At that time I was assigned at the bureau in Ginowan City, site of the Futenma base, so I went straightaway to the crash site the moment it happened and witnessed the horrendous scene. The way that the US military personnel placed restriction on public roads, excluding the local police, media, and residents, made me aware of the reality of their still remaining "occupation mentality." Thereafter, I continued to report on the Futenma issue throughout subsequent assignments in the Tokyo bureau, in the political section, and as a special correspondent in Washington, DC.

But I think my involvement with the military base issue goes back to my elementary school days. My teacher in grade 1 was a survivor of the Himeyuri Student Corps. More than anything else, her arm scarred with gunshot wounds taught me of the horrors of war and preciousness of peace. The memory of her classes, in which she told her own stories, still stays with me. The fact that I was born in Okinawa and grew up feeling war close to me has formed my consciousness, and the fact that I have dealt with the military base issue as a reporter set a foundation of where I stand now.

I aim for elimination of military bases from Okinawa. By that I do not just mean the physical removal of the bases. Essentially, I would like to see elimination of the structural discrimination of Okinawa by Japan. I would like to correct the prevailing misunderstanding that "Okinawa's geographic importance makes the concentration of US military bases inevitable," and ultimately, to see Okinawa self-reliant, free of the influence of military bases.

The situation has not changed. When I read newspapers of decades ago, I am appalled to see that the pages then were dominated by news of US military violence, Okinawan resistance, and the indifference of the Japanese government. The situation now has not changed. But I refuse to give up. I believe that the situation will change, and I am determined to make that change.

I do not have any particular sense of identification as either Okinawan or Japanese. The reason why I tackle the military base issue is not because of my personal background as a resident of Okinawa, but because, from global, universal standards, the Okinawan situation is unfair. As a newspaper reporter, I take it as my responsibility to stand on the side of the weak and to correct injustice.

The reason that the Okinawa military base problem has not been resolved is plainly due to neglect by the Japanese government. There are no votes to be gained by making fundamental change to foreign and security policy. On the contrary, any such endeavor is politically risky. This is why no politician dares touch the issue. The central government often refers to the Okinawan call for a base-free Okinawa as "idealist" and demands Okinawa host more bases, saying we need to be realists. But they have not been able to resolve the Futenma relocation issue at all, fifteen years after an agreement was made to build a replacement base in Henoko. The thinking of government and politicians is frozen, and they do not want to wake up from their "ideal" of Henoko.

## MIYAGI YASUHIRO

b. 1959, Nago City, Okinawa, played a central role in the Nago City Plebiscite Promotion Council (later Council against the Heliport Base) from 1997, and from 1998 to 2006 served as Nago City councillor.

Back in the eighties, I was in Tokyo as a member of a theatrical group. But when the Berlin Wall collapsed, I expected there would be changes in Okinawa, a Cold War island, and went back to Nago, Okinawa, where I was born and brought up. My experience of the movement began as the representative of the citizens calling for a referendum in 1997 on the question of whether or not to construct a new base in Nago City. The opposition won a majority in that referendum, but it was not legally binding, and the mayor of Nago announced that he would accept the base and then resigned. I took up political activity as an elected member of the city assembly and candidate for mayor in order to have the result of that referendum reflected in city government. That activity lasted for nearly ten years till I lost an election, but it decisively changed my life. At present I do not take part in any organized social movement but, based on my more than ten years' experience, I have continued to observe the new base construction problem from a citizen perspective and to publish various things, including a blog. My aim is both to prevent construction of any new base and also, even if in a very small way, to promote Okinawan self-government.

For the ten years after the referendum, there was a majority in prefectural opinion polls against base construction, but a perverse situation applied in which those who were ready to cooperate with the government constituted a majority in the elections of local government heads and assembly members. Okinawans hoped that the change of government from LDP to DPJ would resolve the matter and that hope was betrayed. But the fact that at present the governor and all local mayors oppose any transfer of the base within Okinawa could be described as a late effect of the movement for a change of government. From now on, the DPJ government will most likely apply various pressures, and the outcome remains impossible to predict.

**Figure 12.2.   Miyagi Yasuhiro.**

I am undoubtedly Okinawan. My thinking and my existence are influenced by and constrained by Okinawa's circumstances. During the movement phase, I met many elders who had experienced the Battle of Okinawa. My sense of crisis that that experience might fade away reinforces my determination to prevent base construction.

Okinawa is not calling for immediate return of all US bases. The Japanese and US governments are miscalculating the strength of the Okinawan people's wish to have the base transferred outside Okinawa when their only message is to tell us that in the name of reversion we have to accept construction of a new base and live with it forever and when they keep using economic and other compromise plans to confuse us. Even conservative politicians in Okinawa, once they understood the strength of this sentiment, called for the base to be transferred outside of Okinawa.

I want an end to discrimination against Okinawa that corrodes the constitution at its root and distorts not only Okinawa but the essence of the state of Japan. The United States says it does not situate bases where they are not welcome, but it has continued its military occupation of Okinawa ever since the Second World War, mediated by the government of Japan. People in the United States may not know what is going on in Okinawa. When the United States came to Okinawa in 1945, people of the islands had been brainwashed by Japan, a cult nation, and we were made to say, "Long Live the Emperor!" and for that sake we were dying and being killed. The United States came in then as the antithesis of the cult but has been squatting here ever since. They have gone far beyond their original mission and exceeded any acceptable limit. I would like the United States to end that war once and for all. End the war, and leave.

Japan's is an idealistic constitution, but Okinawa was not part of the process when it was established. Even after the reversion of administrative rights over Okinawa in 1972 it was as if Okinawa was excluded from the application of the constitution by having the bases there in opposition to the will of the Japanese people.

I don't know what the general sentiment is about the relation between the constitution's clauses on the emperor [Articles 1–8] and Article 9 [Renunciation of War], but I think the retention of the emperor system in the form of "symbol of the state and of the unity of the people" meant that the process of reflection on the war was left incomplete. For that reason even to this day ultra-rightist nationalists in Japan launch revisionist campaigns around matters such as how to understand the Battle of Okinawa. In present circumstances, I hold to the complicated view that it is only possible to think about the constitution's Article 9 in conjunction with the Japan-US Security Treaty, and for me as an Okinawan, the brightness shed by Article 9 is pushed into the darkness by the Japan-US Security Treaty.

The right way forward is to be found not in shelves full of books but in the history, livelihood, and struggles of the Okinawan people. The only proper way to solve the present problem is for the governments of Japan and the United States to give up the search for a replacement for the Futenma base, built on land wrongly expropriated from the Okinawan people in war, and to return it to the Okinawan people.

My parents, who made their way from a poor Yambaru village to Nago City, where, despite poverty, they raised me and my four elder brothers and sisters.

## ASHIMINE YUKINE

b. 1971, Matsue City, Shimane, mother, owner of Cafe *Yamagame*, one of the local residents who protest against the plan to construct additional helipads in Camp Gonzales in Yanbaru Forest.

Back in 1994, I was on a biking trip around Yaeyama islands, during which I met a man who is now my husband. Two years after, I visited Okinawa for a camping trip again, and dropped by where he lived, in Kadena Town, and ended up living in Okinawa, till today. When we lived in Kadena, the noise did not bother us as much as it bothered the people in Okinawa City and Chatan Town, where the jet sounds made even ordinary conversation difficult.

We always wanted to live and raise children in a rich natural environment. In the new year of 2002, we found a place we both liked, and as we camped there, the landowner came by, and one thing led to another, and we decided to buy there and build a house. My husband was a carpenter, so we built our own house and cafe. We originally wanted to build a public bath house, but started with a cafe anyway. We were a family of five when we moved to Yanbaru, and now have grown to eight.

When I first saw US military helicopters flying back and forth in the skies over the thick forests I was astonished, and thought, "Wherever you go in Okinawa, there seem to be US bases." I was surprised that where we lived in Yanbaru was actually louder than Kadena. However, my family were all happy to be able to lead an ideal life, the children growing strongly as they played in the rich natural environment.

However, in February 2007, I read in a newspaper that Japan and the United States had agreed to construct six new helicopter takeoff and landing strips, helipads, around the district of Takae in Higashi Village where we were living. Immediately afterward, the Okinawan Defense Bureau conducted what it called an "explanation meeting" at the local hall. Till then, I had had nothing to do with base problems and so I couldn't make

**Figure 12.3.    Ashimine Yukine with her son, age four.**

head or tail of the technical vocabulary used in their leaflets or their ex-
planations.

But since I felt very strongly, "I absolutely oppose any increase in
helipads!" and "I will defend our safe and secure lifestyle!" I set up
and started running study meetings to which I invited experts on the
base problem. I then learned for the first time about the exercises in the
Northern Districts Training Area and the intention to deploy the [MV-22]

Osprey. So, determined to stop this plan, together with others who felt the same way I set up the "Association of Residents against Helipads."

With that, our lives were completely transformed. Till then we had lived totally ordinary, contented lives, but from then, whenever we met talk would be of helipads; there was no escape from it, always and everywhere. We just wanted one thing, for the bases to be removed from Okinawa, and for Okinawan people to be able to lead ordinary, taken-for-granted lives.

Little by little, our movement is spreading, both within Japan and the world. I don't know if the solution to the problems of Futenma and Henoko is near or not but I keep on struggling, convinced that things will turn out for the better.

I am Japanese, but that does not mean that I am full of patriotism. It is hard to say what it is that constitutes identity as Japanese but, anyway, I strongly desire that we stand firmly on our own feet and not just do as the Americans tell us. Most important, I think, is that we raise our level of food self-sufficiency. Even in this opposition movement it is important to solve the base problem that we should produce ourselves more of the food we eat. Little by little, we have been doing this.

I used to think that the government of Japan acted on behalf of the people of Japan, but through involvement in the base problem I came to learn that that was not so. While opposing helipad construction, we were subject to court proceedings under the heading of "provisional ruling over obstruction of traffic" over our sit-in protest and demand for proper explanation and meeting with the Defense Bureau.

Heavens above! It was just unbelievable that the state, which was supposed to protect us, should have brought action against fifteen citizens just because we wanted to protect our livelihood. Among us there were some who had no connection at all with the sit-in, including, most astonishing of all, an eight-year-old girl who had never once even visited the site. So, instead, distrust of the state because "the state does not protect our livelihoods" welled up among us. The outcome of the proceedings was that two of the fifteen were subject of a provisional ruling and proceedings against those two still continue. The state presents virtually nothing by way of evidence. We are angry not only that the meaningless trial has cost us so much time and expense but that taxpayers' money is also wasted on it. It is unbearable that the state keeps insisting on imposing so much of the American bases on Okinawa. I don't think the state even tries to understand Okinawan needs and feelings.

Because of the American bases, Okinawa has to put up with all sorts of things including incidents and accidents caused by US soldiers, accidents and noise nuisance caused by helicopters and fighter planes. Not a day passes without some report of an incident involving the US military appearing in Okinawa's newspapers. Something happens every day. And it is also the case that nearly all the costs involved in maintaining the bases are paid out of Japanese taxes. I want Okinawa to become again a peaceful, safe, and secure island. That is what Okinawans want. As for me personally too, I would like the US to aim for a peaceful world without war.

## YOSHIDA KENSEI

b. 1941, Itoman City, Okinawa, journalist and author.

I consider myself not so much an activist as an Okinawa-born journalist interested in the "Okinawa problem." When I was in middle school and high school, questions concerning the then military government (the occupation), compulsory land acquisition by the military, administrative reversion to Japan, and land problems were much discussed in Okinawa. In the late 1960s, after graduating from the University of Missouri in journalism I returned to Okinawa and began working as a journalist fo-

Figure 12.4.   Yoshida Kensei. *Source:* Satoko Oka Norimatsu.

cused on Okinawa under US military occupation. The main role of *Weekly Okinawa Times*, of which I was chief editor, was to report in English and analyze the Okinawa situation. On my second study trip to Missouri I analyzed Okinawan newspaper editorials on the reversion issue in my master's thesis.

The major fruit of my activities to that point was the book published in 2001 by Western Washington University's Center for East Asian Studies, *Democracy Betrayed: Okinawa under US Occupation*. The book criticized the United States for acting in Okinawa completely contrary to what it publicly and internationally preached in terms of basic human rights.

After that, I wrote a volume based on interviews with former soldiers living in various parts of the United States on their experiences fifty years earlier in the Battle of Okinawa. I also translated *War Is a Racket*, by Smedley D. Butler, a Marine Corps hero whose name is now attached to the Marine HQ in Okinawa. I included it in a book on the US military's propaganda campaign for their "good neighbor" program designed to legitimize the continued basing of US troops after the reversion to Japan of administrative rights, camouflage its unneighborly behavior, and have the government, bureaucrats, and Okinawan people ignore the injustice and accept the bases.

I expected that the return of administrative rights over Okinawa to the sovereign country of Japan would mark a big step toward resolution of the Okinawan problem. With the reversion, there was a noticeable improvement in terms of military land acquisition/compensation issues, base management including the question of poison gas, human rights, economy, education, culture, and so on, compared with the US-administered period. However, as a result of the US-Japan Security Treaty and the Status of Forces Agreement (SOFA) being applied in a concentrated way to Okinawa, military operations and incidents and accidents involving US forces, civilian employees, and families were basically treated as beyond Japan's legal jurisdiction, just as before reversion. In that respect, there was little improvement. The government of Japan does not function as a sovereign state. To the extent that it imposes the Security Treaty and SOFA on Okinawa in breach of its own constitution Okinawa remains a joint military colony of Japan and the United States, and currently there is no prospect of improvement in that situation. I believe that the United States should move the bases not welcome in Japan back either to the US mainland or to its own territory where they will be welcome.

As someone who has worked at the Tokyo office of US media groups (AP, *New York Times*, *Newsweek*) and at the Canadian embassy in Tokyo, who has studied and lectured on Canadian politics, diplomacy, and history at universities in Tokyo and visited the United States and Canada many times and has many friends in both countries, I am not particularly tied to any notion of nationalistic national identity. However, I feel a strong affection for the hometown where I was born and brought up and anger at the military colonial treatment of Okinawa by the United States and Japan.

I am very conscious of the emptying out of democracy and the spread of regional NIMBY-ism ("Not In My Back Yard") in mainland Japan. The government of Japan continues to ignore Okinawan voices on the bases, and while the cities and prefectures of mainland Japan support the US-Japan alliance, they are against any base burden for themselves. The major mass media, which attach greatest weight to circulation, viewer numbers, and advertising revenue, and the Diet, in which Okinawan members are few, do not raise Okinawan voices. If the wishes of Okinawan residents continue to be ignored and risk and burden imposed on Okinawa because it is a small island prefecture, with less than 1 percent of the country's population, it amounts to NIMBY-ism and the negation of democracy. The government is not fulfilling its duty under the constitution to protect the peace and lives of Okinawan people (who are Japanese citizens).

It amounts to a double standard for the United States to have "democracy" as its national principle but not apply it to Okinawa, and to so emphasize military things (maintaining overseas bases and conducting wars) in contradiction to its national principle of "pursuit of international peace." If the United States really believed in peace, democracy, and humanitarianism, it would close down the bases to which the people of Okinawa keep declaring their opposition and withdraw its troops, in accordance with the principle once declared by former Defense Secretary Rumsfeld: "The US does not put bases where they are not welcome."

The United States is immeasurably greater in area than Okinawa, and there are many districts where, for financial reasons, people oppose base realignment and closure. If bases dismantled in Okinawa were transferred to such localities, it would result not only in a reduction of overseas military expenditure but would benefit US security. Taking into consideration the national psychology, and that there are probably no local governments or residents who, sixty-five years after the end of the war, welcome the stationing of US bases, the US should reconsider the maintaining, unchanged, of the US-Japan Security Treaty and the bases. If it does not, it is possible that the US-Japan relationship might even collapse. The American people would never tolerate an agreement conferring extraterritorial status of forces rights where its constitution and laws did not apply or the stationing on its territory of foreign forces paid for by "sympathy" funds akin to foreign aid.

The agreement between the governments of Japan and the United States to transfer Futenma base to Henoko (causing damage to coastal fisheries, danger and noise to residents of local districts, affecting the rare and endangered mammal species of dugong that live in the cobalt-blue coastal waters, and polluting the natural environment in other ways) should also be cancelled. The government of Japan should heed the views of residents in its negotiations with the United States, and the American people should pay more attention to what their government is doing beyond their borders and should make their government desist from double standards.

The Battle of Okinawa occurred because Japan turned Okinawa into a base, stationed military units there, and sacrificed it to protect the "imperial land" (mainland Japan). When Japan lost the Battle of Okinawa with heavy civilian casualties, Okinawa was turned, unchanged, into a US frontline base. When Japan regained Okinawa in 1972, it brought in Self-Defense forces and steadily reinforced them. My worry that Okinawa is placed in the tragic situation of being again a frontline base to protect the imperial lands (the Japanese mainland) influences my thinking and my activities as a journalist. Of course, my heart is also pained over the past murderous behavior of Japan in the Korean peninsula and in China and Southeast Asia, and over the fighting and the harm done since then in the Pacific, Korean, and Vietnam wars, and in the Middle East and inland Asia up to today.

I think the institution of the Japanese emperor, even though now a "symbol," is extremely dangerous in the way it was able to attract popular support, or be politically manipulated, in prewar and wartime. In particular, I think that Articles 6 and 7 of the constitution that spell out the emperor's role in state affairs contain the possibility of justifying political intervention by the emperor in a time of "crisis." Now that more than six decades have passed since the end of the war, it is not clear that many Japanese citizens or Okinawans realize this. Many forget the role played by the emperor or in his name before and during the war, and there is a tendency to support the emperor system. And, even among those who oppose US or Self-Defense Force bases, many ordinary people do not think there is any connection between that and the preamble and Article 9 of the constitution. We need to rethink the constitution, the security treaty, the SOFA, and US wars since the end of the Cold War. The government of Japan places the Security Treaty (and SOFA) above the constitution and so breaches the constitution, its highest precept. The Diet and the Supreme Court are the same. The media ignores the country's reach of the constitution and many mainland people likewise turn a blind eye to it. If the Japanese people protected the constitution and if they were freed from the US-Japan Security Treaty, I think Japan would be respected by foreign countries, including neighbor countries, and would become a friendly, stable, democratic country, and the Okinawa base problem could be solved. The right of self-defense and collective security are recognized under international law. If Japan was to build an exclusively defensive system of security cooperation with its neighbors, without expanding its military power, which is already among the biggest in the world, there would be no need to revise the constitution.

I have no single bedside primer, but I find the constitution's preamble, chapter 2 (Renunciation of War) and chapter 3 (Rights and Duties of Citizens) splendid provisions guaranteeing pacifism, international cooperation, and people's rights against the state.

Article 99 provides that "The Emperor or the Regent as well as Ministers of State, members of the Diet, judges and all other public officials have the obligation to respect and uphold this Constitution." If these were all to stick literally to the constitution, the Okinawan problem should be readily solved.

Ota Masahide is someone who is not just a researcher and politician in the flow of Ryukyu-Okinawa history but one who has a detailed understanding of the Battle of Okinawa, US control of Okinawa post–World War Two, and Japan's Okinawa policy. And as a survivor of the Battle of Okinawa he has constantly called for transformation in Okinawa's present situation.


## CHININ USII

b. 1966, Shuri, Naha City, Okinawa Island, writer.

I have no clear memory of when I first became active in the Okinawa movement. Since I was a child, born and raised in Okinawa, I have been involved in the Okinawan situation. At the time I left Okinawa to go to college in Tokyo, I began asking myself, what is Okinawa, and who am I?

The goal of my activity is for all military bases to be gone from Okinawa, and for the Ryukyus to be decolonized. But I feel uncomfortable if I am called an "activist." All I am doing is just living daily life in Okinawa trying to be true to myself.

I have been acting with "Gathering of Kamaduu gwa" (Kamaduu gwa tachi no tsudoi) since around 2002. Kamaduu gwa was founded in 1997 by women who live and/or work in the neighborhood of the US Marine Corps Air Station (MCAS) at Futenma. When it became known that the Futenma base was to be moved to Henoko, as residents of Ginowan (Futenma), they could not just stand and watch. At the time of the Nago City referendum, they together with women from Nago began going door to door in Nago, appealing to the residents: "Transferring the base to another place in Okinawa doesn't rid Okinawa of it. You don't need to accept the base for the sake of Ginowan. Let's join together and oppose it."

**Figure 12.5.** chinin usii. *Source: Okinawa Taimusu.*

Since then they have continued their movement, at the local level, to rid Okinawa of the bases. According to Kamaduu gwa, what keeps the bases in Okinawa is mainland Japanese public opinion. The majority supports US bases in Japan, but they don't want them nearby. A minority opposes the bases and tells Okinawa, "Wait until we drive all the bases out of Japan," which they don't have the power to do. Together they constitute a force that keeps, for example, Futenma base out of mainland Japan and in Okinawa. In consideration of the whole history of Okinawa-Japan relations, and hoping to elicit some response from the Japanese, they dare to take the position, *"kengai isetsu"* (literally "outside the prefecture," but in the Okinawan context meaning "to mainland Japan" or "Take back the bases you have forced on Okinawa, and get rid of them yourselves"). This position has led to the notion, of course a misunderstanding, that they are not really opposed to the bases or to the Japan-US Security Treaty as such, and has brought down showers of criticism on them, but this has not led them to give up their position. This strength—"Call us what you like, we will continue to be what we are"—finds its origin in the Okinawa women's liberation movement. The Okinawan traditional name "Kamaduu" has recently been found to be derived from Sanskrit, and to mean "beloved one." However, in the modern era, under about a century of "civilizing and Japanizing," it has become degraded to symbolize "coarse, inferior, ignorant Okinawan women." In full awareness of this they choose this name, and in so doing intend to bring the Okinawan language and traditional culture into the antibase movement, thereby transforming it into not only a movement to bring about the return of the land the bases are on, but also a movement for the return and restoration of Okinawa/Ryukyu itself.

Today in Okinawa more and more of the people are becoming aware of their identity and their positionality and are becoming increasingly able to demand from the United States and Japan—and especially from our "intimate enemy" Japan—a position of equality, and to say NO (Stop depending on us!).

One sign of that is that they have forced the prefectural governor to change his position on Futenma base to *kengai isetsu* (move it to mainland Japan).

For Okinawans/Ryukyuans to take that position in full awareness of what it entails means to pass through many complex internal difficulties with our "intimate enemy," the Japanese, and so to be able to say it is one of the concrete acts of "decolonization of consciousness." I believe that this is an extremely important change, and a step forward.

When I heard that the tentative title of this book was "Okinawa, the Japanese Islands That Say 'No,'" I did not understand the meaning. I first thought it was an error in English and that what was meant was,

"Okinawa that the Japanese (main) islands say 'No' to." That is because it is mainland Japan—the government, the bureaucrats, the mass media, and the people who keep saying "no" to the Okinawa that is demanding *kengai isetsu*.

Then, after thinking a little while, I realized that "The Japanese islands saying no" meant Okinawa. Then I felt uncomfortable with the adjective "Japanese" being attached to our islands. "Japanese" reverberates with the meanings "Japan occupies" and "Japan colonizes" Okinawa.

The question about my personal identity, and, to tell the truth, this questionnaire in its entirety, make me feel uneasy. Ever since my college days in Tokyo, I have been getting questions like that over and over. Why, I wonder, am I always put in the position of being subjected to one-directional questions like this? Rather, I believe this is something to be mutually taken up slowly in conversation with someone with whom you have taken the time to develop a relation of trust.

Concerning that gaze which fixes Okinawa in the position of being questioned unilaterally, I am reminded of the Jinruikan (Pavilion of Mankind) incident of 1903. At that time, as its imperial dominion was expanding, Japan, imitating the Western imperial powers, brought people from the various territories it had colonized and put them on display as an academic exhibition. In addition to Ryukyuans (Okinawans), Ainu, native Taiwanese, Koreans, Javanese, and Indians were displayed. Here we see the colony, in the position of power, gazing in curiosity at the colonized, who is reduced to the position of an "exhibit."

This gaze that fixes itself on us is not simply a problem of the past. Of course it is found in "Okinawa boom" tourism, but also, unfortunately, we can feel it in the peace movement and in academic research.

In the Jinruikan incident, another problem was the Ryukyuans who internalized this gaze and demanded, "Do not group us together with those others."

In order not to do this again, I have decided to meet the problem head on and to write these sentences. It is to stand with those people all over the world who are forced to meet the same problem, to stand with those who have become aware of their gaze and are trying to free themselves from it.

And now I will answer the question on my identity. I am registered as a Japanese national, but I am an Okinawan, a Ryukyuan woman.

Then this is my turn. I will ask you who gave me the questions and who are now reading my answers here, "Who are you?"

I have learned a lot from my Okinawan friends, especially Kamadou gwa and Nomura Koya, the author of *Muishiki no shokuminchi shugi— nihonjin no beigun kichi to okinawajin* (*Unconscious Colonialism: The Japanese People's US Bases and Okinawans*). Also I have been influenced by works of Gandhi, Frantz Fanon, Lu Xun, Malcolm X, Haunani-Kay Trask, and bell hooks.

The person who best embodies the moral essence of Okinawa to me is my grandmother.

## KINJO MINORU

b. 1939, Hamahiga Island, Okinawa, sculptor.

Okinawan mass meetings have become common in recent years in Okinawa, and when they take place you are bound to notice the large banner saying "Ryukyu Independence."

In principle, talk of Ryukyu independence has existed for a long time. During the last phases of the Battle of Okinawa two streams of argument were born in the prison camps, one for "return to the fatherland" and the other for independence. Ever since then, these twins have been swept along side by side in the flow of history.

Much of my life was spent in Osaka, in Yamato [mainland Japan]. Young people at that time used to be brought from Okinawa in groups for collective employment in Kansai area, their passports seized by their employers so that they could not go home even for O-Bon or New Year. There was discrimination against Okinawans in terms of lodgings and pay. Young fellows were sometimes caught up in brawls at drinking places.[1]

It was a time when cases of injuries, death, and suicide among Okinawan young people was a social problem. One young Okinawan poured gasoline on the home of the president of the company he worked at, causing the death of the president's wife. In the end he committed suicide while in prison. It was the year after Okinawa's reversion to Japan [1973]. The idea of Okinawan independence was born as a sentiment of resistance against the structural discrimination of Yamato society. Both in Okinawa itself and in mainland Japan, gradually this word spread.

There were some among Okinawan university professors and intellectuals who scorned the idea of independence as just "bar-room independence talk." But following the prison suicide of the young man mentioned above, Okinawan youth in Osaka formed a Gajumaru [Banyan] Association and staked their resistance on their pride as Okinawans and conducted "Eisa Bon-odori" dance at Chishima Ground in Osaka's Taisho ward.[2] However, most of the Uchina (Okinawan) people who came to watch spoke of it as a disgraceful display and took their distance from it in embarrassment.

Figure 12.6.   Kinjo Minoru at his atelier in Yomitan. *Source:* Satoko Oka Norimatsu.

The young people, by contrast, thought of themselves as doing a dance of resistance in order to reclaim their pride. As a high school teacher, I was one of those who supported them.

In Kansai, Eisa dance was an expression of resistance and of liberation from discrimination. At that time, one in four of the people living in Osaka's Taisho ward, or more than 30,000 people, were of Okinawan origin.

Eisa dance, which used to be thought of in terms of inferiority complex and shame, has evolved so that today it is danced proudly at the All-Japan High School Baseball contest at Koshien, even to the extent that the organizing committee has complained. When that happened, the famous TV personality, [the late] Chikushi Tetsuya, protested to the organizing committee.

While this storm raged in Kansai, eventually the "bar-room talk" appeared in Okinawa itself.

On October 21, 1995, at the mass meeting to denounce the rape of the Okinawan girl by US servicemen and the handling of the matter by the governments of Japan and the United States, and again on September 29, 2008, at the mass meeting to denounce the reorganization of US forces in Japan and the adoption of textbooks distorting the history of the Battle of Okinawa, a Declaration of Ryukyu Independence was displayed and handed out in various foreign-language versions, under the banner of "Okinawan Independence."

It begins: "Independence for Ryukyu! Let us take a different path from Japan. Let us take self-determination into our own hands." The Okinawan society of the Ryukyu Arc islands, committed to peace and strong in the arts and performance, culture and sport, chooses the path of solidarity with friends in neighboring countries. The wisdom and know-how to construct Ryukyu society is present in abundance. Let us reclaim our dignity as human beings, our society freed from the oppression of armies, freed from dependence and servitude, poverty and inequality.

Who can know how people respond when we hand them out leaflets at mass meetings that ended with the words

Wake up to the shout of Hiya! (*Hiyamikachiukiri*)
The Yamato world, the future as reversion, is illusion.
Let us islanders of Ryukyu pioneer the new era.
—The Ryukyu Punishment [*Ryukyu Shobun*] of Okinawan Karate Culture

In his book entitled *Okinawa dento karate no hen-yo* [*The Transformation of Okinawan Traditional Karate*], Nohara Koei uses the phrase "the *Ryukyu shobun* [Ryukyu punishment] of karate" in the context of his discussion of the culture of Okinawan karate.[3] Under the political culture of mainland Japan there is a separate entry on karate culture for the Okinawan Karate

Association. Okinawa's karate world comprises two organizations: the "All-Okinawa Karate League" and the "All-Okinawa Karate and Ancient Martial Arts League."

The Yamato [mainland Japan]-based All Japan Karate League (president: Sasakawa Ryoichi) brought pressure to bear through the National Police Agency to compel the Okinawan Federation to join it. Even though most leaders of the mainland All Japan League were pupils or disciples of Okinawan karate figures, they used intimidation to try to force Okinawa to join the All-Japan League, saying that it would not be allowed to participate in the National Athletic Meet unless it did so. On the eve of the 1987 National Athletic Meet, such persuasion failed and negotiations broke down.

Backing their words with political and financial force, [the National League] thus spat on Okinawa's karate world. Nohara analyzes this reliance on force as a *Ryukyu shobun* (Ryukyu punishment). While this confrontation continues to this day, the Okinawan Dojo (training rooms) maintain their Okinawan identity and display pride in Okinawan karate culture. In October 2011, a World Karate Meet will be held in Okinawa as part of the World Uchina (Okinawa) Assembly. Amid the disturbances over the reorganization of US forces in Japan, resistance in accordance with the Okinawa spirit continues.

Eisa and karate give a consciousness of Okinawan culture and enable victory over discrimination and inferiority complex. It happened in 2010 that the victory of the Konan High School in the National High School Baseball championships at Koshien in Hyogo[4] coincided with the mass meeting of 100,000 people to oppose the relocation within Okinawa of Futenma Marine Air Base. I participated in this mass meeting, taking with me a section of my hundred-meter-long, larger than life sculpture on War and Humanity depicting resistance by peasants and their farm animals trying to protect their land against seizure by US forces in the early postwar period. Between forty and fifty people and animals are depicted in that section, "Bayonets and Bulldozers."

Uchina, Cry Not over Discrimination and Oppression—
The gene of resistance is bound to spread!


## URASHIMA ETSUKO

b. 1948, Kagoshima prefecture, Japan, Nago civic activist, author, historian of the antibase movement.

For personal reasons I moved to Okinawa with my then seven-month-old son around May 1990. At first I lived in the base town of Okinawa City

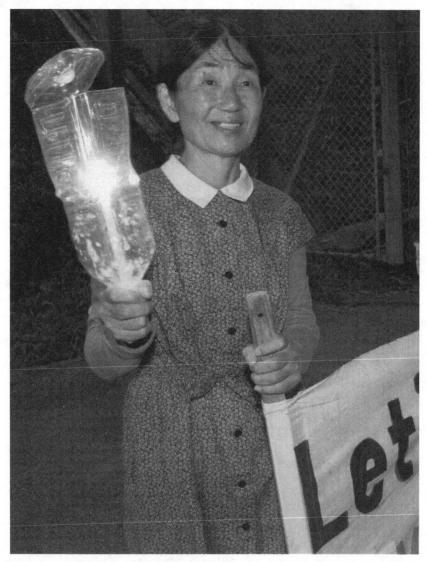

**Figure 12.7. Urashima Etsuko.** *Source:* Toyozato Tomoyuki.

but I took to walking in the mountains, attracted by the nature and scenery of Yambaru that resembled that of Amami island where I had been living till then. Around me, along with the deep attractions of Yambaru nature, I could see with my own eyes how the rare beauty of nature was being ravaged by public works paid for by generous government grants that were poured in to compensate for the US bases. I formed the strong impression that the Okinawa base problem and the environment problem were two sides of the same coin, and the twin problem consciousness I had held since I was young of "peace and environment" became clearer and more deeply and strongly rooted within me.

Along with other friends who were saddened by the destruction of Yambaru nature and who shared the view of the twenty years of Okinawa's reversion to Japan as twenty years of environmental destruction, in May 1992 I founded the Yambaru Protection Liaison Committee, for which I served as general secretary for the next four years, struggling to try to prevent the destruction in however small a way. Unfortunately, that organization had to be wound up while there was still much to be done. But anyway my heart was set on Yambaru and I decided to move to live there.

Around the time of making that move, it happened that I started to work in Sakima Museum, adjacent to Futenma Marine Base. It was just at that time that the question of return of Futenma and its transfer to the Henoko coastal district was much in the news, and I took the opportunity to make my first visit to Henoko. I will never forget the feeling at the moment I first set foot on the uninhabited island of Hirashima. Between the island and Camp Schwab Marine Base lay the translucent, glimmering, emerald green lagoon. The coral, waves, and wind of this sea over unimaginably long months and years had created this sand so white that it seemed almost a crime to step on it.

Scooping up in my fingers this white sand completely free of impurity [I thought of] the Henoko residents who were saying with such fervor "We will protect this." The brilliant whiteness of the sand trickling through my fingers suffused my innermost being. At the same time, the stories I had heard from local people of this island having been used as a base for suicide boat missions during the Battle of Okinawa were also etched on my mind.

In December 1997, Nago citizens conducted a citizens' plebiscite to sound views on whether or not to construct a "heliport" and they were victorious despite the manifold interventions, pressures, and inducements from the governments of Japan and the US state power and money power, sending to the world the message: "No base." Together with the women of Ginowan City (site of the Futenma base) I commuted back and forth to Nago to assist in the plebiscite. We organized ourselves into pairs with the women of Nago's eastern seaboard (the ten districts north of Futami) to participate in the movement, pleading the dangers of Futenma and urging people to vote against the transfer project.

Even though we were victorious in the plebiscite, the Nago City mayor trampled on the will of the people and announced that he would accept the base, then promptly resigned. It was shortly after his successor had been decided at a fresh mayoral election that I was able to make the move to live in the Futami district of the Yambaru of my dreams, thanks to contacts I had made in the movement, and I became a member of the "Ten Districts North of Futami against the Heliport" local civic group. Since the reverberations of the plebiscite success were still continuing, and the newly elected mayor was taking a very cautious attitude even though he was probase, I was thinking I would at last be able to take it easy and fulfill my long-held ambition to write a novel while leading a quiet life in the Yambaru.

However, things were not so simple. The state powers of Japan and the United States pulled out all stops and launched an assault on the local residents, who had neither power nor money and already struggling with aging and depopulation. The days and nights that followed were filled with desperate, all-out efforts to beat back the embers. Apart from the regular movement activities such as sit-ins, signature campaigns, rallies, and *michijune* (street demonstrations) we launched an offensive, adopting creative measures such as sending daily "love letters" to the mayor who seemed unwilling to listen to the voices of citizens or conducting *ugan* (traditional prayer). In the end we adopted all and every possible means, including fierce clashes with the staff and employees of the Okinawa Defense Bureau in canoes and around the offshore survey towers.

I chose to be a writer after I moved to Yambaru, although not so much for money as for my chosen way of life. Writing became a frantic necessity, to report on and give voice to the movement of residents against the construction of the base. It would be hard for me to go about collecting materials and writing from a third-party perspective. I can only write with "I" as subject, of my experiences in my physical engagement as a participant, reporting on the everyday life and bitter struggles, and even when I sometimes have to make a political comment I cannot but write from the "I" perspective.

I think that writing for me has been a way to give shape to how nature is trampled and despoiled by the authorities and to give voice to the voiceless people who are made to live within it while recounting down to the finest detail its beauty and splendor and the sadness and pain. Writing about them has helped me overcome my own difficulties and worries.

Time and again during this fifteen years I have felt "I can't take any more," or "I want to quit the movement." But the reason on such occasions I have not given up is because if our generation destroys this irreplaceable nature which has given life to people from ancient times, nature that forms the basis for future generations yet to be born, we could never be forgiven by those later generations.. The goal of our movement is to hand on to future generations, our children and grandchildren, "peace and nature (the environment)" and it is the responsibility of those now living to strive for this no matter what the difficulties.

I could never have imagined at the outset how long this problem would drag on. Through persevering doggedly as Okinawan governors and Nago mayors ready to accept the construction of a base succeeded one after the other and we were reduced to near despair, the situation now is, I think, quite advantageous. For the first time, a mayor who takes an avowedly antibase stance has been elected. And the governor, who had been ready to accept the base, has been driven by Okinawan opinion to take the position of "move the base somewhere outside Okinawa." All Okinawans are united around "No New Henoko Base" in a way that was never so decisively the case in the past.

And yet, though it is absurd, even though Okinawa's own fate is at stake, we are in a position in which we cannot decide it. I don't know how many times I have felt the bitterness and frustration over the fact that decisions on our fate are taken somewhere beyond our reach. If Okinawa was self-determining, this problem would have been settled by now. The biggest problem is that in fact the determining power is held by the two governments of Japan and the United States and that there will be no resolution until they decide to give up the plan to transfer the base to Henoko. So long as this situation continues, even if the two governments decide to give up the transfer to Henoko, there is no way to stop something similar happening again in the future. There can be no real solution short of putting a stop to this history of being pushed and pulled about by the politics and diplomacy of Japan and the United States and until Okinawa is able to regain the power to determine its own affairs.

Though feeling slightly uncomfortable about it, I define myself as "Zai-Oki" (Okinawa-resident) Japanese. That is because, even though I love Okinawa and share happiness, pain, and sadness with the local people, I must not think that by assimilating as Okinawan I can somehow forget that I am descended from those who once invaded and discriminated against Okinawa. I must not repeat that offense.

I am currently joint representative of "Ten Districts Association." But when I was chosen there was a good deal of friction over the question of whether it could be right for me as "Zai-Oki" Japanese to be representative of the local movement. I worried that it might make it more difficult for local people to take action if an outsider were seen to be taking things into her own hands or taking too prominent a role. But the more I put down roots and formed local ties, the more I came to know that there were many people who were unable to express their support for us because of various considerations but were ready to entrust me with their wishes; so I think

I might have a role to play. But, more than anything, I act for myself and not for anyone else, as I intend to go on living here and I never want to have any base built here.

When I was working on the compilation of Okinawa's prefectural history I listened to many people's experiences of the Battle of Okinawa, and, apart from that, I have had plenty of opportunity to relive war experiences. You could say that one of the driving forces in my antibase activism has been my strong revulsion for war and sense that war must by all means be prevented.

The constitution of Japan is said to be US-made, but I do not agree. After the end of World War II, the losses were so great not only on the defeated side but on the victorious side too that the world filled with the desire that there never be another war. I look on the constitution of Japan as the distillation of that global (and also of course Japanese) wisdom. However, the ideal was subsequently lost sight of and the world saw a reversal back into the era of war.

Even though Okinawa sought reversion to the constitution of Japan (the peace constitution), still today forty years after reversion the constitution of Japan has yet to be applied there. However, when you consider it closely, the situation of "the US-Japan Security Treaty (Anpo) transcends the constitution" applies to the whole country. I think it would be good for the lawless state of Japan as a whole if the constitution of Japan was to be properly applied in Okinawa.

The emperor clause is a major contradiction in the constitution of Japan. It is an alien item implanted there to serve Japan-US political designs. The clauses related to the emperor should be deleted from the constitution and the emperor system should be done away with.

Okinawans have little attachment to or interest in the emperor, but I think discrimination against Okinawa and the emperor system are not unrelated. Many Okinawans were driven to their deaths during the Battle of Okinawa in the name of the emperor. The emperor system and emperor-system-related things lie at the root of all discrimination.

There are so many writings by past Okinawans and present opinion leaders which inspire me and which I use as references when I am writing. But if you ask who have been the greatest influences on me, I would say (though neither is connected to Okinawa) Rachel Carson and Ishimure Michiko.

There is much to be learned from the great figures and those known in history, but I am much more attracted by the great wisdom that flows through the veins of the common people in the marketplace. Many times when conducting interviews I have learned new things from people living extremely ordinary lives, rather than from the words of leaders of the time.

## OTA MASAHIDE

b. 1925 in Kumejima Island (about 100 kilometers west of Okinawa Island), historian. Ota was a nineteen-year old student at the Okinawa Teacher's College in March 1945 on the eve of the US invasion of Okinawa (for his experience of the Battle of Okinawa, see chapter 2). Graduating in 1954 from Waseda University in Tokyo, Ota then completed an MA in journalism at Syracuse University in the United States in 1956. Thereafter he taught at University of the Ryukyus, made numerous visits to teach and research at colleges in the United States, from 1990 to 1998 was governor of Okinawa, and from 2001 to 2007 was a member of the House of Councillors in the Japanese Diet. Marked forever by the tragic experiences of his youth, Ota has written almost one hundred books on various aspects of Okinawan history, culture, and identity, and especially on the Battle of Okinawa. Today he is professor emeritus at the University of the Ryukyus and director of the Ota Peace Research Institute.

My immediate priority after defeat in the war was to gather the remains of my teachers and fellow students. For the first year or so after the war ended,

Figure 12.8. Ota Masahide at his Naha office. *Source:* Satoko Oka Norimatsu.

the US forces put Okinawans into sixteen district encampments (concentration camps) and forbade communication between the camps. Behavior seen as anti-American on the part of Okinawan people was punished by suspension of rations; so leaders of the civil government and teachers, including teachers at the Teachers' College and at the newly set-up foreign language schools, opposed those of us who were collecting remains because they were afraid it might lead to rations for students being cut off. To deal with this, we argued all night long with leaders of the Okinawan government and the schools. That became the first student movement of postwar Okinawa. The result was that a small number of us students could go out on MP [military police] jeeps, under guard, and collect remains. We gathered remains into one large tent and made every effort to return them to their families, but we had no idea how to find people.

Next, I went to Tokyo. In my third year at university, I edited a collection of individual recollections of survivors of the Battle of Okinawa under the title *Okinawa's Youth Brigade* (*Okinawa Kenjitai*) which became a film from Shochiku. I then began a movement to tell the reality of the Battle of Okinawa to as many people as possible. I commissioned a prominent Tokyo sculptor to make the statue "Image of Peace" of three standing figures symbolizing devotion between teachers and students, peace, and friendship. I brought it to Okinawa and had it erected at Mabuni where the student brigade had fought as a memorial for my teachers and classmates.

Once employed by University of the Ryukyus, I started making annual trips to the US National Archives to look for and buy film and photographs of the Battle of Okinawa. I set up the "One Foot" movement in which anyone could contribute as little as one hundred yen and bought as much as possible of such film and photographs. I kept making these annual visits to the United States for about twenty years and gathered a substantial archive which people have since then been able to consult in the Okinawa Prefectural Archives.

The "One Foot" movement grew into a nonprofit called, "Battle of Okinawa One Foot Movement Association." Carrying on the mission of making known the truth about the Battle of Okinawa to a generation with no direct knowledge of it and turning Okinawa into a Mecca for the building of world peace, I made films that spliced together footage from the collection and showed them at screenings and symposiums.

In the process of learning about the battle of Okinawa, one cannot help confronting the question of identity. This is because of the simple reason that the people of Okinawa have been plunged time and again into a situation of identity crisis. After the Satsuma invasion of 1609, Satsuma placed the court of the Ryukyu kingdom under its effective control in order to extract the economic benefits derived from the tribute trade with

China, but kept the reality hidden and made the relationship with China continue unchanged. To conceal this from China, it was strictly forbidden for Okinawans to speak Japanese or dress in Japanese clothing. And when Ryukyu missions of "thanks" went to Edo, they wore Chinese clothing and played Chinese instruments so that Edo could boast of the foreign country under its control. Okinawans were obliged to vacillate in identity, being neither Chinese nor Japanese. In other words, they were put into a situation of loss of identity.

Worse still, the government of Japan thought it would be desirable to abolish Okinawan identity altogether, since it was backward and of little value, and to assimilate it completely to the advanced culture of Japan. That seemed to be the only way for Okinawans to have a national identity as first-class Japanese.

However, ever since Okinawa became a prefecture of Japan in 1879, eight years later than mainland prefectures, its people were subjected by the Meiji government to a heavy-handed and intense education process designed to achieve "*kominka*" (transformation into imperial subjects). George H. Kerr, professor of history at Stanford University, took the view that the abolition of the feudal domains in mainland Japan was different in character from what happened in Okinawa; elsewhere it was a case of creating a modern nation-state on the basis of shared race, language, and culture, but in Okinawa the process was seen exclusively in military and political terms as one of reinforcing Japan's southern gateway.

Okinawans were not seen as being the same race or as fellow countrymen, and the purpose of stationing a detachment of the Kumamoto Sixth Division in Okinawa was not because of the Okinawan people but because they wanted the Okinawan land. In a nutshell, however you look at it, Okinawa was not seen as a part of Japan but as a political and economic colony.

So, to Okinawans, the biggest problem was always that of national identity, how to assimilate to the nation, and for that they had to sacrifice not just their cultural identity but their human identity, giving up their certificate of existence. It was such a heavy price. For that reason, I came to think it necessary for Okinawans to acquire a human identity that would allow them to maintain their own cultural identity, rather than to gain a national identity by assimilation.

From the viewpoint of orientation to a humanistic way of living based on universalist human values, and in order to sweep aside the discriminatory policies of the Japanese and US governments, I want to seek and implement a living environment appropriate for a humanistic way of living.

Okinawans are no different as human beings from Japanese or Americans. And yet in the past they have been treated on countless occasions by mainland Japanese and by Americans as trading goods, like a security or an item to be pawned, that is to say, as a thing or as a means, in order to accomplish the purposes of people of mainland Japan or the US forces.

For example, at the time of the Meiji "Ryukyu disposal," a 400-man detachment of the Japanese army and a 160-man police detachment were stationed in Okinawa in order to reinforce Japan's southern gateway. And again, in the Battle of Okinawa at the end of World War Two, Okinawa was turned into a fortress for the defense of mainland Japan, and almost one-third of the people lost their precious lives. As well, countless irreplaceable cultural items bequeathed us by our ancestors were destroyed by fire. And because before the defeat in the war Okinawa had served as a stepping-off point or base for Japanese aggression against Asia, it was then cut off from Japan and placed under US military control for twenty-seven years. Under the Japan-US Security Treaty of 1951, in exchange for Japan's independence Okinawa was handed to the United States as a military base, Prime Minister Yoshida accepting the use of bases under the Bermuda formula (or 99-year lease).

As a result, not only is 11 percent of Okinawa's land now turned into base, but harbors and coast in twenty-nine places and 40 percent of Okinawa's air space is under US military control. So today, even sixty-six years after the defeat in the war, we still do not enjoy free use of our own land or air or sea. Okinawa can scarcely be seen as part of a sovereign country.

The problems over the transfer of Futenma marine base to Henoko are precisely what Norwegian peace studies scholar Johan Galtung refers to as "structural discrimination." It is common in cases of discrimination for the party that discriminates to have no awareness of itself as discriminating; and mainland prefectures, even though they stress that the Japan-US Security Treaty under which the bases exist is in the national interest, refuse to share Okinawa's burden.

Incidentally, the Japanese national Diet has 712 members, of whom only eight are Okinawan representatives. It would not be so bad if national Diet members who overwhelmingly represent mainland constituencies were to make serious effort to address Okinawan problems as their own; but they make no real effort to do so and just treat them as someone else's problem. So, ironically, Okinawa is always discriminated against in the name of a democracy that is based on majority rule. And that is the biggest factor in prolonging any resolution of the Okinawan base problem. So long as the people of Japan are prepared to sacrifice the people of Okinawa in the interests of their own peace and security I cannot help but doubt their sensitivity as human beings.

When the Battle of Okinawa began on March 26, 1945, I had just completed my foundation year and was about to proceed to second year as student of the Okinawa Teachers' College. But on March 31, under the orders of Lieutenant-Colonel Komaba of the Okinawa Defense Command, all teachers and students of my college were ordered, without exception other than the sick, to report to HQ. Armed with a rifle, 120 rounds of ammunition and two hand grenades, we were then organized into the Blood and Iron Imperial Unit (*Tekketsu Kinnotai*) and sent to war.

Within that unit, I was attached to the twenty-two-man Chihaya detachment responsible for intelligence and propaganda. We made ourselves into groups of two and at the direction of the Defense Command's intelligence section we circulated war information coming from Supreme Headquarters in Tokyo to soldiers and civilians hiding in the caves around Okinawa's main island. The idea was that we would help lift the spirits of the people hiding in caves with no idea of what was happening in the outside world.

However, the situation worsened day by day. By late May, the Shuri castle underground Defense Command was threatened and withdrew to the Kyan peninsula in the south of Okinawa Island. As defeat followed defeat, and led to flight, from June 18 the student corps was dismissed and freed from military orders. However, those of us in the Chihaya Unit were given direct orders from Commander Ushijima Mitsuru to break through enemy lines, regroup at Kunigami district in the north, and resort to guerrilla warfare. In groups of two or three we set out. A group of three, comprising myself, first-year student Nakata, and classmate Yamada, planned to break through the lines, but no sooner had we emerged from the underground site at Mabuni than bombs exploded all around and split us up. My right foot was gashed (by shrapnel) and, unable to walk, I could only crawl on my belly through the rocks.

Under orders to break through to the north at any cost, crawling along with my injured right leg I headed for the caves on the hillside close to where the Defense Command was dug in opposite Mabuni Village. When I went in I found a group of Japanese Army defeated troops hiding there. Their commander, a lieutenant, pressed me for my identity, refusing to accept my repeated protestation that I was a student member of the Blood and Iron brigade. "There cannot be any students in the vicinity of the Headquarters trench, so you must be a spy," he said, poking me in the chest with his bayonet. To be accused of being a spy was beyond my imagination, so, ignoring the pain in my leg, I stood up and protested. Fortunately, I happened to have a pass signed by Lt Colonel Yakumaru Kanemasa of Headquarters Staff Office guaranteeing free entry of Chigusa Unit members to any military sites and requesting the assistance of any commanders. With that, eventually I was able to persuade the officer as to my identity and the crisis passed. But after this I could not forget the shock and bitterness caused by this incident of being mistaken for a spy and started to distrust the old Japanese army and to question the meaning of the Battle of Okinawa.

The loss of so many of my teachers and classmates led me to a decisive turning-point in my effort to understand this war that had been called a holy war. When I think of those buds scattered over the cruel battlefield while still on the brink of adulthood and before they had a chance to flower I find myself overcome with the unbearableness of it. Even after the suicide of the Okinawa Defense Army's Commander General Ushijima and Chief of Staff Cho on June 22, 1945, and the end of organized resistance, I was hiding, uncaptured, around the coast of Mabuni and Gushichan. Day after day, I saw acts by defeated Japanese soldiers of such inhuman cruelty as to make me completely lose faith in humanity. Not only were there countless cases of them mercilessly driving noncombatants from caves or of grabbing food supplies in order to save their own lives, but the spectacle of these soldiers fighting and killing each other over tiny amounts of food or water left me speechless. If only I could survive, I vowed by all means to try to understand how we came to commit such a horrifying and shameful war.

After the war I was living in Ishikawa (now Uruma) City, where the Okinawan civil government was located and where Nakasone Seizen, famous as the leader of the Himeyuri (Lily) Student Brigade, worked. Nakasone believed that there should be a special kind of textbook for Okinawan children who had survived the battle and he wrote with that in mind. On one occasion when I was helping him to Roneo materials, he took delivery by airmail of a copy of the Constitution of Japan and urged me to read it. When I first looked at the new constitution and saw that it prescribed the nonpossession of any army and the resolve never again to go to war I was overcome with emotion. I was in that state of being literally ravaged in mind and body that comes to battlefield survivors, without hope for the future and without joy in life. Having fallen so deeply into distrust of humanity, I could not help but feel the words and sentences of the constitution penetrate to the depths of my being.

It was especially as if the basic principle of the preamble and the war-renouncing precept of Article 9 articulated my deepest desire for peace and antiwar. That unexpected encounter with the new constitution gave me new hope and joy in life. The constitution became in truth the guideline for my subsequent life.

I think this memory and this experience was not uncommon among Okinawans at that time. What a cruel reality it was for Okinawans who had barely survived the war to have to live with military bases, beyond the scope of this profoundly meaningful constitution, and having survived against all odds to be thus placed under the control of a foreign army. It was only natural that the Okinawan people's subsequent movement for reversion to Japan's constitution should have adopted the slogan "Let Us Revert to the Peace Constitution."

## NOTES

1. Kinjo Minoru obtained a passport to go to the mainland in 1957. He went to Kyoto University of Foreign Studies, became a teacher of English, and taught at schools in the Kansai area until he went back to Okinawa in 1994 to focus on his work as a sculptor. In his book *Shitte imasuka Okinawa ichimon itto* (Osaka: Kaiho shuppan sha, 2003), he talks about discrimination against Okinawans in mainland Japan.

2. The Okinawan population in Osaka concentrated in the Taisho district, where from the late nineteenth to early twentieth century they were hired as laborers for construction work on ports and canals and to work at lumbermills around Osaka Bay. (Kinjo, *Shitte imasuka*, 48–53.)

3. Nohara wrote of the three "Ryukyu Punishments"—the first being the forceful incorporation of Ryukyu into Japan in 1879, the second being the US colonization of Okinawa since 1945, and the third being the reversion to Japan in 1972. Karate originated in Okinawa, and Okinawa had two karate organizations, independent from the Japanese national organization. Nohara argues the mainland karate organization threatening the Okinawan organization to join them is another Ryukyu punishment, in a cultural form. Kinjo Minoru, "Mirai e no isan—Ryukyu kyowakoku dokuritsu e no bunkaronteki shian," *Tsubute* (Spring 2009).

4. The High School Baseball Tournament is held every spring and summer at Koshien Stadium in Hyogo, near Osaka. In 2010, Okinawa's Konan High School became the national champion in both spring and summer tournaments, unprecedented in the history of high school baseball in Okinawa.

# 13

~~

# Prospect

## "STOMPING AND KICKING"

At the end of August 2009, hope stirred in the Japanese air as voters united to put a decisive end to five decades of Liberal Democratic Party rule. That hope, however, slowly dissipated as one by one, the Democratic Party of Japan (DPJ) abandoned its preelection pledges and reverted to precisely those clientelist and neoliberal policies it had attacked on the part of its LDP predecessors in order to win office.

Hatoyama Yukio in 2009 came into office promising a government in which politicians would lead and bureaucrats follow; a renegotiated, more equal relationship with the United States; closer ties with neighbor countries, including China; and a Futenma marine base relocated "at least outside Okinawa." Nine months later, he beat an ignominious retreat, unable to resist Washington's adamantine pressures and betrayed by his own government. For Hatoyama's immediate successor, Kan Naoto, the Hatoyama surrender agreement of May 2010 was the basic charter, although the disaster that struck Japan in March 2011 relieved him of pressure to deliver on it. When Japan's third Democratic Party Prime Minister, Noda Yoshihiko, came to office in September 2011, he led a government that was patently subject to bureaucratic direction, had abandoned its reform platform, and promised to hold the US relationship paramount and to implement all agreements entered by his predecessors, including relocating the Futenma base within Okinawa (to Henoko). If Hatoyama's opening address to the Diet (on "protecting life") was naïve and quixotic, he spoke in his own words and offered a vision of progressive change;

two years on, Noda's bland speech was utterly predictable, couched in the words provided him by his bureaucratic minders. Its only "vision" was to reverse the policies on which he and the DPJ had been elected two years earlier, particularly with respect to the US-Japan relationship, Asia, and Okinawa bases.[1]

Noda assumed as his key task the perennial one of Japanese prime ministers: to "deepen" the alliance and make it more "mature." As with previous governments, however, that meant offering more unequivocal Japanese cooperation with American policies, including bases, wars, and the neoliberal agenda promoted as a Trans-Pacific Partnership (TPP). It meant, implicitly if not explicitly, Japan throwing off its constitutional inhibitions and embracing the role of a twenty-first-century client state, rooted in the relationship of conqueror and conquered, occupier and occupied.

The Noda administration quickly signalled its intention to ignore or crush Okinawan dissent and to proceed at all costs with earlier US-Japan agreements on realignment of US forces. Noda's new defense minister, Ichikawa Yasuo, confessed that he was an amateur.[2] Noda's new minister of foreign affairs, Genba Koichiro, declared that he would honor the agreement with the United States on base relocation in order to "reduce the burden on the Okinawan people," and to that end, he would "continue to engage with the people of Okinawa in all sincerity, even if stomped upon and kicked."[3] In other words, Genba portrayed himself and his government as victims of Okinawan "stomping and kicking," a bizarre reversal of roles. He and the Noda government would continue to represent their new base construction as a "lessening" of the burden on Okinawa. *Ryukyu Shimpo* commented, "At the root of the trouble may be glimpsed the gutlessness and discrimination on the part of bureaucrats and politicians who have no sense of shame about ignoring the will of the Okinawan people opposed to any base relocation. The state cannot set aside its mistaken view that it can crush Okinawan society by force."[4]

Meeting President Obama on the sidelines of a United Nations meeting in New York on September 21, 2011, Noda promised that support for the "alliance" would be "even more unwavering" than it had been and that, in order to implement the reorganization plan, he would do his best "to gain the understanding of the Okinawa people." Foreign Minister Genba had only days earlier issued a similar assurance to Secretary of State Clinton.[5]

The embarrassing fact for Noda and Genba, however, was that precisely the opposite message had just been delivered by Okinawan Governor Nakaima to a select audience at George Washington University in Washington, DC, on September 19, 2011. Nakaima declared that for Futenma base to remain as it was was "not an acceptable option" and "the relocation plan of MCAS Futenma must be revised." He made plain that the confrontation between the Japanese state (and its American "ally") and Okinawa was absolute.[6] If the national government were to choose to proceed "against the will of the local citizens," it might lead to "an irreparable rift . . . between the people of Okinawa and the US forces in the prefecture." To a Washington press conference, Nakaima added that the only way base construction in Okinawa could proceed would be by recourse to "bayonets and bulldozers," that is, in the way that the bases had first been built by the US military government in the 1950s.[7] It was time, he said, for the two governments to "stop doing deals and return the bases promptly."[8]

In other words, Okinawa's most senior official, confident in strong Okinawan popular opposition to construction of the new base, believed that base construction could be accomplished only by having the tanks roll through Nago. The alliance, supposedly in the name of democracy, would be called upon to justify crushing democracy. Nakaima's address exposed the Washington audience to the depth of the rift between Japan and the United States on one side and Okinawa prefecture on the other.

While repeating the mantra about lessening the base burden, the Noda administration plainly meant increasing it, by constructing a new base on Okinawa. However, governments for fifteen years—under Hashimoto, Obuchi, Mori, Koizumi, Abe, Fukuda, and Aso of the LDP, and Hatoyama and Kan of the DPJ, had sought to persuade Okinawa to cooperate, using promises, threats, and bribes, all without success. Noda was no more likely than his predecessors to find a way to implement the intergovernmental agreements made, postponed, revised, and postponed again. No amount of "sincerity" on the part of Noda and his ministers seemed likely to succeed where all others had failed. The US-Japan alliance had run aground on the reef of Okinawan resistance.

## OKINAWA AND RAPE, 1995–2011

Late in 2011, an incident occurred that encapsulated in the most vivid way imaginable the nature of the Japan-Okinawa relationship.

In Naha on November 28, the head of the Department of Defense's Okinawa bureau, Tanaka Satoshi, while hosting a reception for a group of ten media representatives, was asked why the government seemed to be delaying the issue of the environmental assessment, the procedural precondition for commencement of works on the Henoko base. He replied, "When you are about to rape someone do you say, 'Now I am going to rape you'?"[9]

With these words, the wheel came full circle—from the 1995 case of the gang rape of the Okinawan child that first roused Okinawans to fury and led the two governments to hastily agree that Futenma would be returned, to this admission at a symbolic level by the government of Japan's top Okinawan official that the "return" would itself take the form of an act of rape upon Okinawa as a whole. Tanaka added to his insult by heaping scorn on the Okinawan desire for a base-free future by saying that a peace-oriented Okinawan island, without bases, was impossible, adding that the reason Okinawa, then the Ryukyu kingdom, had fallen under Japanese control four hundred years earlier had been because of its lack of armed forces.[10]

The comments seemed all too plainly indicative of thinking about Okinawa at high levels of the Japanese government. However figurative, the rape comment stirred a furor comparable to that over the actual rape sixteen years earlier. Tanaka was quickly shunted aside from his job, protest meetings were held, angry statements were adopted in local assemblies, and the Okinawan media seethed with fury. Tanaka's superior, Defense Minister Ichikawa, made things worse when questioned in the Diet on December 1 about the rape analogy by responding that he did not "know in detail" about the 1995 child rape case, which he referred to the next day as an "orgy" (*ranko*) instead of a "rape" (*boko*).[11] For the minister thus to plead ignorance of the single key galvanizing event in Okinawa's recent history and dismiss it as an "orgy" was no less offensive than Tanaka's original statement.

Days later, Ichikawa told a press conference that while he deeply regretted the "somewhat ill-considered" (*keisotsu na*) quality of his remarks, he did not regard the matter as serious enough to warrant his resignation.[12]

Though he hastened the following day to Naha to bow in apology before the governor, Ichikawa also defended himself, saying, "I believe that we need to take a considerable amount of effort to eradicate the pain of the Okinawan people. I know that it will not be easy to regain their trust, but I would like to fulfill my duties."[13] For his part, Prime Minister Noda was "terribly sorry that the feelings of the Okinawan people have been hurt" and he would "redouble his efforts in all sincerity to regain the trust of the Okinawan people."[14] He refused to consider dismissing Ichikawa. In due course, Tanaka was docked forty days' pay, and Ichikawa was rebuked by the Upper House on December 9. Neither was actually dismissed.[15]

For Noda to speak of redoubling his efforts to regain the trust of the Okinawan people and for Ichikawa to speak of continuing to "fulfill my duties" was for the government of Japan to continue in the same vein articulated by Tanaka: to enforce base construction by brushing aside the sentiments of the Okinawan people as "like a little insect that can be crushed,"[16] and violating the Okinawan body politic just as the US servicemen had violated the body of the child fifteen years earlier.

It took the Okinawan media to point out that the Noda government was committed above all, and certainly above any Okinawan constituency, to serve Washington. Responding to repeated insistence that he act before year's end to finalize the environmental impact process, Noda eventually acted, in such a semiclandestine way, at dead of night on the last working day of the year, as to imply that his government was acting shamefully (see chapter 8). His stealth called to mind the predawn attack on the Takae sit-in, exactly a year earlier. Shame and ruthlessness combined in the way his, and earlier, governments acted toward Okinawa.

While frantically trying to hose down Okinawan anger with shallow and empty expressions of regret, Noda was promising Washington that he would serve it at all costs, thus leading his government down the path already noted above that Okinawans call *iraranmii*, into a hopeless cul de sac.

## DEMOCRACY DENIED

Okinawa has successfully blocked one prime minister (Koizumi) between 2001 and 2006, indirectly forced the resignation of another (Hatoyama) in 2010, and since then has stood firm, against Kan and then Noda, on the question of base construction. Although 2010 was the "fiftieth anniversary" of the 1960 US-Japan Security Treaty, the long-awaited bilateral statement to signify the "deepening" of the relationship had to be repeatedly postponed, being issued by the US and Japanese foreign and defense ministers (the "Two plus Two") in only June 2011. Whether the four ministers were doing any more than whistling in the wind remains to be seen; but with no sign of implementation of the agreements of 1996, 2006, 2009, 2010, or 2011, the prospects of base construction taking place in 2012 or thereafter do not seem bright.

What the governments of these two hugely powerful countries seemed unable to accept was that, at least so long as democratic institutions survive, they had no way to persuade or compel a determined Okinawa to submit. Okinawans and their elected representatives have resisted a system that privileges US military and strategic ends over democratic and constitutional principle and that requires the Okinawans to bear permanently the disproportionate burden of the US military presence. By every conceivable democratic means—elections, resolutions (of local assemblies, including the Okinawan Prefectural Assembly and Nago City Assembly), mass "all-Okinawa" meetings, opinion surveys, statements by officials—Okinawans have made clear that no such base will be built. This resistance—fierce, uncompromising, nonviolent, and popularly supported—has showed no sign of weakening.

Both Tokyo and Washington treat Okinawans as an inconvenience and a nuisance, to be persuaded or bought off with the appropriate package of carrots and sticks or, if necessary, subdued by other means. Yet no defense of democracy or of a free world can rest on denial of freedom and democracy in a core territory. If this Okinawan resistance had been in a country out of favor with the United States and Japan, it might have won global acclaim as a heroic expression of popular will, a beacon of courageous, democratic determination. But because the struggle is against two supposed pillars of the global democratic system, such recognition is denied it. The Nago resistance over these years is a victory for democracy first in one city, then in one prefecture, but must remain brittle until it is consolidated at the national level.

In the process, the traditional progressive-conservative divide in Okinawan politics has dissolved such that the conservative governor of Okinawa repeatedly declared through 2011 that the construction would be "difficult," "extremely difficult," "in practice impossible," and eventually (July 2011) that any attempt to build a substitute base for Futenma anywhere within Okinawa would be "*dame*"—unacceptable, that is, he would forbid it.[17] It was another conservative, Naha mayor Onaga Takeshi, who declared from the platform of the historic protest meeting of April 2010 that there was no longer a division between "conservative" and "progressive" but that Okinawa's heart was united (*kokoro ga hitotsu*). The unity Onaga declared that day has not weakened since, and some now refer to it as a chemical change.[18]

Any serious attempt to resolve the "Okinawa problem" would have to begin by setting aside the series of agreements to militarize Oura Bay reached during the high tide of LDP client-state rule and putting an end to the many vain attempts to impose upon Okinawa something its people consistently say that they will not accept. To do that would mean to revisit the formula on which the postwar Japanese state has rested and to begin renegotiating its dependence on the United States. Hatoyama's 2009 vision was denounced and treated with contempt because it promised such reconsideration.

Where exposure of some of the inner workings of the relationship—through the *mitsuyaku*, the WikiLeaks revelations, the Hatoyama confession, and freedom of information legislation—caused only a mild flurry in Tokyo (and Washington), it sent shock waves along the fault lines of the national and regional system beneath Okinawa's islands. In Okinawa, where one-fifth of the main island's land surface, and its most fertile land, remains occupied by US forces nearly four decades after its supposed "reversion" to Japan, more was at stake than elsewhere. DPJ promises to block any new base construction had stirred expectations of a new and more democratic order in which their just demands might at last be met.

It was the Okinawan periphery (joined after the events of March 2011 by the northeastern or Fukushima periphery) that began to set the agenda for the debate on the country's and the region's future.[19]

As ever more shocking details of the secret treaties, lies, intimidation, manipulation, and cover-up of the past four decades are exposed, Okinawans see how they have been tricked and cheated within the state system that incorporated them from 1972. They know now in some detail the deals that Tokyo thrashed out with the Nixon administration in the late 1960s leading to the 1972 reversion and those done by the Democratic Party government in Tokyo with the Obama administration in 2009–2011. For Okinawans, the bitter fact is that, twelve years before the reversion, the Anpo Treaty confirmed the postwar division of Japan into "war state" (American-controlled Okinawa) and "peace state" (demilitarized and constitutionally pacifist mainland Japan). Despite Okinawa's inclusion from 1972 under the Constitution of Japan, with its guarantees of peace, democracy, and human rights, in practice the principles of the Security Treaty (including its secret elements) have always trumped those of the constitution. Detail after detail of recent revelations confirms Tokyo's contempt for Okinawa, its ongoing efforts to neutralize Okinawan democracy, and its readiness to pay almost any price to retain the US forces in Okinawa.

In the Japan of Hatoyama, Kan, and Noda, all major parties are committed, at least formally, to revising the constitution, but none (save the Communist) would revise the security treaty other than to steadily "deepen" it. In Okinawa, by contrast, all parties and the great majority of people are united in demanding that the burden of foreign military presence be lightened and no new base be built.

## BILATERAL TIES DAMAGED

The US-Japan relationship today appears strong. Its closeness and warmth are regularly declared, as if to convey reassurance that all is well. Yet after more than half a century of the US-Japan security relationship from the treaty renewal of 1960, a more unequal, misrepresented, and misunderstood bilateral relationship between two modern states would be difficult to imagine. The Hatoyama era is widely seen in Washington as an aberration, and the reversal to compliance under Kan and Noda is welcomed as normalcy. Pundits generally agree that adjustments that have to be made are to be made essentially by Japan, to make the alliance "mature" in line with the recommendations of the various reports that have been issued from Washington over the years. Yet, however ineffectual, the Hatoyama project was an attempt to equalize and thus to "deepen" the relationship. The formula to which he and then his successors, Kan and Noda, reverted, of bureaucratic rule at home and servility abroad, seemed ill designed to satisfy either constituency in the long term.

The Okinawans' fifteen years of struggle against the two governments have uncovered the deceptive mask of the bilateral relationship more than ever before. Under Republican and Democratic administrations in the United States and LDP and DPJ governments in Japan, the Okinawa base question has been the subject of agreement after agreement, postponement after postponement, failure after failure, feeding irritation on both sides. Each public assurance that the alliance is being deepened, or declaration by a prime minister that he will be even more unwavering in commitment to it, serves less well to conceal the fact that the relationship is seriously challenged due to both countries' underestimation and neglect of the Okinawa's rising democratic expressions and citizenry. Along with truth, the pacifism, human rights, and local autonomy nominally entrenched in the constitution are values for which Okinawans are engaged in a prolonged, fierce struggle. Okinawans insist that the two governments end deception, discrimination, and manipulation, such as Tokyo's recourse to the "deterrence" principle, which is widely dismissed in Okinawa as deceit. Consequently, *"yokushi"* (deterrence) is often sarcastically dismissed in Okinawa as *"yukushi"* (an Okinawan word meaning lies). Okinawans demand that redress and justice for the past and present wrongs be brought forward so that finally the islands are treated with respect. Only then might any truly mature relationship between Japan and the United States be achieved.

## SHIFTS IN PERSPECTIVES

The key policy intellectual of the relationship, Joseph Nye, under whose recommendation the 1995 decision was made to make the stationing of 100,000 US troops in Japan and Korea a permanent feature of the post–Cold War order, remained adamant from then until late 2011 that the "realignment" agenda for the integration of US and Japanese forces and the construction of new facilities to accommodate them must be followed. Under this hat he was the proponent of "hard power." Yet at the same time he wore another hat, as proponent of what he calls a "soft power" role for Japan. While tying Japan's 240,000 Self-Defense Forces ever more closely to their American counterparts by shared intelligence, training, and command, he would expect them to concentrate on nonmilitary contributions to regional and global security, in areas such as climate change, energy, and environment, their "soft" forces being the counterpart of "hard" US military might. The problem with this is twofold: the unequal nature of the relationship and the submission of Japan to strategic objectives (and wars) designed to serve US purposes on the one hand and the commitment of military forces to civil ends on the other. The projected international disaster relief center for Okinawa's Shimoji Island, a joint US-Japan military base, would fall within such parameters.[20] The traumatic experience of 1945, however, seems to have stamped upon Okinawan genes a deep distrust of all military forces, irrespective of flag, a belief that a soldier is a soldier, a military base a military base, and that armies do not defend people.

The Columbia University scholar Gerald Curtis said early in 2011, "The Obama administration has learned from its mistakes and in my view has gotten its Japan policy just about right."[21] It is Japan, he implies, that needs to make legislative and, if necessary, constitutional changes to better serve US strategic ends.[22] Top military and congressional figures—Webb, McCain, Levin, and Jones—did call for a rethink of US foreign policy from late in 2010, and three of them explicitly declared the Henoko project "unrealistic, unworkable, and unaffordable." Their words caused consternation in Tokyo, and the Kan government's key promoter of the Henoko project, Maehara Seiji, rushed to Washington shortly afterward to try to counter them.[23]

An increasing number of US and other Western scholars agree with Webb, McCain, and Levin that, in practical terms, it is "impossible to relocate to Henoko, and that the Marine Corps in Okinawa no longer plays any role in US military strategies." Some (such as Richard Samuels of MIT) believe that "Futenma needs to be closed down ASAP" and that "if Japan can be more responsible towards the US and can say no, that would be an ideal relationship."[24] When Joseph Nye, the principal architect of the policy, conceded in November 2011 that the Henoko project was "unlikely to be acceptable," it was one more, heavier than most, nail in its coffin. Okinawa's "soft power" had proven more than a match for Washington's.[25]

Apart from the well-informed and well-connected few, however, US commentators for the most part paid Okinawa minimal attention, simply assuming that alliance deepening and deterrence made its cooperation imperative, whatever the Okinawan people might think. The Heritage Foundation's Bruce Klingner, for example, commented darkly that the Noda government must either deliver on the promises it had made or else be responsible for Futenma becoming a permanent fixture in Ginowan City, which in turn would stir Okinawan anti-American sentiment and congressional anger. This might in due course even imperil the alliance.[26] What he was demanding was that Okinawan sentiment be either neutralized or crushed, implying that Okinawans had no rights, and that their role was as sacrificial victim for the sake of the alliance. The same anger and impatience that two years earlier Washington had shown to Hatoyama for his attempt to renegotiate the relationship may already have begun to be directed at Noda, even though, unlike Hatoyama, he committed himself fulsomely to doing what Washington demanded. The problem with him was that for all his "good" intentions, he seemed incapable of delivering on them.

## THE "CLIENT" CHALLENGES

This most peculiar of state relationships, in which servility on one side is matched by condescension and contempt on the other, deserves much closer scrutiny than is given it. On the American side, the conviction that Japan is, after all, an American creation and its government a kind of branch office, rooted in the experiences of war and occupation, and that regional and global strategy make imperative the maintenance of the Japanese base system, combines with the pragmatic attraction of the billions of dollars that can be extracted each year in subsidies from the Japanese government. On the Japanese side, it is more difficult to understand how servility should be the unquestioned choice of men and women of intelligence and presumed personal integrity. Those in its grip appear to be convinced that Japan's national interest is best served by it, and that belief seems scarcely shaken by the recent spate of revelations of the harsh and unequal reality of the relationship.

As perhaps nowhere else in contemporary Japan, the Henoko dispute exposes the fabric of the *zokkoku* state and the "alliance" that underpins it. As it continues, it threatens to widen into a movement that could challenge the US base presence in Japan as a whole. Until the US-Japan relationship can be transformed to rest on equality and mutual respect, Japan's sense of selfhood and identity is diminished and its role in the evolution of a regional East Asian or Asian order distorted or blocked. The British specialist Christopher Hughes makes this point:

> For the more that Japan defaults to ready dependence on the United States in security and foreign policy, the more it will simply compound Japanese concerns over the risks of entrapment and abandonment by its ally over issues such as North Korea and the East China Sea, and the more that this will frustrate Japanese ambitions as a major power and engender mutual suspicions within the alliance and thus weaken its basis.[27]

The more Japan itself is subject to Washington's direction, the more it is inclined to compensate by treating Okinawa as its colonial dependency, a surrogate "other" country onto which the contradictions of US base dependency can be downloaded.

# PLACING FUTENMA IN CONTEXT

True, the focus of the struggle has been on the return of Futenma without any new or replacement base in Okinawa, not on the complex of bases woven across the islands as a whole. Even if Futenma were indeed returned to its owners without replacement in Okinawa, the outcome would merely be to reduce Okinawa's percentage of the total US base land in Japan from 74 to 72 percent. But while the focus is indisputably on Futenma and Henoko, that issue is best seen as tactical in the context of a general strategic orientation toward demilitarization, the implementation of the Japanese constitution—especially Articles 9 (peace), 11–40 (human rights and livelihood), and 92–95 (local self-government)—and, given Okinawa's close proximity to China, Taiwan, and Southeast Asia, alternative regional cooperation.

The struggle raises large questions about the nature of Japanese democracy and US strategic planning for its empire of bases across the Pacific. Kent Calder has noted that the hosting of foreign military bases in the territory of a sovereign state is "unusual" and "almost always controversial."[28] They can only be "castles built on sand" and cannot long be stable. Gradually a realization might be spreading, emanating from Okinawa, that to face and begin to resolve the current problem means to revisit the formula on which the postwar Japanese state has rested and to begin renegotiating its dependency on the United States. Despite the inequality of the contest, the fact is that Okinawa has in effect seized the advantage over Tokyo and Washington.

# OKINAWA'S POSITION AND IDENTITY

Over four hundred years, Ryukyu/Okinawa's location on the periphery between successively rival regional empires, then nation-states, then Cold War camps, left it little space for autonomy and virtually none for independence. Now, however, in this third decade of the post–Cold War era, the advance of regional economic integration and the search for a new formula for post–Cold War security and cooperation presents it with a challenge and possible opportunity. The struggle over US base reorganization becomes also a struggle over Okinawan identity and role. As Okinawan political scientist Shimabukuro Jun points out, the root problem of postwar Japan has been that its sovereignty has been just show, *misekake*, empty of substance. Because Anpo (the US-Japan security treaty) de facto overrides *Kenpo*, the peace constitution, with its core principles of peace, human rights, and self-government, Okinawa is essentially a military colony within that system; and its struggle, oriented toward a redefined local autonomy and "regional sovereignty," shares a basic character with the national liberation struggles of the twentieth century.[29]

In a similar vein, Sun Ge, fellow of the Chinese Academy of Social Sciences, sees in the Okinawan struggle a paradoxical combination of isolation and universal significance. She attributes the isolation, "not just to their being sold out time and again by the Government of Japan but to the fact that they have not been able to find deep understanding or support beyond Okinawa," adding that what Okinawans want is not sympathy but "support for their philosophy and action, based on understanding and respect."[30] The universalism is to be found in their orientation toward an identity beyond the nation-state, rooted in the direct democratic formula of federally linked, locally self-governing communities.

According to Sun, outsiders are inclined to see Okinawans as working for independence from US and Japan, return to Ryukyu in history, and self-governance, but the goal of their struggle is higher and richer. As she puts it:

> In a society like Okinawa, the idea of belonging, which is related to sovereignty and identity, can only be relative. Okinawan thinkers are equally on their guard against unconditional attachment to Japan and against Okinawan independence as an absolute. . . . By their refusal to be seen just as victims and their refusal to substitute their position at the periphery for one at the centre, they generate ideas relevant to our future and to the future of humanity.[31]

This quality of transcendence of the conventional categories of state and national self-determination especially attracts Sun's attention. For her, the Okinawan struggles constitute a distillation of the postwar history of East Asia over more than half a century. Okinawa's "internationalist anti-war and pro-peace perspective, its ideology of egalitarianism and opposition to hegemony, and the subtle understanding on the part of Okinawan intellectuals of the problem of identity" all hold broad regional lessons, including for China.[32] Little known and little appreciated, and despite—or perhaps because of—its intense and unequal struggle, Okinawa is seen as having transcended the confines of the nation-state to forge a rich new sense of identity, Okinawa's "bitter freedom" thus becoming universalized as a "new value," that is, a post-nation-state value. To conceive of the "Okinawa problem" in the narrow terms of a base dispute is to miss this deeper significance.

The orientation toward a post-nation-state future is commonly rooted in the sense of a proud, distinctive Ryukyu/Okinawan premodern identity. The memory of the centuries in which the Ryukyu kingdom was a thriving economic and cultural island city-state respected and at peace with its neighbors sharpens the bitterness over the discriminatory treatment meted out to Okinawa at Japanese hands in 1609, 1879, 1945, 1952, 1972, and repeatedly since 1996. As resentment over present discrimination builds, support for some form of Ryukyu/Okinawa independence grows.[33]

Furthermore, China's rise, widely seen in mainland Japan as a threat, is seen more often in Okinawa as an opportunity.[34] The Ryukyu/Okinawa memory of its China relationship is quite different from mainland Japan's memory. For 270 years until 1879, Okinawa/Ryukyu was simultaneously part of the premodern Chinese "tribute" world and of Edo [Japan], national territory and borders meaning little to the people who lived in and travelled between the islands. As Okinawan historian Arasaki Moriteru notes, "China might have sought tribute from its neighbour countries but it was a case of conferring benefit not of controlling or exploiting them economically."[35] The kingdom that retained close and friendly China ties while negotiating treaties with foreign countries and kingdoms through the 1850s was only fully subordinated within the modern Japanese state in 1879.

To the United States, one of the countries that opened diplomatic relations with Ryukyu in the 1850s, it proved convenient to return to that understanding of the islands as different from "Japan proper" in the post-1945 period. MacArthur saw Okinawans as non-Japanese, expected to welcome separation from Japan (even as a militarized US dependency) as liberation. Others in Washington saw the thirtieth parallel north as the border between distinct racial groups: the "Yamato (Japanese)" and the "Ryukyu (Okinawan)." It took a reversion formula that reconciled ongoing US military privilege with nominal Japanese sovereignty for the US to lose interest in the formula of Ryukyu/Okinawa difference.

Few in Okinawa accept the racial profiling on which the distinction/discrimination is based, but dissatisfaction with the second-class treatment meted out to them within the Japanese state nevertheless leads many to look nostalgically to the past and to see in it a hint of a possible future either on a renegotiated and more autonomous basis within the Japanese state or as an independent entity outside it.

Explicit support for independence—whether under the name of Okinawa, Uchina, or Ryukyu—may not be widespread. Nevertheless, in June 2010, a "Declaration of Independence" was issued in the name of "The Federation of Ryukyu Self-Governing Republics." Its initial demands of the Japanese national government included apology and compensation for the abolition of the Ryukyu kingdom and subordination of the islands as Okinawan prefecture in 1879, abolition of the reversion agreements of 1969–1972 (on grounds of dubious legality and the complex of secret deals that enveloped them), and negotiation of a new, autonomous status.[36]

Others point out that although for much of its modern history from 1879, Okinawan languages and cultures were suppressed, if the precedents of Wales and Hawaii were to be followed, Okinawan language revival could be promoted by policy (as the United Nations instructed in 2008).[37] So, although claim to independent sovereign statehood is not so common, and when expressed tends to be wrapped, as Sun Ge notes, in critique of the nation-state, the moral claim for self-government enjoys undoubted widespread support.

The call for renegotiation of the relationship between mainland Japan and Okinawa has another aspect. Okinawans have begun to call on mainlanders not just to lighten or remove the base burden from the Okinawan islands, but to take it upon themselves. Thus, author chinin usii, a member of Okinawan women's group "Gathering of Kamaduu gwa," points to Japan's dependence on Okinawa for its security needs and demands it take upon itself responsibility for hosting the bases and find a site for the relocation of Futenma Air Station.[38] Such demand has been taboo until recent years, since many Okinawans were reluctant simply to transfer their suffering to the mainland, but in recent years, more Okinawans have shed that taboo. Sociologist Nomura Koya argues that the Japanese people, who choose to sustain the US military base presence through their democratic system, have a responsibility to share the base burden equally. Instead, by imposing it in highly unequal manner upon Okinawa, they demonstrate a discriminatory and colonialist mentality.[39] Similarly, political scientist and long-term Okinawa resident Douglas Lummis criticizes many on the mainland for their implicit contradiction in simultaneously supporting Article 9 (the war renunciation clause of the Japanese constitution) and Anpo (the US-Japan Treaty that stipulates the presence of US bases in Japan), ignoring or evading the fact that to do so is to detach the base problem and frame it as an "Okinawa problem" instead of as their own. Like chinin, he argues that so long as the majority of Japanese continue to support Anpo, the Japanese mainland should bear a fair burden of US bases. Criticizing the call for total elimination of the bases in Japan as unrealistic and therefore as tantamount to support for the perpetuation of Okinawa's current burden, he calls for the Okinawan antibase movement to demand the transfer of the bases from Okinawa to the mainland.[40]

Okinawa Governor Nakaima Hirokazu also calls for Futenma Air Station to be relocated elsewhere in Japan. He says, "An equivalent of Futenma Air Station in Tokyo would be a US military base in Hibiya Park."[41] In the US context, that would mean a marine base for Central Park in New York. Such an imaginative formulation is designed to shock mainlanders into realization of the structure of discrimination. It directly challenges the amnesia that has allowed many mainland Japanese to benefit from the peace constitution only through closing their eyes to the sacrifice of Okinawa.

One further aspect to the universalism of the Okinawan identity construct is that it lacks the imperial referent common, whether explicitly or implicitly, to so many mainland identity constructs and is therefore more amenable to accepting a shared Asian or Asia-Pacific identity, such as might be expected to evolve with Japan's participation in a future Asian or Asia-Pacific community. Yamato (mainland) constructions of "Japanese-ness," often centered on the imperial institution, ring hollow in Uchina (Okinawa), and no Okinawan project would conceive of identity in the way one former prime minister, Mori Yoshiro, described Japan in 2000, as "the land of the gods centred on the emperor." The imperial institution is a modern imposition for Okinawa, without historic or cultural roots. And the memory of the Showa emperor's (Hirohito's) insistence in the spring of 1945 that the war be continued, though defeat was inevitable, thus condemning Okinawa to devastation, and of the same emperor's, later admonition to General MacArthur to continue occupying Okinawa for "25 to 50 years or more," the formula that is at the root of their pain, carries a distinct reservation about the institution. Okinawans therefore listen with dismay when some mainland pundits suggest that the disaster of the March 2011 earthquake/tsunami "has made people much more aware of the emperor's existence."[42]

They note, too, the findings of a post-3/11 national opinion poll that found the emperor and the military (the Self-Defense Forces) to be the two institutions most trusted, at 78 and 74 percent, respectively, with an astonishing 22 percent of people actually favoring handing some political power to the emperor, while support for the US bases had grown by 10 percent since 2005, to 57 percent.[43] Such trends were ominous for Okinawa (as several of the contributors to chapter 12, "Turning History Around," note). There are no good reasons for Okinawans to feel positively about the emperor (whose status as "symbol of the state and of the unity of the people" is entrenched in Article 1 of the Constitution) or about the military, whether Japanese or American. Neither is likely to regain trust in Okinawa so long as the memory of 1945 still lives.

## OKINAWA: CITIZEN-RULED DEMOCRACY

Whatever the outcome of the grand struggles under way, Okinawa's history over especially the past fifteen years constitutes a lesson to the rest of Japan—and indeed East Asia and the world—in what it means for people to be citizens, exercising with confidence and determination the sovereignty vested in them under the constitution, exemplary in their commitment to peace and in the resolve never to forget or repeat the crimes of militarism. In Okinawa is to be found a model of democracy in action without peer in East Asia and with few parallels globally. Because of these struggles, Japan's geographical periphery becomes its political core, pointing the way toward an alternative, autonomous, civil-society-led direction for the rest of the country. Here, for the most part unnoticed or unappreciated, one of the most important stories of early twenty-first-century Japan is being told.

## NOTES

1. The Noda government policies—on the Trans-Pacific Partnership (TPP), the consumption tax, the Futenma base transfer, and nuclear energy—were scarcely distinguishable from those of the LDP, with which it was closely cooperating in Diet management. Osamu Watanabe, "Kozo Kaikaku E to Kaiki Suru Hoshu Naikaku," *Shukan Kinyobi* (September 30, 2011).

2. "Defense Chief Calls Himself an Amateur," *Japan Times*, September 4, 2011.

3. See, for example, "Genba gaisho hatsugen fumitsukete iru no wa dare ka," *Ryukyu Shimpo*, September 7, 2011.

4. "Henoko asesu kore ijo guko o kurikaesuna," *Ryukyu Shimpo*, September 6, 2011.

5. For fuller discussion, see Gavan McCormack and Satoko Norimatsu, "Discordant Visitors: Japanese and Okinawan Messages to the US," *Asia-Pacific Journal: Japan Focus* (October 3, 2011), http://japanfocus.org/-Satoko-NORIMATSU2/3611.

6. Nakaima Hirokazu, "Okinawa Governor Nakaima: An Irreparable Rift in Okinawa/Japan/US Relations Would Result from Forceful Construction of Henoko Base," text in English and Japanese at *Peace Philosophy Centre*, September 22, 2011, http://peacephilosophy.blogspot.com/2011/09/okinawa-governor-nakaima-irreparable.html.

7. "Unrealistic Promise on Futenma," *Japan Times*, September 24, 2011.

8. "Okinawa Governor Denies a Japan-US Deal on US Military Realignment Package," *Ryukyu Shimpo*, September 26, 2011 (in English).

9. "Okasu mae ni iu ka' Tanaka boeikyokucho, Henoko hyokasho teishutsu meguri," *Ryukyu Shimpo*, November 29, 2011.

10. "'Bogen' no honshitsu Okinawa besshi no kozoka o kigu," *Ryukyu Shimpo*, December 2, 2011.

11. "Ichikawa bosho, kotetsu shi, seiken wa denaose," editorial, *Asahi Shimbun*, December 6, 2011.

12. "Boeisho jinin ron tsuyomaru," *Mainichi Shimbun*, December 3, 2011.

13. Masami Ito, "Ichikawa Must Straighten Up but Can Stay: Noda," *Japan Times*, December 6, 2011.

14. "Boeisho ni monseki ketsugi teishisei mo kiku mimi naku seifu, hyokasho teishutsu kyoko e,"*Ryukyu Shimpo*, December 10, 2011.

15. Satoshi Okumura, "Decision to Retain Defense Chief Angers Okinawans," *Asahi Shimbun*, December 10, 2011.

16. "'Boeikyokucho bogen," part 3, "Keikaku no hatan ni mukiae," *Okinawa Taimusu*, December 3, 2011.

17. "Futenma isetsu—chiji 'kennai dokomo dame,'" *Okinawa Taimusu*, July 7, 2011.

18. Onaga Takeshi to April 25, 2010, All Okinawa Mass meeting. On the "chemical change," see Yamada Fumihiko, "Okinawa 'mondai' no shinen mukidashi ni natta sabetsusei," *Sekai*, June 2012, p. 98.

19. Satoko Oka Norimatsu, "Fukushima and Okinawa—The 'Abandoned People,' and Civic Empowerment," *Asia-Pacific Journal: Japan Focus* 9, no. 47 (2011), http://japanfocus.org/-Satoko-NORIMATSU/3651.

20. See, for example, Nye's contribution to the following discussion: Tanaka Hitoshi et al., "Nichibei domei 'Chaina kado' de jumyo o nobase," *Bungei Shunju* (May 2010), at esp. 182.

21. Curtis, "Future Directions."

22. For discussion of the various Washington policy think-tank reports of 2000 and 2007 making this point and identified with Joseph Nye and Richard Armitage in particular, see especially Gavan McCormack, "The Travails of a Client State: An Okinawan Angle on the 50th Anniversary of the U.S.-Japan Security Treaty," *Asia-Pacific Journal: Japan Focus* (March 8, 2010), http://japanfocus.org/-Gavan-McCormack/3317.

23. Heianna Sumio, "Maehara shi, Bei gi-in ni genkoan no riko yakusoku," *Okinawa Taimusu*, July 13, 2011.

24. For discussion by the *Ryukyu Shimpo*'s Yonamine Michiyo of experts, including Mike Mochizuki (George Washington University), Morton Halperlin (former deputy assistant secretary of defense), Richard Samuels (MIT), Barry Posen (MIT), and Andrew Bacevich (Boston University and former US Army colonel), see Yonamine, "Economic Crisis." For Samuels and his colleagues, see Eric Heginbotham, Ely Ratner, and Richard J. Samuels, "Tokyo's Transformation: How Japan Is Changing—and What It Means for the United States," *Foreign Affairs* 90, no. 5 (September/October 2011).

25. Joseph Nye, "A Pivot That Is Long Overdue," *New York Times*, November 21, 2011.

26. Bruce Klingner and Derek Scissors, "The US Needs a Real Partner in the New Japanese Prime Minister," Web memo no. 3347, Heritage Foundation, Washington DC, August 30, 2011, http://www.heritage.org/research/reports/2011/08/the-us-needs-a-real-partner-in-the-new-japanese-prime-minister; Bruce Klingner, "Noda seiken e no kitai to kaigi," *Mainichi Shimbun*, October 8, 2011.

27. Christopher Hughes, "Japan's Foreign Policy for a New Age: Realistic Realism," *Asahi Shimbun*, February 26, 2011.

28. Kent E Calder, *Embattled Garrisons: Comparative Base Politics and American Globalism* (Princeton: Princeton University Press, 2007).

29. For a statement of Shimabukuro's position, see Shimabukuro Jun, "Nichibei Anpo no henyo to Okinawa no jichi," in *Okinawa wa doko e mukau no ka* (Okinawa University, December 19, 2010).

30. Sun Ge, "Okinawa ni naizai suru higashi Ajia sengoshi," in *Ajia no naka de Okinawa gendaishi o toinaosu* (Naha: Okinawa University Institute of Regional Studies, 2010), 61, 63.

31. Ibid., 63–64.

32. Ibid., 64. Also see "Okinawa ga wareware no me ni utsuru toki," in *Rekishi no kosaten ni tatte* (Tokyo: Nihon keizai hyoron sha, 2008).

33. Paraphrasing the sentiment expressed by Shimabukuro Jun, "Jichishu to nari kizuna o saisei suru," *Asahi Shimbun*, August 24, 2010.

34. This is a view also shared by the US consul general in Okinawa. Reich, Cable 06NAHA103, "Okinawan Exceptionalism: The China Threat or Lack Thereof," April 26, 2006, *WikiLeaks*. http://wikileaks.org/cable/2006/04/06NAHA103.html.

35. Arasaki Moriteru, "Senkaku shoto (Diaoyu judao) mondai to Okinawa no tachiba," in *Okinawa wa doko e mukau no ka* (Okinawa University, December 19, 2010).

36. On the Declaration of Independence issued by "Ryukyu jichi kyowakoku renpo" (Ryukyu Self-Governing Republican League, the alliance of Amami, Okinawa, Miyako, and Yaeyama islands) on June 23, 2010, see Matsushima Yasukatsu, "'Ryukyu' dokuritsu de 'Heiwa na shima' ni," *Shukan Kinyobi* (July 23, 2010): 22.

37. "Shimakutoba no hi, jugyo de manabu shikumi o," editorial, *Ryukyu Shimpo*, September 18, 2011.

38. chinin usii, "Nihon koso Okinawa kara jiritsu shite," *Asahi Shimbun*, August 24, 2010.

39. Nomura Koya, *Muishiki no shokuminchi shugi: Nihon jin no beigun kichi to Okinawa jin* (Tokyo: Ochanomizu shobo, 2005), 25–41.

40. Douglas Lummis, *Kanameishi: Okinawa to kenpo 9 jo* (Tokyo: Shobunsha, 2010), 169–212.

41. "Governor Nakaima Criticizes the Notification of the Plan to Build the V-shaped Runway at Henoko," *Ryukyu Shimpo* (English web page), June 14, 2011, http://english.ryukyushimpo.jp/2011/06/16/1282/.

42. Sakurai Yoshiko, quoted (from *Shukan Posuto*) in Michael Hoffman, "Extreme Nationalism May Emerge from the Rubble of the Quake," *Japan Times*, May 22, 2011.

43. "The AP-GFK Poll: Japan," July 29-August 10, 2011. http://surveys.ap.org/data%5CGfK%5CAP-Gfk%20Poll%20Japan%20Topline%20FINAL_1st%20release.pdf and http://marketing.gfkamerica.com/pdf/AP-Gfk%20Poll%20Japan%202nd%20release.pdf.

# 14

*⟶*

# The All-Okinawa
# Movement since 2013

## KENPAKUSHO DELEGATION TO TOKYO

With the "normal" democratic avenues to block the unwanted new base exhausted, Okinawans in late January 2013 formed themselves into a delegation, some 150 strong, to deliver to the government in Tokyo what they called a *Kempakusho*, or statement of demand. The delegation comprised thirty-eight city, town, and village heads; forty-one heads of city and town assemblies; twenty-nine members of the prefectural assembly, and the handful of Okinawan members of the national Diet, together with representatives of the Chamber of Commerce and Industry and of the Prefectural Women's Association. Others, even though not joining in the delegation, shared its stance, including the governor, the prefectural branches of the major national political parties (including the conservative coalition partners, Liberal Democratic Party [LDP], and New Komeito), the two prefectural newspapers, and majority opinion in general (according to repeated surveys that found opposition running at levels of 70 percent or more).

Naha City mayor Onaga Takeshi, the conservative and sometime head of the LDP party in Okinawa (later to become governor), spoke for the group, referring bitterly to "the US and Japanese government's trampling on the will of the Okinawan people" and articulating three demands: closure and return of Futenma, abandonment of plans for a Futenma replacement anywhere in Okinawa, and withdrawal of the Osprey (the tilt-rotor MV-22 vertical takeoff and landing, or VTOL) aircraft that the Marine Corps had just (October 2012) introduced.[1]

As Henoko was to be much more than just a "replacement" for Futenma, the Osprey was much more than a mere replacement for conventional military helicopters. It flies twice as fast, carries up to three times as much load, and has an operational radius four times that of the CH-46 helicopter.[2] As we detail above (see pp. 167–172), the government of Japan repeatedly denied any knowledge of its planned introduction to Okinawa until the environmental impact survey was complete and deployment imminent. The Osprey had a checkered history, marked by repeated crashes and forced landings.

Referring to the prime minister's pledge to "take back" Japan, Onaga asked, sarcastically, "Is Okinawa part of that Japan?" To the Okinawan media, he posed the rhetorical question: "can the Japan and the people of Japan that treat the views of Okinawans with such contempt be regarded as a country worthy of the respect of Asia and the world?"[3] The delegation was given short shrift. After a brief and fruitless meeting with the prime minister, its mostly conservative members were shocked to find themselves abused in the streets of Tokyo as "Chinese spies" or "traitors."

Through much of the year that followed, Abe's government set about persuading, splitting, or otherwise neutralizing the Okinawan opposition. On March 22, 2013, Abe formally requested of Governor Nakaima Hirokazu that he grant permission for the Oura Bay reclamation. In April, two prominent Okinawan LDP Diet members surrendered, signaling their readiness to accept the project. In August, Governor Nakaima issued a preliminary permit for rock and coral crushing in Oura Bay. In December, the Okinawa chapter of the LDP itself (including all five national Diet members) dramatically signaled their submission, and eventually Nakaima himself, though assuming the governorship in 2010 on a platform to ask for Futenma replacement elsewhere in Japan but not in Okinawa (see pp. 150–151), famously "turned coat" during a week secreted in a Tokyo hospital. In January 2014, Nago City (which includes Henoko and Oura Bay, the designated new base construction site) returned as its mayor the antibase ("no new base in this city whether on land or on sea") Inamine Susumu, in the process rejecting the extraordinary offer by the LDP secretary general of a 50 billion yen "inducement" fund for city development if only it would elect a probase candidate. The surrender of the Okinawa branch of the LDP provoked a split in the conservative ranks, those submitting to Abe outnumbered by those who followed Onaga Takeshi to merge the progressive camp into what became known as the "All-Okinawa" camp.

Serious preparation for reclamation and construction at the Henoko site followed the Nakaima surrender. At the beginning of July 2014, Abe declared just over half of Oura Bay off limits and initiated the preliminary boring survey. Anticipating protest, he sent auxiliary detachments of police from Japan proper to reinforce the local Okinawan police and, at sea, ordered the national coast guard to send their vessels to fend off the protesting canoes and kayaks.

It was November 2014 before the Okinawan people had the opportunity to register their judgement on Nakaima's reversal. They then, by a massive majority (380,820 to 261,076), dismissed him and chose in his stead former Naha City mayor and Kempakusho leader Onaga Takeshi. Onaga's central platform was his promise to "do everything in my power" to stop the Henoko project. It meant that by December 2014 the prefecture had a governor and a prefectural assembly (or parliament) both committed to stopping the construction works at Henoko and restoring Oura Bay. Just weeks after Onaga's election, all four national Diet Okinawan constituencies dismissed their base-supporting members and installed committed opponents. Two years of Abe government had thus only reinforced prefectural opposition to base construction.

The popular Okinawan resentment against the parliamentary turncoats of 2013 followed. In the election in July 2016 for Upper House of the Diet, Abe's key Okinawan colleague Shimajiri Aiko confronted one of the best-known Okinawan opponents of the base construction, former Ginowan City mayor (two terms, 2003–2010) Iha Yoichi. Though elected in 2010 on an antibase platform, Shimajiri had reversed herself in April 2013 and later that same year helped orchestrate the "surrender" of other conservative Diet members. She was highly appreciated in Abe circles not only for that role but for the views she expressed later: calling for the riot police and coast guard to be mobilized to curb the "illegal, obstructionist activities" of the antibase movement (February 2014), denouncing (anti–base construction) Nago mayor Inamine for "abusing his power" (April 2015), and referring contemptuously to the "irresponsible citizens' movement" (October 2015). With such views, she rose meteorically in the Tokyo establishment, becoming minister for Okinawa in the third Abe cabinet. But to rise in Tokyo was to fall in Okinawa, as Shimajiri, and Abe, learned. By a majority of 100,000 votes, Okinawans in July 2016 ousted her and chose Iha.

Although successive national governments put great effort into persuading local government authorities to cooperate with their base reinforcement plans, they had only limited success. Between 1996 and 2017, no Okinawan who adopted an explicitly pro–Henoko construction stance was returned at election for public office. It is true that candidates supported by the national government (LDP and Komeito) could win elections, but only if and to the extent that they focused their campaign on the economy (jobs) and local issues, avoiding mention of the base question. Not uncommonly, once elected, such LDP-supported Okinawans then switched from opposing to supporting base construction, as in the case of

Shimajiri Aiko and Governor Nakaima discussed above. Thus by 2017 the prefecture itself and the two cities of Naha (the capital) and Nago (site of the Henoko project) were under "All-Okinawa" while "Team Okinawa," more tolerant of new base construction, prevailed in nine other cities.

There could be no doubt that in two forthcoming 2018 elections, for mayor of Nago City (February 2018) and for governor of Okinawa (November 2018), base issues would play a very large role and the campaigns mounted by the national government and by local Okinawan citizens, by Team Okinawa and All-Okinawa, would be fierce. The Abe government, while relishing its nationwide electoral triumph of October 2017, could be expected to take grim note of the fact that three of Okinawa's four seats went to All-Okinawa, including Naha and Nago Cities (as part of Electoral Districts 1 and 3). Not only that, but District No. 1 returned the only Japan Communist Party candidate to win a single seat constituency in the country, and District No. 2 likewise returned the only Social Democratic Party of Japan candidate to do likewise.[4]

## OKINAWA'S ENIGMATIC GOVERNOR

The new (from December 2014) governor, however, was an enigmatic figure. His appeal to Okinawan mass sentiment was based on his "rebirth" as an avatar of All-Okinawa identity politics, transcending the categories of conservative and progressive, "left" and "right," and proclaiming the principle of "identity over ideology." Yet the problem with that All-Okinawa mantra is that identities are commonly multiple. Onaga was both implacable opponent of the national government in certain respects and yet in other respects the quintessential, conservative local government Japanese politician. He was not only Okinawan but, like Prime Minister Abe, a lifelong (to 2014) member of the Liberal Democratic Party and a believer in the Ampo security system and in the need for US bases. While he posed a major challenge, rooted in identity politics, to the government of Japan (and beyond it, to that of the United States), it is not clear how far he could be expected to lead the prefecture against his conservative colleagues and counterparts at the helm of the nation, and whether Okinawan identity could trump ideology and generate a credible democratic politics.

Onaga limited his differences with Tokyo to the three specific *Kempakusho* demands: closure of Futenma, cancellation of any Futenma replacement (i.e., Henoko) within Okinawa, and withdrawal of the MV-22 Osprey aircraft. He remained silent during the summer of nationwide protest against the Abe government's secrecy and security bills in 2015, suggesting that he supported, or at least did not oppose, Abe's controversial interpretation of collective self-defense and security legislation package. He supported the Abe government's scheme to deploy Ground Self-Defense Forces, including offensive surface-to-air, surface-to-ship missile units, along the chain of islands between Taiwan and Kagoshima to pose a threat against the passage of Chinese ships. He also remained silent on the Osprey pad construction protest at Takae (on which see pp. 167–172), and made no visit to the site. When riot police reinforcements were sent from mainland Japan to enforce works at Henoko from late 2015 and at Takae from July 2016, they were sent under the provisions of the National Police Law (1954) at the request of the Prefectural Public Safety Commission. Members of this commission are responsible to and nominated (or dismissed) by the governor, so, at least in theory, Onaga might have dismissed any or all of its five members and appointed others who would represent Okinawan principles. Choosing not to do so,[5] he reserved his criticism for the reliance on force, the "excesses" rather than the act itself. He assured his hosts at the US State and Defense Departments in a February 2017 visit to Washington that he saw the US bases and the security treaty as important "for the defense of freedom, equality, democracy and human rights," formulating his objection to the Henoko project in terms of the damage it might do to the "alliance" if a base had to be imposed by force.[6]

Onaga was, nevertheless, occasionally eloquent and forthright in making the prefecture's case. While Abe and his ministers insisted that the Henoko project amounted to a "burden reduction" for Okinawa, that it was the only way to achieve Futenma return and that it was irreversible, Onaga spoke of an inequitable and increasing burden, building upon the initial illegal seizure of Okinawan land and in defiance of the clearly and often expressed wishes of the Okinawan people; of a struggle for justice and democracy and for the protection of Oura Bay's extraordinary natural biodiversity (which he described as being at least twice as rich in biota as the sea around Galapagos). He quoted the Okinawa Defense Bureau's estimate that there were more than 5,800 kinds of biota in the Bay zone (262 of them in danger of extinction).[7]

It is certain that no other prefectural governor in Japan would ever refer to the national government in the way that Onaga did, as "condescending," "unreasonable," "outrageous" (rifujin), "childish" (otonagenai), and even "depraved" (daraku), or accuse it (before the United Nations Human Rights Commission in Geneva in September 2015) of "ignoring the people's will."[8] It is unlikely that any would lambast the government's weakness in being "completely lacking in ability to say anything to America,"[9] or address the prime minister in terms such as:

Construction of Futenma and other bases was carried out after seizure of land and forcible appropriation of residences at point of bayonet and bulldozer, while Okinawan people after the war were still confined in detention centers. Nothing could be more outrageous than [for you] to try to say to Okinawans whose land was taken from them for what is now an obsolescent base [i.e., Futenma], the world's most dangerous, that they should bear that burden and, if they don't like it, they should come up with an alternative plan.[10]

## IN THE COURTS: THE EXPERTS REPORT (2015)

The political contest between national and prefectural governments, fought through a series of elections, has been matched by the judicial contest, fought in a series of five actions between 2015 and 2017, including referral to the Supreme Court. The proceedings are complex, but demand attention.

Upon assuming office as governor at the beginning of 2015, Onaga set up a "Third Party Commission" of experts to advise him on the legal and environmental questions arising from the consent given by his predecessor to the reclamation of Oura Bay and to identify possible flaws in the legal process that might warrant its cancelation.[11] On July 16, the commission issued an unambiguous finding of multiple procedural "breaches" (*kashi*) in the way the Nakaima administration had made its crucial December 2013 decision. It adopted the common expert view of the Henoko environmental impact assessment (EIA) process as "the worst in the history of Japanese EIA."[12] It found that "necessity for reclamation," a crucial consideration under the 1973 revision to the Reclamation of Publicly Owned Water Surfaces Act (*Koyu suimen umetateho*, 1921), had not been established. Of the six specific criteria under Article 4 of that law for reclamation, the Henoko project failed on three. It did not meet the tests of proof of "appropriate and rational use of the national land," proper consideration for "environmental preservation and disaster prevention," and compatibility with "legally based plans by the national government or local public organizations regarding land use or environmental conservation." It was also incompatible with other laws including the Sea Coast Law (1956) and the Basic Law for Biodiversity (2008).[13]

As the experts committee deliberated during early 2016, the Okinawa Defense Bureau had begun dropping concrete blocks (each weighing between ten and forty-five tons) into Oura Bay as anchors for the works to come. Onaga ordered them to stop (February 16), and Okinawan civil society and nature protection organizations pleaded likewise. Onaga, however, declined to formally cancel the permit for rock and coral crushing issued by his predecessor. Inexplicably, he declared, "unfortunately it is not possible to make a judgement as to destruction of coral."[14]

Following a one-month (August to September 2015) lull in the Oura Bay confrontation while a round of "talks" was conducted, fruitlessly, the government reiterated (through the minister of defense) its stance that there had been no "flaw" in the license Nakaima had granted. It therefore ordered site works resumed. Japan's Department of Defense began scouring the coastal hills and beaches of western Japan, placing orders for millions of tons of soil and sand to dump into Oura Bay. It also ordered an additional hundred-plus riot police from Tokyo to reinforce the mostly local Okinawan forces who till then had been imposing the state's will at the construction site.

On October 13, adopting the commission's recommendation three months after it was released, Onaga formally cancelled (*torikeshi*) the reclamation license, whereupon, its license cancelled, the national government suspended site works. However, the Okinawa Defense Bureau formally complained to the Ministry of Land, Infrastructure, Transport and Tourism (MLITT), protesting that there were no flaws in the Nakaima land reclamation approval of December 2013 and asking MLITT to review, suspend, and nullify Onaga's order under the Administrative Appeal Act.[15] Following a cabinet meeting on October 27, MLITT Minister Ishii Keiichi duly suspended the Onaga order on grounds that otherwise it would be "impossible to continue the relocation" and because in that event "the US-Japan alliance would be adversely affected."[16] To Governor Onaga, he issued first (October 27) "advice," and then, days later (November 6), an "instruction" to withdraw the cancellation order. Onaga refused. On October 29, works at Henoko resumed.

Onaga's next step was the launch, on November 2, of a prefectural complaint against the Abe government with the Central and Local Government Disputes Management Council, a hitherto insignificant review body set up in 2000 by the government's Department of General Affairs. That council called no evidence and took barely six weeks, to December 24, to dismiss the complaint, ruling, mysteriously, that the complaint was "beyond the scope of matters it could investigate."[17]

While this Disputes Council complaint was being heard, on November 17, 2015, the national government (through the MLITT minister) filed suit against the Okinawan government under the Administrative Appeals Act, alleging administrative malfeasance and seeking to have Onaga's order set aside and a "proxy execution" procedure adopted. The presiding judge in this suit, Tamiya Toshiro, had only taken up office in this court two weeks earlier, on October 30, following transfer by the Ministry of Justice from the Tokyo High Court, and there was speculation that his appointment, weeks before the national government suit against the governor was lodged, might have been the result of bureaucratic/judicial collusion designed to ensure Okinawan submission to the base construction plan.[18] On December 25, 2015, the prefecture launched a countersuit in the same Naha branch of the Fukuoka High Court, seeking to have the October ruling by the minister set aside. State and prefectural authorities were thus suing each other over the same matters and in the same Naha court.

The prefecture insisted it was a breach of its constitutional (Articles 92-95) entitlement to self-government for the state to impose the Henoko construction project on it unilaterally and by force. Onaga pointed to what he saw, on expert advice, as fatal flaws in the land reclamation approval process. In his view, the state (the Okinawa Defense Bureau) was adopting a perverse and arbitrary reading of the law, abusing the Administrative Appeal Act by pretending to be just like a "private person" (*ichishijin*) complaining under a law specifically designed to allow individual citizens to seek redress against unjustified or illegal acts by governmental agencies. He noted that while the state sought relief as if it were an aggrieved citizen, it deployed its full powers and prerogatives as a state under the Local Self-Government Law to sweep aside prefectural self-government and assume the right to proxy execution of an administrative act (*gyosei daishikko*). The state, for its part, argued that base (and defense) matters were its prerogative, and that treaty obligations overrode local self-government.

Judge Tamiya rejected applications by the prefecture to call expert witnesses on military and defense matters (who might dispute the need for a Marine Corps presence in Okinawa) or on the environment or environmental assessment law (who might challenge the compatibility of Okinawa's unique biodiversity with large-scale reclamation and militarization). His court showed strong, even exceptional, interest in one matter in particular: securing an explicit statement from Governor Onaga that he would abide by its ruling.[19]

## WAKAI/CONCILIATION (2016)

As the flurry of writs and interrogatories continued, and a tense and sometimes violent confrontation continued between state powers and protesting citizens at the reclamation/construction site, it was hard to imagine where ground for compromise might be found. Yet that is precisely what Chief Justice Tamiya ordered when, on January 29, 2016, he advised the disputing parties to consider an out-of-court settlement. He began with the following exhortation[20]:

At present the situation is one of confrontation between Okinawa and the Government of Japan. So far as the cause of this is concerned, before any consideration of which is at fault both sides should reflect that it should not be like this. Under the 1999 revision to the Local Autonomy Law it was envisaged that the state and regional public bodies would serve their respective functions as independent administrative bodies in *an equal, cooperative relationship* [italics added]. That is especially desirable in the performance of statutory or entrusted matters. The present situation is at odds with the spirit of this revised law.

Essentially, entire Japan, including Okinawa, should reach an agreement on the best solution, and seek cooperation from the United States. Only then the United States would use that as an opportunity for an active cooperation, including a major reform. Instead, if the issue continues to be contested before the courts, and even if the state wins the present judicial action, hereafter it may be foreseen that the reclamation license might be rescinded or that approval of changes accompanying modification of the design would become necessary, and that the courtroom struggle would continue indefinitely. Even then there could be no guarantee that it would be successful. In such a case, as the Governor's wide discretionary powers come to be recognized, the risk of defeat is high. And, even if the state continued to win, the works are likely to be considerably delayed. On the other hand, even if the prefecture wins, if it turns out that the state would not ask for Futenma return because it insists that Henoko construction is the only way forward, then it is inconceivable that Okinawa by itself could negotiate with the US and secure Futenma's return.

Tamiya went on to rebuke and warn the state that, unless it fundamentally changed its strategy, it was heading toward defeat. Drawing attention to the 1999 revision to the Local Autonomy Act that turned the national-prefectural government relationship from instrumental (vertical, superior/inferior) to equal and cooperative, he urged the parties to "conciliate," offering two alternatives, "basic (Plan A)" and "provisional (Plan B)."

Under the "provisional" plan, the state would drop the execution-by-proxy suit and stop site works and the parties would open talks toward a satisfactory resolution (*enman kaiketsu*), while the government would file a less forceful type of lawsuit, to verify the illegality of the permit withdrawal. After the judicial determination, both parties would immediately obey it and promise to each other that they would implement it accordingly.

Under the "basic" plan, Okinawa would reverse its withdrawal of the reclamation permit in exchange for the Japanese government opening negotiations with the United States to have the new base "either returned to Japan or converted into a joint military-civilian airport at some point within thirty years from the time it becomes operational."

There was nothing conciliatory or amicable about either option. There was no reason to think that the "provisional" plan talks that had accomplished nothing till then would somehow offer a path to resolution, while the inclusion of provisos for the defendant (the prefecture) and the plaintiff (the state) to cooperate in the reclamation and subsequent operation of the base under the "basic" plan meant that it was predicated on the contested base at Henoko actually being built and provided to the Marine Corps, probably until at least the year 2045 (or indeed much longer, because there could be no guarantee as to how the government of the United States would respond to any Japanese request at such a remote future date). One retired judge noted,

> The success or failure of diplomatic negotiation with the United States is contingent on the cooperation of a third party, namely the United States. In other words, the paragraph does not describe something that the Japanese government has the authority to execute freely. Thus it fails to adhere to the requisites of a term of settlement, and thus the settlement proposal as a whole lacks validity from a legal standpoint.[21]

On March 4, as directed by Tamiya, the parties came to an out-of-court or "amicable" (*wakai*) settlement.[22] It basically followed the "provisional plan (Plan B)." Site works were halted, both parties withdrew their existing suits under the Administrative Appeals Act, and the state agreed to ask the prefecture under Article 245 of the Local Autonomy Act to cancel the order cancelling the reclamation license and agree to the matter being referred to the Central and Local Government Disputes Management Council in the event of its declining. Tamiya's court saw such a suit as more appropriate to the formally equal relationship between the parties than the execution-by-proxy suit that the Abe government had chosen. The parties would discuss and seek "satisfactory resolution" pending the final outcome of judicial proceedings, and both would then abide by whatever outcome then emerged.

Judge Tamiya combined formal, procedural critique of the Abe government with support for its case, evident in this recommendation of a "solution" that involved construction of the very base that Okinawans were determined to stop. The barb in the "amicable agreement" was the superficially innocuous "sincerity" provision eventually incorporated in Paragraph 9, designed to remove any possible further recourse to the courts once the Supreme Court comes to its decision. It read:

> The complainant and other interested parties and the defendant reciprocally pledge that, after the judgment in the suit for cancellation of the rectification order becomes final, they will immediately comply with that judgment and carry out procedures in accord with the ruling and its grounds,

and also that thereafter they will mutually cooperate and sincerely respond to the spirit of the ruling.[23]

Challenged in the Okinawa Prefectural Assembly on March 8, 2016, as to what this commitment to "cooperate and sincerely respond to the spirit of the ruling" meant, Governor Onaga explained his understanding that, although his October 2015 order might thereby be cancelled, and the Nakaima license restored, in respect of all other matters he would make "appropriate judgement in accord with the law."[24] He did not go into detail, but it would seem to mean that, even if defeated in court, he could still resort to his other sanction: rescission (*tekkai*) of the Nakaima reclamation license. It implied that he could, and evidently would, refuse or obstruct requests from the state for detailed adjustments to the reclamation plan or engineering design.

The March 4 "amicable settlement," shifting the government case against Okinawa from the Administrative Appeals Act, where its position was procedurally weak, to the Local Government Act, where it was stronger, was drawn up and agreed in accord with court directives, so it was neither out-of-court nor, as it turned out, a "settlement," since, no sooner had it been reached, with the government promising "discussions aimed at satisfactory resolution," than Prime Minister Abe insisted anew that Henoko was "the only option," implying that there was nothing to negotiate but Okinawa's surrender.[25] Just three days after agreeing to engage in discussions, and without so much as a preliminary meeting, MLITT Minister Ishii (for the government) sent Governor Onaga a formal request that he retract his cancellation of the Oura Bay reclamation license (i.e., that he restore the license granted by Nakaima in December 2013). It was exactly as prescribed under Paragraph 3 of the agreement, committing the parties to proceed in accord with Article 245 of the Local Autonomy Law, but it was plainly at odds with the prescription under Paragraph 8: that they negotiate.

> Until such time as a finalized court judgement on the proceedings for cancellation of the rectification order is issued, the plaintiff and other interested parties and the defendant will undertake discussions aimed at "satisfactory resolution" (*enman kaiketsu*) of the Futenma airfield return and the current [Henoko] reclamation matter.

On March 14, Governor Onaga responded. He pointed out that the government had given no reason for its request and therefore his cancellation order could not be seen as a breach of the law.[26] So he refused, referring to Ishii's act as "an illegal intervention by the state,"[27] and submitted the matter to the Disputes Management Council. It was, he said, a "pity" that the government had seen fit to issue such a rectification order immediately after entering the amicable agreement.

The five-member Disputes Management Council, since its establish-ment in 2000, had only twice been called upon to adjudicate a dispute and on neither occasion—both matters of relatively minor importance—had it issued any ruling against the government.[28] It was an unlikely avenue for resolution of a major dispute between national and regional govern-ments, especially since it had abstained from doing so just months earlier, in December 2015, without so much as a statement of its reasons.

While the national government insisted there was no alternative to He-noko construction, Onaga told the Disputes Management Council that the project was "a monumental idiocy likely to cause a treasure of humanity to vanish from the earth."[29] There was little or no room for compromise be-tween the prefecture's argument that the Nakaima consent to reclamation was wrongful because it failed to meet the requirements of the Reclama-tion Act and the state's argument that reclamation was within its powers because it had exclusive responsibility for defense and foreign relations.

The council, however, on June 17, 2016, delivered an astonishing judgement: unanimously, it refused to rule on the legitimacy of MLITT Minister Ishii's March order to the Okinawan governor. The panel head, Kobayakawa Mitsuo, told a press conference,

> We thought issuing either a positive or a negative judgement on the rectifica-tion order would not be beneficial in helping the state and local governments create desirable relations.[30]

The panel lamented the "continuing undesirable" state of relations between state and prefecture, and urged "sincere discussions" to reach agreement.[31] Since it issued no ruling, it meant that Governor Onaga's cancellation order remained in place, and that site works could not be resumed. In that sense it might be seen as a victory for the prefecture. But the underlying problem remained: if a commission especially set up to decide on disputes between national and regional governments could not resolve them, who or what could?

## JUDGE TAMIYA'S SPEED TRIAL, 2016

With the door thus closed by the Disputes Management Council, on July 22, 2016, the national government filed a fresh suit with the Naha branch of the Fukuoka High Court (i.e., Judge Tamiya's court), seeking a rul-ing that the Okinawan government comply with the MLITT minister's order and amend (reverse) its revocation of permission for landfill work on Oura Bay. The government rested its case on the grounds of foreign affairs and defense policy it had advanced in the previous hearings. It turned its back on the conciliation process Tamiya had ordered in January and on the Disputes Council's call for "sincere negotiations." Its position that there was no alternative to Henoko construction and therefore nothing to negotiate bordered on contempt of court. As the *Asahi Shimbun* noted in March, the Abe government's actions

> suggest the arrogance that comes from regarding Okinawa as an inferior, despite the High Court's statement that the central government and all local governments are "equals."[32]

As for Okinawa, through its governor and its prefectural assembly, its parliament, and through repeated mass gatherings of its citizens, as well as through its panel of lawyers in the Naha court, it made clear that it accepted, indeed embraced, the principle of equality enunciated by Tamiya and that, as an equal, it ruled out any new base construction on its territory. Governor Onaga insisted (August 5, 2016) that he had exercised his authority properly and that there was no reason why he should submit to a contrary, improper "rectification" directive from the state. At issue, he insisted, were "fundamentals of regional self-government and by extension fundamentals of democracy."[33]

Tamiya adopted an extraordinary "speed trial" schedule. From issue of the writs on July 22 there were just two open days of hearings (August 5 and 19); the prefecture's request to call eight expert witnesses (including Mayor Inamine of Nago City) was summarily dismissed and Onaga himself repeatedly asked only to confirm that he would obey the ruling of the court (a highly irregular query).[34] On September 16, 2016, the Naha branch of the Fukuoka High Court upheld the state's claims in all particulars and ruled that Okinawa's governor was in breach of the law by his cancellation (in July 2015) of the reclamation license on Oura Bay issued by his predecessor almost two years earlier.

Okinawa prefecture lodged an appeal, but few were surprised when, three months later on (December 20), the Supreme Court brusquely dismissed it, having refused to hear any witnesses. Onaga was not formally required to do so by the judgment, but he quickly cancelled his cancellation order, whereupon the state began sending in to the Camp Schwab site a daily convoy of trucks carrying construction equipment and materials. Site works resumed after a hiatus of nearly one year, and on April 25 the government contractors began depositing on the Henoko beach the first large sacks of rock designed to be the foundation of the seawall.

## STATE OF PLAY, 2017

Despite his submission to the court in 2017, Onaga insisted that he was sticking to his pledge to not allow construction of the new base. Standing before the protesters at the gate to Camp Schwab in March 2017, and again before a mass protest rally (of 45,000 people) in Naha in August 2017, he declared that he would "certainly" and "determinedly" use his long-delayed weapon and rescind (*tekkai*) the reclamation license. But he gave no indication as to when he would do so,[35] so that some who had believed in him in 2014 or 2015 found their faith harder to maintain in 2017. As we write, the pressure on Onaga to do as he had repeatedly promised and "rescind" the reclamation permit was palpable, but there was no sign that any such action was imminent.

While still reserving this unused weapon, on July 24, 2017, the Okinawa prefectural government filed a fresh suit in the Naha District Court demanding a halt to the works.[36] The prefecture rested its case on the Fisheries Regulation Law of 2012, under which consent of the governor was required for any alteration to specified fisheries zones. Such permit had been sought from, and granted by, (then) Governor Nakaima in August 2014 for rock and coral crushing in Oura Bay, but it expired in March 2017. Knowing that the prefecture would refuse if asked to renew it, the state declared it no longer necessary. It argued that the governor's or prefectural rights over the Bay were extinguished when the Henoko fisheries cooperative abandoned its fishing rights in the Bay in 2013. The co-op had indeed then voted 94-2 to give up those fishing rights in return for 600 million yen in compensation.[37] However, the prefecture argued that it (the governor) possessed a general entitlement over the coastal region going beyond the rights attaching to the fisheries co-op. It is also the case, although it was not part of the prefecture's case to the court in 2017, that the co-op's 2013 consent was problematic because many of the Henoko fishermen agreed only reluctantly to accept compensation for reclamation in return for abandoning the sea because they felt unable to continue making a living in the face of government determination to press ahead with the base construction. The Okinawan fishing industry had long suffered from red soil runoff pollution from the bases and from rampant development policies. Local newspapers quoted opinions among the participants such as "We cannot fish because of US exercises," "If the country determines something, how can we resist?" and "It resembles the situation in which [in the Battle of Okinawa] people were collectively driven to group suicide." Furthermore, five days after the Henoko meeting, a larger meeting, attended by 150 members of the fishing co-ops of neighboring Ginoza, Kin, and Ishikawa (total members: 316), demanded immediate cancellation of the construction plan.[38] Whatever the Naha court might determine about the law on this, the government case that it could proceed to reclaim the Bay for base construction without prefectural or city consent was a design to evade local, self-governing constitutional democracy.

The outcome of the Naha District Court suit launched in July 2017, fifth in the series that began in 2015, is (as of January 2018) impossible to predict, but the bitter truth is that the longer the proceedings drag on, the closer they come to some point of irreversibility. Even in the unlikely event of the prefecture "winning," and a prefectural license being held necessary, the state could then simply apply for it, however belatedly, and Governor Onaga had stated that he would comply, provided only that the procedural formalities were met.[39] Some within the base opposition camp suggest that it is not that Governor Onaga wants the new base to be built; he does indeed want to stop it, but not to the extent of fighting against the national government to do so. If possible, he would like the national government itself to call a halt, out of consideration for his views and for the sentiment of the people of Okinawa.[40] Unlike the action that went to the Supreme Court in 2016, this is one court action that the state had no incentive to hasten. So long as works continue, time favors the state.

While he awaited the outcome of the court action on coral crushing, and kept promising *tekkai*, Onaga also exercised other, lesser, options for trying to halt seawall construction. Each revision to the design that affected city or prefecture required consent, and either Governor Onaga or Nago City mayor Inamine (or both) could simply say no. Under an ordinance adopted by the Okinawan Prefectural Assembly in 2015, the prefectural authorities could, if they so chose, stop and inspect every truckload (or shipload) of soil or sand being imported from outside the prefecture (and at least in principle forbid entry) because of the fear of pathogens (including Argentine ants) being introduced into the island's environment.[41] Other ordinances empower the prefecture to protect important "natural monuments" in Oura Bay such as hermit crabs, and historically important cultural relics such as "anchor stones" dating back to the premodern Ryukyu era.[42] No one doubted that Mayor Inamine, whose jurisdiction included both construction sites, would refuse permission for works to divert the Mija River outlet to Oura Bay (one of many late "adjustments" to the plan). However, although the coastal area of Oura Bay was declared worthy of the strictest conservation status as rank 1 under prefectural Guidelines on the Conservation of the Natural Environment, neither the prefecture nor the city had any way even to enter and inspect, let alone to protect, their own seas and coast.

The Henoko works also encounter serious design problems. Civic applications under freedom of information secured evidence that the state's engineering design was being repeatedly and substantially revised. Both the technical difficulties of reclaiming deep waters (60-plus meters) of Oura Bay and the stubbornness of the civic resistance seem to have been beyond the state's anticipation. Three "works yards" adjacent to the construction site at Henoko and part of the original design had to be abandoned in recognition of the fact that Nago mayor Inamine would never agree to them. Worries over the possibility of site subsidence or liquefaction called for the state's contractors to need to undertake "boring surveys" of nineteen sites not part of the original design, and the attrition caused by the daily Schwab gate civic protest continued to cause significant delays and cost overruns. In five months the seawall that was supposed to stretch for 300 meters had reached only 100, ceasing before the Bay's sudden plunge into very deep waters.[43] If the project does indeed go ahead, and assuming the delivery of materials proceeds by road, as spelled out in the original plan, it would mean Okinawa being subjected to more than three million ten-ton trucks loaded with sand and soil from all over western Japan, at the rate of approximately 2,800 truckloads per day (approximately thirty times greater than the mid-2017 rate).[44] Quite apart from the potentially devastating ecological consequences of introducing sand and soil from many parts of the country, in logistical terms it was a nightmare, threatening to overwhelm the island's port and road system.

Because of the continuing Camp Schwab gate-front protest and the growing chaos on the roads in the vicinity, the state late in 2017 shifted its strategy so as to commence delivery of construction materials by sea as well as by road.[45] One shipload could carry the equivalent of 190 ten-ton trucks,[46] and if significant quantities of fill could be delivered by sea, at multiple ports across northern Okinawa, it would be much more difficult for citizens to mobilize effective protest. In June, the Okinawa Defense Agency asked the prefectural authorities for permission to use the port facilities at the tiny hamlet of Oku (population 174) in Kunigami village at the far northern point of Okinawa Island for unloading materials. The prefecture, after due consideration, consented in September, and delivery commenced in November 2017.

The issue of that permit seemed to many a plain breach of the governor's commitment to use "all means at my disposal" to prevent reclamation. On November 15, a defensive governor confronted civic critics at the prefectural offices. Yamashiro Hiroji, probably the best-known figure of the anti–base construction protest and therefore "public enemy number one" to the Abe government, distanced himself from the governor and demanded an explanation. The governor referred in deferential terms to the long civic protest ("for 1,000 days") and to Yamashiro's "illegal and wrongful" treatment by the state, but he insisted that on a strict understanding of the relevant law (the Port and Harbor Act, 1950) and provided the procedures laid down were observed, he had had no alternative but to consent. He protested, however, that the prefectural complaint based on the Reclamation Law was a different matter.[47] That suit would continue in the courts, and he would still, at the appropriate moment, rescind the permit that underlay ongoing construction.

It was a narrowly legalistic defense. As some pointed out, it was inconceivable that the Japanese state could ever be defeated in court.[48] Disappointment spread, even in the ranks of All-Okinawa, at the governor who kept saying he would do "everything in my power" to stop Henoko construction while procrastinating about actually rescinding the reclamation permit and now had given de facto support for construction by endorsing the use of Oku port for delivery of materials. The people of Oku ward unanimously adopted a resolution calling on him to cancel the Oku port use license.[49] He was said to be "contemplating a major decision over matters including the possible cancelation of the harbor use permit."[50]

### STATE VIOLENCE AND CIVIC RESISTANCE

While court battles engaged a small army of lawyers and officials, on the front lines, at Henoko and Takae, state forces directly confront citizen protesters. A ten-year encampment at the Henoko fishing harbor put paid to the first design for a floating heliport base in 2005. In the second, continuing, phase, the core protest camp shifted a couple of kilometers from the fishing harbor to the gate to Camp Schwab base. From July 2014, that Camp Schwab gate site became the main access route to the construction site. This phase of the protest now approaches its fourth year.

On an average day, the core protest group at the gate may be between sixty and one hundred or so protesters, but on special occasions there are many more, especially on days when core protesters are supplemented by All-Okinawa–chartered buses bringing volunteers from throughout the island. The impromptu exchange of experience and ideas, interspersed with performances of song or dance, grew during 2016 to such an extent that the gathering declared itself "Henoko University" and organized a series of "lectures" by activists and scholars.

From March 2016, during the nine-month lull in Oura Bay works, the focus of struggle shifted from Henoko to the N-1 entrance gate to the Marine Corps' Northern Training Area in the Yambaru forest (Takae hamlet; population 150), about 40 kilometers away. Under the 1996 agreement, about half (4,000 hectares) of the vast Northern Training Area, spanning Higashi and Kunigami villages and known to the Americans as Camp Gonsalves, was to be returned "within five to seven years." The actual return took place twenty years later, in December 2016.

Furthermore, as at Henoko, Takae "reversion" meant substitution and military upgrading, not simply handover. The Japanese state agreed in 1996 to construct new helipads for the Marine Corps to replace those located within the land to be returned to Okinawa. There were to be six helipads, substantial structures 75 meters in diameter and fed by access roads built by clear-felling forest. When the detailed plan was settled, the village assembly unanimously protested against it (February and July 2006) and set up a roadside protest "sit-in" camp the following year. As it had done at Henoko, the government proceeded to impose its agenda by crushing the opposition, resorting to various devices including SLAPP-type (strategic lawsuit against public participation) restraining court orders (pp. 167-172). An environmental impact study was conducted (2007–2012), but, like that for Henoko, it was conducted by the contractors themselves and was neither independent nor scientific. One crucial detail—that the "helipads" were to be used not by the conventional CH-46 helicopter but by the ear-crushingly noisy and dangerous VTOL Osprey—was kept from the public until the process was over. In February 2015, two "Osprey pads" were completed and handed over to the Marine Corps. The Higashi Village Assembly adopted unanimously a resolution declaring that the construction contravened the wishes of the local community and banning US aircraft from using them. Days later, on February 25, the Osprey began training flights.

From July 22, 2016, as the construction process went to accelerated mode, the government stepped up its assault on the people of Takae, creating in effect a "lawless" zone.[51] Its forces periodically swept aside protest tents and vehicles and closed or limited traffic on Highway 70.[52] Where the original (2006) plan had been to build one helipad at a time so as to minimize damage to the forest, henceforth all four that remained would be built simultaneously, cutting the estimated time for works completion from thirteen to six months. It meant quadrupling the daily number of trucks employed in delivering materials and equipment, and sending major police reinforcements from mainland Japan to help stave off the Okinawan opposition. As *Ryukyu Shimpo* pointed out, it was the sort of mobilization of force with which a major assault on a yakuza gangster headquarters might be launched.[53] For the people carrying on the resistance, mostly elderly, the experience of being overwhelmed by state force, outnumbered roughly five to one, was "akin to martial law" as novelist Medoruma Shun put it.[54]

Officially, the process of reversion was one of "burden reduction," but the experience of the people of Takae was of life made virtually unbearable. The Ospreys flew roughly twice as often as the CH-46 they replaced,[55] ignored the agreed 150-meter height limitation and flew as low as 60 meters over the village,[56] and became especially feared because of their emergency landings, high-risk night parachute drops, and refueling and equipment hauling exercises. The level of noise in excess of sixty decibels increased twelvefold over the five years of Osprey deployment from

2012.[57] In the vicinity of Takae Primary School, sixty decibels was exceeded in 2016 on 6,887 occasions.[58] Increasingly night training flights were conducted, especially terrifying when conducted without lights.[59] And such is the level of concentration in Okinawa of US military facilities in Japan that reversion of half of the Northern Training Area merely reduced the Okinawan proportion of American base land from 74 to 71 percent.

When the rare and protected resident of the Yambaru forest, the Noguchigera woodpecker, began to die mysteriously, locals suspected that the avian nervous system too (like the human) could not cope with the disturbance brought by the Osprey.[60] The US military enjoyed priority over all the forest dwellers, not only human but animal, avian, insect, or botanical, and so the once peaceful, biodiverse, forested environment became a virtual war zone. The Okinawa Prefectural Assembly (for the first time) adopted a resolution calling for immediate halt to the works.[61] A local newspaper conducted a door-to-door survey of opinion among local residents and found opposition running at 80 percent, with not one soul in favor.[62]

As the bitter contest continued, costs skyrocketed. The 613 million yen budgeted for construction of the Osprey pads blew out by more than fifteen times to 9,400 million yen (roughly $80 million) before the works were "completed" and handed over in December 2016. Likewise, the initial budget of 5.9 billion yen for preliminary construction works at Henoko was raised ten times over eighteen months to 13.9 billion, an increase of 2.3 times, with policing the largest item at roughly 70 percent of the total.[63] When the summer rains came at Takae in 2017, the fill began to leak and flow into the neighboring sea, polluting it and requiring further, remedial work.[64] But since the state treated Henoko and Takae as colonial construction projects carried out in hostile territory, neither environmental impact nor cost warranted serious consideration.

Following a series of crashes and forced landings around the world, in December 2016, one of the Futenma-based Ospreys crashed into the sea off Okinawa's north shore near Nago City, and on August 5, 2017, another crashed, killing its crew of three, off the northeast coast of Australia. Japanese foreign minister Kono Taro asked for the Osprey to be grounded, but the United States refused, and after a two-day hiatus, the remaining Futenma Ospreys (reduced to twenty-two) resumed their place in Okinawan skies.[65] Even the Okinawan branch of the national ruling coalition party, Komeito, protested to the Okinawan Defense Bureau calling for it to be suspended and described it as "shameful" for Japan as a state to be thus rudely ignored.[66] On October 11, 2017, a "conventional" Marine Corps helicopter (CH-53) crash-landed in flames on a farm in Takae hamlet. Again Okinawan protests were dismissed, further feeding Okinawa outrage.

## RULE OF LAW

As his government in July 2014 had effectively amended the constitution by the simple device of adopting a new interpretation, so in 2015 it showed scant respect for the relevant laws in the way it addressed Henoko reclamation. Constitutional lawyers who in 2015 overwhelmingly condemned Abe's de facto revision of the constitution in respect to security laws, from 2016 criticized as manipulation or breach of the law the way the Abe government was proceeding in the judicial dispute with Okinawa prefecture.

Furthermore, as we note above (pp. 53–54), ever since the Supreme Court held in the Sunagawa case in 1959 that the judiciary would not pass judgment on matters pertaining to the security treaty with the United States because of their being "highly political," the treaty has in effect been elevated above the constitution and immunized from any challenge at law. By the time the Supreme Court turned its attention to Henoko in 2016, that principle was deep in its DNA. The court proceedings were at odds with the Tamiya advice to both parties in January 2016 as to the significance of the 1999 revision to the Local Autonomy Law, whereby state and regional public bodies were to carry out their respective functions "in an equal, cooperative relationship." Former Okinawa University president and specialist in environmental law Sakurai Kunitoshi conveyed the view of many Okinawans when he declared that the 2016 Supreme Court decision was "appalling," showing

> that it was not a custodian of the constitution, that the local self-government law was nothing but a scrap of paper and that the Japan-US Security Treaty was superior to the constitution.[67]

The Henoko problem during 2015–2017 was thus repeatedly referred to the judiciary. Chief Cabinet Secretary Suga repeatedly insisted that Japan was a law-governed state, a *hochi kokka*, as he put it,[68] but it was not clear that Abe's Japan did in fact enjoy the division of powers and independence of the judiciary that are the hallmark of a modern, constitutional state. While the citizenry remained resolutely nonviolent and exercised the right of civil disobedience only after exhausting all legal and constitutional steps to oppose the base project, coast guard and riot police flaunted their violence, dragging away protesters (quite a few of whom are in their seventies and eighties), dunking canoeists in the sea (or dumping them on remote shores), pinning down one protest ship captain till he lost consciousness, and on a number of occasions causing injuries to protesters requiring hospital treatment.[69]

If laws were broken at Henoko and at Takae, there is a strong prima facie case for thinking that the government, police, and the Japan Coast Guard were the guilty parties. The police and coast guard mobilization to enforce a government construction project may well have been in breach of the provisions of the Police Duties Execution Act and the Coast Guard Act. The mobilization of Self-Defense Forces helicopters to transport construction equipment was probably counter to the Self-Defense Law and the Coast Guard Law lacked any provision that could justify the organ supposedly entrusted with the defense of Japan's shores and bays in treating protesting canoeists and kayakers as enemies of the state. Yamashiro's snipping of a strand of barbed wire seemed trivial when compared to the state's clear-felling without permit of an estimated 24,000 forest trees.[70] Many of the trucks used by contractors for the state at Takae lacked license plates and were therefore in breach of Okinawan road traffic law. When riot police brought in from Osaka abused protesters as *dojin* and *shinajin* (natives or Chink/Chinese), the government refused to treat it as hate speech,[71] and when Prime Minister Abe, opening the special session of the Diet in September 2016, conveyed special appreciation for the work being done by police and military personnel, he drew a standing ovation.[72]

Citizens nonviolently exercising what they believed to be their fundamental last resort right to protest face the full panoply of state force, including SLAPP and the special criminal law (and punitive detention as in the Yamashiro case). Ultimately the state acts not as a responsible instrument of democratic rule but as an instrument of force at the disposal of government. LDP party chief Ishiba Shigeru expressed what was probably the shared view within government when he wrote of the burgeoning Okinawan protest movement in his blog (on November 29, 2013) that after all there was little difference in substance between vociferous demonstrators and terrorists.[73] Abe's government was intent on compelling the protest movement, both civic and institutional, to surrender by sowing despair.

As the government chafed under the continuing delays in its projects to construct the bases at Henoko and Takae, it sought to allocate blame. The sixty-four-year-old Okinawa prefecture retired former public servant Yamashiro Hiroji became the target of state outrage, Japan's "public enemy number one," so to speak.[74] He was renowned as master choreographer of the resistance, conducting the assembly of protesting citizens day after day, month after month, in song, dance, and debate. His wit and resolute nonviolence irritated the servants of the state.

Yamashiro, like many others during the suspension of works at Henoko under the court-ordered conciliation process, shifted the focus of his protest to Takae. On October 17, 2016, he was detained during a brief flurry. Initially the prosecutors sought an order for his detention for having been caught red-handed inflicting damage to property (cutting a strand of barbed wire to gain access to the construction site). Two other charges were later added: "forcible obstruction of public business" (Yamashiro and others were alleged to have piled up 1,400 concrete blocks in January 2016 to try to obstruct entry to Camp Schwab base) and "shaking [a contractor] by the shoulder causing bruising."[75]

Of the three charges, the wire cutting caused damage estimated at about $20 that was quickly repaired. The concrete blocks were swiftly removed by police and caused zero obstruction, so that the only potentially serious charge was that of assault causing injury. In the context of daily melees, continuing over many months and in all weather, and the overwhelming preponderance of force on the side of the state and its contractors, premeditation seemed improbable, while the number of protesters who had suffered bruising or other injury by being summarily grabbed, beaten, detained, thrown aside, in some cases leading to hospitalization, was not known but was certainly greater than the one upon whose bruises the court was deliberating in 2017.[76]

Yamashiro was held, treated as a suspected terrorist, for five months in solitary confinement; denied repeated requests for bail; forbidden visitors (including his family); subject to what can only be described as deliberate humiliation (forced to submit to "body searches" twice daily); interrogated daily (for at least the first half of that time); and, despite his serious illness being well-known, refused even the right to take delivery of a pair of socks while he was at the Nago police cell.[77] Only after widespread protest did the authorities eventually relax that rule, but then only to allow one pair of socks, which had to be short and which he was forbidden to wear inside his cell. It was a trivial enough matter, but illustrative of the state's bureaucratic sadism.

One American specialist on Japanese law pointed out that Yamashiro's prolonged detention contravened Japan's obligations under the International Covenant on Civil and Political Rights (notably Articles 9, 14, and 15,[78] which require release pending trial). In like vein, a group of Japanese criminal law specialists insisted that Yamashiro's detention was "unlawful," being inter alia a breach of Article 34 of the constitution banning lengthy detention without probable cause.

In civil suits too, based on constitutional principle, Okinawans tend to find themselves without remedy when they confront the encroachments of the state upon their lives or livelihood. Between 2002 and 2015, courts issued altogether seven judgments in the attempt to stop the intolerable levels of noise and nuisance emanating from Futenma base, repeatedly accepting evidence (in the words of the Naha District Court in June

2015) that the 2,200 plaintiffs of Ginowan City did indeed suffer "mental distress, poor sleep, and disruption to their daily lives" from "serious and widespread" violations that "could not be defended on any ground of public interest" but refused the relief they sought of a stoppage of the pain. Monetary compensation was all the court was prepared to consider. It ordered victims be paid 754 million yen (approximately $9 million) in compensation.

Resident groups in the five municipalities in the vicinity of Kadena US Air Force base have launched similar suits in three sets of "noise" proceedings, 1982–1988, 2000–2009, and 2011–2017. In the last of these suits, 22,000 claimants were awarded damages of 30 billion yen (ca. $267 million).[79] Noise levels not only did not abate but intensified, reaching in excess of 100 (occasionally an astounding 113) decibels in parts of Yomitan Village, Kadena City, and Okinawa City. Residents of those towns and villages are systematically deprived of the quality of life supposedly guaranteed them by the constitution and are subjected in their daily life to high levels of stress and sleeplessness, or to suspension of class in the schools.[80]

As with Futenma, courts are ready to compensate but claim they have no jurisdiction to order a stop to the nuisance or even a ban on night flights. In effect they concede that the US military is beyond and above the law, and the government of Japan is complicit in enforcing its ongoing illegality and the accompanying suffering of its people. Responding to Chief Cabinet Secretary Suga, *Ryukyu Shimpo* commented, "How could a government that enforces continuing illegality upon the citizens of one of its regions be considered a law-ruled state?"[81]

## SECURITY

The role of "base island" long imposed on the Okinawan people by the US and Japanese governments has meant for them not just deprivation of sovereignty and territory but deprivation of personal security in the name of national security. Between the reversion of Okinawa to Japan in 1972 and 2015, by official count US forces and their dependents and civil employees had been responsible for 5,896 criminal incidents, one tenth of them (574) crimes of violence including rape. Indelibly etched on the Okinawan collective memory are not just the 1995 rape case but many others going back to the rape/murder of six-year-old Yumiko-chan in 1955 and the crash of a fighter jet onto Miyamori Primary School in 1959 (killing seventeen people, including eleven children). Countless resolutions of protest over the years have been met with countless promises of better behavior.

After the current phase of Okinawan protest was triggered by the rape case of 1995, at least a dozen or more reported cases of US military rapes happened in Okinawa. Again, in April 2016, the rape and murder of a twenty-year-old Okinawan woman (to which an American ex-Marine base worker confessed) shocked, saddened, and outraged Okinawa. A protest and mourning meeting on May 25 adopted five demands (essentially the demands of the 2013 *Kempakusho*): drastic overall reduction of US bases, basic revision of the US-Japan SOFA (Status of Forces Agreement), closure and return of Futenma, withdrawal of Ospreys, and abandonment of base construction at Henoko. Two days later, the prefectural assembly made almost identical demands, but added that *all* Marine Corps bases and soldiers (i.e., not just Futenma but also the large, sprawling bases at Camp Schwab, Camp Hansen, and the Northern Training Area) should be closed and withdrawn from the island. It was the first time for such a demand to issue from the prefecture's parliament. Shortly after that, a prefectural mass meeting on June 19 brought together 65,000 mourning citizens in somber mood under a blazing 35-degree sun, where they listened silently to the victim's father ask for prefectural unity to demand withdrawal of *all* bases. Protesters declared that the people's anger "has gone beyond any limit." A coalition of sixteen organizations making up the "Okinawa Women Act against Military Violence" announced the same demand, for the withdrawal of *all* military bases and armed forces (thereby including also the massive US Air Force base at Kadena and Japan's own Self-Defense Force units). By early 2017, Okinawan sentiment was reaching well beyond the All-Okinawa and *Kempakusho* 2013 demands, with their exclusive focus on US bases and aircraft, to demand the removal from Okinawa of all appurtenances of the military, whether American or Japanese.[82]

## STRUGGLE WITHOUT END

For two decades from 1996, the "irresistible force" of the nation state has confronted the "immovable object" of the Okinawan resistance in a grand if massively unequal struggle. Never in modern Japanese history had the national government concentrated such effort on trying to bend the government and people of a region to its will. The project the "strong" state attempts to push through has been repeatedly delayed by the determined, nonviolent resistance of the "weak" (Okinawa). The more Abe resorts to deceit, intimidation, or violence, the more the resistance stiffens and the Okinawan demands widen and deepen. By refusing to listen to them, Abe pushes the relationship between state and prefecture toward open clash, weakens the US military ties that he is intent on strengthening, irritates the Pentagon he is committed to serving, and exposes Japan to the world as a state that denies basic democratic principle and human rights to the people of one of its prefectures.

By any conventional reckoning, with his hands on the levers of state power Abe should long ago have been able to bring Okinawa to heel, crushing its motley and minuscule flotilla of canoes and kayaks and its army of resolutely nonviolent Okinawans. Yet the contest continues. Twenty years have passed since Tokyo and Washington first promised Futenma return "within 5 to 7 years," i.e., by 2003. In 2016, as the twentieth anniversary of the original agreement passed, Admiral Harry Harris, commander of US Pacific forces, told Congress that the likely completion and handover date would be fiscal year 2025.[83] But he added that the situation at the Henoko site was not improving and that protest was "continuing to escalate."[84]

When US and Japanese government representatives meet on formal occasions, they tend to "celebrate" the "alliance" as a beacon of shared commitment to freedom, democracy, basic human rights, and the rule of law. Okinawans point out, however, that their experience is of being denied all of these. In the era of the Trump presidency, the absurdity of the pretense is simply more blatant than before. For all Abe's grandiloquent oratory before the United Nations or the US Congress about shared universal values and "proactive contribution to peace," Okinawans experience his government as fundamentally opposed to them, to pacifism, and to the constitution.

As of late 2017, however, the All-Okinawa movement faces its greatest challenge. For years, even for decades, Okinawans have not faltered, declaring on every conceivable occasion that they oppose the construction of any new base on their islands and insisting that existing bases be wound up and returned. National governments have never wavered in opposing this, none more determinedly so than that of Abe Shinzo. Treating Okinawan democratic sentiment as a barrier to be overcome, it not only refuses to listen but is ruthless in crushing the nonviolent resistance (for which it seems to enjoy the support of a majority of mainland citizens). The All-Okinawa movement has been the avatar of majority Okinawan sentiment since 2013, especially since the election of Onaga Takeshi as governor in December 2014, and the majority of Okinawans have trusted Governor Onaga to do as he constantly pledges: prevent the construction of any new base. His record, however, three years into his term as governor, shows a pattern of successive procrastination, reluctance to endorse or associate with the mass protest movement, and reliance on judicial resolution even as the record shows that to be futile. Despite his pledge to prevent construction, he appears to have no effective strategy. Consequently, the construction project on Oura Bay advances inexorably.

The K9 seawall at Henoko, complete by November 2017, was ready to transport reclamation materials. Construction of two additional seawalls got underway in that same month.

The prospect of reclamation and base construction looms now larger than ever. The state seems able to take with impunity whatever steps it deems necessary, while the people are more and more constrained. With the opening in November 2017 of a new front, the port of Oku, it seemed there was no prospect of end to the Okinawan struggle. For twenty years, Okinawans had succeeded in blocking and delaying and forcing change in the base construction plan, but the decisive moment in this contest might be at hand.

## NOTES

1. "Kempakusho," *Sekai* (March 2013): 154.
2. "Osprey's Arrival Foments Distrust," *Japan Times*, July 24, 2012.
3. Editorial, *Ryukyu Shimpo*, January 29, 2013.
4. Okinawa Electoral District No. 3 went to All-Okinawa's Denny Tamaki of the People's Life Party, headed by Ozawa Ichiro, and No. 4 went to the LDP-supported and avowedly pro–base construction Nishime Kosaburo (of Team Okinawa).
5. Onaga, "Chinjutsusho," August 3, 2016, Statement to Fukuoka Court, Okinawa prefecture home page, and (on Galapagos) "Henoko kakunin sosho, umetate zehi de honshitsu tsuke," editorial, *Ryukyu Shimpo*, August 3, 2016.
6. Kihara Satoru, "Hobei de 'oru Okinawa' o itsudatsu shita Onaga chiji," *Ari No Hitokoto*, February 7, 2017.
7. Figures given by Onaga, "Chinjutsusho."
8. "Henoko koji, ichinen chudan, Bei kaiheitai toppu ga shogen," *Ryukyu Shimpo*, March 17, 2016.
9. Onaga Takeshi, "Okinawa wa shinkichi o kobamu," *Sekai* (January 2016): 73.
10. "Onaga chiji, Abe shusho kaidan zenbun (boto hatsugen)," *Okinawa Taimusu*, May 19, 2015.
11. Full title: "Third Party Commission on the Procedure for Approval of Reclamation of Public Waters for the Construction of a Futenma Replacement Airfield."
12. For an analysis by a prominent member of the panel, delivered immediately after submission of the formal report, see Sakurai Kunitoshi and Gavan McCormack, "To Whom Does the Sea Belong? Questions Posed by the Henoko Assessment," *Asia-Pacific Journal: Japan Focus* (July 19, 2015), http://apjjf.org/2015/13/29/Sakurai-Kunitoshi/4346.html/.
13. Ibid.
14. "Implicitly" because Okinawan newspapers showed photographs that seemed to leave little doubt about coral being crushed by concrete blocks. "Zenkoku seron chosa, min-i ni soi 'Henoko dannen' o," editorial, *Ryukyu Shimpo*, April 21, 2015.

15. Press conference by Defense Minister Nakatani Gen, http://www.mod .go.jp/e/pressconf/2015/10/151027.html/, October 13, 2015.

16. "Tokyo overturns Futenma works plan," *Japan Times*, November 1, 2015.

17. "Kokoku sosho teiki, Onaga chiji kaiken," *Ryukyu Shimpo*, December 26, 2015.

18. Kyodo news agency reports of high-level bureaucratic/judicial collusion through a secret planning group headed by Chief Cabinet Secretary Suga Yoshihide, and including Foreign Minister Kishida Fumio, Defense Minister Nakatani Gen, and Tezuka Makoto, head of the Justice Ministry's Litigation Bureau and a specialist in out-of-court settlements, were carried in *Chugoku Shimbun, Okinawa Times*, and other papers, on March 24, under the heading (*Chugoku Shimbun*) "Henoko wakai no butaiura, Suga-shi shudo, gokuhi no chosei, sosho furi no kyu tenkai," and taken up again later in articles or editorials. For a convenient resume, Kihara Satoru, "Wakai no butaiura—Abe seiken to saibancho ga gokuhi ni sesshoku?" *Ari No Hitokoto*, March 25, 2016.

19. "Dai shikko sosho dai yon kai koto benron," *Ryukyu Shimpo*, February 16, 2016. See also discussion in Kihara Satoru, "Henoko saiban judai kyokumen (2) 'mizukara torikesu' wa riteki hanshin koi," *Ari No Hitokoto*, February 17, 2016.

20. Major documents, in Japanese only, are to be found on the Okinawa prefecture home page, including both the January 29 conciliation proposal and the March 4 agreement.

21. Nakasone Isamu, "Henoko: the 'amicable settlement,'" in Gavin McCormack, "'Ceasefire' on Oura Bay: The March 2016 Japan-Okinawa 'Amicable Agreement' Introduction and Six View from within the Okinawan Anti-Base Movement," *Asia-Pacific Journal: Japan Focus* (April 1, 2016), http://apjjf.org/2016/07/McCormack .html/.

22. Chiji koshitsu Henoko shin kichi kensetsu mondai taisakuka, "Wakai joko," March 4, 2016.

23. The tortuous prose of Article 9 confirmed several courtroom oral exchanges to the same effect. Onaga was repeatedly asked for assurances. "Will you abide by the judgment?" to which he replied, repeatedly, "*Shitagau*" ("I will follow it").

24. "Chiji, haiso demo kengen koshi, Henoko zesei shiji, keiso-i ni uttae e," *Ryukyu Shimpo*, March 9, 2016.

25. Reiji Yoshida, "Tokyo settles lawsuits, halts landfill at Henoko," *Japan Times*, March 4, 2016.

26. "Ken, keiso-i ni fufuku moshide 'zesei shiji' no torikeshi kankoku motome," *Ryukyu Shimpo*, March 14, 2016.

27. "Henoko isetsu, keiso-shori i ni shinsa moshide hasso, Okinawa ken," *Asahi Shimbun*, March 14, 2016.

28. "Keiso-i handan wa yosoku konnan," *Okinawa Taimusu*, November 2, 2015.

29. "Shin kichi 'sodai na guko,' chiji, keiso-i de umetate hihan, kuni 'shonin ni kashi nai,'" *Ryukyu Shimpo*, April 23, 2016.

30. "Panel refrains from supporting Okinawa in base relocation spat," *Mainichi Shimbun*, June 18, 2016.

31. "Keiso-i tekihi handan sezu, jichi o kobamu kuni e no keikoku da," *Ryukyu Shimpo*, June 18, 2016. For documents from the hearings, see Okinawa prefecture home page: http://www.pref.okinawa.lg.jp/site/chijiko/henoko/.

32. "Abe looks down nose at Okinawa despite court's advice on issue," *Asahi Shimbun*, March 10, 2016.

33. "Okinawa, Henoko sosho, chiji 'zesei shiji ukeru iwarenai,'" NHK News web, August 5, 2016.

34. Matsunaga Kazuhiro, quoted in "Henoko, iho kakunin sosho, Okinawa ken wa zenmen-teki ni arasou shisei, jokoku fukamaru ugoki mo," *Okinawa Taimusu*, August 20, 2016.

35. "Umetate shonin tekkai e, Onaga chiji 'kanarazu', ketsui futatabi, kenmin taikai," *Ryokyu Shimpo*, August 13, 2017, http://ryukyushimpo.jp/news/en try-554729.html/.

36. Okinawa prefecture, "Chiji koshitsu Henoko shin kichi kensetsu mondai taisakuka," July 24, 2017, http://www.pref.okinawa.jp/site/chijiko/henoko/documents/01_sojogaiyou.pdf.

37. See Urashima Etsuko, "A Nago Citizen's Opinion on the Henoko Marine Base Construction Project," *Asia-Pacific Journal: Japan Focus* (November 25, 2013).

38. "Ginoza nado gyokyo, Henoko isetsu ni hantai," *Okinawa Taimusu*, March 17, 2013.

39. Kihara Satoru, "'Gansho hasai sashitome sosho' wa yugai mueki, sono yottsu no riyu," *Ari No Hitokoto*, July 25, 2017.

40. Such would seem to be the position adopted by Nakasone Isamu. See "Rondan: Ken no gansho hasai sashitome teiso—meikai na sentaku datta no ka," *Ryukyu Shimpo*, August 4, 2017, and Takara Sachika, "'Tekkai' shincho Chiji ni gimon," *Okinawa Taimusu*, August 31, 2017.

41. See Gavan McCormack, "To the Courts! To the Streets! Okinawa at December 2015," *Asia-Pacific Journal: Japan Focus* (December 7, 2015), http://apjjf.org/Gavan-McCormack/4405.

42. Ibid. The discovery of seventeen culturally significant earthen- and stoneware objects in the Oura Bay site vicinity was announced in November 2015.

43. "Kisha kaisetsu, Henoko chakko kara 5 kagetsu," Ryukyu Asahi Hoso, http://www.qab.co.jp/nws/2017092794932.html/.

44. Assuming average truck load rate of about 80 percent.

45. "Henoko shin kichi: ken, gogan henko de boeikyoku ni shokai, raigetsu kaito o yokyu," *Okinawa Taimusu*, September 27, 2017.

46. "Kisha kaisetsu," op. cit.

47. "Oki minato kara no kaijo hannyu 'arata na jitai ga dete kite iru' Onaga Takeshi okinawa kenchiji, burasagari kaiken," *Ryukyu Shimpo*, November 15, 2017.

48. Sato Manabu, "Ampo no jijitsu hasshin o," *Ryukyu Shimpo*, November 24, 2017.

49. "Oku minato shiyo hantai kumin ketsugi," *Ryukyu Shimpo*, November 29, 2017.

50. "'Oku shiyo torikeshi mo' Onaga shi, Henoko koji de uttae," *Tokyo Shimbun*, December 1, 2017.

51. "Ho keishi no chakurikutai koji 'hochi kokka' no na ni ataisezu," *Ryukyu Shimpo*, August 2, 2016.

52. Watase Natsuhiko and Morizumi Takashi, "Kyukyu hanso tsuzuku kogi genba," *Shukan Kinyobi* (August 5, 2016): 42–43.

53. Ryota Nakamura, "Riot squad sent to subdue Takae protesters similar in scale to that sent to eradicate yakuza gangsters," *Ryukyu Shimpo*, July 18, 2016.

54. Quoted in Jon Letman, "Fighting to Save a Remote Okinawan Forest," *Honolulu Civil Beat*, August 12, 2016.

55. "Chakurikutai senko teikyo, hazubeki taibei juzoku da," editorial, *Ryukyu Shimpo*, February 19, 2015.

56. "Osupurei kunren jissai wa 60m, seifu setsumei 150m," *Ryukyu Shimpo*, February 14, 2017.

57. "Seifu no kotoba to gyakko, Beigunki no zatsuon 5 nen de 12-bai, Okinawa, Takae, Osupurei haibi go," *Okinawa Taimusu*, October 4, 2017.

58. "Shin kichi kensetsu 'Henoko' zehi aratamete tou," editorial, *Ryukyu Shinbun*, October 19, 2017.

59. Night flights increased to 400 during the month of June 2016, up by eightfold over 2014 (Okinawa Defense Bureau, quoted in Letman, op. cit.).

60. "Higashi-son de Noguchigera mado ni shototsushi, kotoshi yon-wa me," *Oknawa Taimusu*, October 29, 2014.

61. Okinawa Prefectural Assembly, "Beigun hokubu kunrenjo heripaddo kensetsu ni kansuru ikensho," July 21, 2016.

62. "Chakurikutai hantai, Takae 80%, sansei kaito wa zero, Honshi ga 2-ku jumin anketo," *Ryukyu Shimpo*, August 3, 2016.

63. Mori Takao, "Okinawa, Henoko, Takae kono hantoshi amari no tokuchoteki doko," *Kagakuteki Shakaishugi*, September 2017.

64. Ibid.

65. "'Osupurei go-oki de tsuiraku' hiko teishi, kizen to semare," editorial, *Okinawa Taimusu*, August 8, 2017.

66. "Komeito, 'kokka to shite do shiyo mo nai' tsuiraku kogi de hihan," *Ryukyu Shimpo*, August 8, 2017.

67. Sakurai Kunitoshi, interviewed in "Kireme nai sochi ronjiyo," *Ryukyu Shimpo*, December 26, 2016.

68. "Kuni 'hochi kokka' de yusaburi," editorial, *Ryukyu Shimpo*, October 25, 2016.

69. Details on this and other cases in "'All Japan' versus 'All Okinawa'—Abe Shinzo's Military First-ism," *Asia-Pacific Journal: Japan Focus* (March 16, 2015). On Shimabukuro Fumiko, see "Henoko 85-sai josei kega, ichiji ishiki ushinau," *Ryukyu Shimpo*, November 22, 2014.

70. Details in Okinawan media, July-August 2016. See especially "Takae doji chakko mubo na keikaku wa akiraka ni," *Okinawa Taimusu*, August 28, 2016; "Heripaddo koki tanshuku, Nichibei ryo seifu wa mori mo kowasu no ka," *Okinawa Taimusu*, August 29, 2016; and (24,000 trees felled) "Letter of concern and request, Inscription of Yambaru forest as a world natural heritage site," December 1, 2016, in Yoshikawa and McCormack, op. cit.

71. "Cabinet: No need for Tsuruho to apologize over 'dojin' issue," *Asahi Shimbun*, November Beer 22, 2016.

72. "Abe's instruction of diet ovation for SDF criticized," *Japan Times*, September 27, 2016.

73. "Kussaku sagyo ni chakushu, mohaya 'kyofu seiji' da, banko chushi shi min-i o toe," *Ryukyu Shimpo*, editorial, August 18, 2014.

74. For earlier version of the following discussion of the Yamashiro case, see Gavan McCormack and Sandi Aritza, "The Japanese State versus the People of Okinawa: Rolling Arrests and Punitive Detention," *Asia-Pacific Journal: Japan Focus* (January 5, 2017), http://apjjf.org/2017/02/McCormack.html/.

75. "Activists Protesting US Base Relocation in Okinawa Arrested," *Mainichi Shimbun*, November 30, 2016.

76. For a list of incidents of "Violence, Detention, and Arrests in Henoko, Okinawa in 2014–15," see All Okinawa Council et al., "Joint Submission to United Nations, Human Rights Council: Violation of Freedoms of Expression and Peaceful Assembly in Okinawa, Japan," December 11, 2015, in Hideki Yoshikawa and Gavan McCormack, "Okinawa: NGO Appeal to the United Nations and to US Military and Government over Base Matters, December 2015 and December 2016," *Asia-Pacific Journal: Japan Focus* (December 2016).

77. "'Kutsushita no sashiire mitomete' 'pantsu to issho' Okinawa kenkei ni 100 nin ga uttae," *Okinawa Taimusu*, December 12, 2016. And for Yamashiro's account, Gavan McCormack and the Asia-Pacific Jounal Report, "There Will Be No Stopping the Okinawa Resistance—an Interview with Yamashiro Hiroji," *Asia-Pacific Journal: Japan Focus* (August 1, 2017), http://apjjf.org/2017/15/McCormack.html/.

78. Lawrence Repeta, "The Silencing of an Anti-US Base Protester in Okinawa," *Japan Times*, January 4, 2017.

79. "Hiko sashitome kikyaku," *Ryukyu Shimpo*, extra, February 23, 2017. See also Kyodo, "Japanese Government Ordered to Pay Record Damages in US Base Noise Suit," *Japan Times*, February 23, 2017.

80. "Kadena bakuon ka jumin no himei ga kikoeru," editorial, *Okinawa Taimusu*, November 12, 2017.

81. "Futenma soon sosho, hochi kokka to ieru no ka," *Ryukyu Shimpo*, June 12, 2015. See also "Futema soon sosho iho jotai o hochi suru na," *Okinawa Taimusu*, June 12, 2015.

82. "Datsu gunji no seron keisei o," *Ryukyu Shimpo*, April 23, 2017.

83. Admiral Harry Harris, commander-in-chief US Pacific forces, congressional evidence quoted in "Beigun no honne, hirogaru hamon, Bei shireikan no Henoko isetsu okure hatsugen," *Okinawa Taimusu*, March 3, 2016.

84. Quoted in Heianna Sumiyo, "Harisu Beigun shireikan 'hantai undo kakudai shite iru' Nakatani shi ni Henoko okure kenhien tsutatsu," *Okinawa Taimusu*, February 25, 2016.

# Bibliography

Ahagon, Shoko, and Douglas Lummis. "I Lost My Only Son in the War: Prelude to the Okinawan Anti-Base Movement." *Asia-Pacific Journal: Japan Focus* (June 7, 2010). http://japanfocus.org/-Ahagon-Shoko/3369.

Aldous, Christopher. "'Mob Rule' or Popular Activism: The Koza Riot of December 1970 and the Okinawan Search for Citizenship." In *Japan and Okinawa: Structure and Subjectivity*, edited by Glenn D. Hook and Richard Siddle, 148–66. London, New York: Routledge, 2003.

Allen, Matthew. *Identity and Resistance in Okinawa*. Lanham, MD: Rowman & Littlefield, 2002.

———. "Wolves at the Back Door—Remembering the Kumejima Massacres." In *Islands of Discontent: Okinawan Responses to Japanese and American Power*, edited by Laura Hein and Mark Selden, 39–64. Lanham, MD: Rowman & Littlefield, 2003.

Ambassador MacArthur to Department of State. "Cable No 4393." *Foreign Relations of the United States* 18 (June 24, 1960): 377–84.

Arakawa, Akira. *Okinawa: Togo to hangyaku*. Tokyo: Chikuma shobo, 2000.

Arasaki, Moriteru. *Okinawa gendaishi*. 2nd ed. Tokyo: Iwanami shoten, 2005.

———. "Senkaku shoto (Diaoyu judao) mondai to Okinawa no tachiba." In *Okinawa wa doko e mukau no ka*. Okinawa University, December 19, 2010.

Arasaki, Moriteru, Jahana Naomi, Matsumoto Tsuyoshi, Maedomari Hiromori, Kameyama Norikazu, Nakasone Masaji, and Ota Shizuo. *Kanko kosu de nai Okinawa: Senseki, kichi, sangyo, shizen, sakishima*. 4th ed. Tokyo: Kobunken, 2008.

Arashiro, Toshiaki. *Junia ban Ryukyu Okinawa shi*. Itoman: Henshu kobo toyo kikaku, 2008.

Arashiro, Yoneko. "Okinawa jimoto shi shasetsu ni miru Okinawa sen ninshiki." In *Pisu nau Okinawa sen: Musen no tame no sai teii*, edited by Ishihara Masaie. Kyoto: Horitsu bunkasha, 2011.

Armitage, Richard L., and Joseph S. Nye. "The U.S.-Japan Alliance: Getting Asia Right through 2020." Washington, DC: Center for Strategic and International Studies, February 2007.

"Atlas of the World's Languages in Danger." UNESCO Publishing. http://www.unesco.org/culture/en/endangeredlanguages/atlas.

Boei mondai kondankai. "Nihon no anzen hosho to boeiryoku no arikata—21 seiki e mukete no tenbo." Tokyo: Okura sho insatsu kyoku, 1994.

Calder, Kent E. _Embattled Garrisons: Comparative Base Politics and American Globalism._ Princeton: Princeton University Press, 2008.

Center for Strategic and International Studies. "Japan-U.S. Alliance at Fifty—Where We Have Been; Where We Are Heading." In Pacific Forum CSIS Conference: The Japan-U.S. Alliance at Fifty. Washington, DC, January 15, 2010.

Chinen, Kiyoharu. "Nago shicho sen hitotsu ni natta min-i." _Sekai_ (March 2010): 20–24.

chinin, usii. _Usii ga yuku—shokuminchi shugi o tanken shi, watashi o sagasu tabi._ Naha: Okinawa Taimusu sha, 2010.

Clinton, Bill. "Remarks by the President to the People of Okinawa (July 21, 2000)." Okinawa Prefecture Military Affairs Division. http://www3.pref.okinawa.jp/site/view/contview.jsp?cateid=14&id=681&page=1.

Clinton, Hillary Rodham. "Remarks with Japanese Foreign Minister Katsuya Okada after Their Meeting." Honolulu, January 12, 2010.

Clinton, Secretary of State, Secretary of Defense Gates, Minister for Foreign Affairs Matsumoto, and Minister of Defense Kitazawa. "Joint Statement of the Security Consultative Committee 'Toward a Deeper and Broader U.S.-Japan Alliance: Building on 50 Years of Partnership.'" June 21, 2011.

Curtis, Gerald. "Future Directions in US-Japan Relations." Background paper for the "New Shimoda Conference—Revitalizing Japan-US Strategic Partnership for a Changing World." February 2011.

Department of Defense. "Futenma Replacement Facility Bilateral Experts Study Group Report." August 31, 2010.

———. "Joint Press Conference with Japanese Defense Minister Toshimi Kitazawa and Secretary of Defense Robert Gates." Tokyo, October 21, 2009.

———. "Quadrennial Defense Review." February 2010.

———. "US Stationed Military Personnel and Bilateral Cost Sharing 2001 Dollars in Millions—2001 Exchange Rates" (July 2003). http://www.defense.gov/pubs/allied_contrib2003/chart_II-4.html.

Department of Defense, Office of International Security Affairs. "United States Security Strategy in the East Asia-Pacific Region." Washington, DC, 1995.

Dierkes, Julian. _Postwar History Education in Japan and the Germanys—Guilty Lessons._ New York: Routledge, 2010.

Driscoll, Mark. "When Pentagon 'Kill Machines' Came to an Okinawan Paradise." _Counterpunch_, November 2, 2010.

"Eirei ka inujini ka." Ryukyu Asahi Broadcasting, 2010.

Eisenhower, Dwight D. "Memorandum for the Record." _Foreign Relations of the United States, 1958–60_ 18 (April 9, 1958).

Field, Norma. _In the Realm of a Dying Emperor: Japan at the Century's End._ New York: Vintage, 1993.

Figal, Gerald. "Waging Peace on Okinawa." In *Islands of Discontent: Okinawan Responses to Japanese and American Power*, edited by Laura Hein and Mark Selden, 65–98. Lanham, MD: Rowman & Littlefield, 2003.

Francis, Carolyn Bowen. "Omen and Military Violence." In *Okinawa: Cold War Island*, edited by Chalmers Johnson, 109–29. Cardiff: Japan Policy Research Institute, 1999.

Fujiwara, Akira, ed. *Okinawa sen to tenno sei*. Tokyo: Rippu shobo, 1987.

Fukuchi, Hiroaki. "Okinawa no 'nihon fukki.'" *Shukan Kinyobi* (May 12, 2006): 30–33.

Furutachi, Ichiro, and Satoko Norimatsu. "US Marine Training on Okinawa and Its Global Mission: A Birds-Eye View of Bases from the Air." *Asia-Pacific Journal: Japan Focus* (May 2, 2010). http://japanfocus.org/-Satoko-Norimatsu2/3363.

Gabe, Masaaki. *Okinawa henkan wa nan datta no ka*. NHK Bukkusu, 2000.

Gekkan Okinawa Sha. *Laws and Regulations during the U.S. Administration of Okinawa, 1945–1972*. Naha: Ikemiya shokai, 1983.

Green, D. S. "Report on the Medical Topography and Agriculture of the Island of Great Lew Chew." In *Narrative of the Expedition of an American Squadron to the China Seas and Japan, Performed in the Years 1852, 1853, and 1854, under the Command of Commodore M. C. Perry, United States Navy*, 22–37. Washington: A.O.P. Nicholson, 1856.

Green, Michael. "Japan's Confused Revolution." *Washington Quarterly* 33, no. 1 (2009): 3–19.

Hara, Kimie. *Cold War Frontiers in the Asia-Pacific: Divided Territories in the San Francisco System*. Abingdon: Taylor & Francis, 2006.

———. "The Post-War Japanese Peace Treaties and China's Ocean Frontier Problems." *American Journal of Chinese Studies* 11, no. 1 (April 2004): 1–24.

Hatoyama, Yukio. "My Political Philosophy." *Voice*, September 2009 (August 13, 2009).

———. "Policy Speech by Prime Minister Yukio Hatoyama at the 174th Session of the Diet." Prime Minister of Japan and His Cabinet, January 29, 2010.

Hayashi, Hirofumi. *Okinawa sen ga tou mono*. Tokyo: Otsuki shoten, 2010.

———. *Okinawa sen: Kyosei sareta "shudan jiketsu,"* Rekishi Bunka Library. Tokyo: Yoshikawa kobunkan, 2009.

———. *Okinawa sen to minshu*. Tokyo: Otsuki shoten, 2001.

Heginbotham, Eric, Ely Ratner, and Richard J. Samuels. "Tokyo's Transformation: How Japan Is Changing—and What It Means for the United States." *Foreign Affairs* 90, no. 5 (September/October 2011): 138–48.

Hein, Laura, and Mark Selden, eds. *Islands of Discontent: Okinawan Responses to Japanese and American Power*. Lanham, MD: Rowman & Littlefield, 2003.

Honda, Masaru. "Kensho: Kore ga mitsuyaku da." *Sekai* (November 2009): 164–75.

Hook, Glenn D., and Richard Siddle, eds. *Japan and Okinawa: Structure and Subjectivity*. London, New York: Taylor & Francis, 2002.

Ida, Hiroyuki. "Kanbo kimitsuhi yaku san oku en ga Okinawa chijisen ni nagarekonda shoko." *Shukan Kinyobi* (October 22, 2010): 20–21.

Iha, Yoichi. "Futenma isetsu to Henoko shin kichi wa kankei nai." *Shukan Kinyobi* (January 15, 2010): 28–29.

Iha, Yoichi, and Satoko Norimatsu. "Why Build a New Base on Okinawa When the Marines Are Relocating to Guam?: Okinawa Mayor Challenges Japan and the US." *Asia-Pacific Journal: Japan Focus* (January 18, 2010). http://japanfocus.org/-Norimatsu-Satoko/3287.

Inamine, Keiichi. "Okinawa as Pacific Crossroads." *Japan Quarterly* (July–September 2000): 10–16.

Inoue, Kiyoshi. *"Senkaku" retto—Tsuriuo shoto no shiteki kaimei.* Tokyo: Daisan shokan, 1996.

"Interview—Fukushima Mizuho zendaijin ga kataru Hatoyama Yukio. Ozawa Ichiro. Kan Naoto." *Shukan Kinyobi* (June 18, 2010): 14–17.

Ishihara, Masaie. "Okinawa ken heiwa kinen shiryokan to 'Heiwa no Ishiji' no imi suru mono." In *Soten Okinawa sen no kioku*, 308–23. Tokyo: Shakai hyoronsha, 2002.

——. *Okinawa no tabi: Abuchira gama to Todoroki no go.* Tokyo: Shueisha, 2007.

——. "Okinawa sen o netsuzo shita engoho no shikumi." In *Pisu nau Okinawa sen: Musen no tame no sai teii*, edited by Masaie Ishihara, 24–39. Kyoto: Horitsu bunkasha, 2011.

Ishihara, Masaie, Arashiro Toshiaki, Oshiro Masayasu, and Yoshihama Shinobu. *Okinawa sen to beigun kichi kara heiwa o kangaeru.* Tokyo: Iwanami shoten 2008.

Ishihara, Masaie, Oshiro Masayasu, Hosaka Hiroshi, and Matsunaga Katsutoshi. *Soten Okinawa sen no kioku.* Tokyo: Shakai hyoronsha, 2002.

Ishii, Akira. "Chugoku no Ryukyu/Okinawa seisaku—Ryukyu/Okinawa no kizoku mondai o chushin ni." *Kyokai Kenkyu*, no. 1 (2010): 71–96.

Ishiyama, Hisao. *Kyokasho kentei: Okinawa sen "shudan jiketsu" mondai kara kangaeru.* Tokyo: Iwanami shoten, 2008.

Jahana Naomi, "Okinawa sen no ato o tadoru." In Arasaki et al., *Kanko kosu de nai Okinawa: Senseki, kichi, sangyo, shizen, sakishima*, 37–112. Tokyo: Kobunken, 2008.

——. *Shogen Okinawa "shudan jiketsu" Kerama shoto de nani ga okita ka.* Tokyo: Iwanami shoten, 2008.

Janamoto, Keifuku. "Guntai ga ita shima: Kerama no shogen." 38 min. Naha: Okinawa sen kiroku firumu 1 fito undo no kai, 2009.

Japan, and United States. "Treaty of Mutual Cooperation and Security between Japan and the United States of America." *Ministry of Foreign Affairs* (January 1960).

Japan Communist Party. "Okinawa no beigun kichi mondai o sekai ni uttaemasu." http://www.jcp.or.jp/seisaku/gaiko_anpo/2002117_okinawa_uttae.html.

Japan-U.S. Security Consultative Committee (2 + 2). "Cooperation in Response to the Great East Japan Earthquake" (June 21, 2011). http://www.mofa.go.jp/mofaj/area/usa/hosho/pdfs/joint1106_03.pdf.

Johnson, Chalmers. "The Heliport, Nago, and the End of the Ota Era." In *Okinawa: Cold War Island*, edited by Chalmers Johnson, 215–32. Cardiff: Japan Policy Research Institute, 1999.

——. "The 1995 Rape Incident and the Rekindling of Okinawan Protest against the American Bases." In *Okinawa: Cold War Island*, edited by Chalmers Johnson, 109–29. Cardiff: Japan Policy Research Institute, 2009.

Kamata, Satoshi. "Shattering Jewels: 110,000 Okinawans Japanese State Censorship of Compulsory Group Suicides." *Asia-Pacific Journal: Japan Focus* (January 3, 2008). http://www.japanfocus.org/-Kamata-Satoshi/2625.

Kerr, George H. *Okinawa: The History of an Island People*. Rutland, Tokyo: Charles E. Tuttle, 2000.

Kikuno, Yumiko, and Satoko Norimatsu. "Henoko, Okinawa: Inside the Sit-In." *Asia-Pacific Journal: Japan Focus* (February 22, 2010). http://japanfocus.org/-Norimatsu-Satoko/3306.

Kinjo, Minoru. "Mirai e no isan—Ryukyu kyowakoku dokuritsu e no bunkaron-teki shian." *Tsubute* (Spring 2009).

———. *Okinawa kara Yasukuni o tou*. Nara: Uda shuppan kikaku, 2006.

———. *Shitte imasuka Okinawa ichimon itto*. Osaka: Kaiho shuppan sha, 2003.

Kinjo, Shigeaki. "*Shudan jiketsu*" *o kokoro ni kizande*. Tokyo: Kobunken, 1995.

Kitaoka, Shinichi. "The Secret Japan-US Security Pacts: Background and Disclosure." *Asia Pacific Review* 17, no. 2 (2010): 10–25.

Kristensen, Hans M. . "Nihon no kaku no himitsu." *Sekai* (December 2009): 177–83.

Kunimori, Yasuhiro. *Okinawa sen no nihon hei: 60 nen no chinmoku o koete*. Tokyo: Iwanami shoten, 2008.

Kurihara, Keiko. *Nerawareta shudan jiketsu: Oe Iwanami saiban to jumin no shogen*. Tokyo: Shakai hyoronsha, 2009.

Lee, Peter. "High Stakes Gamble as Japan, China and the U.S. Spar in the East and South China Seas." *Asia-Pacific Journal: Japan Focus* (October 25, 2010). http://japanfocus.org/-Peter-Lee/3431.

Levin, Carl, John McCain, and Jim Webb. "Senator Levin, McCain, Webb Call for Re-examination of Military Basing Plans in East Asia" (May 11, 2011). http://webb.senate.gov/newsroom/pressreleases/05-11-2011-01.cfm.

Lummis, Douglas. *Kanameishi: Okinawa to kenpo 9 jo*. Tokyo: Shobunsha, 2010.

Maeda, Sawako. "Yureru Yaeyama no kyokasho erabi." *Peace Philosophy Centre* (2011). http://peacephilosophy.blogspot.com/2011/09/blog-post_16.html.

Maeda, Tetsuo. "*Juzoku*" *kara* "*jiritsu*" *e—Nichibei Anpo o kaeru*. Tokyo: Kobunken, 2009.

———. "Minshuto wa senshu boei o homuru no ka." *Sekai* (November 2010): 113–20.

Maedomari, Hiromori. "'Kichi izon keizai' to iu shinwa." *Sekai* (February 2010): 203–9.

Magosaki, Ukeru. *Nichibei domei no shotai*. Tokyo: Kodansha gendai shinsho, 2009.

Maher, Kevin. *Ketsudan dekinai nippon (The Japan That Can't Decide)*. Tokyo: Bunshun shinsho, 2011.

Makishi, Yoshikazu. "Kushi-wan Henoko kaijo e no shin gunji kuko keikaku." In *Okinawa wa mo damasarenai*, 100–110. Tokyo: Kobunken, 2000.

———. "SACO goi no karakuri o abaku." In *Okinawa wa mo damasarenai*. Tokyo: Kobunken, 2000.

Matsunaga, Katsutoshi. "Shin okinawa heiwa kinen shiryokan mondai to hodo." In *Soten Okinawa sen no kioku*, 131–210. Tokyo: Shakai hyoronsha, 2002.

Matsushima, Yasukatsu. "Yuimaru Ryukyu no jichi—'Ryukyu' dokuritsu de 'heiwa na shima' e." *Shukan Kinyobi* (July 23, 2010).

McCormack, Gavan. "Ampo's Troubled 50th: Hatoyama's Abortive Rebellion, Okinawa's Mounting Resistance and the US-Japan Relationship (Part 2)." *Asia-Pacific Journal: Japan Focus* (May 31, 2010). http://japanfocus.org/-Gavan-McCormack/3366.

———. "The Battle of Okinawa 2009: Obama vs Hatoyama." *Asia-Pacific Journal: Japan Focus* (November 16, 2009). http://japanfocus.org/-Gavan-McCormack/3250.

———. *Client State: Japan in the American Embrace*. New York: Verso, 2007.

———. "Ideas, Identity and Ideology in Contemporary Japan: The Sato Masaru Phenomenon." *Asia-Pacific Journal: Japan Focus* (November 1, 2010). http://japanfocus.org/-Gavan-McCormack/3435.

———. "Okinawa and the Structure of Dependence." In *Japan and Okinawa: Structure and Subjectivity*, edited by Glenn D. Hook and Richard Siddle, 93–113. London, New York: RoutledgeCurzon, 2003.

———. "The Travails of a Client State: An Okinawan Angle on the 50th Anniversary of the U.S.-Japan Security Treaty." *Asia-Pacific Journal: Japan Focus* (March 8, 2010). http://japanfocus.org/-Gavan-McCormack/3317.

McCormack, Gavan, and Satoko Norimatsu. "Discordant Visitors: Japanese and Okinawan Messages to the US." *Asia-Pacific Journal: Japan Focus* (October 3, 2011). http://japanfocus.org/-Satoko-NORIMATSU2/3611.

McCormack, Gavan, Satoko Norimatsu, and Mark Selden. "Okinawa and the Future of East Asia." *Asia-Pacific Journal: Japan Focus* (January 10, 2011). http://japanfocus.org/-Satoko-NORIMATSU2/3468.

McCormack, Gavan, Sakurai Kunitoshi, and Urashima Etsuko. "Okinawa, New Year 2012: Tokyo's Year End Surprise Attack." *Asia-Pacific Journal: Japan Focus* (January 7, 2012). http://japanfocus.org/-Urashima-Etsuko/3673.

McCormack, Gavan, Manabu Sato, and Etsuko Urashima. "The Nago Mayoral Election and Okinawa's Search for a Way beyond Bases and Dependence." *Asia-Pacific Journal: Japan Focus* (February 16, 2006). http://japanfocus.org/-Etsuko-Urashima/1592.

McNeil, David. "Implausible Denial: Japanese Court Rules on Secret US-Japan Pact over the Return of Okinawa." *Asia-Pacific Journal: Japan Focus* (October 10, 2011). http://japanfocus.org/-David-McNeill/3613.

Minister for Foreign Affairs Ikeda, Minister of State for Defense Kyuma, Secretary of Defense Perry, and Ambassador Mondale. "The SACO Final Report, December, 2, 1996."

Minister for Foreign Affairs Okada, Minister of Defense Kitazawa, Secretary of State Clinton, Secretary of Defense Gates. "Joint Statement of the U.S.-Japan Security Consultative Committee Marking the 50th Anniversary of the Signing of the U.S.-Japan Treaty of Mutual Cooperation and Security." Ministry of Foreign Affairs. January 19, 2010.

Ministry of Defense. "National Defense Program Guidelines" (December 17, 2010). http://www.mod.go.jp/e/d_act/d_policy/national.html.

———. "Zainichi Beigun churyu keihi futan no suii." http://www.mod.go.jp/j/approach/zaibeigun/us_keihi/suii_table_53-60.html.

Ministry of Foreign Affairs. "Iwayuru 'mitsuyaku' mondai ni kansuru chosa kekka" (March 9, 2010). http://www.mofa.go.jp/mofaj/gaiko/mitsuyaku/kekka.html.

———. "Japan-U.S. Security Consultative Committee (2 + 2)" (2011). http://www.mofa.go.jp/region/n-america/us/security/scc/index.html.

Mitchell, Jon. "Beggars' Belief: The Farmers' Resistance Movement on Iejima Island, Okinawa." *Asia-Pacific Journal: Japan Focus* (June 7, 2010). http://japan focus.org/-Jon-Mitchell/3370.

———. "US Military Defoliants on Okinawa: Agent Orange." *Asia-Pacific Journal: Japan Focus* (September 12, 2011). http://japanfocus.org/-Jon-Mitchell/3601.

Miyagi, Yasuhiro, and Inamine Susumu. "'Unacceptable and Unendurable': Local Okinawa Mayor Says No to US Marine Base Plan." *Asia-Pacific Journal: Japan Focus* (October 17, 2011). http://japanfocus.org/-Miyagi-Yasuhiro/3618.

Miyazato, Seigen. "Okinawa kenmin no ishi wa meikaku de aru." *Sekai* (January 2009): 157–63.

Mo, Banfu. "Nitchu shototsu no yoha o kakudai sasete wa naranai." *Sekai* (December 2010): 116–23.

Morrow, J. "Observations on the Agriculture, Etc, of Lew Chew." In *Narrative of the Expedition of an American Squadron to the China Seas and Japan, Performed in the Years 1852, 1853, and 1854, under the Command of Commodore M.C.Perry, United States Navy*, 14–20. Washington, DC: A.O.P. Nicholson, 1856.

Nakasone, Hirofumi, and Hillary Rodham Clinton. "Agreement between the Government of Japan and the Government of the United States of America Concerning the Implementation of the Relocation of III Marine Expeditionary Force Personnel and Their Dependents from Okinawa to Guam." Tokyo, February 17, 2009.

Narusawa, Muneo. "Beigun no kaku haibi to nihon." *Shukan Kinyobi* (March 26, 2010): 18–19.

———. "Shin seiken no gaiko seisaku ga towareru Okinawa kichi mondai." *Shukan Kinyobi* (September 25, 2009): 13–15.

———. "Showa tenno to Anpo joyaku." *Shukan Kinyobi* May 1 (2009): 11–17.

Niihara, Shoji. "Ampo joyaku ka no 'mitsuyaku.'" *Shukan Kinyobi* (June 19, 2009): 20–21.

Nishitani, Osamu. "Jihatsuteki reiju o koeyo—Jiritsuteki seiji e no ippo." *Sekai* (February 2010).

Nishizato, Kiko. "Higashi Ajia shi ni okeru Ryukyu Shobun." *Keizaishi Kenkyu* 13 (February 2010): 67–129.

Nomura, Koya. *Muishiki no shokuminchi shugi: Nihon jin no beigun kichi to Okinawa jin*. Tokyo: Ochanomizu shobo, 2005.

Norimatsu, Satoko. "Hatoyama's Confession: The Myth of Deterrence and the Failure to Move a Marine Base Outside Okinawa." *Asia-Pacific Journal: Japan Focus* (February 13, 2011). http://www.japanfocus.org/-Norimatsu-Satoko/3495.

———. "Fukushima and Okinawa—The 'Abandoned People,' and Civic Empowerment." *Asia-Pacific Journal: Japan Focus* 47 (2011). http://japanfocus.org/-Satoko-NORIMATSU/3651.

Nozaki, Yoshiko. *War Memory, Nationalism and Education in Postwar Japan, 1945–2007: The Japanese History Textbook Controversy and Ienaga Saburo's Court Challenges*. Florence: Routledge, 2008.

Nozaki, Yoshiko, and Mark Selden, "Japanese Textbook Controversies, Nationalism, and Historical Memory: Intra- and Inter-National Conflicts." *Asia-Pacific Journal: Japan Focus* (June 15, 2009). http://japanfocus.org/-Yoshiko-Nozaki/3173.

Odanaka, Toshiki. "Sunagawa jiken jokokushin to Amerika no kage: Shihoken dokuritsu e no oson kodo." *Sekai* (August, 2008): 113–21.

Okinawa Prefectural Government Military Affairs Division, "US Military Base Issues in Okinawa." http://www3.pref.okinawa.jp/site/contents/attach/24600/2011.6%20Eng.pdf.

Okinawa Prefectural Peace Memorial Museum. *Sogo Annai*. Itoman: Okinawa kosoku insatsu kabushiki gaisha, 2001.

Okinawa Prefecture Peace and Gender Equity Promotion Division. "Heiwa no Ishiji kokumei sha su." http://www3.pref.okinawa.jp/site/view/contview.jsp?cateid=11&id=7623&page=1.

Okinawa Taimusu, ed. *Idomareru Okinawa sen: "Shudan jiketsu" kyokasho kentei mondai hodo tokushu*. Naha: Okinawa Taimusu sha, 2008.

Onaga, Takeshi. "Okinawa wa 'yuai' no soto na no ka." *Sekai* (February 2010): 149–54.

Osawa, Masachi. "Fuhenteki na kokyosei wa ika ni shite kanoka." *Sekai* (August 2000): 150–59.

Oshiro, Masayasu. "Okinawa sen no shinjitsu o megutte." In *Soten: Okinawa sen no kioku*, 15–60. Tokyo: Shakai hyoronsha, 2002.

Ota, Masahide. *The Battle of Okinawa: The Typhoon of Steel and Bombs*. Nagoya: Takeda Printing Company, 1984.

———. "Governor Ota at the Supreme Court of Japan." In *Okinawa: Cold War Island*, edited by Chalmers Johnson, 205–14. Cardiff: Japan Policy Research Institute, 1999.

———. *Konna Okinawa ni dare ga shita: Futenma isetsu mondai saizen saitan no kaiketsu saku*. Tokyo: Dojidaisha, 2010.

———. *Okinawa no irei no to: Okinawa sen no kyokun to irei*. Naha: Naha shuppansha, 2007.

———. *Shisha tachi wa imada nemurezu*. Tokyo: Shinsensha, 2006.

———. *Soshi Okinawa sen*. Tokyo: Iwanami shoten, 1982.

———. *This Was the Battle of Okinawa*. Naha: Naha shuppansha, 1981.

Ota, Masahide, and Satoko Norimatsu. "'The World Is Beginning to Know Okinawa': Ota Masahide Reflects on His Life from the Battle of Okinawa to the Struggle for Okinawa." *Asia-Pacific Journal: Japan Focus* (September 20, 2010). http://japanfocus.org/-Norimatsu-Satoko/3415.

Ota, Masahide, and Sato Masaru. "Taidan Okinawa wa mirai o do ikiru ka." *Sekai* (August 2010): 118–25.

———. *Tettei toron Okinawa no mirai*. Tokyo: Fuyo shobo shuppan, 2010.

Ota Peace Research Institute. "Okinawa kanren shiryo—Okinawa sen oyobi kichi mondai." Naha: Ota Peace Research Institute, 2010.

Packard, George R. *Edwin O. Reischauer and the American Discovery of Japan*. New York: Columbia University Press, 2010.

———. "Some Thoughts on the 50th Anniversary of the US-Japan Security Treaty." *Asia-Pacific Review* 17, no. 2 (2010): 1–9.

Rabson, Steve. "'Secret' 1965 Memo Reveals Plans to Keep US Bases and Nuclear Weapons in Okinawa after Reversion." *Asia-Pacific Journal: Japan Focus* (December 21, 2009). http://japanfocus.org/-Steve-Rabson/3294.

Ryukyu Asahi Broadcasting, and Satoko Norimatsu. "Assault on the Sea: A 50-Year U.S. Plan to Build a Military Port on Oura Bay, Okinawa." *Asia-Pacific Journal: Japan Focus* (July 5, 2010). http://japanfocus.org/-Ryukyu_Asahi_Broadcasting-/3381.

Saito, Mitsumasa. "American Base Town in Northern Japan. US and Japanese Air Forces at Misawa Target North Korea." *Asia-Pacific Journal: Japan Focus* (October 4, 2010). http://japanfocus.org/-Saito-Mitsumasa/3421.

Sakurai, Kunitoshi. "COP 10 igo no Okinawa." In *Okinawa wa doko e mukau no ka.* Okinawa University, December 19, 2010.

———. "The Guam Treaty as a Modern 'Disposal' of Ryukyus." *Asia-Pacific Journal: Japan Focus* (September 21, 2009). http://japanfocus.org/-Sakurai-Kunitoshi/3223.

———. "The Henoko Assessment Does Not Pass." *Asia-Pacific Journal: Japan Focus* (March 5, 2012). http://japanfocus.org/events/view/131.

———. "Japan's Illegal Environmental Impact Assessment of the Henoko Base." *Asia-Pacific Journal: Japan Focus* (February 27, 2012). http://japanfocus.org/-John-Junkerman/3701.

———. "Nokoso subarashii Okinawa no shizen o mirai sedai ni." In *Shinpojiumu— Okinawa no seibutsu tayosei no genjo to kadai*, 55–67. Naha: Okinawa University Institute of Regional Studies, 2010.

Sato, Eisaku, and Richard Nixon. "Agreed Minute to Joint Communiqué of United States President Nixon and Japanese Prime Minister Sato Issued on November 21, 1969," reproduced in Shunichi Kawabata and Nanae Kurashige, "Secret Japan-U.S. Nuke Deal Uncovered," *Asahi Shimbun*, December 24, 2009.

———. "Joint Statement by Japanese Prime Minister Eisaku Sato and U.S. President Richard Nixon." Washington, DC, November 21, 1969.

Sato, Manabu. "Forced to 'Choose' Its Own Subjugation: Okinawa's Place in U.S. Global Military Realignment." *Asia-Pacific Journal: Japan Focus* (August 2, 2006). http://japanfocus.org/-Sato-Manabu/2202.

———. "Obama seiken no Amerika—Keizai to gaiko seisaku no henka." In *Okinawa 'Jiritsu' e no michi o motomete*, edited by Miyazato Seigen, Arasaki Moriteru, and Gabe Masaaki, 83–94. Tokyo: Kobunken, 2009.

Sato, Masaru. "Chugoku teikokushugi ni taiko suru ni wa." *Chuo Koron* (November 2010): 70–81.

Secretary of State Rice, Secretary of Defense Rumsfeld, Minister of Foreign Affairs Aso, and Minister of State for Defense Nukaga. "United States-Japan Roadmap for Realignment Implementation" (May 1, 2006). http://www.mofa.go.jp/region/n-america/us/security/scc/doc0605.html.

Security Consultative Committee. "Interim Report" (2005). http://www.mofa.go.jp/mofaj/area/usa/hosho/pdfs/gainenzu.pdf.

———. "Transformation and Realignment for the Future, October 29, 2005."

Shimabukuro, Jun. "Nichibei Anpo no henyo to Okinawa no jichi." In *Okinawa wa doko e mukau no ka.* Okinawa University, December 19, 2010.

Shimoji, Yoshio. "Futenma: Tip of the Iceberg in Okinawa's Agony." *Asia-Pacific Journal: Japan Focus* (October 24, 2011).

Shimojima, Tetsuro. *Chibichiri gama no shudan jiketsu: Kami no kuni no hate ni.* Tokyo: Gaifusha, 2000.

——. *Okinawa Chibichiri gama no "shudan jiketsu."* Iwanami booklet. Tokyo: Iwanami shoten, 1992.

Shindo, Eiichi. "Bunkatsu sareta ryodo." *Sekai* (April 1979): 31–51.

Shinohara, Hajime. "Toranjishon Dai Ni Maku E." *Sekai* (November 2010): 85–91.

"Sino-Japanese Relations: Vice-Premier Teng Hsiao-Ping's Press Conference in Tokyo 25 October 1978." *Survival* 21, no. 1 (1979): 42–44.

Smits, Gregory. "Examining the Myth of Ryukyuan Pacifism." *Asia-Pacific Journal: Japan Focus* (September 13, 2010). http://japanfocus.org/-Gregory-Smits/3409.

Suda, Shinichiro, Yabe Koji, and Maedomari Hiromori. *Hondo no ningen wa shiranai ga, Okinawa no hito wa minna shitte iru koto—Okinawa beigun kichi kanko gaido.* Tokyo: Shoseki johosha, 2011.

Suganuma, Unryu. *Sovereign Rights and Territorial Space in Sino-Japanese Relations: Irredentism and the Diaoyu/Senkaku Islands.* Honolulu: University of Hawaii Press, 2000.

Sun Ge. "Okinawa ga wareware no me ni utsuru toki." In *Rekishi No Kosaten Ni Tatte.* Tokyo: Nihon keizai hyoron sha, 2008.

——. "Okinawa ni naizai suru higashi Ajia sengoshi." In *Ajia no naka de Okinawa gendaishi o toinaosu*, 52–64. Naha: Okinawa University Institute of Regional Studies, 2010.

Taira, Kamenosuke. "Okinawa fuzai no 'fukki' ni i o tonaeta Yara Chobyo." *Shukan Kinyobi* (July 15, 2011).

Taira, Koji. "The Okinawan Charade: The United States, Japan and Okinawa: Conflict and Compromise, 1995–96." *Japan Policy Research Institute* (January 1997). http://www.jpri.org/publications/workingpapers/wp28.html.

Takahashi, Tetsuro. *Okinawa beigun kichi deta bukku.* Okinawa tanken sha, 2011.

Tanaka, Hitoshi, John Dower, Tsuyoshi Sunohara, and Joseph Nye. "Nichibei domei 'Chaina kado' de jumyo o nobase." *Bungei shunju* (May 2010): 178–88.

Tanaka, Nobumasa. "Desecration of the Dead: Bereaved Okinawan Families Sue Yasukuni to End Relatives' Enshrinement." *Asia-Pacific Journal: Japan Focus* (May 7, 2008). http://www.japanfocus.org/-Nobumasa-Tanaka/2744.

——. *Dokyumento Yasukuni sosho: Senshi sha no kioku wa dare no mono ka.* Tokyo: Iwanami shoten, 2007.

Tanji, Miyume. *Myth, Protest and Struggle in Okinawa.* New York: Routledge, 2006.

Terashima, Jitsuro. "Noriki no ressun, tokubetsu hen, (94), joshiki ni kaeru ishi to koso—Nichibei domei no saikochiku ni mukete." *Sekai* (February 2010): 118–25.

——. "The Will and Imagination to Return to Common Sense: Toward a Restructuring of the US-Japan Alliance." *Asia-Pacific Journal: Japan Focus* (March 15, 2010). http://japanfocus.org/-Jitsuro-Terashima/3321.

Togo, Kazuhiko, and Sato Masaru. "Gaimu kanryo ni damasareru Okada gaisho." *Shukan Kinyobi* (March 26, 2010): 14–17.

Toyoshita, Narahiko. *Anpo joyaku no seiritsu: Yoshida gaiko to tennno gaiko.* Tokyo: Iwanami shoten, 1996.

Tsushima-maru Memorial Museum. "Tsushima maru gekichin jiken towa." http://www.tsushimamaru.or.jp/jp/about/about1.html.

Uemura, Hideaki. "The Colonial Annexation of Okinawa and the Logic of International Law: The Formation of an Indigenous People." *Japanese Studies* 23, no. 2 (September 2003): 107–24.

Ueunten, Wesley Iwao. "Rising Up from a Sea of Discontent: The 1970 Koza Uprising in U.S.-Occupied Okinawa." In *Militarized Current: Toward a Decolonized Future in Asia and the Pacific,* edited by Setsu Shigematsu and Keith L. Camacho, 91–124. Minneapolis: University of Minnesota Press, 2010.

United Nations Human Rights Committee. "International Covenant on Civil and Political Rights." ccpr/C/JPN/CO/5 (HRC 2008). Geneva, 2008.

United States Congress House Committee on Armed Services. "Report of a Special Subcommittee of the Armed Services Committee, House of Representatives: Following an Inspection Tour, October 14 to November 23, 1955." Washington, DC: GPO, 1956.

Urashima, Etsuko. "Okinawa Yanbaru, kaze no tayori (10) Ikusa yo wa tsuzuku." *Impaction* 170 (August 2009): 128–41.

———. "Okinawa Yanbaru, kaze no tayori (21) 'Kokusaku' ni honro sareru ikari." *Impaction* 161 (2011): 118–32.

Urashima, Etsuko, and Gavan McCormack. "Electing a Town Mayor in Okinawa: Report from the Nago Trenches." *Asia-Pacific Journal: Japan Focus* (January 25, 2010). http://japanfocus.org/-Gavan-McCormack/3291.

US Department of the Navy. "Guam and CMNI Military Relocation—Environmental Impact Statement." November 2009.

US Government Accountability Office. "Defense Management—Comprehensive Cost Information and Analysis of Alternatives Needed to Assess Military Posture in Asia." Washington, DC, May 2011.

US Institute of Peace. "Congressional Commission on the Strategic Posture of the United States Issues Final Report" (May 2009). http://www.usip.org/print/newsroom/news/congressional-commission-the-strategic-posture-the-united-states-issues-final-report.

US Pacific Command. "Guam Integrated Military Development Plan." July 11, 2006.

"U.S. Policy in the Ryukyu Islands, Memorandum of Conversation." U.S. National Archives, July 16, 1965, Record Number 79651.

VAWW-NET Japan. "Kyokasho ni iwanfu ni tsuite no kijutsu o." http://www1.jca.apc.org/vaww-net-japan/history/textbook.html.

Vine, David. "Smearing Japan." *Foreign Policy in Focus* (April 20, 2011). http://www.fpif.org/articles/smearing_japan.

Wakaizumi, Kei. *The Best Course Available: A Personal Account of the Secret US-Japan Okinawa Reversion Negotiations.* Honolulu: University of Hawaii Press, 2002.

Watanabe, Osamu. "Kozo kaikaku e to kaiki suru hoshu naikaku." *Shukan Kinyobi* (September 30, 2011): 15–17.

Watanabe, Tsuyoshi. "'Jihatsuteki reiju' no jubaku o tachikiru Okinawa." *Sekai* (December 2010): 41–51.

Webb, Jim. "Observations and Recommendations on US Military Basing in East Asia, May 2011" (May 2011). http://webb.senate.gov/issuesandlegislation/foreignpolicy/Observations_basing_east_asia.cfm.

Weiner, Tim. *Legacy of Ashes: The History of the CIA.* New York: Doubleday, 2007.

Yakabi, Osamu. *Okinawa Sen, beigun senryo shi o manabi naosu: Kioku o ikani keisho suruka.* Yokohama: Seori shobo, 2009.

Yamaguchi, Masanori. "'Media ichigeki Hato o sagi ni saseta' ote media 'Nichibei domei fukashin' hodo." *Shukan Kinyobi* (June 11, 2010): 24–25.

Yamane, Kazuyo, ed. *Museums for Peace Worldwide.* Kyoto: Organizing Committee of the Sixth International Conference of Museums for Peace, 2008.

Yonamine, Michiyo. "Economic Crisis Shakes US Forces Overseas: The Price of Base Expansion in Okinawa and Guam." *Asia-Pacific Journal: Japan Focus* (February 28, 2011). http://www.japanfocus.org/-Yonamine-Michiyo/3494.

Yonetani, Julia. "Contested Memories—Struggles over War and Peace in Contemporary Okinawa." In *Japan and Okinawa: Structure and Subjectivity,* edited by Glen Hook and Richard Siddle, 188–207. London, New York: RoutledgeCurzon, 2003.

———. "Making History from Japan's Margins—Ota Masahide and Okinawa." Dissertation, Australian National University, 2002.

———. "Playing Base Politics in a Global Strategic Theater: Futenma Relocation, the G-8 Summit, and Okinawa." *Critical Asian Studies* 33, no. 1 (2001): 70–95.

Yoshida, Kensei. "Anpo kichi no shima Okinawa." *Meru Magajin Oruta* (December 20, 2009). http://www.alter-magazine.jp/backno/backno_72.html.

———. *Democracy Betrayed: Okinawa Under U.S. Occupation.* Bellingham: Center for East Asian Studies, Western Washington University, 2001.

———. "Okinawa and Guam: In the Shadow of U.S. and Japanese 'Global Defense Posture.'" *Asia-Pacific Journal: Japan Focus* (June 28, 2010). http://japanfocus.org/-Yoshida-Kensei/3378.

———. *Okinawa no kaiheitai wa Guamu e iku.* Tokyo: Kobunken, 2010.

———. "A Voice from Okinawa (18)—Futenma Kichi No Kigen." *Meru Magajin Oruta* (January 20, 2011). http://www.alter-magazine.jp/backno/backno_85.html#08.

Yoshida, Yutaka. *Ajia taiheiyo senso.* Tokyo: Iwanami shoten, 2007.

Yoshikawa, Hideki. "Dugong Swimming in Uncharted Waters: US Judicial Intervention to Protect Okinawa's 'Natural Monument' and Halt Base Construction." *Asia-Pacific Journal: Japan Focus* (February 7, 2009). http://japanfocus.org/-Hideki-YOSHIKAWA/3044.

# Index

317

# About the Authors

*From left: McCormack, Norimatsu, and Ota Masahide. Naha, Okinawa, 2013.*

**Gavan McCormack** is emeritus professor at the Australian National University and author of a number of studies of modern and contemporary East Asia. He is a graduate of the University of Melbourne (law) and University of London (Chinese), with a PhD from University of London in 1974. He has been a regular visitor to Japan over half a century since 1962 and has been a visiting professor at a number of Japanese universities. His most recent book was *Client State: Japan in the American Embrace* (2007), which was also translated and published in Japanese, Korean, and Chinese.

**Satoko Oka Norimatsu** is director of the Peace Philosophy Centre (www .peacephilosophy.com), based in Vancouver, Canada. She is a graduate of Keio University (BA in literature, 1990) and the University of British Columbia (MBA, 2001). After teaching at UBC Centre for Intercultural Communication, she established her peace education organization in 2007. She writes, speaks, and teaches on issues such as the military colonization of Okinawa, Japanese imperialism, war memory, and historical reconciliation. She leads historical study tours, including a US-Japan joint students' trip to Hiroshima and Nagasaki. She is a regular contributor to the Okinawan newspaper *Ryukyu Shimpo*, and her publications in Japanese include *Let's Talk about War — Let's Talk about What War Really Is*, coauthored with Oliver Stone and Peter Kuznick (Kinyobi, 2014).

Both authors are editors of the *Asia-Pacific Journal: Japan Focus* (www.apjjf .org), which in 2008 was awarded the inaugural Ikemiyagi Shui Prize (by the Okinawan daily *Ryukyu Shimpo*) for the dissemination to the world of information and analysis concerning Okinawa.

# ASIA/PACIFIC/PERSPECTIVES

## Series Editor: Mark Selden

*Social and Political Change in Revolutionary China: The Taihang Base Area in the War of Resistance to Japan, 1937–1945*
    by David S. G. Goodman
*Rice Wars in Colonial Vietnam: The Great Famine and the Viet Minh Road to Power*
    by Geoffrey C. Gunn
*Islands of Discontent: Okinawan Responses to Japanese and American Power*
    edited by Laura Hein and Mark Selden
*Masculinities in Chinese History*
    by Bret Hinsch
*The Rise of Tea Culture in China: The Invention of the Individual*
    by Bret Hinsch
*Women in Early Imperial China, Second Edition*
    by Bret Hinsch
*Chinese Civil Justice, Past and Present*
    by Philip C. C. Huang
*Local Democracy and Development: The Kerala People's Campaign for Decentralized Planning*
    by T. M. Thomas Isaac with Richard W. Franke
*Hidden Treasures: Lives of First-Generation Korean Women in Japan*
    by Jackie J. Kim with Sonia Ryang
*North Korea: Beyond Charismatic Politics*
    by Heonik Kwon and Byung-Ho Chung
*A Century of Change in a Chinese Village: The Crisis of the Countryside*
    by Juren Lin, edited and translated by Linda Grove
*Postwar Vietnam: Dynamics of a Transforming Society*
    edited by Hy V. Luong
*From Silicon Valley to Shenzhen: Global Production and Work in the IT Industry*
    by Boy Lüthje, Stefanie Hürtgen, Peter Pawlicki, and Martina Sproll
*Resistant Islands: Okinawa Confronts Japan and the United States*
    by Gavan McCormack and Satoko Oka Norimatsu
*The Indonesian Presidency: The Shift from Personal towards Constitutional Rule*
    by Angus McIntyre
*Nationalisms of Japan: Managing and Mystifying Identity*
    by Brian J. McVeigh
*The Korean War: A Hidden History*
    edited by Tessa Morris-Suzuki
*To the Diamond Mountains: A Hundred-Year Journey through China and Korea*
    by Tessa Morris-Suzuki
*To Hell and Back: The Last Train from Hiroshima*
    by Charles Pellegrino